AI Utilization for Marketing Content Creation

Albérico Travassos Rosário
https://orcid.org/0000-0003-4793-4110
Universidade Europeia, Portugal

Rui Nunes Cruz
https://orcid.org/0000-0002-5773-6049
Universidade Europeia, Portugal

IGI Global
Scientific Publishing
Publishing Tomorrow's Research Today

Vice President of Editorial — Melissa Wagner
Director of Acquisitions — Mikaela Felty
Director of Book Development — Jocelynn Hessler
Production Manager — Mike Brehm
Cover Design — Jose Rosado

Published in the United States of America by
IGI Global Scientific Publishing
701 East Chocolate Avenue
Hershey, PA, 17033, USA
Tel: 717-533-8845 | Fax: 717-533-7115
Website: https://www.igi-global.com E-mail: cust@igi-global.com

Library of Congress Cataloging-in-Publication Data

(CIP Data Pending)
ISBN13: 979-8-3693-9994-1
Isbn13Softcover: 979-8-3693-9995-8
EISBN13: 979-8-3693-9996-5

British Cataloguing in Publication Data
A Cataloguing in Publication record for this book is available from the British Library.

Table of Contents

Detailed Table of Contents

This literature review analyzes current research on artificial intelligence (AI) in marketing, focusing on ethical considerations and managerial applications. Recent studies cover a range of AI applications, including customer engagement, personalization, and brand loyalty, alongside the ethical challenges AI poses, such as data privacy, transparency, and fairness. The review identifies core theoretical frameworks such as social identity theory and affordance theory that underpin these discussions. Findings highlight that while AI can enhance consumer experiences and drive brand loyalty, it also requires ethical oversight to ensure responsible data usage and avoid potential consumer mistrust. This review contributes to a deeper understanding of AI's dual role in marketing as both an enhancer of consumer engagement and a domain for ethical scrutiny

This chapter will examine the revolutionary role of Artificial Intelligence (AI) in today's marketing and more specifically digital department. It will explore how AI can be used to improve financial results, decrease human errors, and improve customer experience through data analysis. The chapter will also discuss the difficulties that may be provoked by using AI, such as the need for qualified staff, privacy issues, and high implementation costs. Additionally, it will evaluate how AI will affect the digital marketing landscape. The chapter will conclude by discussing possible future AI trends, including augmentation reality and automation enhancements, and how these advancements may influence the marketing department.

In today's data-driven world, businesses must leverage big data and AI to stay competitive. This chapter explores how AI, combined with big data analytics, enables marketers to make real-time, informed decisions that enhance customer engagement and optimize marketing strategies. Key methodologies such as machine learning and behavioral analytics transform vast amounts of data into actionable insights. AI facilitates predictive analytics, hyper-personalization, and automated decision-making, while Customer Data Platforms (CDPs) offer a unified view of customers. Behavioral analytics helps track consumer interactions across digital touchpoints, improving segmentation and engagement. Real-world case studies from e-commerce, retail, and finance show how AI-driven marketing leads to business growth and ROI. However, ethical challenges like data privacy, algorithmic bias, and transparency must be addressed to maintain consumer trust. This chapter provides marketing professionals, researchers, and business leaders with crucial insights into leveraging AI and big data for success.

As the digital marketing landscape evolves, advertisers and publishers must continually adapt their content creation strategies to remain competitive. This chapter explores effective strategies for content creation, addressing both advertiser and publisher perspectives. We delve into content strategies across various marketing channels, focusing on key aspects such as content marketing, keyword harvesting, ad copy optimization, multilingual content generation, and more. By integrating traditional methods with advanced technologies, this chapter serves as a comprehensive guide for marketers aiming to enhance their content strategies.Recent insights reveal that early adopters of GenAI have been significantly better prepared to leverage its potential. Early adopters are three times more likely to have a fully functioning project planning process with dedicated tools for content marketing. They are also three times more likely to have a formal, analytics-driven approach to balancing content supply and demand and a high level of automation for content fulfillment and distribution.

OTAs have increasingly adopted advanced technologies to deliver more personalized and efficient services. In Portugal, where tourism plays a crucial economic role, this technological shift presents an opportunity to enhance competitiveness and offer customers a more distinctive experience. This study examines the use and future perceptions of technology and artificial intelligence in the tourism, with a particular focus on the accommodation platforms, exploring perspectives from both consumers and companies, namely channel managers, short-term rental management companies, and accommodation owner. A mixed-methods approach was employed, enabling the collection of both quantitative and qualitative results, which reveal a predisposition from both individuals and companies to adopt artificial intelligence, along with high expectations for the future, although some concerns persist, particularly regarding the lack of human contact.

Artificial Intelligence (AI) is being utilized to solve structural problem and consumer diversity in rural marketing in India. By using AI together with machine learning and predictive algorithms, market penetration andcliente engagement are greatly increased, as well as delivery efficiency. With the exception of rural areas, infrastructure needs to be in place, and technology has to be perceived as positive. Quantitative analysis of the impact of AI on supply chain efficiency, consumer engagement, and productivity of the Indian tech providers, rural marketers and consumers is carried out using SPSS, and these data were used for this research. Perceived usability and top infrastructure readiness are the factors that affect the effectiveness of AI. This implies that policy for upgrading infrastructure, training programs and tech funding to encourage rural growth and economic results. With this, AI can be used to run valuable agricultural supply chains, personalized offering, digital payments, increase incomes, employment opportunities, and long term social welfare benefits.

This study investigates the impact of AI-driven personalization on email marketing performance, comparing it with traditional methods across key performance indicators including open rates, click-through rates (CTR), and conversion rates. Using empirical data, the findings reveal that AI-powered email campaigns significantly outperform traditional campaigns, achieving improvements of 42% in open rates, 71% in CTR, and 68% in conversion rates. These results highlight the effectiveness of AI's ability to analyze real-time customer behavior and dynamically tailor content, enhancing engagement and driving better business outcomes. While the study confirms and extends existing literature, limitations such as a relatively small sample size, focus on quantitative metrics, and reliance on proprietary AI tools suggest directions for future research. Overall, this research underscores the transformative potential of AI personalization in optimizing email marketing strategies and offers practical and theoretical insights for digital marketers.

Preface

In the last decade, Artificial Intelligence has moved from a specialized technological discipline to a transformative force reshaping the foundations of modern marketing. What began as a collection of computational techniques has evolved into an ecosystem of intelligent systems capable of understanding, predicting, personalizing, and even co-creating consumer experiences. Today, AI influences not only how brands communicate, but how they think, operate, and strategize. The rapid expansion of machine learning, natural language processing, generative AI, and big data analytics has pushed marketers into a new era—one defined by automation, real-time insights, hyper-personalization, and a reconfiguration of the relationship between companies and consumers.

This book brings together a diverse set of contributions that collectively map this transformation. It provides a comprehensive and multidimensional exploration of how AI is integrated into marketing, how it shapes consumer perceptions, and how it redefines entire sectors from tourism to rural markets. Across these chapters, the reader encounters not only technical and methodological advancements, but also the ethical, social, and strategic implications of this shift toward intelligent marketing ecosystems.

The structure of the book follows a deliberate progression—from macro-level reflections on ethics and strategy to highly specific applications and sectoral analyses. This organization provides coherence to a field that is inherently fragmented and fast-moving, offering readers a way to understand both the breadth and depth of AI's impact on marketing practice. What emerges is a landscape where creativity meets computation, where authenticity coexists with automation, and where human decision-making is augmented rather than replaced by intelligent systems.

CHAPTER OVERVIEWS

Chapter 1: Artificial Intelligence in Marketing: A Literature Review on Ethical Implications and Managerial Strategies

The opening chapter provides the conceptual and ethical foundation for the entire volume. It situates AI within a broader transformation that has redefined decision-making processes, consumer analysis, and strategic management. Drawing on a systematic bibliometric review of 175 documents, the chapter charts the evolution of AI-driven marketing research, identifies global trends, and highlights the countries and institutions leading this scholarly development.

Beyond mapping the academic landscape, the chapter confronts the ethical challenges that underpin AI adoption: transparency, algorithmic bias, consumer privacy, and responsible data management. It explores how marketers must navigate this tension between innovation and responsibility, outlining managerial strategies that balance technological advancement with trust, accountability, and long-term sustainability. By beginning with ethics, the book anchors all subsequent discussions in a framework that emphasizes human-centric and responsible AI design.

Chapter 2: The Integration of AI into the Marketing Department

Following the broad strategic overview, the second chapter turns inward—into the structure, functions, and decision-making processes within marketing departments. It provides a detailed examination of how AI reshapes internal workflows, from predictive analytics to customer segmentation, task automation, and content personalization.

The chapter outlines the theoretical lenses that help explain AI adoption, including the Technology Acceptance Model (TAM) and Diffusion of Innovation (DOI). These frameworks illuminate not only the opportunities created by AI, but also the organizational barriers—skills gaps, resistance to change, technological uncertainty, and the strategic alignment required for successful integration.

By focusing on the inner workings of the marketing function, this chapter builds a bridge between conceptual strategy and operational reality. It demonstrates how AI becomes embedded in processes, competencies, and organizational culture—reshaping how marketers perceive consumers, design experiences, and measure value.

Chapter 3: Harnessing Big Data and AI – Unlocking Predictive Insights for Smarter Marketing Decisions

Big data is the lifeblood of AI, and this chapter explores that relationship with depth and clarity. It chronicles the historical evolution of AI in marketing—from rule-based systems to contemporary predictive models—and highlights how data has transformed from a passive resource into an active driver of strategic decision-making.

The chapter illustrates the power of real-time analytics, machine learning algorithms, and customer data platforms (CDPs) to generate actionable insights. Through examples of behavioral analysis, forecasting models, and automated segmentation, it shows how predictive intelligence enhances targeting precision, campaign optimization, and consumer understanding.

Ethical considerations are revisited here as well, reinforcing the necessity of data governance, privacy protection, transparency, and fairness. This reflection creates continuity with the first chapter, emphasizing that analytical capabilities must always be accompanied by responsible practices.

Chapter 4: Artificial Intelligence in Marketing: A Literature Review on Ethical Implications and Managerial Strategies

A review that complements the previous chapter by offering a research-based perspective on AI content generation. Using a PRISMA-guided literature review, it analyzes the main academic contributions on how AI supports or transforms digital content production.

The chapter identifies key themes emerging in the literature, including automation of repetitive tasks, optimization of content performance, personalization at scale and the growing relevance of human–AI collaboration. A simple conceptual model is introduced to show how AI enhances content creation through automation, optimization, personalization and creative augmentation.

The review highlights the benefits discussed across studies—greater speed, improved accuracy and deeper targeting—but also recalls the risks, such as reduced authenticity or over-reliance on automation. It concludes that the strongest content strategies emerge when AI is used to support, not replace, human creativity.

Chapter 5: Authenticity in Marketing Strategies – Human vs. AI-Created Promotional Campaigns

As AI begins to produce content at scale, the question of authenticity becomes central. This chapter confronts that challenge by presenting an experimental comparison between human-created and AI-generated marketing campaigns. Grounded in authenticity theory, the study examines emotional resonance, trust, consumer perception, and brand loyalty.

The findings are nuanced: while human-created campaigns often evoke stronger emotional connections, AI-generated campaigns can match or even exceed trust levels when well-designed. The chapter concludes that authenticity is not inherent to the creator but depends on emotional relevance, cultural resonance, and perceived sincerity. This work deepens the understanding of how consumers interpret AI-generated content and reinforces the importance of ethical and strategic content design.

Chapter 6: A Comprehensive Literature Review on the Influence of Artificial Intelligence on Consumer Engagement and Brand Loyalty in Digital Marketing

Continuing the exploration of consumer perception, this chapter moves from authenticity to engagement and loyalty. Through a systematic bibliometric review, it examines how AI technologies—recommendation engines, chatbots, personalization algorithms, sentiment analysis—shape long-term interactions between brands and consumers.

It identifies AI as a catalyst for immersive, tailored, and emotionally resonant experiences that foster loyalty. Yet it also highlights risks: over-automation, personalization fatigue, and privacy concerns. The chapter thus provides a balanced view that aligns technological promise with psychological complexity.

Chapter 7: Artificial Intelligence in Online Travel Agencies: Perspectives of Consumers, Channel Managers, and Accommodation Managers

The first sector-specific chapter applies AI concepts to the tourism and accommodation industry, examining how consumers, property managers, and channel managers perceive and adopt AI. It combines quantitative and qualitative methodologies to assess personalization, automation, platform competitiveness, and the evolving role of human contact in digital service experiences.

This chapter illuminates how AI reshapes an industry dependent on trust, experience, and service quality. It also highlights tensions—automation versus human touch, efficiency versus empathy—that echo throughout the book.

Chapter 8: Leveraging Artificial Intelligence to Drive Sustainable Rural Marketing in India

This chapter explores AI's role beyond urban and digital-native contexts. Focusing on rural India, it examines how machine learning and predictive analytics enhance supply chain efficiency, consumer engagement, and socioeconomic development in regions marked by infrastructural constraints. This unique perspective extends the book's scope, demonstrating AI's potential to address societal challenges, reduce inequalities, and support inclusive economic growth. It underscores that AI adoption is not merely a technological endeavor but a social and developmental one.

Chapter 9: Assessing the Influence of AI-Driven Personalization on Email Marketing Performance: An Empirical Comparison with Traditional Approaches

This study examines how AI-driven personalization influences the effectiveness of email marketing compared to traditional campaign approaches. Focusing on key performance indicators—open rates, click-through rates, and conversion rates—the analysis draws on empirical data to demonstrate that AI-powered campaigns consistently achieve substantially higher engagement and performance. The findings attribute these gains to AI's capacity to process real-time customer behavior and dynamically customize email content, thereby strengthening audience engagement and improving business outcomes. While reinforcing and extending prior research on digital marketing personalization, the study also acknowledges limitations related to sample size, emphasis on quantitative measures, and dependence on proprietary AI systems. Overall, it highlights the significant strategic value of AI personalization and provides both practical implications for marketers and a foundation for future academic inquiry.

FINAL REFLECTION

"AI Utilization for Marketing Content Creation" offers a panoramic view of AI's transformative influence across marketing ecosystems. Each chapter adds a new dimension—ethical, strategic, technical, perceptual, or contextual—allowing readers to appreciate the complexity and opportunity embedded in the ongoing AI revolution.

This book is designed for scholars, practitioners, students, and innovators who seek not only to understand AI, but to engage critically with its implications. By bringing together rigorous research, practical insights, and sectoral applications, it provides a foundation for navigating the future of AI-enabled marketing—one that values innovation, responsibility, and human connection.

As you embark on the chapters ahead, we invite you to explore this evolving landscape with curiosity, critical reflection, and an openness to new possibilities. The future of marketing is neither purely human nor purely artificial—it is a collaboration, and this book is a guide to understanding that partnership.

Chapter 1
Artificial Intelligence in Marketing:
A Literature Review on Ethical Implications and Managerial Strategies

Albérico Travassos Rosário
https://orcid.org/0000-0003-4793-4110
GOVCOPP, School of Business Sciences of Setúbal, Polytechnic Institute of Setúbal, Portugal

Rui Cruz
https://orcid.org/0000-0002-5773-6049
UNIDCOM/IADE, Universidade Europeia, Portugal

Luis Andrade
https://orcid.org/0000-0001-8615-5473
Universidade Europeia, Portugal

ABSTRACT

This literature review analyzes current research on artificial intelligence (AI) in marketing, focusing on ethical considerations and managerial applications. Recent studies cover a range of AI applications, including customer engagement, personalization, and brand loyalty, alongside the ethical challenges AI poses, such as data privacy, transparency, and fairness. The review identifies core theoretical frameworks such as social identity theory and affordance theory that underpin these discussions. Findings highlight that while AI can enhance consumer experiences and drive brand loyalty, it also requires ethical oversight to ensure responsible data

DOI: 10.4018/979-8-3693-9994-1.ch001

usage and avoid potential consumer mistrust. This review contributes to a deeper understanding of AI's dual role in marketing as both an enhancer of consumer engagement and a domain for ethical scrutiny

INTRODUCTION

The emergence of artificial intelligence (AI) represents one of the most transformative technological advancements of the 21st century. AI innovations are revolutionising how industries operate and innovate. Initially, AI was a concept rooted in computer science. However, it has rapidly evolved over the past decade due to advancements in machine learning, natural language processing, and big data analytics (Verma et al., 2021). This growth has enabled AI technology adoption across various sectors, including healthcare, finance, manufacturing, and retail, where automation and intelligent systems increasingly integrate into daily operations. In addition, Vlačić et al. (2021) found that these technologies have been adopted in the marketing industry, allowing companies to collect and analyse substantial consumer data, personalise customer experiences, and optimise their campaigns in significant ways. As a result, AI's adoption has transformed marketing into a data-driven, highly responsive field, facilitating more thoughtful decision-making and more effective strategies for engaging target audiences.

The growing reliance on AI in marketing has shifted toward more sophisticated, data-centric approaches. With the ability to process large-scale consumer data, AI systems give marketers more profound insights into customer preferences, behaviours, and purchasing patterns (Chintalapati & Pandey, 2022). Tools such as recommendation engines, predictive analytics, and real-time customer interaction platforms have allowed marketers to move from reactive strategies to proactive, predictive ones. Leveraging AI enables companies to deliver more targeted advertising, improve customer segmentation, and refine product offerings based on real-time feedback (Huang & Rust, 2021). Moreover, AI helps automate routine marketing tasks like email campaigns and social media management, freeing time for creative strategy development and innovation. The increasing integration of AI tools highlights the technology's potential to redefine the scope and impact of modern marketing strategies.

AI's impact on marketing has reshaped traditional marketing strategies and driven innovations that enhance customer relationships, increase efficiency, and provide predictive insights. AI has become central to many marketing operations, from automated content creation and personalised advertisements to advanced customer segmentation and sentiment analysis (Sterne, 2017). However, as AI-driven tools become more integral to marketing, ethical concerns regarding data privacy, algorithmic bias, and transparency have surfaced. These concerns have prompted the need for responsible management and AI applications (Feng et al., 2021). This literature review provides a comprehensive analysis of the ethical implications of AI in marketing alongside the managerial strategies required to navigate this evolving field. Using a systematic bibliometric literature review (LRSB) of 175 documents, this paper synthesises existing research to explore how AI is redefining marketing while addressing the ethical and strategic challenges it presents.

METHODOLOGICAL APPROACH

This study utilises a systematic bibliometric literature review (LRSB) to explore the ethical implications and managerial strategies associated with using artificial intelligence (AI) in marketing. The LRSB method allows for a quantitative analysis of published literature, offering insights into the distribution of knowledge, key trends, and influential works within the field. The Preferred Reporting Items for Systematic Reviews and Meta-Analyses (PRISMA 2020) framework guided the methodology to ensure a transparent and replicable review process. PRISMA was selected due to its structured approach to identifying, screening, and synthesising relevant literature, enhancing the findings' rigour and reliability (Haddaway et al., 2022). Following PRISMA's procedure allowed the systematic capturing of a broad scope of publications while filtering down to the most pertinent studies related to AI's role in marketing strategies.

The Scopus database was utilised to gather and select pertinent materials, following the guidance of Rosário & Casaca (2023) and Rosário et al. (2023, 2021). Scopus is highlighted as one of the most extensive abstract and citation databases, offering various sources, such as conference proceedings, books, and journal articles, and encompassing both international and regional research areas. The platform ensures high data quality through an independent Content Selection and Advisory Board, which enforces a stringent content selection and regular re-assessment protocol.

Unlike conventional literature reviews, the Systematic Bibliometric Literature Review (LRSB) approach provides a more structured and thorough analysis of the research landscape on a specific subject, as indicated by Rosário & Casaca (2023) and Rosário et al. (2023, 2021). This approach emphasises refining article selection to include only those works that directly address the research question. It also establishes a clear audit trail, enabling readers to evaluate the selected studies' methodology, findings, and overall quality.

The LRSB method follows a detailed protocol for screening and selecting sources to ensure the data's reliability and relevance. This protocol is divided into three phases and six steps, as shown in Table 1, by the methodologies detailed by Rosário & Casaca (2023) and Rosário et al. (2023, 2021).

Table 1. Process of systematic LRSB.

Fase	Step	Description
Exploration	Step 1	formulating the research problem
	Step 2	searching for appropriate literature
	Step 3	critical appraisal of the selected studies
	Step 4	data synthesis from individual sources
Interpretation	Step 5	reporting findings and recommendations
Communication	Step 6	Presentation of the LRSB report

Source: adapted *Rosário & Casaca (2023); Rosário et al. (2023, 2021).*

The researchers utilised the Scopus database to identify and select credible sources broadly acknowledged by the academic and scientific community. It is worth noting a limitation of this study: it focused solely on the Scopus database, excluding other academic and scientific databases, and restricted its search to publications available up to September 2024. The search strategy emphasised peer-reviewed academic and scientific publications.Parte superior do formulário

The selection process began with a comprehensive search of the Scopus database, using the search term "artificial intelligence" in the title, abstract, and keywords. This initial search identified 605,271 documents. A secondary search query was applied to narrow the focus to marketing applications: TITLE-ABS-KEY "artificial intelligence" AND TITLE-ABS-KEY "marketing," which reduced the dataset to 4,794 documents. This step was crucial in identifying literature that explicitly linked AI with marketing practices, ensuring the relevance of the documents to the study's aims. Finally, the search further refines by adding the keyword "marketing strategy," which limited the dataset to 175 documents directly related to AI-driven marketing strategies. These results formed the core of the systematic review, and the researchers subsequently analysed them for relevance and quality.

Specific inclusion and exclusion criteria were applied to ensure the relevance and rigour of the documents analysed in the final report (see Table 2). The researchers included only articles published in peer-reviewed journals that addressed the intersection of marketing strategy and brand development. To keep the dataset focused, they excluded publications unrelated to business, marketing, or branding fields. This systematic selection process ensured the final literature set was high-quality and closely aligned with the research objectives. Table 2 provides a summary of the search process.

Table 2. Screening Methodology.

<table>
<tr><th>Database Scopus</th><th>Screening</th><th>Publications</th></tr>
<tr><td>Meta-search</td><td>Keyword: Artificial Intelligence</td><td>605,271</td></tr>
<tr><td>First Inclusion Criterion</td><td>Keyword: Artificial Intelligence, Marketing</td><td>4,794</td></tr>
<tr><td>Second Inclusion Criteria</td><td>Keyword: Artificial Intelligence, Marketing
Exact Keyword: Marketing Strategy</td><td rowspan="2">175</td></tr>
<tr><td>Screening</td><td>Keyword: Artificial Intelligence, Marketing
Exact Keyword: Marketing Strategy
Until October 2024</td></tr>
</table>

Source: own elaboration

Content and thematic analysis methods were utilised to identify, assess, and present the range of documents, following the approach outlined by Rosário & Casaca (2023) and Rosário et al. (2023, 2021). Strict selection criteria were applied to include only relevant, high-quality academic sources. The researchers included studies that specifically focused on luxury brands and consumer behaviour. Document eligibility was assessed based on alignment with the research topic, methodological rigour, and publication in peer-reviewed sources (see Figure 1).

Figure 1. PRISMA 2020 flow diagram for the systematic literature search.

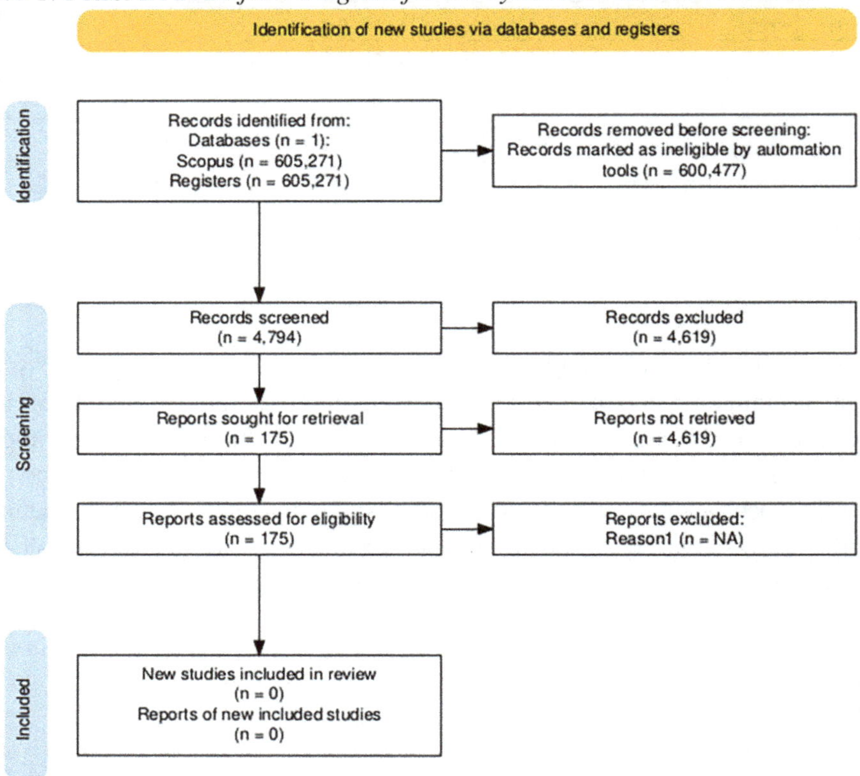

Subsequently, 175 scientific and academic documents indexed in Scopus were analysed using a combination of narrative and bibliometric approaches, as detailed by Rosário & Casaca (2023) and Rosário et al. (2023, 2021). These methods were applied to examine the documents' content and identify recurring themes that were directly relevant to the research questions.

Of the 175 documents selected, 83 were conference proceedings, 47 were journals, 40 were book series, and 5 were books.

PUBLICATION DISTRIBUTION

Peer-reviewed articles on Artificial Intelligence in Marketing on Ethical Implications and Managerial Strategies, September 2024. The year 2024 has the highest number of peer-reviewed publications, reaching 39. Figure 2 summarises the peer-reviewed literature published until September 2024.

Figure 2. Documents by year

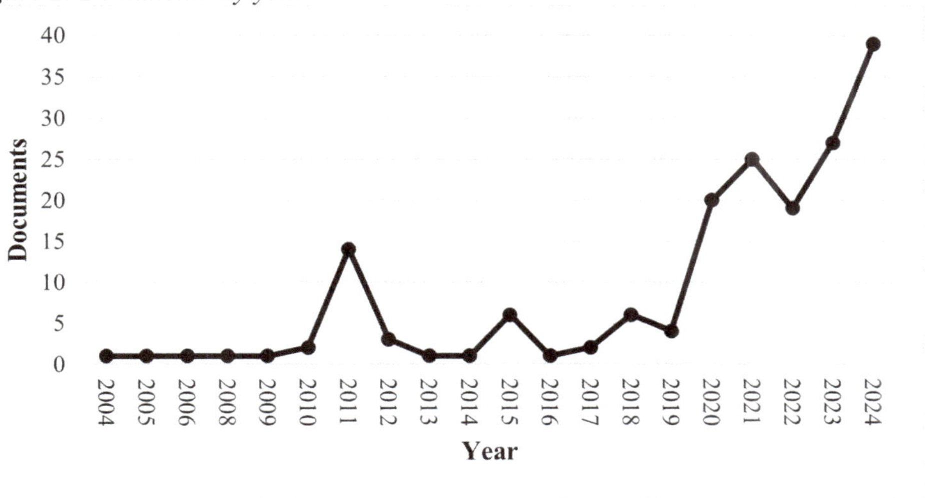

Source: own elaboration

Figure 3 displays the countries exhibiting the highest levels of scientific output in specific research areas, with particular emphasis on China, India, the USA, and Indonesia, which boast the most significant number of publications.

Figure 3. Scientific production by country.

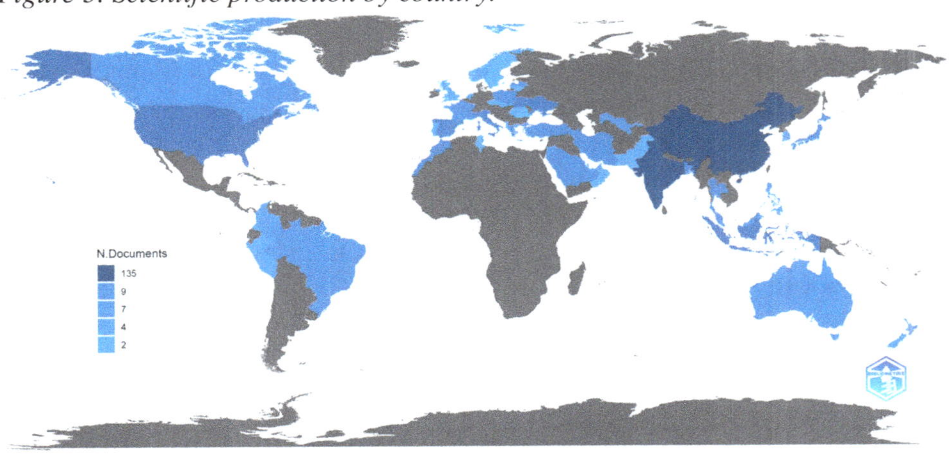

Table 3 and Figure 3 visually illustrate the top 10 nations making notable scientific contributions in the examined domains. This investigation aims to identify countries that prioritise studying luxury brands and their consumption.

Table 3. Top 10 countries by number of publications.

Country	Number of Publications
CHINA	135
INDIA	104
USA	25
INDONESIA	20
SPAIN	15
UKRAINE	14
ITALY	12
JAPAN	11
MOROCCO	11
BAHRAIN	9

Source: own elaboration

Publications were sorted out as follows: Advances In Intelligent Systems And Computing (8); 2011 2nd International Conference On Artificial Intelligence Management Science And Electronic Commerce Aimsec 2011 Proceedings (8); Lecture Notes In Networks And Systems (7); Lecture Notes In Computer Science Including Subseries Lecture Notes In Artificial Intelligence And Lecture Notes In Bioinformatics (7); Communications In Computer And Information Science (5); ACM International Conference Proceeding Series (4); Procedia Computer Science (3); Journal Of The Academy Of Marketing Science (3); Journal Of Physics Conference Series (3); Ceur Workshop Proceedings (3); with 2 (Studies In Big Data; Strategic Direction; Smart And Sustainable Interactive Marketing; Mobile Information Systems; Lecture Notes On Data Engineering And Communications Technologies; Lecture Notes In Electrical Engineering; Journal Of Business Research; International Conference On Electrical Computer Communications And Mechatronics Engineering Iceccme 2023; Information Switzerland; IFIP Advances In Information And Communication Technology; IEEE Access; Computers In Human Behavior), and the remaining publications with 1 document.

The subject areas covered by the 82 scientific or academic documents were Computer Science (142), Engineering (59), Business, Management and Accounting (37);

Mathematics (34); Decision Sciences (30); Economics, Econometrics and Finance (17); Physics and Astronomy (13); Materials Science (10); Social Sciences (7); Medicine (7); Energy (5); Psychology (4); Arts and Humanities (4); Neuroscience (3); Environmental Science (2); Earth and Planetary Sciences (2); Agricultural and Biological Sciences (2); Multidisciplinary (1); Chemistry (1); Chemical Engineering (1); and Biochemistry, Genetics and Molecular Biology (1).

The most quoted article was "A Strategic Framework for Artificial Intelligence in Marketing" by Huang & Rust (2021), with 499 quotes published in the Journal of the Academy of Marketing Science 7,190 (SJR), the best quartile (Q1), and with H index (207). In this article, "The authors develop a three-stage framework for strategic marketing planning, incorporating multiple artificial intelligence (AI) benefits: mechanical AI for automating repetitive marketing functions and activities, thinking AI for processing data to arrive at decisions, and feeling AI for analysing interactions and human emotions."

In Figure 4, we can analyse citation changes for documents published up to September 2024. The period ≤2014-2024 shows a positive net growth in citations with an R2 of 72%, reaching 983 in 2024.

Figure 4. Evolution of citations between ≤2014 and 2024.

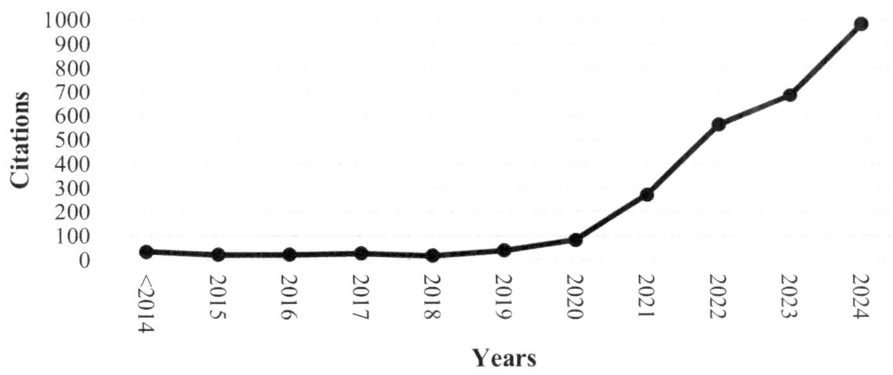

Source: own elaboration

The h-index measures the productivity and impact of published works by identifying the highest number of articles each has received at least an equal number of citations. Seventeen of the documents considered for the h-index received at least 17 citations.

Citations of all scientific and academic documents from the period ≤2014 to September 2024, with a total of 2,746 citations; of the 175 documents, 71 were not cited. The self-citation of documents in ≤2014 to September 2024 was 59.

Using the main keywords "Artificial Intelligence in Marketing on Ethical Implications and Managerial Strategies, "the bibliometric analysis revealed key indicators of the evolving landscape of scientific and academic information within the documents, as shown in Figure 5. The researchers derived these insights using VOSviewer scientific software, focusing specifically on the primary search terms: "Artificial Intelligence," "Marketing," and "Marketing Strategy."

Figure 5. Network of all keywords

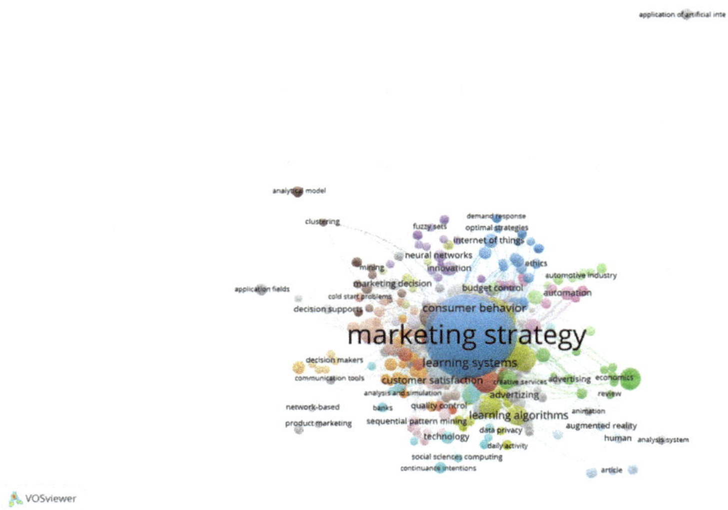

This study builds on a thorough review of scientific and academic literature exploring Artificial Intelligence in Marketing on Ethical Implications and Managerial Strategies. Figure 6 provides a detailed examination of the interrelated keywords, highlighting the connections between critical terms across the academic articles. This analysis helps identify the topics covered in these studies and offers valuable insights into potential avenues for future research. Furthermore, Figure 7 illustrates a substantial number of co-citations and units, enhancing the analysis of the cited references and supporting the overall findings.

Figure 6. Network of Linked Keywords

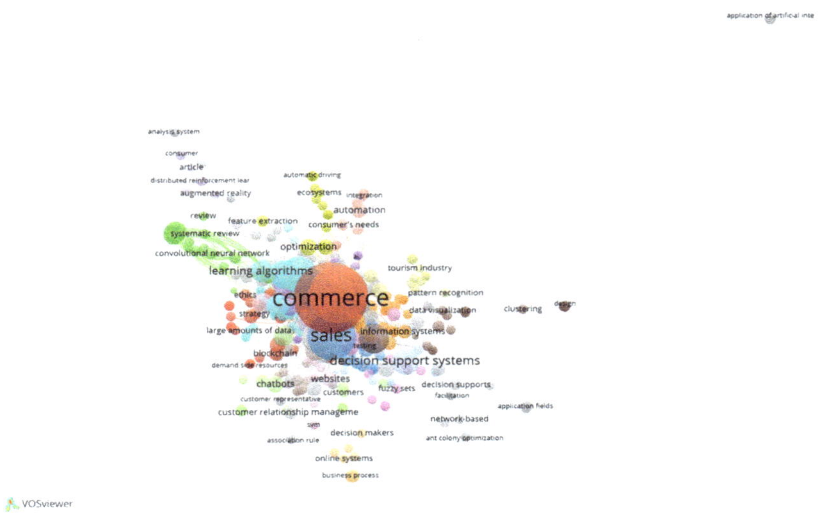

Figure 7. Network of co-citation

THEORETICAL PERSPECTIVES

In recent years, the integration of AI into marketing has grown significantly. Businesses increasingly leverage AI technologies to enhance customer engagement, streamline operations, and optimise marketing strategies (Jhaveri et al., 2023). AI-driven tools like machine learning algorithms, chatbots, and predictive analytics have become central to marketing efforts. They enable companies to deliver personalised content, automate processes, and make data-informed decisions (Mdoe et al., 2023). This growth and adoption have led to increased research on the application of AI in marketing and its potential impacts and challenges. This literature review section synthesises data from the identified 175 sources.

Defining the Main Concepts

Artificial Intelligence

Artificial intelligence (AI) is a branch of computer science focused on creating systems and technologies capable of simulating human cognitive processes such as learning, reasoning, problem-solving, and decision-making. Although there is no standard definition of AI, Samoili et al. (2020) describe it as "machines that behave like humans or are capable of actions that require intelligence" (p.7). AI encompasses a wide range of subfields, including machine learning, natural language processing, and neural networks, which allow systems to adapt, predict, and improve through exposure to new data (Ponomarenko et al., 2024). AI systems analyse vast amounts of information, identify patterns, and execute tasks with high accuracy, often surpassing human capabilities in speed and scalability.

AI transforms marketing by enhancing data analysis, automating repetitive tasks, and improving customer interaction through personalised content and predictive insights. Tools like recommendation engines, chatbots, and predictive analytics are examples of how AI is applied to make marketing more efficient and effective (Rama Krishna et al., 2023; Salkovska et al., 2023). They enable businesses to precisely reach target audiences and optimise decision-making based on real-time data. As AI continues to evolve, its potential to revolutionise marketing strategies is substantial (Özkaynak et al., 2024). Its ability to process and interpret large-scale consumer data will be at the forefront of digital marketing innovation.

Marketing

Marketing is the strategic process by which organisations create, communicate, and deliver value to consumers with the ultimate goal of promoting and selling products or services. Its history dates back 200 years, when Thomas Barrett invented persuasion, awareness, and promotion techniques (Sheth, 2021; Cillo & Rubera, 2024). Marketing involves understanding customer needs and behaviours, market research, brand positioning, product development, and campaigns to generate awareness and drive consumer engagement. Modern marketing integrates traditional approaches, such as print advertising and in-store promotions, and digital tactics, such as social media marketing, search engine optimisation (SEO), and email campaigns (Abdulla & Hussain, 2024; Kurolov, 2022). Developing a strategy that balances long-term brand equity with short-term sales objectives, using data to inform decision-making, and adapting to changing market conditions is central to effective marketing (Djasurovna et al., 2024; Zeeshan & Saxena, 2020). In today's digital era, marketing has become increasingly data-driven, relying on advanced tools and technologies, including AI, to collect consumer insights, analyse trends, and automate workflows (Ziakis & Vlachopoulou, 2023). This shift allows marketers to craft personalised, real-time customer experiences, building stronger relationships between brands and their audiences while optimising resource allocation and marketing performance across various platforms.

Theoretical Frameworks on AI Adoption in Marketing

Theoretical frameworks provide a structured approach to understanding the underlying principles and dynamics that influence AI adoption in marketing. Applying established theories can help comprehend how marketers and consumers interact with AI-driven tools and the implications of these interactions on marketing strategies (Doanh et al., 2023; Narayanasamy et al., 2019). Two relevant frameworks in this context are Social Identity Theory and Affordance Theory. They offer valuable insights into how AI shapes the marketing landscape and influences consumer behaviour. These theories help explain the psychological and perceptual factors that drive the adoption and effectiveness of AI technologies in marketing.

Social Identity Theory

Henri Tajfel and John Turner developed the Social Identity Theory (SIT) in the 1970s. However, Raskovic and Takacs-Haynes (2021) trace its origins back to Henri Tajfel's early research in the 1950s on the influence of social categorisation on perceptions, followed by his exploration of the cognitive basis of prejudice in the 1960s. His work on minimal social categorisation in the early 1970s and group-based social comparisons in the mid-1970s also provided foundational concepts. SIT argues that individuals define themselves based on their membership in social groups (Hodson & Earle, 2017). According to this theory, a person's self-concept is closely tied to their identification with various groups, whether based on nationality, gender, profession, or brand loyalty. The theory explains how individuals derive pride and self-esteem from the success and status of the groups they associate with, leading to in-group favouritism and out-group discrimination (Charness & Chen, 2020). In addition, SIT highlights the psychological mechanisms that drive group behaviour, including categorisation, identification, and comparison. Individuals tend to categorise themselves and others into social groups, identify with these groups, and compare their group to others to maintain positive self-perceptions.

SIT is highly relevant in explaining the adoption of AI in marketing, especially in understanding consumer behaviour and brand loyalty in the digital age. AI-driven marketing tools leverage data on social identities to create more personalised and targeted content that resonates with specific consumer groups (Liu et al., 2020). For example, AI can analyse consumer data to identify patterns of group behaviour, enabling brands to tailor their messaging and positioning to align with the identities of their target audiences. AI-enhanced tools such as customer segmentation and personalised advertising can reinforce consumers' sense of belonging to specific brand communities, strengthening brand loyalty (Rather & Hollebeek, 2019). Moreover, AI systems can track how social identities evolve, giving marketers real-time insights into how consumers' group affiliations influence purchasing behaviour (Selenko et al., 2022). Consequently, they can leverage these insights to create dynamic and relevant marketing strategies that capitalise on the psychological principles of SIT.

Affordance Theory

Psychologist James J. Gibson originally introduced the Affordance Theory. It refers to the concept that an object or environment provides particular action possibilities or “affordances” based on its properties and the individual's capabilities (Blewett & Hugo, 2016). In essence, affordances are the potential uses or actions a person perceives in an object or system. The theory highlights the relationship between users and the technological tools they interact with (Volkoff & Strong, 2017). Researchers have widely applied it in various fields, including design, human-computer interaction, and organisational studies. Affordances are not intrinsic features but rather emerge through the interaction between the user's goals and the object's capabilities, meaning that what one person sees as a possibility for action may differ from another based on their context and knowledge.

Affordance Theory helps explain how AI tools provide marketers with new possibilities for action and strategy. AI offers multiple affordances to marketing professionals, such as automating routine tasks, providing predictive analytics, and delivering personalised content at scale (Keller et al., 2019). Marketers perceive these affordances based on their understanding of the technology and its alignment with their strategic goals. For example, AI's ability to analyse large datasets allows marketers to gain deeper insights into customer behaviour and preferences, leading to more informed decision-making (Liu & Chen, 2024). Similarly, AI-driven chatbots afford real-time customer service, enabling businesses to enhance customer experience and engagement. The concept of affordance is critical in explaining how marketing teams adopt and use AI technologies (Lin et al., 2022). It emphasises that the value of AI lies not just in its technical capabilities but in how users recognise and leverage these capabilities within their specific marketing contexts.

Applications of AI in Marketing

AI applications in marketing have transformed how businesses engage with consumers, optimise strategies, and drive growth. Leveraging AI innovations, such as advanced machine learning algorithms and data analytics, enables marketers to make more informed decisions, personalise customer experiences, and automate critical processes (Patil et al., 2024; Hidri et al., 2020; Sakas et al., 2022). Integrating AI across various marketing functions enhances efficiency and provides valuable insights that lead to more targeted and effective campaigns (Wilendra et al., 2024). Below are vital applications of AI in marketing that demonstrate its broad and impactful role in the industry.

Customer Engagement

AI-driven technologies enhance customer engagement by facilitating meaningful interactions between brands and their audiences. Businesses use machine learning algorithms to analyse customer behaviour and preferences in real time, allowing for timely and relevant communication (Kunekar et al., 2024; Peruchini et al., 2024). For instance, Gabelaia (2023) found that AI can track how users interact with digital content, enabling marketers to identify patterns that indicate a customer's interests and needs. With this insight, brands can create tailored experiences, such as personalised recommendations and targeted content, fostering a deeper connection with customers (Albán Bartra et al., 2021; Chen et al., 2020). In addition, AI-powered tools can automate engagement efforts (Hsu & Liou, 2021). This would ensure that businesses maintain consistent and effective communication across various platforms, from social media to email marketing, ultimately leading to stronger customer relationships and increased engagement rates.

Brand Loyalty

AI significantly influences brand loyalty by enabling companies to provide personalised experiences that resonate with individual consumers. AI leverages data analytics, which helps brands understand their customer's preferences, habits, and feedback, allowing for tailored interactions that enhance satisfaction (James et al., 2021; Rodriguez-Sarmiento et al., 2024). For example, AI can analyse purchase history and browsing behaviour to suggest products that align with customers' tastes, creating a sense of understanding and connection (Huang & Rust, 2021). Moreover, AI-driven loyalty programs can dynamically adapt to customer behaviour, offering rewards aligning with purchasing patterns and encouraging repeat business (Liu & Chen, 2021; Lv, 2022). As a result, when customers feel valued and understood, their likelihood of developing loyalty toward a brand increases. The sense of being valued and understood contributes to long-term customer retention and advocacy.

Personalisation

Personalisation is a crucial application of AI in marketing that transforms how businesses communicate with customers. According to Rao et al. (2018), AI enables marketers to create highly personalised content and recommendations by analysing vast amounts of data, including demographic information, browsing history, and purchase patterns. This tailored approach enhances the customer experience by ensuring that marketing messages are relevant and timely, significantly improving engagement rates (Kushnarevych & Kollárová, 2023; Lee, 2021). In addition, personalised marketing campaigns, driven by AI insights, can dynamically adjust in real-time, responding to user interactions and preferences (Irani & Nozari, 2024). This strategy enhances the overall effectiveness of marketing strategies and customer satisfaction.

Predictive Analytics

AI-powered predictive analytics allows marketers to forecast future consumer behaviours and trends based on historical data. Businesses employing machine learning algorithms can analyse patterns in customer interactions, purchase histories, and market dynamics to identify potential future actions (Adi Pratama et al., 2024; Wu et al., 2021). This capability enables organisations to make data-driven decisions about inventory management, marketing strategies, and customer engagement efforts (Tianyuan & Moro, 2021). Predictive analytics can help determine which products are likely in demand, allowing companies to optimise inventory and reduce waste (Al Khaldy et al., 2023; Tian et al., 2018; Kadu & Joshi, 2022). Furthermore, brands can proactively engage with their audiences through targeted marketing campaigns by anticipating customer needs, improving customer satisfaction and increasing conversion rates.

Customer Segmentation

AI enhances customer segmentation by providing deeper insights into consumer behaviours and preferences, allowing marketers to categorise audiences more effectively. Traditional segmentation methods rely on broad demographic criteria. AI enables more nuanced groupings based on intricate behavioural data (Agrawal et al., 2024; Jha et al., 2020). AI can identify distinct customer segments with common traits or preferences by analysing purchasing habits, online interactions, and social media activity (Septiana Putra et al., 2023; Kasahara et al., 2017). This advanced segmentation allows marketers to tailor their strategies to specific groups, delivering targeted messages and offers that resonate more effectively (Su, 2018; Thamaraiselvi et al., 2024). As a result, businesses can optimise their marketing efforts, allocate resources efficiently, and achieve higher engagement and conversion rates in their campaigns.

Chatbots and Virtual Assistants

AI-powered chatbots and virtual assistants have revolutionised customer service by providing real-time support and information. These AI-driven tools can handle various inquiries, from answering frequently asked questions to guiding customers through complex processes while operating 24/7 (Youn & Jin, 2021). Chatbots leverage natural language processing to understand and respond to customer queries conversationally, enhancing the overall user experience (Huang et al., 2021; Chica et al., 2023). In addition, they can collect valuable data on customer preferences and issues, which can inform marketing strategies and product development (Liu, 2021; Khatibi et al., 2011). As a result, businesses that implement AI chatbots and virtual assistants can significantly improve customer satisfaction, streamline operations, and reduce response times (Khondakar et al., 2024). These practices help free human agents to focus on more complex tasks.

Marketing Automation

AI plays a critical role in marketing automation by streamlining repetitive tasks and enhancing the efficiency of marketing campaigns. Businesses can automate various processes using AI-driven tools, including email marketing, social media posting, and lead nurturing (Gupta & Tomar, 2021; Kordon, 2010). This automation allows marketers to focus on strategic planning and creativity. For instance, AI can analyse customer behaviour to trigger automated email responses based on user actions, such as abandoned shopping carts or recent purchases (Martínez-Rolán & Piñeiro-Otero, 2022). This level of automation saves time and resources and ensures that customers receive timely and relevant communications (Manis & Madhavaram, 2023; Kumar et al., 2024). Organisations that integrate AI into marketing automation improve their responsiveness to consumer needs and optimise the overall effectiveness of their marketing strategies.

Ad Targeting

AI helps analyse consumer data to deliver personalised advertisements to the right audience at the right time. Through machine learning algorithms, AI can identify patterns in user behaviour, preferences, and demographics (Otero & Gutiérrez, 2015). Marketers can then use these insights to segment their audiences more precisely. This targeted approach ensures that advertisements reach individuals most likely interested in the promoted product or service (Hatano et al., 2019; He, 2022). Moreover, AI enables dynamic ad placements that can adapt in real time based on user interactions, maximising the relevance of the content shown (Hsieh et al., 2011; Kumar et al., 2021). As a result, AI-driven ad targeting improves the efficiency of marketing campaigns and enhances return on investment (ROI) by increasing conversion rates and reducing wasted ad spend.

Managerial Strategies for AI Implementation in Marketing

Implementing AI in marketing requires a strategic approach to realise its full potential. Marketing leaders must focus on integrating AI technologies to align with broader business goals while ensuring that teams across the organisation are equipped to utilise these tools effectively (Hu, 2011; Chen et al., 2022). AI-driven strategies should enhance marketing processes' efficiency and support continuous improvement through data analysis and informed decision-making (Charles et al., 2024). Below are critical managerial strategies that provide a framework for successfully incorporating AI into marketing operations.

Data-Driven Decision Making

Incorporating content marketing and storytelling in a marketing strategy can help brands engage consumers by providing value beyond product offerings. Modern-day consumers expect more from brands than advertisements, including informative, entertaining, or inspiring content. Content marketing enables brands to meet this demand by producing blogs, videos, articles, and social media posts that align with the brand's values and mission while addressing the target audience's interests (Roy et al., 2022). Storytelling is a critical component of content marketing that allows brands to humanise their identity by crafting narratives that resonate emotionally with consumers (Chen et al., 2023). Through stories that reflect the brand's history, values, or customer experiences, brands can create a lasting impression, which is vital for building brand loyalty. Therefore, an effective marketing strategy should include content marketing and storytelling to facilitate an ongoing conversation between the brand and its audience (Mochla et al., 2023). These elements help keep the brand prominent in consumers' minds and foster long-term engagement. As a result, these opportunities contribute to brand-building by adding depth to the brand's image, making it more relatable and memorable to consumers.

AI Integration into Marketing Processes

Seamless integration of AI into existing marketing workflows is crucial for maximising its potential. Marketers should view AI not as a standalone tool but as a complement to existing functions like content creation, customer relationship management (CRM), and analytics (Abebe et al., 2018; Abbasi & Esmaili, 2024). Marketing leaders must work closely with IT teams to embed AI technologies into processes where they can add the most value (Alammal & Al Mubarak, 2023; Sarath Kumar Boddu et al., 2022). For example, Davenport et al. (2020) explain that integrating AI into CRM systems can enhance customer interactions by providing personalised content and automating routine tasks such as lead nurturing and customer follow-ups. When fully integrated into core marketing operations, AI enhances the department's ability to operate efficiently, make data-backed decisions, and scale initiatives with minimal human intervention.

Cross-Functional Collaboration

Effective AI implementation in marketing requires collaboration across various departments, particularly between marketing, IT, and data science teams. Each team brings unique expertise (Jianjun, 2020). Marketers understand consumer behaviour and campaign objectives, IT professionals ensure the technical infrastructure can support AI tools, and data scientists can provide insights into data patterns and algorithm performance (Kavitha Devi & Venkatesh, 2010; Maharani & Gozali, 2015; Noor, 2022). Encouraging cross-functional collaboration ensures that AI technologies are implemented correctly and optimised to meet marketing goals. This approach helps marketers use AI tools to their fullest potential by translating technical capabilities into actionable marketing strategies (Setor, 2021; Lee, 2004).

In addition, fostering collaboration helps avoid silos, ensuring that AI initiatives align with overall business objectives.

Performance Monitoring and Optimisation

AI-driven marketing strategies require ongoing monitoring to assess their effectiveness and make necessary adjustments. Managers must establish key performance indicators (KPIs) that reflect short-term and long-term marketing goals (Cui, 2024). AI tools often assist in tracking these metrics, such as customer engagement, conversion rates, and ROI. Business managers can continuously monitor performance and identify areas where AI-driven campaigns succeed, as well as areas where improvements are needed (Durmus Senyapar et al., 2024; Li, 2024). Regular assessment allows businesses to fine-tune AI algorithms, ensuring that marketing initiatives remain agile and responsive to changing consumer behaviours or market trends (Meng & Beninsig, 2024; Lee et al., 2020; Senecha & Srivastava, 2022). The cycle of monitoring, feedback, and optimisation is critical for maintaining the relevance and efficiency of AI-powered marketing strategies.

Scalability and Flexibility

As AI continues to evolve, marketing strategies must remain scalable and flexible. AI solutions should be chosen with an eye toward future growth, ensuring they can adapt to increasing data volumes, expanding customer bases, and more complex marketing needs (Li et al., 2023; Fu et al., 2018; Shen et al., 2011). Managers must prioritise AI tools that can be easily scaled to handle more extensive operations or changing marketing landscapes. For example, AI can manage increased customer interactions, automate more complex tasks, and provide deeper insights through more extensive data sets as businesses grow. Flexibility is equally essential (Gallego et al., 2024; Lei et al., 2021). AI technologies should be adaptable enough to integrate with emerging marketing trends or shifts in consumer behaviour without requiring a complete overhaul of the system (Gore & Kumar Mishra, 2023; Yaiprasert & Hidayanto, 2023). A scalable and flexible AI strategy allows marketing teams to grow and innovate alongside the technology.

Change Management

Successful AI implementation requires effective change management to ensure smooth organisational adoption. Marketing teams may face resistance when integrating AI technologies, as employees might feel threatened by automation or need help interacting with new systems (Kaur et al., 2020). Managers must guide their teams through this transition by fostering a culture that embraces innovation and providing comprehensive training on AI tools and their benefits (Tsai et al., 2006; Songsangyos et al., 2015). Clear communication about how AI will enhance, rather than replace, human roles can help alleviate concerns and encourage buy-in from staff (Alawadh et al., 2023; Liang et al., 2019). A structured change management process equips teams to adapt to AI technologies, enabling smoother implementation and long-term success in marketing initiatives.

Ethical Implications of Implementing AI in Marketing

The rise of AI in marketing presents multiple ethical implications that businesses must carefully navigate. While AI offers immense potential for improving efficiency, personalisation, and customer engagement, its use also raises critical concerns regarding the treatment of consumer data, fairness in decision-making, and the impact on individuals and society (Benjelloun & Kabak, 2024). This section explores the key ethical dilemmas associated with AI implementation in marketing, highlighting businesses' complexities in balancing innovation with ethical responsibility.

Data Privacy

Data privacy is one of the most pressing ethical concerns in AI-driven marketing. AI systems rely on large volumes of personal data to function effectively, including customer demographics, browsing history, purchase patterns, and sensitive information such as location data or social media activity (Makhlooqa & Mubarakb, 2024; Sun, 2023). This vast collection of personal data raises concerns about how marketers gather, store, and use this information (Qian & Gao, 2011). Many consumers are unaware of the extent of data collection and usage, which often leads to a breach of trust between them and businesses. In addition, the risk of data breaches or unauthorised access increases with AI since these systems often handle and process data at unprecedented scales (Xie & He, 2022; Yang et al., 2020). Consumer data becomes vulnerable when companies fail to ensure robust security measures, leading to potential financial and reputational damage (Zhang et al., 2020). Furthermore, the need for clear global standards on data privacy adds complexity. Different regions enforce varying levels of protection, leaving consumers exposed in jurisdictions with weaker regulations.

Bias and Discrimination

AI systems are susceptible to bias and discrimination, which presents significant ethical challenges in marketing. Since historical data trains AI algorithms, the AI system can perpetuate or even amplify any biases present in that data (Leavy et al., 2020; Xu, 2022; Singhal et al., 2024). For example, if past marketing campaigns disproportionately targeted specific demographics, an AI system may continue to favour these groups, potentially leading to discriminatory outcomes (Schwartz et al., 2022; Liu, 2024). This tendency requires revision in product recommendations, pricing strategies, and ad targeting to prevent the exclusion or unfair treatment of marginalised groups (Sung et al., 2022). Biases may arise from the data and the AI algorithms' design. Human developers may unintentionally encode their biases into the system (Nazer et al., 2023; Zhang et al., 2022; Xiao, 2012). This unintentional bias can lead AI systems to make decisions reinforcing existing social inequalities, undermining fairness and inclusivity in marketing practices (Zhang, 2024; Naufal et al., 2017). The opacity of AI decision-making processes presents a challenge, making it difficult for practitioners to detect and address bias once embedded in the system.

Transparency

The issue of transparency in AI-driven marketing involves the opacity of algorithms and the decision-making processes behind AI applications. AI systems often function as "black boxes," making decisions that users, consumers, or developers do not understand or explain (Felzmann et al., 2020; Buhas et al., 2024; Zhang & Huang, 2015). The lack of transparency can erode trust between consumers and companies, as individuals may feel uncomfortable or suspicious when they cannot understand how or why certain advertisements or content target them. In marketing, AI is frequently used to personalise customer experiences, but without transparency, consumers may not fully grasp the extent to which their data is being used or manipulated (Schmidt et al., 2020; Carloman et al., 2024; D'Aniello et al., 2016). Moreover, the complexity of AI algorithms makes it difficult to audit or hold companies accountable for the outcomes of their AI systems, especially when harmful or unintended consequences arise (Daneshjou et al., 2021; Olena et al., 2024). This challenge creates ethical issues in maintaining transparent customer relationships and ensuring AI systems operate clearly and understandably.

Manipulation and Autonomy

AI's ability to predict and influence consumer behaviour raises ethical concerns about manipulation and the erosion of consumer autonomy. AI-powered marketing strategies, particularly those using predictive analytics, can create highly targeted content designed to influence purchasing decisions, sometimes without the consumer being fully aware of the extent of the influence (de Marcellis-Warin et al., 2022; Elhajjar, 2024). While traditional marketing has always aimed to persuade consumers, AI's capacity to process large amounts of data and predict behaviour with high accuracy introduces a new level of precision in shaping choices. This heightened precision can blur the line between persuasion and manipulation in marketing (Blauth et al., 2022; Papavasileiou & Tsadiras, 2011; Prada Segura & Velandia Daza, 2021). Consumers may find themselves guided toward decisions that align with a company's interests but may not be in their best personal interest (Rita et al., 2021). This influence can undermine autonomy, as individuals lose the ability to make independent choices based on unbiased information (Hacker, 2023; Patel & Modi, 2020; Wang & Zhong, 2024). The ethical challenge here revolves around how much impact is too much and where the boundary lies between acceptable marketing practices and manipulative tactics that exploit consumer vulnerabilities.

Consent and Informed Choice

The ethical issue of consent and informed choice in AI marketing arises from the often opaque data collection processes characterising AI systems. AI requires vast amounts of consumer data to function effectively. However, many consumers must know how much their data is collected, shared, or used (Farid et al., 2024; Eriksson et al., 2020). In many cases, consent must be adequately obtained or embedded within lengthy, unclear privacy policies that consumers may need to fully understand (Roy et al., 2024). The lack of explicit consent prompts questions about whether consumers are truly informed about how their personal information is used, especially when shared with third parties or applied to purposes beyond the initial agreement (Cohen, 2019; El Koufi & Belangour, 2023).

Moreover, the dynamic nature of AI systems, which continually adapt and evolve, allows data usage to change over time. This variability further complicates the issue of informed consent, as it becomes challenging for consumers to stay fully aware of how their data may be used in the future (Cohen & Slottje, 2024; Saadi & Azdimousa, 2024; Wang & Xu, 2011). The lack of transparency and clear communication can make consumers feel deceived or exploited, as they may need to fully understand or agree with how companies leverage their data in marketing strategies.

Job Displacement and Workforce Impact

Implementing AI in marketing raises significant ethical concerns regarding job displacement and the broader impact on the workforce. AI technologies are increasingly capable of automating tasks previously performed by human workers, such as data analysis, content creation, and customer service interactions (Neary et al., 2018; Fu & Fu, 2011; Trandafili et al., 2013). While this can lead to increased efficiency and cost savings for businesses, it also threatens to reduce the need for human labour in specific roles (Lazaroiu & Rogalska, 2023). As AI continues to evolve, marketing professionals may find their skills becoming obsolete, leading to job losses or the need for significant retraining (Tiwari, 2023; Gao et al., 2023; Wang et al., 2022). This shift affects individual workers and has broader societal implications, such as increased unemployment and economic inequality (Tsai, 2024; Wahbeh & Abuelrub, 2021). The rapid pace of AI adoption in marketing can leave workers unprepared for the transition, creating ethical concerns about how businesses manage the human impact of technological advancements (Chen & Tang, 2022; Gupta & Chokshi, 2020; Wang & Lim, 2011). Furthermore, the rise of AI could lead to a devaluation of human creativity and strategic thinking as companies increasingly rely on machines to generate insights and solutions that were once the domain of human marketers.

CONCLUSION

The emergence of AI has significantly altered the marketing field by offering businesses numerous tools and capabilities to engage customers and optimise strategies. AI has become integral to modern marketing, with applications like predictive analytics, marketing automation, customer segmentation, and personalised experiences becoming standard practices. These AI-driven tools allow businesses to analyse vast amounts of consumer data in real time, making it easier to create targeted, relevant marketing campaigns that resonate with individual preferences. AI-powered chatbots and virtual assistants enhance customer engagement by providing 24/7 support and personalised interactions. Moreover, companies leverage AI to streamline processes, boost efficiency, and drive better decision-making through data-driven insights. To fully capitalise on AI's potential, businesses must implement robust managerial strategies, including integrating AI into marketing processes, promoting cross-functional collaboration, and ensuring scalability and flexibility to adapt to changing market dynamics. Continuous performance monitoring and optimisation are also critical for maintaining the effectiveness and fairness of AI systems as they evolve.

However, the rapid adoption of AI in marketing introduces a series of ethical considerations that marketers must carefully manage to maintain consumer trust and ensure fairness. For instance, data privacy is a crucial concern. AI systems often rely on large datasets containing personal information, which can lead to misuse or breaches. In addition, the risk of bias and discrimination in AI algorithms, where automated systems can perpetuate or amplify existing societal biases, raises serious concerns about fairness in marketing practices. Transparency is another critical issue since the decision-making processes of AI systems are often opaque. The lack of clarity prevents consumers from understanding how companies use their data or why AI systems make confident decisions. The lack of transparency can undermine consumer trust, mainly when companies use AI systems to manipulate or influence consumer behaviour without consumers' full awareness. Marketers must also prioritise consent and informed choice to ensure consumers fully understand how their data will be used. Finally, the workforce impact of AI, including job displacement and the need for upskilling, poses additional ethical considerations. Balancing innovation and ethical responsibility is essential as businesses integrate AI into their operations. Achieving this balance enables businesses to deploy AI systems in ways that are transparent, fair, and respectful of consumer rights. Addressing these challenges allows companies to establish and maintain consumer trust and build sustainable, ethically sound AI-driven marketing strategies that benefit businesses and their customers.

Contributions to theories and practices in Artificial Intelligence (AI) in marketing, specifically concerning ethical implications and managerial strategies, have grown significantly in recent years.

(i) Theoretical Contributions

a) Ethical Frameworks for AI in Marketing Researchers have developed frameworks that identify the ethical dimensions of AI usage in marketing, including privacy, fairness, transparency, and accountability. These frameworks help outline the boundaries of ethical AI, ensuring that consumer rights are respected while leveraging AI capabilities. Researchers have advanced theories to differentiate between acceptable and manipulative practices, such as persuasive versus exploitative AI-driven personalisation, to provide a clearer understanding of ethical AI marketing; b) Theories on Consumer Perception and Trust

Researchers have proposed theoretical models to explore consumer perceptions of AI-driven interactions, focusing on trust, satisfaction, and perceived value. Understanding how transparency in AI operations affects trust has led to the concept of "trustworthiness heuristics," where clear communication of AI involvement can positively impact consumer behaviour. Research has expanded on the "uncanny valley" in AI communication, theorising how overly human-like AI interactions can evoke discomfort or mistrust, affecting brand perception. c) Value creation through AI-enhanced personalisation.

Researchers have developed theories around AI-driven customer journey mapping, demonstrating how AI can optimize consumer touchpoints for better experiences. Specifically, it includes understanding how predictive analytics can impact customer lifetime value and satisfaction, focusing on maintaining an ethical balance in personalization. Contribution to theories like "predictive personalisation ethics", exploring when personalisation goes beyond helpful suggestions into unethical manipulation, has influenced guidelines for ethical data use;

(ii) Practical Contributions

Advances in AI-based segmentation have allowed marketers to target consumers with higher accuracy. Practical guidelines on ethical segmentation involve defining target groups and understanding the ethical impact of excluding or including specific demographics. Companies are creating managerial playbooks that outline when and how to use AI insights, focusing on ethical targeting, avoiding bias, and ensuring AI outputs are fair and non-discriminatory; d) Mitigating AI Bias Tools and strategies for identifying and correcting AI biases in marketing are now standard. Organizations have established best practices for bias audits and ongoing AI evaluation cycles to maintain ethical standards as AI systems evolve; e) Integrating human oversight with AI automation.

Managerial strategies increasingly focus on a hybrid AI-human approach, where AI handles data-driven insights while human experts make final decisions to balance efficiency and ethics.

Guidelines emphasise the role of human oversight in sensitive AI-driven decisions, such as pricing strategies or personalised content delivery, to prevent ethical breaches;

(iii) Emerging Ethical Considerations: a) AI and Consumer Autonomy

The debate on consumer autonomy and AI has led to developing autonomy-preserving marketing strategies. Specifically, it involves designing AI recommendations to frame them as options rather than definitive choices, thereby maintaining consumer control.

Managers develop strategies that encourage transparency in nudging practices by highlighting when an AI-driven suggestion is made and allowing consumers to opt in or out; b) The Role of AI in Sustainability and Ethical Consumerism AI is contributing to the rise of sustainable and ethical consumerism, where AI-driven analytics predict and influence consumer behaviour toward more sustainable choices. Organizations are establishing guidelines to ensure that AI-driven sustainability messages are accurate and not "greenwashed." Managers are increasingly using AI to monitor and report on sustainable marketing practices, ensuring ethical compliance with brand promises and consumer expectations.

(iv) Managerial Strategies for AI Implementation: a) Training and Development

Practical contributions have seen the development of training programs for marketers to understand AI ethics and how to utilise AI tools responsibly. Specifically, it includes training on ethical decision-making processes in data analysis, targeting, and automation. Leadership strategies involve creating a cross-disciplinary AI ethics team within the organisation to oversee AI-related marketing initiatives; b) Adoption of AI Ethics Technology Introduction of AI ethics technology, such as platforms that assess the ethical implications of AI campaigns before launch. These technologies assist managers in identifying potential ethical pitfalls in segmentation, targeting, and personalisation. Companies are encouraged to implement algorithmic transparency tools where consumers can understand the logic behind AI-driven offers or ads, contributing to a more ethical and consumer-friendly approach.

By integrating these theoretical and practical contributions, companies aim to balance AI's innovative potential in marketing with ethical standards, fostering sustainable, fair, and consumer-centric business practices.

Exploring the future lines of investigation in AI for marketing, particularly around ethical implications and managerial strategies, is critical to navigating the evolving landscape. (i) There is a growing need to develop industry-specific ethical guidelines for AI in marketing. Research can focus on creating frameworks that consider unique challenges across industries (e.g., healthcare, finance, fashion) where AI usage in marketing has different ethical impacts. Further refinement of ethical AI frameworks that consider cultural and regional variations is essential. Specifically, it involves understanding how ethical considerations vary across global markets and adjusting AI strategies to align with these diverse ethical perspectives. (ii) Researchers are exploring predictive ethics, designing AI systems to forecast potential ethical dilemmas based on consumer data, and marketing tactics to provide a proactive approach to ethical AI management. Specifically, it involves developing AI systems that can anticipate not only consumer behaviour but also potential ethical breaches, enabling early intervention and strategic adjustments to prevent ethical issues; and (iii) Investigating how AI can ethically influence consumer behaviour towards sustainable and ethical choices is a crucial area. Explicitly, it examines the fine line between using AI to provide beneficial nudges that encourage ethical consumption and avoiding manipulative practices that could undermine consumer autonomy. Research could explore AI's capacity to analyse consumer data to predict ethical consumption patterns, creating models that encourage sustainable behaviour without exploiting consumer vulnerabilities.

By advancing these future lines of investigation, researchers and practitioners can better navigate the ethical complexities of AI in marketing, developing strategies that are not only innovative but also responsible, fair, and consumer-focused.

ACKNOWLEDGEMENT

We want to express gratitude to the Editor and the Arbitrators. They offered precious suggestions or improvements. The GOVCOPP Research Center of the University of Aveiro and UNIDCOM supported the authors.

REFERENCES

Abbasi, R., & Esmaili, M. (2024). Identifying the applications of artificial intelligence in online marketing. In *Smart and Sustainable Interactive Marketing* (pp. 32–54). IGI Global., DOI: 10.4018/979-8-3693-1339-8.ch003

Abdulla, A., & Hussain, O. B. (2024). AI-enabled business process optimization and digital marketing. *2024 IEEE International Conference on Interdisciplinary Approaches in Technology and Management for Social Innovation, IATMSI 2024.*

Abebe, R., Adamic, L. A., & Kleinberg, J. (2018). Mitigating overexposure in viral marketing. *32nd AAAI Conference on Artificial Intelligence, AAAI 2018.*

Adi Pratama, R., Auliya Khadija, M., Noviana Paradhita, A., & Nurharjadmo, W. (2024). AI-Driven Predictive Analytics to Enhance Digital Marketing Strategies in Domain and Hosting Business. *2024 International Conference on Data Science and Its Applications, ICoDSA 2024.*

Agrawal, V., Kaswan, K. S., & Kumar, S. (2024). An optimised deep learning model for fast and accurate brain tumour segmentation. *AIP Conference Proceedings.*

Al Khaldy, M. A., Al-Obaydi, B. A. A., & al Shari, A. J. (2023). The Impact of Predictive Analytics and AI on Digital Marketing Strategy and ROI. In *Studies in Big Data* (Vol. 136, pp. 367–379). Springer Science and Business Media Deutschland GmbH., DOI: 10.1007/978-3-031-42455-7_31

Alammal, A. H., & Al Mubarak, M. (2023). Artificial Intelligence in Marketing: Concerns and Solutions. In Internet of Things (Vol. Part F1270, pp. 101–113). Springer Science and Business Media Deutschland GmbH. https://doi.org/DOI: 10.1007/978-3-031-35525-7_7

Alawadh, H. M., Alabrah, A., Meraj, T., & Rauf, H. T. (2023). Discourse analysis-based credibility checks to online reviews using deep learning-based discourse markers. *Computer Speech & Language*, *78*, C7–C101450. DOI: 10.1016/j.csl.2022.101450

Albán Bartra, C., Alcántara Sánchez, D., & Sagástegui Cruz, J. (2021). Sports Marketing and Its Relationship in the Value Creation for the Customers of Sports Center, Trujillo, 2019. Advances in Intelligent Systems and Computing.

Benjelloun, A., & Kabak, S. (2024). *Ethical Challenges and Management Implications of Artificial Intelligence in Digital Marketing*. Lecture Notes in Networks and Systems.

Blauth, T. F., Gstrein, O. J., & Zwitter, A. (2022). Artificial intelligence crime: An overview of malicious use and abuse of AI. *IEEE Access : Practical Innovations, Open Solutions*, *10*, 77110–77122. DOI: 10.1109/ACCESS.2022.3191790

Blewett, C., & Hugo, W. (2016). Actant affordances: A brief history of affordance theory and a Latourian extension for education technology research. *Critical Studies in Teaching and Learning*, *4*(1), 55–76. DOI: 10.14426/cristal.v4i1.50

Buhas, V., Ponomarenko, I., Kazak, O., & Korshun, N. (2024). AI-Driven Sentiment Analysis in Social Media Content. *CEUR Workshop Proceedings*.

Carloman, A. N., Bermudo, U. V. W., Estilloso, E. M., & Llantos, O. E. (2024). Bundle AI: An Application of Multiple Constraint Knapsack Problem (MCKP) Through Genetic Algorithm (GA). Procedia Computer Science.

Charles, V., Rana, N. P., Pappas, I. O., Kamphaug, M., Siau, K., & Engø-Monsen, K. (2024). The Next 'Deep' Thing in X to Z Marketing: An Artificial Intelligence-Driven Approach. *Information Systems Frontiers*, *26*(3), 851–856. DOI: 10.1007/s10796-023-10462-x

Charness, G., & Chen, Y. (2020). Social identity, group behavior, and teams. *Annual Review of Economics*, *12*(1), 691–713. DOI: 10.1146/annurev-economics-091619-032800

Chen, H., Yu, S., Huang, F., Zhu, B., Gao, L., & Qian, C. (2020). Spatio-temporal Analysis of Retail Customer Behavior Based on Clustering and Sequential Pattern Mining. 2020 3rd International Conference on Artificial Intelligence and Big Data, ICAIBD 2020 C7 – 9137465.

Chen, J., Frankwick, G. L., & Zhang, Z. (2022). Adopting Artificial Intelligence to Manage a Turbulent Environment: An Abstract. In Developments in Marketing Science: Proceedings of the Academy of Marketing Science (pp. 223-224). Springer Nature. https://doi.org/DOI: 10.1007/978-3-030-89883-0_61

Chen, N., Li, Z., & Tang, B. (2022). Can digital skills protect against job displacement risk caused by artificial intelligence? Empirical evidence from 701 detailed occupations. *PLoS One*, *17*(11), e0277280. PMID: 36346798

Chica, M., Cordon, O., Robles, J. F., Garrido, A., Mingot, J., & Damas, S. (2023). Zio: an artificial intelligence digital twin to build virtual markets. *Proceedings of the 2023 IEEE Conference on Artificial Intelligence, CAI 2023*.

Chintalapati, S., & Pandey, S. K. (2022). Artificial intelligence in marketing: A systematic literature review. *International Journal of Market Research*, *64*(1), 38–68. DOI: 10.1177/14707853211018428

Cillo, P., & Rubera, G. (2024). Generative AI in innovation and marketing processes: A roadmap of research opportunities. *Journal of the Academy of Marketing Science*. Advance online publication. DOI: 10.1007/s11747-024-01044-7

Cohen, I. G. (2019). Informed consent and medical artificial intelligence: What to tell the patient? Geo. LJ, p. 108, 1425.

Cohen, I. G., & Slottje, A. (2024). Artificial intelligence and the law of informed consent. In Research Handbook On Health, AI, and the Law (pp. 167-182). Edward Elgar Publishing.

Cui, R. (2024). Optimisation of cross-border e-commerce marketing strategy based on deep learning model. Applied Mathematics and Nonlinear Sciences, 9(1 C7-20230176). https://doi.org/DOI: 10.2478/amns.2023.2.00176

D'Aniello, G., Gaeta, A., Gaeta, M., Lepore, M., Orciuoli, F., & Troisi, O. (2016). A new DSS based on situation awareness for smart commerce environments. Journal of Ambient Intelligence and Humanized Computing, 7(1), 47-61. DOI: 10.1007/s12652-015-0300-0

Daneshjou, R., Smith, M. P., Sun, M. D., Rotemberg, V., & Zou, J. (2021). Lack of transparency and potential bias in artificial intelligence data sets and algorithms: A scoping review. *JAMA Dermatology*, *157*(11), 1362–1369. DOI: 10.1001/jamadermatol.2021.3129

Davenport, T., Guha, A., Grewal, D., & Bressgott, T. (2020). How artificial intelligence will change the future of marketing. *Journal of the Academy of Marketing Science*, *48*(1), 24–42. DOI: 10.1007/s11747-019-00696-0

De Marcellis-Warin, N., Marty, F., Thelisson, E., & Warin, T. (2022). Artificial intelligence and consumer manipulations: From consumer's counter algorithms to firm's self-regulation tools. *AI and Ethics*, *2*(2), 259–268. DOI: 10.1007/s43681-022-00149-5

Djasurovna, E. S., Obitovich, K. M., & Akramovich, A. I. (2024). Navigating the Digital Landscape: Enhancing Service Discovery and Portability in Digital Marketing Strategies. Lecture Notes in Computer Science (including subseries Lecture Notes in Artificial Intelligence and Lecture Notes in Bioinformatics)

Doanh, D. C., Dufek, Z., Ejdys, J., Ginevičius, R., Korzynski, P., Mazurek, G., & Ziemba, E. (2023). Generative AI in the manufacturing process: Theoretical considerations. *Engineering Management in Production and Services, 15*(4), 76–89. DOI: 10.2478/emj-2023-0029

Durmus Senyapar, H. N., Colak, I., & Bayindir, R. (2024). AI-Driven Smart Homes and Smart Grids: Marketing Strategies for Seamless Integration and Consumer Adoption. 12th International Conference on Smart Grid, icSmartGrid 2024.

El Koufi, N., & Belangour, A. (2023). Artificial Intelligence Techniques Applied in Precision Marketing: A Survey. *International Conference on Electrical, Computer, Communications and Mechatronics Engineering, ICECCME 2023.*

Elhajjar, S. (2024). Unveiling the marketer's lens: Exploring experiences and perspectives on AI integration in marketing strategies. *Asia Pacific Journal of Marketing and Logistics.* Advance online publication. DOI: 10.1108/APJML-04-2024-0485

Eriksson, T., Bigi, A., & Bonera, M. (2020). Think with me, or think for me? On the future role of artificial intelligence in marketing strategy formulation. *The TQM Journal, 32*(4), 795–814. DOI: 10.1108/TQM-12-2019-0303

Farid, Y., Chang, C., Marcasciano, M., Di Meglio, F., Rodríguez-Mantilla, I., Nanni, J., & Chen, H. C. (2024). Consent 2.0: Informed choices in the age of artificial intelligence. *Surgery, 175*(5), 1454–1455.

Felzmann, H., Fosch-Villaronga, E., Lutz, C., & Tamò-Larrieux, A. (2020). Towards transparency by design for artificial intelligence. *Science and Engineering Ethics, 26*(6), 3333–3361.

Feng, C. M., Park, A., Pitt, L., Kietzmann, J., & Northey, G. (2021). Artificial intelligence in marketing: A bibliographic perspective. *Australasian Marketing Journal, 29*(3), 252–263. DOI: 10.1016/j.ausmj.2020.07.006

Fu, D., & Fu, K. (2011). Notice of Retraction: Research on European marketing strategies of Huawei and its enlightenment on Chinese enterprise. 2011 2nd International Conference on Artificial Intelligence, Management Science, and Electronic Commerce, AIMSEC 2011—Proceedings C7-6011335, pp. 3254–3258. DOI: 10.1109/AIMSEC.2011.6011335

Fu, M., Wong, C. M., Zhu, H., Huang, Y., Li, Y., Zheng, X., & Vong, C. M. (2018). DAlim: Machine learning-based intelligent lucky money determination for large-scale e-commerce businesses. Lecture Notes in Computer Science (including subseries Lecture Notes in Artificial Intelligence and Lecture Notes in Bioinformatics)

Gabelaia, I. (2023). *The Impact of User-Generated Content on Customer Purchase Intentions of Online Shoppers*. Lecture Notes in Networks and Systems.

Gallego, V., Lingan, J., Freixes, A., Juan, A. A., & Osorio, C. (2024). Applying Machine Learning in Marketing: An Analysis Using the NMF and k-Means Algorithms. Information (Switzerland), 15(7 C7 - 368). DOI: 10.3390/info15070368

Gao, Y., Wang, J., Li, Z., & Peng, Z. (2023). The social media big data analysis for demand forecasting in the context of globalisation: Development and case implementation of innovative frameworks. *Journal of Organizational and End User Computing*, *35*(3). Advance online publication. DOI: 10.4018/JOEUC.325217

Gore, S., & Kumar Mishra, P. (2023). Improvisation of Food Delivery Business by Leveraging Ensemble Learning with Various Algorithms. International Conference on Self-Sustainable Artificial Intelligence Systems, ICSSAS 2023, Proceedings.

Gupta, A., & Tomar, K. (2021). Enhancing marketing strategies and analytics through artificial intelligence. Proceedings of 2nd International Conference on Computation, Automation and Knowledge Management, ICCAKM 2021, C7-9357763.

Gupta, S., & Chokshi, S. (2020). Digital Marketing Effectiveness Using Incrementality. *Communications in Computer and Information Science*.

Hacker, P. (2023). Manipulation by algorithms. Exploring the triangle of unfair commercial practice, data protection, and privacy law. *European Law Journal*, *29*(1-2), 142–175.

Haddaway, N. R., Page, M. J., Pritchard, C. C., & McGuinness, L. A. (2022). PRISMA 2020: An R package and Shiny app for producing PRISMA 2020-compliant flow diagrams, with interactivity for optimised digital transparency and Open Synthesis. *Campbell Systematic Reviews*, *18*(2), e1230. DOI: 10.1002/cl2.1230

Hatano, D., Kuroki, Y., Kawase, Y., Sumita, H., Kakimura, N., & Kawarabayashi, K. I. (2019). Non-zero-sum Stackelberg budget allocation game for computational advertising. Lecture Notes in Computer Science (including subseries Lecture Notes in Artificial Intelligence and Lecture Notes in Bioinformatics)

He, Q. (2022).. . *Design of Marketing Data Mining System Based on AI Lecture Notes on Data Engineering and Communications Technologies*, *129*, 133–140. DOI: 10.1007/978-3-030-99616-1_18

Hidri, A., Selmi, A., & Hidri, M. S. (2020). Discovery of Frequent Patterns of Episodes within a Time Window for Alarm Management Systems. IEEE Access, 8 C7 - 8955801, 11061-11073. DOI: 10.1109/ACCESS.2020.2965647

Hodson, G., & Earle, M. (2017). Social Identity Theory (SIT). In *Encyclopedia of Personality and Individual Differences*. Springer., DOI: 10.1007/978-3-319-28099-8_1185-1

Hsieh, M. Y., Kung, C. Y., Lai, C. S., & Chen, C. T. (2011). Using the QFD to make the most potential marketing strategy by applying innovative wireless technology in a hypercompetitive era. *Key Engineering Materials*.

Hsu, S. F., & Liou, S. (2021). Artificial Intelligence Impact on Digital Content Marketing Research. 2021 9th International Conference on Orange Technology, ICOT 2021

Hu, Y. (2011). Notice of Retraction: Research on the improvement of market competitiveness based on customer value. 2011 2nd International Conference on Artificial Intelligence, Management Science, and Electronic Commerce, AIMSEC 2011—Proceedings C7 - 6010645, 1455–1458. DOI: 10.1109/AIMSEC.2011.6010645

Huang, M. H., & Rust, R. T. (2021). A strategic framework for artificial intelligence in marketing. Journal of the Academy of Marketing Science, pp. 49, 30–50. DOI: 10.1007/s11747-020-00749-9

Huang, M. H., & Rust, R. T. (2021). A strategic framework for artificial intelligence in marketing. *Journal of the Academy of Marketing Science*, *49*(1), 30–50. DOI: 10.1007/s11747-020-00749-9

Huang, S. Y. B., Lee, C. J., & Lee, S. C. (2021). Toward a unified theory of customer continuance model for financial technology chatbots. Sensors, 21(17 C7-5687). DOI: 10.3390/s21175687

Irani, H. R., & Nozari, H. (2024). *Smart and sustainable interactive marketing*. IGI Global., DOI: 10.4018/9798369313398

James, C. M., Manoj, D., Pious, G. M., Jose, J. P., & Jeyakrishnan, V. (2021). *Lopels is the AI-based multi-vendor loyalty platform*. Advances in Intelligent Systems and Computing.

Jha, N., Parekh, D., Mouhoub, M., & Makkar, V. (2020). Customer Segmentation and Churn Prediction in Online Retail. Lecture Notes in Computer Science (including subseries Lecture Notes in Artificial Intelligence and Lecture Notes in Bioinformatics).

Jhaveri, M., Chirputkar, A., & Ashok, P. (2023). The efficacy of artificial intelligence in making the best marketing decisions. International Conference on Innovative Data Communication Technologies and Application, ICIDCA 2023—Proceedings.

Jianjun, M. (2020). Research on collaborative filtering recommendation algorithms based on user behaviour characteristics. Proceedings: 2020 International Conference on Big Data and Artificial Intelligence and Software Engineering, ICBASE 2020 C7-9403763.

Kadu, S., & Joshi, B. (2022). Text-Based Sentiment Analysis Using Deep Learning Techniques. In Studies in Big Data (Vol. 113, pp. 81-100). Springer Science and Business Media Deutschland GmbH. DOI: 10.1007/978-3-031-10869-3_5

Kar, A. K., & Khatwani, G. (2014). *A group decision support system for selecting a social CRM*. Advances in Intelligent Systems and Computing.

Kasahara, H., Iiyama, M., & Minoh, M. (2017). Transportation mode inference using environmental constraints. Proceedings of the 11th International Conference on Ubiquitous Information Management and Communication, IMCOM 2017 C7 - 83

Kaur, J., Arora, V., & Bali, S. (2020). Influence of technological advances and change in marketing strategies using analytics in the retail industry. *International Journal of System Assurance Engineering and Management*, *11*(5), 953–961. DOI: 10.1007/s13198-020-01023-5

Kavitha Devi, M. K., & Venkatesh, P. (2010). Kernel-based collaborative-recommender system for e-purchasing. Sadhana. *Academy Proceedings in Engineering Sciences*, *35*(5), 513–524. DOI: 10.1007/s12046-010-0035-8

Keller, R., Stohr, A., Fridgen, G., Lockl, J., & Rieger, A. (2019). Affordance-experimentation-actualisation theory in artificial intelligence research: a predictive maintenance story. In Affordance-Experimentation-Actualization Theory in Artificial Intelligence Research: a Predictive Maintenance Story.

Khatibi, V., Iranmanesh, H., & Keramati, A. (2011). A neuro-IFS intelligent system for marketing strategy selection. *Communications in Computer and Information Science*.

Khondakar, M. F. K., Sarowar, M. H., Chowdhury, M. H., Majumder, S., Hossain, M. A., Dewan, M. A. A., & Hossain, Q. D. (2024). A systematic review on EEG-based neuromarketing: recent trends and analysing techniques. Brain Informatics, 11(1 C7 - 17). DOI: 10.1186/s40708-024-00229-8

Kordon, A. (2010). Marketing computational intelligence in industry. 2010 IEEE World Congress on Computational Intelligence, WCCI 2010 - 2010 IEEE Congress on Evolutionary Computation, CEC 2010 C7 - 5586356

Kumar, V. V., Devi, G. D., Ajay, U., Sharun, M., & Yukesh, P. (2023). Enhancing smallholder farmer livelihoods through AI-based e-commerce marketing for agricultural products. 2nd International Conference on Sustainable Computing and Data Communication Systems, ICSCDS 2023: Proceedings

Kumar, V., Ashraf, A. R., & Nadeem, W. (2024). AI-powered marketing: What, where, and how? International Journal of Information Management, p. 77 C7-102783. DOI: 10.1016/j.ijinfomgt.2024.102783

Kumar, V., Ramachandran, D., & Kumar, B. (2021). Influence of new-age technologies on marketing: A research agenda. Journal of Business Research, pp. 125, 864–877. DOI: 10.1016/j.jbusres.2020.01.007

Kunekar, P., Usman, M., Veena, C. H., Singla, A., Anute, N., & Polke, N. (2024). Enhancing Advertising Initiatives: Using Machine Learning Algorithms to Engage Targeted Customer. Proceedings of International Conference on Communication, Computer Sciences and Engineering, IC3SE 2024.

Kurolov, M. O. (2022). A systematic mapping study of using digital marketing technologies in health care: The state of the art of digital healthcare marketing. *ACM International Conference Proceeding Series*

Kushnarevych, A., & Kollárová, D. (2023). Development of Artificial Intelligence as a Breakthrough for Personalization in Marketing. *International Conference on Electrical, Computer, Communications and Mechatronics Engineering, ICECCME 2023*. DOI: 10.1109/ICECCME57830.2023.10252550

Lazaroiu, G., & Rogalska, E. (2023). How generative artificial intelligence technologies shape partial job displacement and labour productivity growth. *Oeconomia Copernicana, 14*(3), 703–706.

Leavy, S., O'Sullivan, B., & Siapera, E. (2020). Data, power and bias in artificial intelligence. arXiv preprint arXiv:2008.07341.

Lee, J. H. (2021). Changes in marketing brought by AI Proceedings, 2021 21st ACIS International Semi-Virtual Winter Conference on Software Engineering, Artificial Intelligence, Networking, and Parallel/Distributed Computing, SNPD-Winter 2021 C7-9403452.

Lee, V. C. S. (2004). An alternative methodology for mining seasonal patterns using self-organising maps. Lecture Notes in Computer Science (including subseries Lecture Notes in Artificial Intelligence and Lecture Notes in Bioinformatics)

Lee, V. H., Hew, J. J., Leong, L. Y., Tan, G. W. H., & Ooi, K. B. (2020). Wearable payment: A deep learning-based dual-stage SEM-ANN analysis. Expert Systems with Applications, p. 157 C7-113477. DOI: 10.1016/j.eswa.2020.113477

Lei, L., Taorong, G., Jindou, Y., Feixiang, G., Tao, X., Tao, C., & Songsong, C. (2021). Research on the strategy of adjustable load resources participating in the distributed trading market. 2021 IEEE 2nd International Conference on Big Data, Artificial Intelligence and Internet of Things Engineering, ICBAIE 2021 C7 - 9389883

Li, Y. (2024). Optimising the Omni Channel Marketing Strategy of Green Clothing by Integrating Artificial Intelligence and Big Data. *ACM International Conference Proceeding Series*

Li, Y., Chan, J., Peko, G., & Sundaram, D. (2023). Mixed emotion extraction analysis and visualisation of social media text. *Data & Knowledge Engineering*, *148*, C7–C102220. DOI: 10.1016/j.datak.2023.102220

Liang, L. Q., Yu, C. H., & Zhou, X. (2019). The index system of mobile health applications is based on the AHP-Fuzzy comprehensive evaluation method—2019 IEEE Symposium Series on Computational Intelligence, SSCI 2019 C7-9002886.

Lin, X., Shao, B., & Wang, X. (2022). Employees' perceptions of chatbots in B2B marketing: Affordances vs. disaffordances. *Industrial Marketing Management*, *101*, 45–56.

Liu, J. (2024). Marketing strategy matching algorithm under artificial intelligence. *3rd IEEE International Conference on Distributed Computing and Electrical Circuits and Electronics, ICDCECE 2024*.

Liu, L., & Chen, J. (2024). Marketing affordance of social media for product innovation: The role of organisational structures. *Marketing Intelligence & Planning*.

Liu, Q. (2021). Research on the Intelligent Analysis and Visualization of Webcast Entrepreneurship Data under the E-commerce Mode. Proceedings of the 5th International Conference on I-SMAC (IoT in Social, Mobile, Analytics and Cloud), I-SMAC 2021

Liu, S., Hu, X., Wang, S. H., Zhang, Y. D., Fang, X., & Jiang, C. (2020). Mixing patterns in social trust networks: A social identity theory perspective. *IEEE Transactions on Computational Social Systems*, *8*(5), 1249–1261. DOI: 10.1109/TCSS.2020.3021179

Liu, Y., & Chen, W. (2021). Optimisation of Brand Marketing Strategy of Intelligent Technology under the Background of Artificial Intelligence. *Mobile Information Systems*, *2021*, C7–C9507917. DOI: 10.1155/2021/9507917

Lv, H. (2022). Smart Product Marketing Strategy in a Cloud Service Wireless Network Based on SWOT Analysis. *Wireless Communications and Mobile Computing*, *2022*, C7–C7539860. DOI: 10.1155/2022/7539860

Maharani, W., & Gozali, A. A. (2015). Collaborative Social Network Analysis and Content-Based Approach to Improve the Marketing Strategy of SMEs in Indonesia. *Procedia Computer Science*.

Makhlooqa, A., & Mubarakb, M. A. (2024). Artificial intelligence and marketing: Challenges and opportunities. In Technological Innovations for Business, Education and Sustainability (pp. 3-16). Emerald Publishing. DOI: 10.1108/978-1-83753-106-620241001

Manis, K. T., & Madhavaram, S. (2023). AI-enabled marketing capabilities and the hierarchy of capabilities: Conceptualisation, proposition development, and research avenues. *Journal of Business Research, 157*, C7–C113485. DOI: 10.1016/j.jbusres.2022.113485

Martínez-Rolán, X., & Piñeiro-Otero, T. (2022). Surfing on big data: automation and data mining as a marketing strategy. In *Organisational Innovation in the Digital Age* (pp. 63–85). Springer International Publishing., DOI: 10.1007/978-3-030-98183-9_3

Mdoe, A., Mishra, A., & Motahar Hossain, M. (2023). How blockchain and artificial intelligence are changing SME marketing strategies. *Proceedings of the 2023 International Conference on Advanced Computing and Communication Technologies, ICACCTech 2023.*

Meng, X., & Beninsig, M. A. (2024). Intelligent application utilising facial recognition to determine marketing strategies for shopping mall customers. Proceedings of SPIE, The International Society for Optical Engineering.

Narayanasamy, S. S. A. L., Hajamydeen, A. I., & Ishak, Z. (2019). The theoretical framework of digital marketing and its future availability in Malaysia. 2019 IEEE 9th International Conference on System Engineering and Technology, ICSET 2019—Proceeding C7 – 8906342.

Naufal, A., Kurniawati, A., & Hasibuan, M. A. (2017). Decision support system of SMB Telkom University roadshow location prioritisation with weighted sum model method. 2016 2nd International Conference of Industrial, Mechanical, Electrical, and Chemical Engineering, ICIMECE 2016 C7 - 7910428

Nazer, L. H., Zatarah, R., Waldrip, S., Ke, J. X. C., Moukheiber, M., Khanna, A. K., & Mathur, P. (2023). Bias in artificial intelligence algorithms and recommendations for mitigation. *PLOS Digital Health*, *2*(6), e0000278.

Neary, B., Horák, J., Kovacova, M., & Valaskova, K. (2018). The future of work: Disruptive business practices, technology-driven economic growth, and computer-induced job displacement. *Journal of Self-Governance and Management Economics*, *6*(4), 19–24.

Noor, N. (2022). Halal Service Marketing: A Strategic Perspective. In Contributions to Management Science (pp. 11–29). Springer Science and Business Media Deutschland GmbH. DOI: 10.1007/978-3-030-98160-0_3

Olena, C., Tetiana, T., Violeta, A., Viktoria, K., & Leonid, P. (2024). Use of Artificial Intelligence in the Formation of the Marketing Strategy of the Enterprise—Lecture Notes in Networks and Systems.

Otero, E. L., & Gutiérrez, R. C. (2015). *Using social media advertising to increase the awareness, promotion and diffusion of public and private entities*. Advances in Intelligent Systems and Computing.

Özkaynak, Ü., Ercan, Ş., İspir, F. B., Gençoğlu, M. T., & Tanyıldızı, E. (2024). Artificial Intelligence-Based Marble Block Analysis System for Sustainable Green Transformation. 32nd IEEE Conference on Signal Processing and Communications Applications, SIU 2024—Proceedings.

Papavasileiou, V., & Tsadiras, A. (2011). Time variations of association rules in market basket analysis. *IFIP Advances in Information and Communication Technology*.

Patel, M., & Modi, K. (2020). Exploring Online Ad Images using Deep-Learning Approach. Proceedings of the International Conference on Intelligent Computing and Control Systems, ICICCS 2020 C7-9121175.

Patil, S. M., Kharat, A. M., Jain, S., Tripathi, V. V. R., Bisen, G. K., & Joshi, A. (2024). Investigating the Influence and Function of Artificial Intelligence in Contemporary Marketing Management: Marketing in the AI Era. *Proceedings of the 3rd International Conference on Advances in Computing, Communication and Applied Informatics, ACCAI 2024*.

Peruchini, M., da Silva, G. M., & Teixeira, J. M. (2024). Between artificial intelligence and customer experience: a literature review on the intersection. Discover Artificial Intelligence, 4(1 C7 - 4). DOI: 10.1007/s44163-024-00105-8

Ponomarenko, I. V., Pavlenko, V. M., Morhulets, O. B., Ponomarenko, D. V., & Ukhnal, N. M. (2024). Application of artificial intelligence in digital marketing. *CEUR Workshop Proceedings*.

Prada Segura, J. A., & Velandia Daza, J. L. (2021). *Mobile Application to Market Inventories of Small Merchants in the San Victorino Sector in Bogotá: A Strategy Against COVID*. Advances in Intelligent Systems and Computing.

Qian, J., & Gao, C. (2011). The application of Data Mining in CRM. 2011 2nd International Conference on Artificial Intelligence, Management Science and Electronic Commerce, AIMSEC 2011—Proceedings C7 – 6010697.

Rama Krishna, S., Rathor, K., Ranga, J., Soni, A., Srinivas, D., & Anil Kumar, N. (2023). Artificial Intelligence Integrated with Big Data Analytics for Enhanced Marketing. 6th International Conference on Inventive Computation Technologies, ICICT 2023, Proceedings

Rao, H. K., Zeng, Z., & Liu, A. P. (2018). Research on personalised referral service and big data mining for e-commerce with machine learning. 2018 4th International Conference on Computer and Technology Applications, ICCTA 2018

Raskovic, M., & Takacs-Haynes, K. (2021). (Re)discovering social identity theory: An agenda for multinational enterprise internalisation theory. *Multinational Business Review*, *29*(2), 145–165. DOI: 10.1108/MBR-02-2020-0031

Rather, R. A., & Hollebeek, L. D. (2019). Exploring and validating social identification and social exchange-based drivers of hospitality customer loyalty. *International Journal of Contemporary Hospitality Management*, *31*(3), 1432–1451. DOI: 10.1108/IJCHM-10-2017-0627

Rita, S., Kim-Phuc, T., & Sébastien, T. (2021). Long-Term Demand Forecasting System for Demand-Driven Manufacturing. *IFIP Advances in Information and Communication Technology*.

Rodriguez-Sarmiento, L. F., Galpin, I., & Sanchez-Riaño, V. (2024). Mapping Brand Territories Using ChatGPT. *Communications in Computer and Information Science*.

Rosário, A. T., Lopes, P. R., & Rosário, F. S. (2023). Metaverse in Marketing: Challenges and Opportunities. In Khang, A., Shah, V., & Rani, S. (Eds.), *Handbook of Research on AI-Based Technologies and Applications in the Era of the Metaverse* (pp. 204–227). IGI Global., DOI: 10.4018/978-1-6684-8851-5.ch010

Rosário, A., & Casaca, J. (2023). Relationship marketing and customer retention: A systematic literature review. *Studies in Business and Economics*, *18*(3), 44–66. DOI: 10.2478/sbe-2023-0044

Rosário, A., Moreira, C., & Macedo, P. (2021). Competitive dynamics of strategic groups in the Portuguese banking Industry, Cuadernos de Gestión, 21(2), 1-15. ISSN: 1131-6837. DOI: 10.5295/cdg.180975ac

Roy, B., D'Souza, M. S., Bhattacharjee, S., Acharjee, P. B., Thorat, S., & Bhayani, T. (2024). Role of Artificial Intelligence in Influencing Impulsive Buying Behaviour. TQCEBT 2024, 2nd IEEE International Conference on Trends in Quantum Computing and Emerging Business Technologies 2024

Saadi, S., & Azdimousa, H. (2024). *Artificial Intelligence and Green Marketing: What Link?* Lecture Notes in Networks and Systems.

Sakas, D. P., Giannakopoulos, N. T., Kanellos, N., & Migkos, S. P. (2022). Innovative Cryptocurrency Trade Websites: Marketing Strategy Refinement via Digital Behavior. *IEEE Access : Practical Innovations, Open Solutions*, *10*, 63163–63176. DOI: 10.1109/ACCESS.2022.3182396

Salkovska, J., Batraga, A., Kaibe, L., & Kellerte, K. (2023). Use of Artificial Intelligence in the Digital Marketing Strategy of Latvian Companies—Lecture Notes in Networks and Systems.

Samoili, S., Cobo, M. L., Gómez, E., De Prato, G., Martínez-Plumed, F., & Delipetrev, B. (2020). AI Watch. Defining Artificial Intelligence. Towards an operational definition and taxonomy of artificial intelligence.

Sarath Kumar Boddu, R., Santoki, A. A., Khurana, S., Vitthal Koli, P., Rai, R., & Agrawal, A. (2022). An analysis to understand the role of machine learning, robotics and artificial intelligence in digital marketing. Materials Today: Proceedings, pp. 56, 2288–2292. DOI: 10.1016/j.matpr.2021.11.637

Schmidt, P., Biessmann, F., & Teubner, T. (2020). Transparency and trust in artificial intelligence systems. *Journal of Decision Systems*, *29*(4), 260–278.

Schwartz, R., Schwartz, R., Vassilev, A., Greene, K., Perine, L., Burt, A., & Hall, P. (2022). Towards a standard for identifying and managing bias in artificial intelligence (Vol. 3, p. 00). US Department of Commerce, National Institute of Standards and Technology.

Selenko, E., Bankins, S., Shoss, M., Warburton, J., & Restubog, S. L. D. (2022). Artificial intelligence and the future of work: A functional-identity perspective. *Current Directions in Psychological Science*, *31*(3), 272–279. DOI: 10.1177/09637214221091823

Senecha, N., & Srivastava, R. (2022). Mentor EduTech: Charting new territories through social media marketing. *Emerald Emerging Markets Case Studies*, *12*(2), 1–32. DOI: 10.1108/EEMCS-09-2021-0310

Septiana Putra, M. F., Aswie, A., Edbert, I. S., & Suhartono, D. (2023). Hybrid Approaches for Customer Segmentation and Product Recommendation. *2023 International Conference on Informatics, Multimedia, Cyber and Information Systems, ICIMCIS 2023*

Setor, T. (2021). Information System-Marketing Manager Dyad Presence in Top Management Teams: A Study on Demographic Diversity, Power Disparity and Organizational Performance. *SIGMIS-CPR 2021: Proceedings of the 2021 Computers and People Research Conference.*

Shen, H., Han, Y., Zhang, Z., & Zeng, Z. (2011). Notice of Retraction: Marketing strategies for Chinese public legal services companies. 2011 2nd International Conference on Artificial Intelligence, Management Science and Electronic Commerce, AIMSEC 2011 - Proceedings C7 - 6011125, 3105-3108. DOI: 10.1109/AIMSEC.2011.6011125

Sheth, J. (2021). New areas of research in marketing strategy, consumer behaviour, and marketing analytics: The future is bright. *Journal of Marketing Theory and Practice*, *29*(1), 3–12. DOI: 10.1080/10696679.2020.1860679

Singhal, K., Singh, J. N., & Sharma, V. (2024). Enabling Autonomous Digital Marketing: A Machine Learning Approach for Consumer Demand Forecasting. Proceedings of the International Conference on Computing, Power, and Communication Technologies, IC2PCT 2024

Songsangyos, P., Iamamporn, S., & Kongsomlap, T. (2015). A development of decision support system model for sale planning. Proceedings 2015 International Conference on Science and Technology, TICST 2015 C7-7369381.

Sterne, J. (2017). *Artificial intelligence for marketing: practical applications.* John Wiley & Sons.

Su, Q. (2018). Research on influencing factors of consumer behaviour based on Wechat Stores. *ACM International Conference Proceeding Series.*

Sun, L. L. (2023). *Analysis of E-Commerce Live Broadcast Marketing Strategy Based on Big Data Algorithm.* Lecture Notes in Electrical Engineering.

Sung, E. C., Danny Han, D. I., Bae, S., & Kwon, O. (2022). What drives technology-enhanced storytelling immersion? The role of digital humans. *Computers in Human Behavior*, *132*, C7–C107246. DOI: 10.1016/j.chb.2022.107246

Thamaraiselvi, P., Masih, J., Giri, P., Sridevi, J., Karim Shaikh, I. A., & Prasad, M. V. R. (2024). Analysis of Social Media Marketing Impact on Customer Behaviour Using AI & Machine Learning. *Proceedings of 9th International Conference on Science, Technology, Engineering and Mathematics: The Role of Emerging Technologies in Digital Transformation, ICONSTEM 2024*

Tian, J., Zhang, Y., & Zhang, C. (2018). *Predicting consumer variety-seeking through weather data analytics*. Electronic Commerce Research and Applications., DOI: 10.1016/j.elerap.2018.02.001

Tianyuan, Z., & Moro, S. (2021). *Research Trends in Customer Churn Prediction: A Data Mining Approach*. Advances in Intelligent Systems and Computing.

Tiwari, R. (2023). The impact of AI and machine learning on job displacement and employment opportunities. *International Journal of Engineering Technologies and Management Research*, *7*(1).

Trandafili, E., Biba, M., & Xhuvani, A. (2013). Profiling social network users with machine learning. *CEUR Workshop Proceedings*.

Tsai, C. Y., Wang, J. C., & Chen, C. J. (2006). A change detection model for credit card usage behaviour. International Conference on Computational Intelligence, Man-Machine Systems and Cybernetics—Proceedings.

Tsai, H. Y. (2024). Bp Neural Network Research on Enterprise Marketing Strategy Combination. *2024 IEEE International Conference on Information Technology, Electronics and Intelligent Communication Systems, ICITEICS 2024*

Verma, S., Sharma, R., Deb, S., & Maitra, D. (2021). Artificial intelligence in marketing: Systematic review and future research direction. *International Journal of Information Management Data Insights*, *1*(1), 100002. DOI: 10.1016/j.jjimei.2020.100002

Vlačić, B., Corbo, L., Silva, S. C., & Dabić, M. (2021). The evolving role of artificial intelligence in marketing: A review and research agenda. *Journal of Business Research*, *128*, 187–203. DOI: 10.1016/j.jbusres.2021.01.055

Volkoff, O., & Strong, D. M. (2017). Affordance theory and how to use it in IS research. In *The Routledge Companion to management information systems* (pp. 232–245). Routledge.

Wahbeh, S. Y., & Abuelrub, E. E. (2021). Liberty Dental Clinic—the secret behind the most expensive smile creators. In *Corporate Success Stories in the UAE: The Key Drivers behind their Growth* (pp. 93–107). Emerald Group Publishing Ltd., DOI: 10.1108/978-1-80043-578-020211007

Wang, G. A., & Lim, Y. T. (2011). Notice of Retraction: Research on China's Alibaba development. 2011 2nd International Conference on Artificial Intelligence, Management Science and Electronic Commerce, AIMSEC 2011 - Proceedings C7 - 6011136, 2295-2301. DOI: 10.1109/AIMSEC.2011.6011136

Wang, H., Kang, B., Peng, L., & Shi, Y. (2022). Analysis and Research on the Marketing Strategy of Agricultural Products Based on Artificial Intelligence. *Mathematical Problems in Engineering*, *2022*, C7–C7798640. DOI: 10.1155/2022/7798640

Wang, X., & Xu, J. (2011). Notice of Retraction: The study on staff management of service shops. 2011 2nd International Conference on Artificial Intelligence, Management Science and Electronic Commerce, AIMSEC 2011 - Proceedings C7 - 6011303, 3567-3570. DOI: 10.1109/AIMSEC.2011.6011303

Wang, X., & Zhong, W. (2024). Evolution and innovations in animation: A comprehensive review and future directions. Concurrency and Computation: Practice and Experience, 36(2 C7 - e7904). DOI: 10.1002/cpe.7904

Wilendra, W., Nadlifatin, R., & Kusumawulan, C. K. (2024). ChatGPT: The AI Game-Changing Revolution in Marketing Strategy for the Indonesian Cosmetic Industry. Procedia Computer Science.

Wu, G., Tan, G., Deng, J., & Jiang, D. (2021). Distributed reinforcement learning algorithm of operator service slice competition prediction based on zero-sum Markov game. *Neurocomputing*, *439*, 212–222. DOI: 10.1016/j.neucom.2021.01.061

Xiao, D. (2012). Statistics and analysis of bank customers' financial consumption behaviours. Proceedings: 2012 5th International Symposium on Computational Intelligence and Design, ISCID 2012

Xie, D., & He, Y. (2022). Marketing Strategy of Rural Tourism Based on Big Data and Artificial Intelligence. *Mobile Information Systems*, *2022*, C7–C9154351. DOI: 10.1155/2022/9154351

Xu, H. (2022). Intelligent automobile auxiliary propagation system based on speech recognition and AI-driven feature extraction techniques. *International Journal of Speech Technology*, *25*(4), 893–905. DOI: 10.1007/s10772-022-09958-9

Yaiprasert, C., & Hidayanto, A. N. (2023). AI-driven ensemble three machine learning to enhance digital marketing strategies in the food delivery business. *Intelligent Systems with Applications*, *18*, C7–C200235. DOI: 10.1016/j.iswa.2023.200235

Yang, Y., Liu, S., Li, Y., & Jia, J. (2020). Big data marketing: Review and prospect. Xitong Gongcheng Lilun yu Shijian. *Xitong Gongcheng Lilun Yu Shijian*, *40*(8), 2150–2158. DOI: 10.12011/1000-6788-2020-1187-09

Youn, S., & Jin, S. V. (2021). "In AI, we trust?" The effects of parasocial interaction and technopian versus luddite ideological views on chatbot-based customer relationship management in the emerging "feeling economy.". Computers in Human Behavior, p. 119 C7-106721. DOI: 10.1016/j.chb.2021.106721

Zeeshan, M., & Saxena, K. (2020). Explorative Study of Artificial Intelligence in Digital Marketing. In Lecture Notes on Data Engineering and Communications Technologies (Vol. 49, pp. 968-978). Springer Science and Business Media Deutschland GmbH. DOI: 10.1007/978-3-030-43192-1_107

Zhang, B. (2024). Innovative exponential TODIM-CoCoSo framework for uncertain multiple-attribute group decision-making in the effectiveness evaluation of short video marketing strategies. *Journal of Intelligent & Fuzzy Systems*, *46*(2), 4029–4042. DOI: 10.3233/JIFS-236767

Zhang, C., & Huang, Z. (2015). Mining tourist motive for marketing development via twice-learning. *Applied Artificial Intelligence*, *29*(2), 119–133. DOI: 10.1080/08839514.2015.993554

Zhang, J., Wang, Y., Wang, Z., Wang, H., & Lv, X. (2020). Evaluation and classification of travel value of passengers between Wuhan and Yichang based on large samples. Proceedings of 2020 IEEE International Conference on Information Technology, Big Data and Artificial Intelligence, ICIBA 2020 C7-9276961.

Zhang, Y., Pan, K., Huo, Y., Deng, B., & Fu, Y. (2022). Analysis of Power Marketing Strategy Based on Computer Artificial Intelligence Technology. EEI 2022, 4th International Conference on Electronic Engineering and Informatics

Ziakis, C., & Vlachopoulou, M. (2023). Artificial Intelligence in Digital Marketing: Insights from a Comprehensive Review. Information (Switzerland), 14(12 C7 - 664). DOI: 10.3390/info14120664

ADDITIONAL READING

Beccalli, E., Elliot, V., & Virili, F. (2020). *Artificial Intelligence and Ethics in Portfolio Management.* In *Springer Proceedings in Business and Economics*, 19-30. DOI: DOI: 10.1007/978-3-030-47355-6_2

Han, R., Lam, H. K. S., Zhan, Y., Wang, Y., Dwivedi, Y. K., & Tan, K. (2021). Artificial intelligence in business-to-business marketing: A bibliometric analysis of current research status, development, and future directions. *Industrial Management & Data Systems*, *121*(10), 2467–2497. DOI: 10.1108/imds-05-2021-0300

Hermann, E. (2021). Leveraging Artificial Intelligence in Marketing for Social Good—An Ethical Perspective. *Journal of Business Ethics*, •••, 1–19. DOI: 10.1007/s10551-021-04843-y PMID: 34054170

Mogaji, E., Soetan, T. O., & Kieu, T. (2020). The implications of artificial intelligence on the digital marketing of financial services to vulnerable customers. *Australasian Marketing Journal*, *29*(3), 235–242. DOI: 10.1016/j.ausmj.2020.05.003

Saura, J. R., Ribeiro-Soriano, D., & Palacios-Marqués, D. (2021). Setting B2B digital marketing in artificial intelligence-based CRMs: A review and directions for future research. *Industrial Marketing Management*, *98*, 161–178. DOI: 10.1016/J.INDMARMAN.2021.08.006

Shaik, M. (2023). Impact of artificial intelligence on marketing. *East Asian Journal of Multidisciplinary Research*, *2*(3). Advance online publication. DOI: 10.55927/eajmr.v2i3.3112

Stone, M., Aravopoulou, E., Ekinci, Y., Evans, G., Hobbs, M., Labib, A., Laughlin, P., & Machtynger, L. (2020). Artificial intelligence (AI) in strategic marketing decision-making: A research agenda. *The Bottom Line (New York, N.Y.)*, *33*(3), 183–200. DOI: 10.1108/bl-03-2020-0022

Vaio, A. D., Palladino, R., Hassan, R., & Escobar, O. (2020). Artificial intelligence and business models in the sustainable development goals perspective: A systematic literature review. *Journal of Business Research*, *121*, 283–314. DOI: 10.1016/J.JBUSRES.2020.08.019

Yadav, A., & Sondhi, H. (2023). *Systematic Literature Review on Sustainable Marketing and Artificial Intelligence. 2023 10th International Conference on Computing for Sustainable Global Development (INDIACom)*, 583-588. DOI: N/A. Link

KEY TERMS AND DEFINITIONS

Artificial Intelligence: a set of technologies that enable computers to perform various advanced functions, including the ability to see, understand, and translate spoken and written language, analyse data, make recommendations, and more.

Brand Loyalty: refers to a consumer's enduring positive attitude towards a familiar brand and their commitment to consistently purchasing the brand's products and/or services despite any shortcomings, competitor actions, or shifts in the market environment.

Chatbots: a computer program that simulates husimulation with an end user.

Customer Engagement: the way a company creates a relationship with its customer base to foster brand loyalty and awareness.

Data Analytics: converts raw data into actionable insights.

Data-Driven: a strategic concept that can be applied to any business.

Ethical: the philosophical study of moral phenomena.

Personalisation: consists of tailoring a service or product to accommodate specific individuals.

Search Engine Optimization: the set of strategies to enhance and improve a website's positioning on organic results pages, disregarding sponsored links on search engines, generating conversions, be they a lead, a purchase, a form submission, scheduling an appointment, or others.

Social Identity Theory: the feeling of an individual to fit in (belong) to a specific social group (segments, categories).

Chapter 2
The Integration of AI Into the Marketing Department

Maria-Alexandra Foka
https://orcid.org/0009-0002-3728-3334
The American College of Greece, Greece

ABSTRACT

This chapter will examine the revolutionary role of Artificial Intelligence (AI) in today's marketing and more specifically digital department. It will explore how AI can be used to improve financial results, decrease human errors, and improve customer experience through data analysis. The chapter will also discuss the difficulties that may be provoked by using AI, such as the need for qualified staff, privacy issues, and high implementation costs. Additionally, it will evaluate how AI will affect the digital marketing landscape. The chapter will conclude by discussing possible future AI trends, including augmentation reality and automation enhancements, and how these advancements may influence the marketing department.

INTRODUCTION

Introduction of Artificial Intelligence

In this age of digitalization, the convergence of contemporary technologies has set off a disruptive wave of digitalization that is affecting many industries. Industry 4.0, or i4.0, was defined as a technological revolution for businesses to advance their technology and change other aspects. Artificial intelligence (AI) and other technologies are all categorized under this umbrella. More specifically AI is the

DOI: 10.4018/979-8-3693-9994-1.ch002

ability of a computer system or device, through the use of an Artificial Neural Network (ANN) system installed within to think and learn in a manner that is as close to that of a human as possible to enhance human capabilities by automating tasks and to solve complex problems arising from both business environments and life.

Artificial Intelligence in marketing can also be examined through several theoretical lenses, such as the Technology Acceptance Model (TAM), which explains how perceived usefulness and ease of use affect AI adoption by marketers (Ma et al., 2024). Another valuable framework is the Diffusion of Innovation Theory, which provides insight into how new technologies like AI are gradually adopted across organizations (Abdalla et al., 2024). Including these perspectives offers a deeper understanding of the strategic drivers and barriers in AI integration.

Introduction of the Marketing Department

The marketing department operates in a dynamic and uncertain environment as demand, customer behavior, technological advances, and other external factors constantly evolve. This creates uncertainty in the department and it makes it hard to predict new trends and needs due to the extensive data analyses required. In order to overcome these difficulties, Marketing recognizes the capabilities that AI can offer for collecting and analyzing data to use them in the decision-making process (Burgess, 2018). The growing field of artificial intelligence applications in marketing has included in-depth analyses of consumer purchasing patterns (Chatterjee et al., 2020) and the development of client demands through data analysis. According to (Williams, 2023) by utilizing AI, marketers can acquire more profound insights into their target audience and enhance their ability to categorize and guide customers to the next phase of their journey, ensuring optimal customer experience.

Why Artificial Intelligence is Important in the Marketing Department

Artificial Intelligence is very crucial in marketing as it enables companies to make data-driven decisions. Customer insights can be easily collected with the use of AI tools by analyzing vast amounts of data in order to provide a full customer profile to businesses. In that way, companies can have a better understanding of customer behavior, preferences, and needs. Additionally, marketers can better understand their customers future behavior by using AI technology to find patterns in data. AI can also be used for the making of personalized content, marketing marketing messages, recommendations, and for the automation of tasks, such as scheduling social media posts. By using AI tools, marketing departments will have the opportunity to make insight-driven decisions based on real-time data, guaranteeing a unique customer experience and a competitive advantage over rivals across other industries.

RESEARCH METHODOLOGY

This chapter in order to investigate the integration and the impact of Artificial Intelligence (AI) in the marketing domain, uses a quantitative research design with a literature-based approach. This method offers a thorough understanding of the positives, difficulties, and future trends related to AI by reviewing and combining knowledge from academic sources, online articles, case studies, and industry reports.

The Data collection process in order to ensure the reliability and relevance of the materials involves several steps. Initially, sources were selected through a literature search conducted on academic databases such as Google Scholar, Scopus, Web of Science, and Elicit. Additionally, case studies and examples were gathered from reliable publications, including the ones focused specifically on marketing.

To refine the search specific keywords were used to ensure relevant and focused results such as, "Artificial Intelligence", "Challenges of AI in Marketing", "Personalization", and "Future Trends". Then the chosen materials were evaluated for their reliability and relevant results in order to guarantee a comprehensive understanding. All findings were organized into categories to facilitate a structured examination of AI's impact on the marketing department. This method ensures a deep and thorough analysis, collecting data from a variety of reliable sources.

Impact of AI on the Marketing Department

Better user experience: When the content of an advertisement aligns with the consumer's desires, they are more likely to become loyal customers of a specific brand. AI tools through their applied technologies, can collect data with key elements such as location, historical data, and past behavior to determine which content is most suitable.

Additionally, in retail, Augmented Reality (AR) ads can be utilized, allowing customers to try products before purchasing without visiting the store. This means fewer unhappy customers, fewer returns, and greater customer engagement.

Predictive Customer Behavior: Artificial Intelligence provides the ability to business personalize experiences for customers based on their past behavior, while it can also predict behavior for both existing and new users. Using a data management platform that collects secondary data, AI can collect information about users from across the internet. This allows businesses to formulate effective marketing strategies, focusing on potential customers who are more likely to purchase in the future.

Real-Time Customer Support: Fast replies to customer requests with the use of chatbots. Chatbots are automated tools that give the customer the impression of real-time personal assistance. These chatbots have the potential to completely transform the way businesses interact with customers. The ultimate goal of chatbots is to replace traditional user interfaces commonly used in computers and connected devices.

With the use of chatbots, companies have the opportunity to collect valuable data about customers' needs and preferences, as well as access to their social account insights. In that way, businesses can properly address customers by offering personalized solutions and offers creating a more personal relationship with them.

Marketing Recommendation System: Another powerful application of AI in marketing is the Marketing Recommendation System, which uses AI-advanced technology to create personalized product recommendations for customers. While some of the existing systems already use similar technology, the latest AI tools are expected to deliver high-quality information and advisory services comparable to those provided by sales specialists.

Core AI Technologies in Marketing

Artificial Intelligence in marketing relies on several foundational technologies, each playing a distinct role in how campaigns are designed, optimized, and delivered. Machine Learning (ML) enables predictive analytics, segmentation, and dynamic pricing by detecting patterns in large datasets. Natural Language Processing (NLP) powers chatbots, sentiment analysis, and content personalization, helping marketers understand and respond to customer emotions and preferences. Computer Vision supports visual search, image recognition, and AR-powered product testing, enhancing customer engagement and interaction.

These technologies, when combined, give marketers the ability to create more targeted, adaptive, and data-driven campaigns. However, their effectiveness depends heavily on data quality and ethical usage. Poor data governance or biased training datasets can lead to misinterpretations, discriminatory outcomes, or manipulative practices. Recognizing both the potential and the risks of these technologies is essential for building sustainable and trustworthy AI-driven marketing strategies.

POSITIVE ASPECTS OF ARTIFICIAL INTELLIGENCE IN THE MARKETING DEPARTMENT

Artificial Intelligence can offer many benefits in the Marketing Department, from simplifying basic tasks to handling complex processes in various ways, which some can be seen below.

Better Customer Experience by Data Analysis

Businesses with the use of AI can take customer experience to another level, by providing personalized content and improving satisfaction, and retention. With AI tools, businesses can create product recommendations and targeted messaging to individual customers, based on their interests and behaviors (Haleem et al., 2022). Additionally, AI allows direct communication across channels such as social media platforms, e-mail, and chatbots by using insights from Natural Language Processing (NLP) and machine learning. This personalization fosters customer loyalty, satisfaction, and long-term relationships (Ahana Priyanka et al., 2023).

For instance, Amazon's constant sales are a major factor in its enormous success as an e-commerce platform. Amazon has benefited greatly from AI, especially in its ability to recommend products to customers based on their browsing or past purchases ("Top picks for you" and "Buy it again") and other users' experiences ("Customers also bought these items") (The Role of AI in Marketing and How to Use It, n.d.).

Decrease in Human Errors

AI has decreased human error, especially in the most important domains. Additionally, this technology can create and optimize pleasant and pertinent content for recipients in various email formats. AI is unquestionably there to avoid human interaction and, as a result, to eliminate the possibility of human error. Many companies worry that their employees won't be able to secure customer information and other critical company data because data security breaches happen often. Through learning, adapting, and responding to an organization's cybersecurity requirements, AI can help with a variety of issues. AI can replace many of the cut-and-burn resources typically needed to create and carry out a marketing plan.

For example, HubSpot is an AI tool that helps reduce human errors in email marketing making it difficult for marketers to make any mistakes. This allows them to focus on planning and strategy while AI ensures accuracy.

Financial Benefits

More effective marketing campaigns can be created if businesses use AI to analyze Data. These campaigns reduce costs and increase revenue and profitability. AI automation tools also decrease labor expenses and improve lead generation methods to boost Return on Investment (ROI) (IBM, 2024). Personalized marketing campaigns driven by real-time customer insights, enhance customer experience, improve retention rate, and reduce turnover caused by negative advertising. Integrating AI-powered solutions enhances a company's market penetration, operational efficiency, and competitive position.

For instance, a small business that uses AI tools can create personalized campaigns focused on people who have shown some interest in the product before, to increase sales and cut costs. AI automation tools can also offer the company a more effective real-time communication through chatbots and reduce labor expenses. All these strategies will lead the company to a higher position in the market.

According to a 2023 McKinsey report, companies integrating AI into marketing have experienced campaign performance increases of 15–25% and cost reductions of up to 30%, especially in customer acquisition.

Improved Productivity and Efficiency

The automation of everyday tasks and processes with the help of AI tools allows businesses to focus on strategic programs. Well-structured strategic plans lead to improved productivity, enhanced efficiency, as well as cost savings. It is impossible to overestimate the impact of AI on increasing these factors, as it has completely transformed numerous industries. From data processing and analysis to customer service management, AI-powered systems can carry out automated tasks that would otherwise require human intervention. Additionally, these tools facilitate the creation of highly personalized and customized products, which ultimately increase customer satisfaction while reducing labor expenses. By examining customer patterns, AI can also assist businesses in predicting trends and making well-informed decisions about inventory optimization. Overall, businesses can boost productivity and improve the quality of their products and services by integrating AI into main operational procedures.

Netflix is a significant example of a business that has profited from automation thanks to AI. Netflix uses AI tools to analyze user data, including viewing preferences and history, to provide personalized content recommendations (Antonyuk, 2024). In addition to improving customer satisfaction, this automation lowers the expenses related to producing undesired content. AI also helps Netflix predict trends, maximize production investments, and provide its audience with higher-quality content.

Measuring ROI and Long-Term Value

One of the most critical advantages of AI in marketing lies in its ability to make business performance measurable with unprecedented precision. Traditional marketing efforts often struggled with attributing specific outcomes to campaigns.

In contrast, AI-powered platforms track the full customer journey across multiple channels, enabling a more accurate calculation of Return on Investment (ROI).

Key performance indicators (KPIs) frequently used include:

Conversion Rate – percentage of prospects who become paying customers after interacting with an AI-driven touchpoint.

Customer Lifetime Value (CLV) – long-term profitability per customer, enhanced through AI personalization and retention strategies.

Return on Ad Spend (ROAS) – revenue generated per dollar spent on AI-powered advertising.

Engagement Metrics – such as click-through rates, open rates, or dwell time, which highlight how AI-optimized content resonates with audiences.

Additionally, advanced attribution models powered by AI can assign proportional value to each step in the customer journey, helping companies identify which touchpoints deliver the greatest impact. This allows businesses to optimize resource allocation, reduce wasted advertising spend, and maximize profitability.

For example, a global e-commerce retailer using AI-driven programmatic advertising improved its campaign ROI by 32% in one quarter, primarily because the system automatically reallocated budget to the highest-performing ad placements in real time. Similarly, a financial services company leveraged AI for predictive customer segmentation and reported a 27% increase in cross-sell revenue, alongside improved CLV.

The long-term implication is that companies can shift from viewing marketing as a cost center to recognizing it as a data-driven investment, directly tied to measurable growth and sustainability.

NEGATIVE ASPECTS OF ARTIFICIAL INTELLIGENCE IN THE MARKETING DEPARTMENT

Despite the many positive aspects that AI offers in the marketing department, there are also some negative ones that concern both businesses and customers.

High Cost of Implementation

Before making a decision, businesses should weigh the return on investment because the initial cost of implementing the technology can be high (Ahana Priyanka et al., 2023). Additionally, the initiation and development of AI technology requires a substantial investment in software, hardware, and training programs to educate the team on how to use AI effectively. Maintenance costs are also significant as AI technology constantly evolves and requires system updates and upskilling needs for the staff members.

For instance, small and medium businesses, adopting AI may be difficult with these expenses. (Advantages and Disadvantages of Artificial Intelligence in Digital Marketing, 2024). These businesses have small budgets that are often not enough to invest in the needed software, hardware, training programs, and most importantly maintenance costs. As a result, these businesses cannot keep up with the competition and push out of the market.

Privacy Concerns and Data Security

One of the biggest challenges marketers need to face when using AI tools is ensuring privacy and data security. Targeted advertisements are created based on customer profiles which are created from customer insights such as their browsing behavior, purchase behavior, and social media activity. However, if this data collection falls into the wrong hands, customers may experience severe privacy violations, identity theft, or other threats. A business's strong relationship with customers when AI is used is only possible if trust exists. Trust is built when businesses prioritize secured systems against cyber threats, maintain transparency in their data collection processes, and ensure AI tools follow regulatory laws around data protection.

Example of data theft on Facebook in April 2019: The data of about 533 million Facebook users was compromised in this instance of data leakage. Profile names, ID numbers, email addresses, and phone numbers were among the information that was leaked. The attacker used a version of the contact importer function that was accessible before September 2019 to scrape people's Facebook profiles. The purpose of the feature was to assist users in connecting with friends by using their contact lists (Breachsense, n.d.).

In addition to privacy, legal compliance with data protection regulations such as the GDPR (General Data Protection Regulation) and the EU AI Act (2024) is crucial. These regulations classify AI applications based on risk and enforce accountability, transparency, and security standards. Marketing teams must implement AI in ways that are transparent and explainable, using mechanisms like Explainable AI (XAI) to clarify how decisions are made to customers and regulators.

Lack of Skilled Personnel

To establish AI technology tools, businesses need to have skilled personnel who can manage these systems. Lack of skilled personnel, or difficulties in finding employees with these kinds of abilities is a significant challenge that marketers need to overcome. This affects not only small businesses but even large ones that are still figuring out solutions (Crabill, 2023). The integration of AI technology in today's world is crucial as it can transform businesses by offering efficiency and accuracy. However, businesses must invest in training programs to help their employees cope with the change and face competition. If this fails chances of bankruptcy or general failure of the company are high.

For example, a mid-size company wants to integrate AI technology tools into its system to improve its marketing department and boost sales. However, they struggle to find personnel with the desired knowledge to use these systems. Without skilled staff, the company cannot fully benefit from AI technology and will probably fall behind larger companies that have successfully integrated AI tools. Eventually, sales will start decreasing and the company will be on the brink of failure.

To overcome the skills gap, companies are encouraged to adopt cross-functional training programs that combine marketing knowledge with AI literacy. Collaborations with academic institutions and the use of certifications from reputable online platforms (e.g., Coursera, Google AI) can accelerate workforce readiness.

Lack of Common Sense

AI technology does not have the ability to understand human emotions; however, it can be programmed and trained to recognize and identify them, though it is still far from feeling them. While this tool lacks emotions, it also lacks common sense (De Bruyn et al., 2020). Something that is easy for people to understand might not be comprehensible to AI which can lead to several challenges. For instance, AI may recommend products to customers based on their previous purchasing history but without the ability to understand the reasons behind those purchases. Furthermore, AI's reliance on historical data means it may fail to catch emerging trends or shifts in customer behavior, as it cannot adapt as flexibly as humans to changing environments. Lastly, while AI offers valuable tools to businesses for data analysis, its struggle with the lack of common sense can limit its effectiveness in creating truly personalized marketing strategies.

For instance, a strong example of weak AI's common sense could be YouTube. YouTube is a platform that uses AI tools to recommend videos to its users based on their recently viewed history and engagement patterns. However, sometimes AI may misunderstand the context of users' content, leading to controversial recommendations. For instance, a user may watch a video based on political issues, but the recommended videos after might be unrelated to their interests or even inappropriate, due to the inability of AI to comprehend the intent behind this search. This lack of common sense can negatively affect user experiences, and raise serious ethical concerns. It also highlights the limitations of AI in making context-aware and common sense-based decisions, factors that are critical for creating a truly personalized user experience.

Algorithmic Bias and AI-Related Errors

While AI reduces human errors, it also introduces new categories of mistakes rooted in algorithmic design. AI models can replicate and even amplify historical biases present in training data, leading to discriminatory outcomes in targeted marketing campaigns. For instance, an AI system may favor certain demographic groups for high-value product recommendations while systematically excluding others, not because of intent but due to biased datasets.

Additionally, AI "black box" models often lack transparency, which makes it difficult for marketing teams to identify and correct errors. These algorithmic failures not only harm brand reputation but can also trigger legal and ethical consequences. Companies must therefore establish bias auditing, explainability mechanisms, and regular monitoring to minimize such risks.

Integration and Over-Reliance Challenges

Another major limitation is the difficulty of integrating AI tools with existing marketing systems such as CRM platforms, data warehouses, or legacy databases. Integration requires high levels of interoperability, clean data flows, and continuous technical maintenance. Without proper alignment, AI systems may underperform or even disrupt workflows.

Furthermore, businesses risk becoming overly dependent on AI-generated insights. Over-reliance can reduce the creative and strategic flexibility of marketers, leading to a "technology lock-in" where decisions are dictated solely by algorithms rather than human judgment. If AI systems fail or produce misleading outputs, organizations without strong human oversight may face strategic blind spots or reputational damage.

ETHICAL CONSIDERATION

Despite the fact that AI presents a opportunity to revolutionize marketing, it is important to consider the ethical implications of its application. AI in marketing has been on the rise as more and more businesses are looking to incorporate AI in their marketing strategies in a bid to enhance and automate their marketing processes. (Ahana Priyanka et al., 2023).

Privacy and Security

AI algorithms collect and use a vast amount of personal data in personalized marketing and this raises major data privacy concerns. Although this improves personalization, it also raises questions about the collection, storage, and use of data, which could violate consumer privacy if not handled securely and transparently ("Exploring the Ethical Implications of AI-Powered Personalization in Digital Marketing," 2024). Moreover, marketing teams must ensure compliance with legal frameworks such as the GDPR and the EU AI Act, and adopt Explainable AI (XAI) practices to maintain consumer trust.

Bias in AI Algorithms

Another ethical worry is BIA in AI algorithms. There are numerous ways in which an algorithm can be biased. Even if sensitive data like gender, race, or sexual orientation are removed, all other existing data from which AI systems learn to make decisions, may still contain biased human actions or represent historical injustices. Additionally, a source of bias could also be the inaccuracy of data sampling, this could be an outcome of groups that are either over or under represented in the training data that AI tools follows to make actions (Manyika et al., 2019). Establishing internal auditing procedures for algorithmic fairness is a critical step for companies using AI in marketing.

Manipulative Practices

AI has a high degree of accuracy in predicting consumer behavior, which could allow for overly persuasive strategies that take advantage of weaknesses in consumers. Hyper-personalized advertisements, for example, can press people into buying unnecessary items, going against moral principles in the name of profit.

Loss of Human Interaction

Lastly, there is a chance that customer interactions will become less human. Chatbots and virtual assistants driven by AI are efficient, but in some situations, they might not have the empathy and comprehension that customers want, which could undermine customer satisfaction and brand trust.

Accountability and Transparency

AI systems in marketing frequently function as "black boxes," indicating that their decision-making processes are not consistently transparent or comprehensible. The absence of transparency can hinder businesses in rationalizing their AI-driven decisions to stakeholders or customers. To guarantee ethical AI utilization, enterprises must delineate explicit accountability for decisions rendered by AI systems and ensure transparency in their operations for consumers. This may involve elucidating the process of recommendation generation or the utilization of data in a manner comprehensible to non-technical audiences (Benkert, 2019).

Regular reporting and disclosure on AI-based decisions can strengthen accountability and mitigate ethical risks.

Ethical Implications of Automation

The growing automation of marketing functions, driven by AI, could result in workforce displacement. Although AI can improve efficiency, it also presents ethical dilemmas regarding job displacement in industries dependent on conventional marketing positions. Companies must acknowledge the social responsibility of reconciling technological progress with employee welfare, potentially providing reskilling initiatives for those impacted by automation. Many companies are now establishing ethical guidelines and AI ethics boards to proactively address these dilemmas.

Consumer Autonomy and Responsible AI Guidelines

Beyond issues of privacy and bias, one of the most pressing ethical concerns in AI-driven marketing is the erosion of consumer autonomy. AI's ability to hyper-personalize recommendations and advertisements can subtly steer individuals toward certain purchasing decisions, limiting their freedom of choice. While personalization enhances convenience, it also raises questions about manipulation versus empowerment: at what point does helpful guidance become undue influence?

A widely cited example is the Cambridge Analytica scandal (2018), where data-driven micro-targeting was used to influence voter behavior. This case highlights how AI-enhanced personalization, when misused, can have consequences far beyond commercial transactions—affecting politics, society, and democracy itself.

To prevent such misuse, businesses must adopt responsible AI frameworks guided by the following principles:

Transparency: clearly communicate how customer data is collected, processed, and used in marketing decisions.

Fairness: actively audit algorithms to detect and mitigate bias.

Explainability: provide customers with understandable reasons behind personalized recommendations.

Consent & Control: allow consumers to opt out of data collection and personalization features.

Accountability: establish internal AI ethics boards or committees to oversee responsible AI practices.

By embedding these guidelines, organizations not only minimize ethical risks but also strengthen trust and long-term brand loyalty, which are increasingly becoming competitive differentiators in the age of AI-powered marketing.

THE IMPACT OF AI

The Impact of AI on Customers

Evolved technology and the power of the internet have brought numerous advantages to consumers, such as personalized recommendations, reduced shopping time, real-time support, and many others (Jordan & Mitchell, 2015). The integration of AI has taken all this experience one step forward for customers by offering:

Firstly, automated payments, improved search engine quality, and customer assistance available anytime needed, are factors, that can reduce shopping time even more, making it more convenient.

Secondly, mass-scale hyper-personalization and after-sale communication with consumers, add additional value to the customer journey making the experience for them feel unique and personalized each time.

Lastly, the ability to virtually test the product under consideration, the elimination of the category learning process, and finally the utilization of benchmarking against other users all contributed to the reduction of post-purchase dissonance. This new dimension of the consumer-brand relationship was brought about by the construction of surprise and delight (Jarek & Mazurek, 2019).

These improvements contribute not only to user satisfaction but also to deeper emotional engagement with brands through AI-enhanced storytelling and interactive tools.

The Impact of AI in Marketing to the Competitive Environment

Buyers Power

Buyer's power refers to the ability of customers to influence product prices based on their purchasing behavior. Integrating AI into the marketing department can increase and decrease buyers' power. AI can offer customers a wide variety of customized products which makes it more difficult for them to switch to another supplier, and also allows businesses to enhance customer support and loyalty. As a result, buyers power decreases and the company has more control over the prices. On the other hand, AI also allows customers access to more information and a bigger variety of products and makes it easier to compare competitor's services, which can easily increase their power. AI enables deeper segmentation and dynamic pricing strategies that can balance buyer power depending on data control.

Suppliers Power

Suppliers have the power to influence prices and control the variety of goods and services available to buyers. AI in marketing gives businesses the opportunity to have access to better insights into pricing and market trends enabling stronger negotiations with the suppliers and an improved optimization of the supply chain. As a result, AI in the marketing department reduces the supplier's power by allowing businesses to find alternative suppliers. However, it can enhance the communication and the relationships among both sides. Additionally, AI can enhance demand forecasting, strengthening negotiation positions with suppliers.

Threat of Substitute Products or Services

Several product options make the threat of substitutes increase but when there are limited options the threat decreases. One of the biggest advantages AI offers to the marketing department is the ability to customize products that businesses can offer to customers based on their insights. This provides consumers with a wide range of products to choose from. Additionally, AI helps to speed up innovation which keeps businesses ahead of other substitutes and improves cost efficiency. As a result, AI in marketing reduces the threat of substitute products as all these factors make it difficult for customers to choose other alternatives. AI also facilitates continuous innovation and user feedback loops, which are key in retaining market share against substitutes.

Threat of New Entrances

The threat of new entrances increases when the entrance to the market is easy and decreases when it's more difficult. AI in marketing makes it harder for new competitors to enter new markets, as companies already have loyal customers formed due to customized products and personalized experiences. It also increases the costs of entrance and gives a significant data advantage to established businesses making it more difficult for new competitors to enter the market and survive. With AI-driven personalization becoming the standard, new entrants must invest heavily to compete—raising entry barriers.

Rivalry Among the Existing Competitors

Rivalry among the existing competitors refers to the degree of competitiveness between companies in a market. Businesses with the use of AI can automatically increase competitiveness in the market. This is a result of the advanced tools for personalization that AI technology offers marketers in order to target customers more effectively. Additionally, AI automation tools lower operational costs, which can lead to increased pricing and force companies to change their strategies to remain competitive. As companies adopt AI automatically gain an advantage, increasing the competitiveness of the market.

It is also important to highlight that AI-driven differentiation strategies offer a powerful means of sustaining competitive advantage. By integrating AI into the core of customer relationship management and campaign personalization, companies can deliver unique value propositions that are harder for competitors to replicate.

FUTURE TRENDS OF AI IN THE MARKETING DEPARTMENT

AI has the power to transform how marketers communicate with customers, from understanding their needs and behavior to creating more personalized content for targeted engagement. All these advancements have already made a noticeable impact on the marketing domain, an impact that is expected to be more intense over time as technology evolves. In the future, AI in marketing is expected to notably transform automation, personalization, and the decision-making process (Patrecia Meliana, 2024). It will also become an essential tool for businesses to survive the competitive environment.

Emerging innovations include not just technical efficiency, but creative augmentation through generative AI models.

Automation Improvements

AI is expected to transform routine tasks through automation. With the use of chatbots is expected that by 2028 85% of the communication with customers will be accomplished without human interaction. This will provide immediate and accurate responses to customers to common issues, enhancing overall efficiency. Moreover, AI can predict behaviors, customize communication, and resolve issues by analyzing large volumes of data in a short time, providing a more unique experience to consumers. However, to gain customer trust, businesses must address several challenges related to chatbots. Interactions need to remain empathic while ensuring data privacy and security. Striking the ideal balance between automation and human interaction will be crucial.

For instance, Photobuck has already incorporated AI tools in its communication services. In cooperation with Zendesk AI, they built a communication tool with chatbots that support and answer common customer questions 24/7. This has significantly improved their response time by 14% and all positive ratings by 3%. (Photobucket Delivers 24/7 Member Support with Messaging, 2022)

Advanced automation also involves Agentic AI, where systems like AutoGPT can plan and execute complex, multi-step campaigns autonomously.

New Level of Personalization

Personalization will also reach new levels. Over time, AI tools will gain the power to analyze a broader variety of data and insights in a shorter period than nowadays, enabling highly customized marketing campaigns. This will allow businesses to offer a unique, personalized experience to customers throughout their journey, significantly enhancing engagement and satisfaction. Additionally, consumers will enjoy a more consistent experience across websites, mobile apps, social media, and even in physical stores, as AI will facilitate seamless personalization across various platforms. With AI algorithms dynamically changing and adjusting recommendations and content based on customer behavior and actions, real-time adaption is set to become a standard.

For example, businesses with advanced AI tools and future technological advantages will be able to have a complete customer profile in just seconds, Jasper.AI for instance, is an AI tool that helps businesses create tailored marketing campaigns (Jasper, 2023).

Artificial Intelligence with Augmentation Reality

Augmentation Reality (AR) is a technology that blends digital information with the real world, enhancing customer experience. An emerging trend of the future is the combination of AI tools with AR technology, which will allow customers to engage and see through victuals how their lives would be with the addition of a product. As these technologies advance, the merging of AI and AR will bring closer the real and the virtual world and transform how companies communicate with their customers and how customers receive their relationship with the brand.

For instance, Spotify is already exploring the potential of the integration of AR with AI. This could lead to a new kind of music experience that reacts to the movement of a user's phone, like a small window where the picture of the song actually is, which will display visuals that sync with the song and take the listening experience to a whole new level.

Another emerging trend is the rise of Generative AI technologies, such as ChatGPT, DALL·E, and Midjourney, which are increasingly used in marketing for content creation, copywriting, and visual design. These tools empower marketers to produce high-quality, personalized content at scale, reducing both time and cost. Furthermore, Agentic AI systems like AutoGPT represent the next evolution, where AI agents can autonomously plan and execute multi-step marketing tasks, transforming traditional workflows.

The Changing Role of Marketing Professionals

As AI continues to evolve, the future of marketing will not only be defined by new technologies but also by the shifting responsibilities of marketing professionals. While automation takes over repetitive tasks such as data collection, segmentation, and basic content creation, human marketers are increasingly expected to focus on strategic thinking, creative direction, and ethical oversight.

This transition introduces both opportunities and challenges. On one hand, job displacement is a legitimate concern, particularly for roles centered on routine execution (e.g., entry-level data analysts or campaign managers). On the other hand, AI is also creating demand for new skill sets—such as AI literacy, data governance expertise, prompt engineering, and ethical AI auditing.

Forward-thinking companies are investing in upskilling and reskilling programs, ensuring that their marketing teams are prepared to collaborate effectively with AI tools. Universities and online learning platforms are also adapting curricula to include marketing analytics, machine learning basics, and responsible AI practices.

A practical example is Unilever, which introduced an internal AI training program for its marketing staff. Instead of replacing employees, the company empowered them to use AI tools for consumer insights, campaign optimization, and sustainability reporting. As a result, Unilever reported 30% faster campaign execution times and a significant boost in employee satisfaction, since staff felt they were acquiring future-proof skills rather than being sidelined.

Looking ahead, the human–AI partnership is expected to be the norm rather than the exception. Marketers will serve as strategic orchestrators, guiding AI systems toward outcomes that align with brand values, customer expectations, and societal responsibilities.

AI INTO DIGITAL MARKETING

AI's rapid evolution has appeared as a transformative force for several sectors with digital marketing being one of the most affected ones. AI has the power to completely transform digital marketing and reshape business outreach strategies through its ability to analyze vast amounts of data, recognize behavior patterns, and predict future trends. However, the relationship between AI and digital marketing needs further exploration, and it has already been the subject of numerous studies, as the rapid advancements of AI tools especially the introduction of ChatGPT and Google Bard, alongside the constantly changing environment, can be life-changing for businesses (Van Esch & Stewart Black, 2021).

AI has enabled digital marketing and revolutionized the way businesses create content for campaigns, generate leads, reduce costs, and others which are all explained below (Dr. N.Thilagavathy, 2021).

Implications of AI in Digital Marketing

Advertising: Businesses rely a lot on the advertising of their products as it is a way to attract new customers keep the already ones and build fame, but it can also be one of the most challenging tasks a business must do, as it hides many dangers and high costs. AI has made this task extremely easier as it can do most of the job on its own, from the extraction of the data to the creation of a full effective advertising message. The AI tools evaluate all the collected data and separate them into categories based on consumers' interests. This allows businesses to easily create a framework and truly understand their customers' desires to completely satisfy them (AI in Digital Marketing - the Ultimate Guide, n.d.).

Moreover, AI supports real-time ad placement and bidding (programmatic advertising), enabling marketers to deliver the right message to the right person at the right moment, maximizing ROI. Platforms like Google Ads use AI to adjust bids and predict which ads are most likely to perform better, reducing cost-per-click and increasing conversions.

Content Creation: Technology tools can now create content from scratch by collecting customer data from their previous purchasing behavior. By that businesses save a lot of time and resources. AI can evolve complete advertisements based on customer needs and focus on satisfying their desires. Furthermore, AI tools can write reports based on data and information. BBC News, The New York Times, and the Washington Post are significant examples of using this way of journalism, also, Facebook uses AI for detecting fake posts and news (AI in Digital Marketing - the Ultimate Guide, n.d.).

In addition, generative AI models like GPT and DALLE can be used to automate blog writing, image generation, and even video scripts—tools that empower marketers to scale content creation without compromising creativity.

AI in Graphic Design: AI tools like Canva and Adobe Sensei are revolutionizing graphic design by offering intelligent suggestions on color schemes, designs, and placement, which makes it simpler to generate unique ideas. In this sense, these tools consider user preferences and design trends to recommend elements that, among other things, are likely to have the intended effect, thereby promoting higher levels of creativity and time management.

For example, Adobe Sensei can suggest alternative ways for something to look or behave; it can even perform repetitive tasks without the need for human intervention, freeing up humans to work on more strategic facets of their jobs. AI is used by Canva, an online graphic design tool, to display design templates that satisfy a user's project specifications. It can even suggest particular elements one might require based on past user behavior and current design trends.

With the help of these tools, one can eliminate the majority of design work, which makes it easier to produce high-quality designs fast.

AI and SEO Optimization

AI-driven SEO tools help businesses better understand search intent, optimize keywords, and structure content to rank higher in search engine results. Tools such as SurferSEO and MarketMuse use machine learning to recommend keyword strategies and anticipate ranking opportunities. Predictive SEO powered by AI can even identify emerging search trends before competitors, creating a first-mover advantage. The challenge lies in the constant evolution of search algorithms, which can limit the accuracy of AI predictions.

AI in Social Media Marketing

AI is deeply embedded in social media, from content recommendation engines to targeted advertising. Platforms like Hootsuite Insights and Sprinklr use natural language processing (NLP) and sentiment analysis to monitor customer opinions in real time. The opportunity lies in hyper-targeted engagement, but the risk comes from opaque algorithms that control visibility, sometimes amplifying bias or misinformation.

AI in Email Marketing

Email marketing achieves one of the highest ROI rates among digital channels, and AI further enhances its performance. Platforms like HubSpot and Mailchimp AI Assistant optimize subject lines, segment audiences, and personalize campaigns at scale. Marketers can automatically test multiple variations of emails and deploy the most effective ones. However, over-automation can make communication feel impersonal, reducing authenticity and trust.

ANALYTICS AND OPTIMIZATION DRIVEN BY AI

Analyzing User Behavior:

Two examples of tools that use machine learning algorithms to analyze user behavior on websites are Google Analytics and Hotjar. Users have access to both of these tools. By tracking how users interact with different sections of a website, analytics tools driven by artificial intelligence can pinpoint areas that might need improvement. For example, they can monitor which pages have higher bounce rates and then suggest changes that will increase the amount of time users spend on the page in question. The gathering of information about how users navigate a website, the kinds of pages they view, how long they stay on the site, and when they leave is the focus of a user behavior analysis. There are several methods for gathering this data. Artificial intelligence-based tools are able to identify patterns and trends in such data that are not immediately apparent.

An AI tool could be used, for example, to find out that a large percentage of users often decide to leave their shopping carts on a specific page. This can be accomplished by looking into user behavior. Designers are able to find problems with the page, like unclear navigation, slow loading times, or insufficient product information, by examining this behavior. After that, they can make the required changes to make the page better.

AI-driven platforms such as Crazy Egg and Mixpanel offer additional behavioral insights by using heatmaps and funnel analysis to identify friction points in the customer journey. These data-rich visualizations can reveal drop-off moments in real-time, allowing marketers to make faster UX improvements.

A/B Test

A/B testing, which is also occasionally referred to as split testing or bucket testing, is a technique that involves contrasting two different versions of a website or application with one another in order to determine which one is more successful. It accomplishes this by randomly displaying two different versions of a page to users and then employing statistical analysis to determine which of the two variations achieves better results in terms of achieving your conversion goals (Optimizely, 2019).

AI A/B testing tools are heading in the direction of being an extraordinary resource for website design and content optimization. As a standard method of alternative testing, it entails making and comparing different versions of a website by hand in order to determine which one performs better. In order to constantly test out different designs and configurations, AI can automate this process. It can swiftly identify the best combinations of user engagement and conversion rates, allowing for rapid iteration and improvement. In order to ensure consistency among participants and comply with regulations governing human subjects research, AI-adapted A/B testing automates the production and analysis of test variations. This program, for example, alters web pages using machine learning by generating a large number of permutations of its commands, some of which include content changes. AI systems can also monitor user actions in real-time, finding out which variants work best for certain objectives like lowering bounce rates or increasing click-through rates. AI-driven A/B testing guarantees peak website performance by continuously optimizing the design using real-time data.

Modern AI tools like Google Optimize and Adobe Target now go beyond traditional A/B testing by implementing multivariate testing and Bayesian algorithms to increase test accuracy. These allow marketers to run dozens of variations simultaneously while reducing the time needed to reach statistically significant conclusions.

EFFECTS OF AI FOR WEB DESIGN

Speed and Efficiency

These artificial intelligence tools have significantly reduced the amount of time that is required to design and create websites. They do this by automating tasks that are repetitive and by making intelligent design suggestions. As a result of this improved performance, designers are able to focus their attention on strategic and creative aspects of design, which ultimately leads to a quicker completion of the project and a reduction in costs. Using design tools that are powered by artificial intelligence, many aspects of web design can be done in an automatic or semi-automated manner. Some examples of these aspects include the generation of templates, the selection of color palettes, and some image optimization responsibilities. As a result, the amount of manual input that is required during the design process is reduced, which in turn makes it easier for designers to complete projects in a shorter amount of time. In a similar vein, artificial intelligence is useful for completing complex tasks that would otherwise require a significant amount of time and would necessitate a high level of professionalism in addition to a greater amount of experience. For instance, AI can analyze how users interact with websites or improve their content in order to achieve better search results on Google, among other things. Using artificial intelligence, designers are able to focus on more strategic aspects of their work, such as developing innovative design concepts and creating engaging user experiences. This is made possible by AI's ability to automate repetitive tasks. Not only does this result in an improvement in the quality of the final product, but it also results in an increase in job satisfaction for designers, as they can devote more time to activities that are both creative and fulfilling.

AI platforms like Wix ADI (Artificial Design Intelligence) and Bookmark's AIDA use user-provided inputs to automatically generate entire websites tailored to business type and customer goals, demonstrating AI’s potential to streamline web creation processes.

Data Driven Decisions

Artificial intelligence analytics provides designers with insights that they can act upon based on user data to improve design decision making and continuously advance the design process. Because of this information, they can determine whether or not the site is effective, which enables them to make continuous adjustments while maintaining their focus on the user experience when they are building sites. To successfully implement an effective web design, data-driven decision-making is an essential component. Tools that use artificial intelligence collect and analyze massive amounts of user data, which provides valuable insights into user behavior and preferences. Having this kind of understanding is helpful when it comes to making design decisions, which enable websites to become more engaging to users in addition to converting them. A large number of metrics, including user interactions, click-through rates, bounce rates, and conversion rates, can be monitored by AI analytics tools. These tools can gather this information. When designers examine this kind of information, they might be able to identify patterns or trends that indicate the areas in which modifications are required. When this occurs, it means that AI-based systems can investigate what is causing a high bounce rate on a specific web page and suggest possible design alternatives that could enhance user retention. This is the case if the bounce rate is high. Further, predictive analytics powered by AI can anticipate user needs and recommend UX improvements before problems occur, a shift from reactive to proactive design strategies.

For example, using machine learning algorithms, Google Analytics analyzes user behavior and offers insights into how users interact with a website. With the aid of these insights, designers can determine which components best engage users and increase conversions, enabling ongoing optimization and development.

To measure the success of AI integration, marketers must track performance using specific Key Performance Indicators (KPIs). Examples include conversion rate, customer lifetime value (CLV), return on ad spend (ROAS), and engagement rates. For instance, companies have reported conversion increases of up to 90% and campaign ROI improvements exceeding 60% following AI adoption. Establishing a KPI dashboard enables continuous monitoring and strategic adjustment.

DIFFICULTIES AND LIMITATIONS

Data Quality Dependence

The quality of the user data is the primary factor determining how effective AI is at creating websites. The quality of the design may suffer if the details that are provided are either inaccurate or insufficient. For artificial intelligence to function effectively, data of high quality and relevance must be gathered. When it comes to the success of AI-driven web design, data quality is an essential component. To make well-informed decisions and provide useful recommendations, artificial intelligence algorithms require data that is both accurate and comprehensive. If the data is inaccurate, out of date, or incomplete, the artificial intelligence tools may generate results that are less than optimal, which may result in poor design choices and decreased user engagement. To ensure that the data is of a high quality, it is necessary to have reliable data collection and management practices. These practices include validating the accuracy of the data, removing any inconsistencies or errors, and regularly updating the sources of the data as part of the process. In the same vein, this enables us to collect a variety of data types, which enables artificial intelligence algorithms to conduct a comprehensive analysis of the actions and behaviors of users.

The integration of data governance frameworks and ethical data sourcing is essential to maintain data integrity and avoid algorithmic bias. Without this, even the most advanced AI systems can make inaccurate or discriminatory decisions.

Decrease in the Human Touch

Websites can lose the creativity and attachment that come with being designed by humans if they rely too heavily on instruments that are powered by artificial intelligence. Despite the fact that artificial intelligence can assist in the execution of a number of geometrical constructions quickly and unobtrusively, it is not capable of reading the deeply ingrained emotions of users or telling the story about a brand in the manner that is required from a human point of view. AI tools are very effective at eliminating repetitive tasks and optimizing design components in accordance with data. They also can eliminate monotonous jobs. Nevertheless, they might be missing out on the creative and emotional aspects that are brought about by the artistic touch of man. In the event that it is about emotion design, then human designers are in a better position to comprehend it because they are aware of how different color schemes, images, or typefaces can be associated with different sensations or feelings that users have within them. These kinds of insights are helpful in the development of websites, which can interact with visitors on a more personal level and tell an engaging story about the brand. It is essential to strike a balance between the use of artificial intelligence (AI) automation and human creativity in web design to preserve the human element. While artificial intelligence tools can handle tasks that are data-driven and repetitive, human designers can concentrate on the creative and emotional aspects of design. This approach to working together ensures that websites are not only effective and data-driven, but also visually appealing and emotionally engaging for their users.

Combining AI design tools with human-centered design principles ensures that digital experiences remain empathetic, inclusive, and brand-consistent. The future of web design lies in this collaborative synergy.

Data Governance and Ethical Data Management

While data quality is a recognized limitation, it is equally important to address the broader issue of data governance. AI systems rely on massive volumes of structured and unstructured data, and without strong governance frameworks, the risk of poor data handling can undermine marketing performance.

Data governance involves policies, standards, and controls that ensure data is accurate, consistent, secure, and ethically sourced. For example, the lack of a unified governance system may result in duplicate customer profiles across platforms, inconsistent records, or even regulatory violations. Such weaknesses can produce biased algorithms, leading to unfair targeting or exclusion of specific groups.

The consequences of poor governance include:

Distorted insights → campaigns based on incomplete or biased data.

Legal exposure → violations of GDPR, the EU AI Act, or CCPA.

Loss of trust → consumers losing confidence in brands that mishandle data.

To mitigate these risks, organizations are encouraged to adopt data governance frameworks such as DAMA-DMBOK (Data Management Body of Knowledge) or ISO standards for data quality. Key best practices include:

Implementing data lineage systems to track the origin and use of customer data.

Conducting routine data audits to detect inconsistencies.

Establishing ethical sourcing guidelines to avoid collecting sensitive data without explicit consent.

Using Explainable AI (XAI) to provide clarity on how customer data influences marketing decisions.

By embedding governance into AI-driven marketing, companies can ensure compliance with regulations, avoid reputational damage, and maintain a trust-based relationship with consumers—a critical factor in sustainable brand success.

OPPORTUNITIES OFFERED BY AI IN DIGITAL MARKETING

Voice User Interfaces

Voice user interfaces (VUIs) enable users to interact with a product in a hands-free, eyes-free manner. This is made possible through visual assistants such as Siri, Google Assistant, and Alex, which are perfect examples of VUIs. These systems respond to voice or speech commands, acting in specific ways to fulfill users' needs while at the same time allowing them to focus their attention elsewhere (What Are Voice User Interfaces (VUI)?, 2017).

Accessibility and user interaction can be significantly enhanced by integrating VUIs for websites with the help of AI. Today, many users rely on voice commands for their online interactions, which is why voice search optimization and intuitive interfaces have become extremely important for businesses. Furthermore, integrating AI to enable seamless navigation to websites and quick access to information makes websites more convenient and time-efficient for customers. Another reason VUIs are likely to succeed is that these systems use natural language (NLP), allowing users to interact and communicate with these tools in a controversial language, and effortlessly gain access to the information they need. Lastly, VUIs improve the level of engagement with customers as these systems provide a more user-friendly experience to consumers in a more natural environment.

VUI integration is also expected to grow across smart homes, automotive systems, and retail, which means brands must optimize not just for textual SEO but for voice search intent. Structured data markup and natural question-based content become critical components of AI-driven content strategy.

AI-Driven SEO

The process of optimizing a website in order to improve its visibility and ranking in search engine results pages (SERPs) is referred to as search engine optimization, of which SEO is the practice. The use of relevant keywords, the creation of high-quality content, the establishment of backlinks, and the guaranteeing of technical aspects such as the website's speed and its compatibility with mobile devices are all techniques that are involved. Increasing the amount of organic traffic and improving user engagement are the goals of this endeavor (Keever, 2024).

Search Engine Optimization (SEO) is very important for websites as it determines their position on the web and how difficult or easy users can find it through search engines. With the integration of AI, SEO content can be more friendly. This guarantees that websites are optimized for the most popular and pertinent keywords, increasing their exposure and bringing in more natural visitors. This could happen with AI as it has the power to detect and suggest relevant keywords and topics. By examining user behavior, industry trends, and search engine algorithms, AI-driven SEO solutions are transforming how websites are optimized for search engines and raising their ranks. Additionally, large volumes of data may be analyzed by AI systems to determine the factors that affect search engine results. This involves looking at user interaction data, keywords, and content quality. Lastly, AI after analyzing and understanding these factors can provide suggestions for improving a website, such as identifying better keywords, enhancing UI and UX, and producing excellent content.

A relevant case study is Sephora, which uses AI-driven chatbots and facial recognition tools to personalize customer experiences both online and in-store. This has resulted in an 11% increase in conversion rates and improved customer satisfaction scores (Rayome, 2018).

EPILOGUE

In conclusion, the integration of AI into the marketing department can be challenging and brings significant changes to businesses, affecting everything from their strategies to the way they communicate with their customers.

AI offers numerous advantages to businesses including the ability to analyze massive amounts of data, deliver customized experiences, and automate routine tasks all of which drive efficiency, and embrace customer satisfaction.

On the other hand, implementing AI can also bring challenges to businesses, especially to small and medium-sized ones. High implementation costs, data privacy issues, and the need for skilled personnel can create substantial barriers for these companies to overcome. However, as the marketplace continues to evolve the adoption of AI tools is becoming increasingly vital for businesses to remain competitive and survive in today's dynamic environment.

AI is a technology that has not yet reached its maximum capabilities. While it already offers significant advantages, both to humans in their everyday lives and businesses. AI tools must be used wisely, as their misuse can easily impact human interactions and decision-making. These tools are essential for companies across all departments as they can help with time-saving and data analyses but also AI tools have the power to transform not just the marketing department but the entire organization. Companies that adopt this technology thoughtfully will have the greatest opportunity to place themselves as leaders in the market.

Furthermore, the future of AI in marketing must emphasize ethical responsibility, algorithmic transparency, and inclusive design. Businesses are encouraged to establish AI governance frameworks that align with regulatory requirements (such as GDPR and the AI Act), ensuring fair and accountable AI use. Strategic implementation of AI should also include ongoing employee training and evaluation metrics that measure impact beyond profits—such as trust, satisfaction, and sustainability.

REFERENCES

Abdalla, A. A., Bhat, M. A., Tiwari, C. K., Khan, S. T., & Wedajo, A. D. (2024). Exploring ChatGPT adoption among business and management students through the lens of diffusion of Innovation Theory. *Computers and Education: Artificial Intelligence*, *7*, 100257. DOI: 10.1016/j.caeai.2024.100257

Advantages and Disadvantages of Artificial Intelligence in Digital Marketing. (2024, August 5). Dentsu. https://www.dentsu.com/id/en/insights/our-blog/artificial-intelligence-in-digital-marketing

AI in Digital Marketing - The Ultimate Guide. (n.d.). Digital Marketing Institute........ . . . https://digitalmarketinginstitute.com/blog/ai-in-digital-marketing-the-ultimate-guide#

Antonyuk, S. (2024, March 21). *All about Netflix Artificial Intelligence: the Truth behind Personalized Content*. Litslink. https://litslink.com/blog/all-about-netflix-artificial-intelligence-the-truth-behind-personalized-content

Benkert, C.-L. (2019). *Ethics & AI: Identifying the ethical issues of AI in marketing and building practical guidelines for marketers*. https://essay.utwente.nl/78303/1/Benkert_BA_BMS.pdf

Breachsense. (n.d.). *5 Data Breach Examples (& Causes to Avoid in 2023)*. Www.breachsense.com. https://www.breachsense.com/blog/data-breach-examples/

Chatterjee, S., Nguyen, B., Ghosh, S. k., Bhattacharjee, k., & Chaudhuri, S. (2020). Adoption of artificial intelligence integrated CRM system: An empirical study of Indian organizations. *The Bottom Line (New York, N.Y.)*, *33*(4), 359–375. DOI: 10.1108/Bl-08-2020-0057

Crabill, J. (2023, December 6). The Pros And Cons Of AI In Marketing: Focusing On The eLearning Niche. ELearning Industry. https://elearningindustry.com/advertise/elearning-marketing-resources/blog/pros-and-cons-of-ai-in-marketing-tips-for-elearning-marketers

De Bruyn, A., Viswanathan, V., Beh, Y. S., Brock, J. K.-U., & Von Wangenheim, F. (2020). Artificial Intelligence and marketing: Pitfalls and opportunities. *Journal of Interactive Marketing*, *51*(1), 91–105. DOI: 10.1016/j.intmar.2020.04.007

Dr, N., & Thilagavathy, E. P. K. (2021). Artificial Intelligence on digital Marketing-An overview. *NVEO - NATURAL VOLATILES & ESSENTIAL OILS Journal | NVEO*, *8*(5), 9895–9908. https://www.nveo.org/index.php/journal/article/view/2772

Exploring the Ethical Implications of AI-Powered Personalization in Digital Marketing. (2024).. . *Data Intelligence*. Advance online publication. DOI: 10.3724/2096-7004.di.2024.0055

Gharib, M., Fakhry, A. E., Ali, A. M., & Abdelhafeez, A., & Hussam Elbehiery. (2024). Single Valued Neutrosophic Sets for Analysis Opinions of Customer in Waste Management. *International Journal of Neutrosophic Science*, *23*(3), 175–185. DOI: 10.54216/ijns.230315

Haleem, A., Javaid, M., Qadri, M. A., Singh, R. P., & Suman, R. (2022). Artificial Intelligence (AI) Applications for marketing: a literature-based Study. *International Journal of Intelligent Networks, 3*(3), 119–132. sciencedirect. https://www.sciencedirect.com/science/article/pii/S2666603022000136

IBM. (2024, July 25). *AI in Marketing | IBM*. Ibm.com. https://www.ibm.com/think/topics/ai-in-marketing

Jarek, K., & Mazurek, G. (2019). Marketing and Artificial Intelligence. *Central European Business Review*, *8*(2), 46. DOI: 10.18267/j.cebr.213

Jasper. (2023). *Jasper (formerly jarvis) - #1 AI writing assistant*. Www.jarvis.ai. https://www.jasper.ai/

Jordan, M. I., & Mitchell, T. M. (2015). Machine learning: Trends, perspectives, and prospects. *Science*, *349*(6245), 255–260. DOI: 10.1126/science.aaa8415 PMID: 26185243

Keever, S. (2024, August 12). Council Post: AI Is Driving The Future Of SEO: How To Adapt. *Forbes*. https://www.forbes.com/councils/forbesagencycouncil/2024/02/02/ai-is-driving-the-future-of-seo-how-to-adapt/

Lakshmipriyanka, A., Harihararao, M., Prasanna, M., & Deepika, Y. (2023). A study on artificial intelligence in marketing. *International Journal for Multidisciplinary Research*, *5*(3), 1–12.

Ma, J., Wang, P., Li, B., Wang, T., Xiang, S. P., & Wang, D. (2024). Exploring User Adoption of ChatGPT: A Technology Acceptance Model Perspective. *International Journal of Human-Computer Interaction*, *41*(2), 1–15. DOI: 10.1080/10447318.2024.2314358

Macumber, R., & Durga, V. (2024). Google, SEO and helpful content: How artificial intelligence can be helpful for e-commerce websites. *Journal of Digital & Social Media Marketing.*, *12*(3), 206–206. DOI: 10.69554/rjuw9313

Manyika, J., Silberg, J., & Presten, B. (2019, October 25). *What Do We Do About the Biases in AI?* Harvard Business Review. https://hbr.org/2019/10/what-do-we-do-about-the-biases-in-ai

Meliana, P. (2024, June 4). *The future of marketing: AI transformations by 2025.* ContentGrip; ContentGrip. https://www.contentgrip.com/future-ai-marketing/

Optimizely. (2019). *A/B Testing.* Optimizely.com. https://www.optimizely.com/optimization-glossary/ab-testing/

Photobucket delivers 24/7 member support with messaging. (2022, March 29). Zendesk. https://www.zendesk.com/customer/photobucket/

Rayome, A. (2018). How Sephora is leveraging AR and AI to transform retail and help customers buy cosmetics Beauty retailer Sephora followed customer technology trends to command the cosmetic industry worldwide. Here's an inside look at its successful digital transformation. https://steepnews24.wordpress.com/wp-content/uploads/2018/02/sephora_cover_story_final.pdf

TechTarget. (2023, May). *What is IS (information system or information services)? - Definition from WhatIs.com.* WhatIs.com. https://www.techtarget.com/whatis/definition/IS-information-system-or-information-services

The AI Revolution: How Artificial Intelligence is Reshaping Marketing Strategies – IJSREM. (2024). Ijsrem.com. https://ijsrem.com/download/the-ai-revolution-how-artificial-intelligence-is-reshaping-marketing-strategies/

The Role of AI in Marketing and How to Use It. (n.d.). Www.invoca.com. https://www.invoca.com/blog/ai-marketing-how-to-use-it

Van Esch, P., & Stewart Black, J. (2021). Artificial Intelligence (AI): Revolutionizing Digital Marketing. *Australasian Marketing Journal, 29*(3), 199–203. DOI: 10.1177/18393349211037684

What are Voice User Interfaces (VUI)? (2017, February 9). The Interaction Design Foundation; Interaction Design Foundation. https://www.interaction-design.org/literature/topics/voice-user-interfaces?srsltid=AfmBOorp7OT2tCl_5LmnxBvcF46rCLw9l33qTL_1K3zfXRG-6arv3j60

Williams, K. (2023, July 27). *The Pros and Cons of AI in Marketing: An Analysis.* SurveySparrow. https://surveysparrow.com/blog/the-pros-and-cons-of-ai-in-marketing/

Yadav, B. (2024). Role of Artificial Intelligence in Marketing: A Paradigm Shift. *IJFMR240111924, 6*(1). https://www.ijfmr.com/papers/2024/1/11924.pdf

Chapter 3

Harnessing Big Data and AI:

Unlocking Predictive Insights for Smarter Marketing Decisions

Rajkumar Jagdale
https://orcid.org/0000-0002-4074-1095
Vishwakarma University, Pune, India

Abdul Hannan R. Dalal
https://orcid.org/0009-0005-0866-9723
Vishwakarma University, Pune, India

ABSTRACT

In today's data-driven world, businesses must leverage big data and AI to stay competitive. This chapter explores how AI, combined with big data analytics, enables marketers to make real-time, informed decisions that enhance customer engagement and optimize marketing strategies. Key methodologies such as machine learning and behavioral analytics transform vast amounts of data into actionable insights. AI facilitates predictive analytics, hyper-personalization, and automated decision-making, while Customer Data Platforms (CDPs) offer a unified view of customers. Behavioral analytics helps track consumer interactions across digital touchpoints, improving segmentation and engagement. Real-world case studies from e-commerce, retail, and finance show how AI-driven marketing leads to business growth and ROI. However, ethical challenges like data privacy, algorithmic bias, and transparency must be addressed to maintain consumer trust. This chapter provides marketing professionals, researchers, and business leaders with crucial insights into leveraging AI and big data for success.

DOI: 10.4018/979-8-3693-9994-1.ch003

1. INTRODUCTION

Digital transformation created an exceptional data growth explosion which transformed business-customer relationships completely. Organizations gain extensive amounts of data from everything customers do online including buying activities and social media use and interactions. The fundamental obstacle of data analysis is not related to accessing data but in developing significant conclusions from it. History-based intuition and past market performance cannot sustain modern businesses in this high-speed data-dominated age. The market industry now requires artificial intelligence (AI) together with big data analytics for marketing purposes to convert unprocessed information into useful insights. AI-based marketing tools composed of machine learning algorithms and natural language processing and predictive analytics help marketers study intricate consumer actions to predict upcoming market directions and deliver personalized engagements for large numbers of people through advanced methods. The use of modern technical systems enables organizations to improve consumer relationships and maximize advertising results that lead to increased business expansion.

AI systems combined with big data have transformed marketing processes through distributed automatic operations that use real-time decisions. The analysis of vast dataset required weeks to complete in previous processing methods. The real-time algorithms within AI-based marketing systems process extensive amounts of structured along with unstructured data to select target audiences better and optimize marketing campaigns. CDPs operate by merging various data sources to generate unified customer profiles in order to drive this change. Through behavioural analytics businesses acquire user behaviour data for the purpose of monitoring digital behaviour to deliver personalized content to customers. Companies must understand all ethical problems that emerge from their marketing AI deployment. Consumer trust depends on dealing with ethical problems that involve protecting privacy data through removing algorithmic bias and ensuring complete clarity in data use. The chapter explores marketing applications of big data and AI through methodological descriptions of case studies and ethical analytics which display business implementation of advanced technology for better choices.

2. LITERATURE REVIEW

2.1 Historical Evolution of AI in Marketing

The integration of artificial intelligence (AI) into marketing did not occur overnight; rather, it has evolved through a series of technological and strategic advancements over several decades. Understanding this evolution provides important context for how contemporary AI applications in marketing have developed and matured.

2.2 Early Stages: Rule-Based Systems and CRM Automation (1980s–1990s)

AI's earliest influence on marketing can be traced back to the 1980s and 1990s, when expert systems and rule-based decision engines were introduced in business software. These early systems operated based on predefined logic, often used in customer relationship management (CRM) and basic email automation. For instance, businesses could trigger customer follow-ups based on rule-based criteria like purchase frequency or cart abandonment.

These tools, while limited in adaptability, represented the initial move toward automated decision-making and personalized communication, laying the groundwork for today's intelligent systems.

2.3 Emergence of Data-Driven Marketing and Web Analytics (2000s)

The 2000s marked a critical turning point, as digital platforms like Google Analytics (2005) and customer data management systems became mainstream. Marketers began leveraging behavioral tracking and web analytics to understand user journeys. While not fully AI-based, these tools introduced data-centric thinking, which is fundamental to AI marketing.

Simultaneously, machine learning algorithms began to surface in recommendation systems, most notably pioneered by Amazon and Netflix, where user behavior data was used to predict preferences and drive engagement.

2.4 Rise of Social Media and Real-Time Engagement (2010–2015)

The rise of platforms like Facebook, Twitter, and Instagram between 2010 and 2015 significantly changed the landscape. These platforms enabled vast, real-time datasets, pushing marketers toward sentiment analysis, real-time bidding, and personalized targeting. AI began to be applied more deeply through natural language processing (NLP) to analyze customer feedback and generate dynamic content.

Sentiment analysis is widely used to extract insights from customer reviews across platforms like Amazon, helping businesses refine strategies based on consumer feedback (Jagdale, Shirsat, & Deshmukh, 2019). In their study, Naïve Bayes and SVM achieved accuracies of 98.17% and 93.54% respectively for classifying camera reviews (Jagdale et al., 2019).

During this period, the use of AI in programmatic advertising took off, with AI optimizing ad placements and budgets in real time. Marketing automation platforms such as HubSpot and Marketo incorporated AI features for lead scoring and email personalization.

2.5 Modern Era: Predictive and Generative AI (2016–Present)

From 2016 onward, AI in marketing has become more sophisticated and impactful. Deep learning, predictive analytics, and AI-powered chatbots have enabled businesses to deliver hyper-personalized customer experiences. Customer Data Platforms (CDPs) emerged to consolidate multichannel data and feed AI models for improved segmentation and targeting.

The recent integration of generative AI technologies (e.g., ChatGPT, DALL·E) has introduced new possibilities such as automated content creation, AI-generated visuals, and conversational marketing at scale.

Companies today use AI to optimize every stage of the customer journey — from dynamic pricing, automated A/B testing, and customer sentiment monitoring to real-time product recommendations.

3. THE ROLE OF BIG DATA AND AI IN MARKETING

Organizations now transform their marketing operations through artificial intelligence (AI) working together with big data analytics to access extensive databases for choosing superior business insights. Organizations apply AI-driven marketing approaches to examine substantial big data collections containing both structured and unstructured data in order to obtain superior customer insights along with personalized customer interactions. Big data analytics serves as the foundation for artificial intelligence applications since this method allows marketers to find significant consumer behaviour patterns (Chen, Chiang, & Storey, 2012). Through implementation of predictive score modeling business operations gain the capability to predict customer demands which guides their strategic changes (Davenport & Ronanki, 2018). AI marketing tools became more precise and efficient in their operations through expanded consumer data acquisition during the advancement of machine learning algorithms (Wedel & Kannan, 2016). Organizations must preserve transparent privacy practices when implementing these technologies because they generate ethical along with privacy-related worries according to Smith, A. and Jones, B. (2023).

3.1 Machine Learning as a Catalyst for Predictive Insights

Predictive marketing receives support from machine learning (ML) because it enables real-time analysis of data to determine customer preferences. The organization of customers according to their behavioural actions by AI systems through supervised and unsupervised learning enables better market identification approaches (Erevelles, Fukawa, & Swayne, 2016). Organizations employing predictive analytics with machine learning enhance their price strategy development while gaining better understanding of market trends along with improving customer relationship techniques (Delen & Demirkan, 2013). AI-powered automation methods improve marketing operational performance and minimize human errors during marketing operations (Mupa & Nkomo, 2024). Studied research shows technology businesses experience superior conversion performances while earning elevated return on investment once they deploy machine learning algorithms according. Accurate machine learning model operation and relevance require continuous monitoring and model readjustments according to Patil (2024).

3.2 Customer Data Platforms and Data Integration

The technology revolution has introduced Customer Data Platforms (CDPs which enable companies to unite consumer data from numerous contact points (Latifi, 2024). Businesses can use CDPs to build universal customer profiles through one platform which integrates multiple data sources starting from social media up to website and e-commerce transactions (Rahaman, 2024). CDP integration allows marketers to create precise customer segments which helps them produce specific recommendations and targeted communication messages (Lamplugh 2024). AI-powered analytics assists organizations in locating their most valuable clients while forecasting customer abandonment risks and building marketing plans which are data-based (Davenport & Ronanki, 2018). Bytecat platform processing capability extends CDP efficacy through its ability to handle unstructured text like social media mood expressions (Wirtz, Tuzovic, & Kuppelwieser, 2014). Though efficient marketing and advertisement functions attract consumers to CDPs, companies must follow data protection rules to preserve client trust Smith, A. and Jones, B. (2023).

3.3 Behavioural Analytics and Consumer Insights

The technology revolution has introduced Customer Data Platforms (CDPs which enable companies to unite consumer data from numerous contact points (Latifi, 2024). Businesses can use CDPs to build universal customer profiles through one platform which integrates multiple data sources starting from social media up to website and e-commerce transactions (Rahaman, 2024). CDP integration allows marketers to create precise customer segments which helps them produce specific recommendations and targeted communication messages (Lamplugh 2024). AI-powered analytics assists organizations in locating their most valuable clients while forecasting customer abandonment risks and building marketing plans which are data-based (Davenport & Ronanki, 2018). The power of CDPs gets stronger through AI because it enables the analysis of unstructured data such as social media sentiment (Wirtz, Tuzovic, & Kuppelwieser, 2014). Though efficient marketing and advertisement functions attract consumers to CDPs, companies must follow data protection rules to preserve client trust Smith, A. and Jones, B. (2023).

3.4 Predictive Analytics and Data-Driven Decision-Making

Using predictive analytics powered by AI allows organizations to forecast rates of customer behaviour therefore improving their marketing efficiency (Latifi, 2024). Dados de pesquisa processados pelo machine learning modelos permitem identificar paterns and generate useful data insights about future marketing ventures. The predictive modeling approach creates substantial worth to business organizations in retail and finance sectors because it enhances inventory administration and customer delight (Chen et al., 2012). Organizations employing predictive analytics solutions with AI power reach better customer retention results together with higher customer engagement numbers (Erevelles et al., 2016). High-quality data inputs represent the main requirement for predictive analytics success and data governance stands necessary to achieve marketing success with AI-based solutions (Patil, 2024).

3.5 Ethical Considerations in AI-Driven Marketing

Before conducting benefit analysis of AI and big data organizations need to solve ethical matters regarding consumer privacy protection and data security together with algorithmic bias problems Smith, A. and Jones, B. (2023). Open AI model frameworks together with preventive measures against discriminatory marketing campaign biases represent essential elements for companies (Keikhosrokiani, 2024). Customer privacy matters due to data collection have intensified their public discussion because consumers lack knowledge about how their information will be used (Wirtz et al., 2014). The General Data Protection Regulation (GDPR) operates with other regulatory structures to defend customer rights through ethical data handling measures (Latifi, 2024). Businesses that embrace ethical AI deployment use customer relationships to build brand reputation (Davenport & Ronanki, 2018). Rahaman (2024) argues that modern businesses should develop responsible AI approaches to achieve innovation and ethical compliance in their operations.

4. THE INTERSECTION OF BIG DATA AND AI IN MARKETING

4.1 Defining Big Data and AI in the Context of Marketing

Marketing underwent a massive transformation thanks to big data together with artificial intelligence (AI) to improve business operations regarding consumer information acquisition and analysis. The substantial amounts of organized and unorganized data coming from various sources including social media activities and internet purchases and customer evaluations and internet-connected devices constitute big data (Gandomi & Haider, 2015). The datasets described by Chen et al. (2012) exhibit three properties: Volume, Velocity and Variety so complex analytical techniques are essential for extraction of meaningful insights. AI consists of machine learning and natural language processing and deep learning approaches that enable big data processing to help organizations automate systems and execute predictive analytics and immediate decision-making processes. Marketers leverage AI and big data to create an effective collaboration which delivers predictions about consumer preferences and personalized marketing content management of their programs (Wedel & Kannan, 2016).

4.2 The Significance of Data-Driven Marketing in Today's Landscape

The digital revolution resulted in unprecedented data growth which remarkable businesses must adopt data-driven marketing as their competitive tool (Davenport & Ronanki, 2018). Marketing practices in previous times depended mainly on instinct and past knowledge together with large customer clusters. AI-powered marketing gives companies a chance to work with live customer data that supports the delivery of customized marketing solutions and automatic advertisement selection and proactive monitoring of buyer response patterns (Erevelles, Fukawa, & Swayne, 2016). Companies rely on predictive analytics as well as AI-powered chatbots and recommendation engines to deliver customized messaging and offers for each customer through their historical and current interaction data. The personalization tool operated by Amazon through AI algorithms reviews customer ordering patterns alongside their browsing activities before developing customized product solutions which grow business sales and enhance user involvement (Patil, 2024). Marketing strategies based on data enhance customer satisfaction at the same time as maximizing ROI to create lasting brand loyalty.

4.3 An Overview of the Relationship Between Data, Analytics, and Marketing Performance

Data analytics and marketing performance align in a complex manner through business exploration of artificial intelligence analytics tools for tracking key performance indicators (KPIs) and budget optimization and customer targeting strategy development (Delen & Demirkan, 2013). Using AI-driven marketing platforms enables businesses to examine client conduct while making trend forecasts and generating implementable insights that direct resource distribution effectively (Wirtz, Tuzovic, & Kuppelwieser, 2014). The crucial function of Customer Data Platforms (CDPs) is to merge data from multiple channels so customers can gain a comprehensive view of themselves which improves both segmentation strategies and personalized services (Latifi, 2024). Companies that integrate Google Analytics and IBM Watson and Salesforce Einstein into their operations can track their marketing campaigns live to optimize performance and elevate their engagement results through data-dependent changes (Rahaman, 2024). The automation of regular marketing tasks through AI improves efficiency while increasing operational scale by cutting both employee workload and costs (Keikhosrokiani, 2024). Organizations can boost their marketing results through AI but must handle ethical matters related to privacy of user data and algorithm biases as well as regulatory requirements in order to keep customer trust Smith, A. and Jones, B. (2023).

The table 1 below provides a clear comparison between traditional marketing and AI-driven marketing approaches, illustrating the fundamental shift from manual, intuition-based decision-making to automated, data-driven strategies that leverage artificial intelligence for enhanced efficiency and effectiveness. Traditional marketing relied heavily on broad customer segmentation, past experiences, and manual data collection methods, often leading to generalized messaging that lacked personalization and real-time adaptability. In contrast, AI-driven marketing leverages machine learning algorithms, predictive analytics, and customer data platforms (CDPs) to collect and process vast amounts of data in real time, allowing businesses to gain deeper insights into consumer behavior and preferences. This real-time data processing enables hyper-personalization, where marketing efforts are tailored to individual customer needs, significantly improving engagement and customer satisfaction. Additionally, AI enhances decision-making by automating tasks such as ad targeting, campaign optimization, and content personalization, reducing the reliance on human intuition and minimizing errors. With AI, businesses can dynamically adjust their strategies based on predictive insights, ensuring that marketing efforts remain relevant and effective. Moreover, AI-powered marketing strategies are more efficient, enabling real-time adjustments, faster execution, and automated responses to market trends, ultimately leading to improved customer experiences, increased retention rates, and higher conversion rates. By integrating AI into marketing, companies can optimize their efforts, enhance brand loyalty, and drive business growth in an increasingly competitive digital landscape.

Table 1. Traditional Marketing vs. AI-Driven Marketing Approaches

Factor	Traditional Marketing	AI-Driven Marketing
Data Collection	Manual, survey-based	Automated, real-time data collection
Customer Segmentation	Broad, generalized segmentation	Granular, behaviour-based segmentation
Decision-Making	Intuition-based strategies	Data-driven, predictive decision-making
Personalization	Limited personalization	Hyper-personalized, AI-driven recommendations
Efficiency	Slower execution	Faster, real-time adjustments based on AI insights
Marketing Strategy	Based on past experiences	Dynamic strategy optimization using AI
Customer Engagement	One-size-fits-all approach	AI-powered personalized customer interactions

5. MACHINE LEARNING AS A CATALYST FOR PREDICTIVE INSIGHTS

5.1 Understanding Machine Learning and Its Relevance in Marketing

Machine learning (ML) is a subset of AI that enables systems to learn from data, identify patterns, and make predictions without explicit programming. In marketing, ML algorithms analyze consumer data to anticipate purchasing behaviour, segment audiences, and optimize advertising strategies (Chen et al., 2012). One of the most significant advantages of ML in marketing is its ability to process vast amounts of customer data in real time, allowing businesses to adapt their marketing strategies dynamically (Erevelles et al., 2016). Companies use supervised learning for tasks such as customer churn prediction and sentiment analysis, while unsupervised learning helps uncover hidden customer segments based on behavioural similarities (Davenport & Ronanki, 2018). Advanced ML models, including deep learning and reinforcement learning, are increasingly being employed to improve customer engagement through personalized experiences, predictive lead scoring, and automated content generation .

5.2 Techniques for Implementing Machine Learning in Analyzing Customer Behaviour

Several ML techniques play a crucial role in analyzing customer behaviour and predicting future trends. Natural Language Processing (NLP) is widely used for social media sentiment analysis, chatbots, and personalized content recommendations (Wirtz et al., 2014). NLP algorithms extract consumer sentiments from online reviews, helping brands understand public perception and refine their messaging (Rahaman, 2024). Businesses also rely on clustering algorithms (e.g., K-Means, DBSCAN) to segment customers based on shared characteristics, allowing for more targeted marketing efforts (Keikhosrokiani, 2024). Additionally, decision tree algorithms (e.g., Random Forest, XGBoost) enhance marketing automation by ranking potential leads based on conversion probability (Latifi, 2024). AI-powered recommendation engines, such as those used by Netflix and Spotify, leverage collaborative filtering techniques to deliver personalized content suggestions based on user preferences and historical interactions (Patil, 2024).

5.3 Case Studies Demonstrating Successful Machine Learning Applications in Marketing Campaigns

Several companies have successfully implemented machine learning to revolutionize their marketing strategies. Amazon, for instance, utilizes ML-based recommendation engines that analyze customer purchase history and browsing behaviour to suggest products that align with individual preferences, resulting in a 35% increase in sales from personalized recommendations alone (Patil, 2024). Similarly, Netflix applies ML algorithms to its content recommendation system, analyzing user viewing patterns to predict and promote content that aligns with individual tastes, significantly improving user engagement and retention (Rahaman, 2024). In the financial sector, American Express uses ML-driven fraud detection systems to identify suspicious transactions based on spending behaviours, enhancing both security and customer trust (Keikhosrokiani, 2024).

In the retail industry, Walmart uses AI-powered demand forecasting tools to predict inventory needs based on customer purchasing trends, reducing operational costs and minimizing product shortages (Davenport & Ronanki, 2018). AI-driven advertising platforms, such as Google Ads and Facebook Ads, employ ML algorithms to optimize ad targeting in real time, ensuring that businesses reach the most relevant audience segments (Wedel & Kannan, 2016). The automotive industry is also leveraging ML for predictive maintenance marketing, where companies like Tesla use AI to analyze vehicle data and provide proactive maintenance recommendations, enhancing customer satisfaction (Erevelles et al., 2016).

These case studies illustrate the transformative power of machine learning in modern marketing, enabling companies to enhance personalization, optimize engagement, and maximize ROI. However, despite its many advantages, the deployment of ML-driven marketing strategies must be accompanied by ethical considerations, particularly in data privacy, fairness in AI models, and regulatory compliance Smith, A. and Jones, B. (2023)

6. CUSTOMER DATA PLATFORMS (CDPS) AND THEIR ROLE IN DATA INTEGRATION

6.1 Explanation of Customer Data Platforms and Their Functionalities

Customer Data Platforms (CDPs) have emerged as essential tools for businesses looking to unify, analyze, and activate customer data for marketing and personalization. A CDP is a centralized system that collects customer data from various sources, organizes it into structured profiles, and makes it accessible for marketing, sales, and customer service teams (Latifi, 2024). Unlike traditional data management systems, CDPs focus specifically on customer-centric data integration, allowing businesses to create a 360-degree view of their consumers (Rahaman, 2024). These platforms are designed to handle first-party, second-party, and third-party data, making them highly effective in consolidating fragmented customer information across multiple channels (Davenport & Ronanki, 2018). Key functionalities of CDPs include data ingestion, identity resolution, segmentation, analytics, and real-time activation, ensuring that businesses can leverage customer insights effectively (Keikhosrokiani, 2024).

Table 2. Key Features of Customer Data Platforms (CDPs) in AI-Driven Marketing

Feature	Function
Centralized Data Management	Unifies customer data from multiple sources (e.g., websites, apps, social media)
Real-Time Insights	Provides actionable insights instantly for dynamic marketing adjustments
AI-Powered Segmentation	Uses machine learning to group customers based on behaviour and preferences
Personalization Engine	Delivers tailored recommendations and targeted advertisements
Predictive Analytics Integration	Forecasts customer needs and optimizes campaign strategies
Privacy and Compliance	Ensures adherence to GDPR, CCPA, and other data regulations

The table 2 above provides a structured overview of the key functionalities of Customer Data Platforms (CDPs), which have become indispensable tools for AI-driven marketing strategies by enabling businesses to aggregate, manage, and utilize customer data efficiently. CDPs serve as centralized data hubs that collect information from multiple sources, including websites, mobile apps, CRM systems, social media, and offline transactions, ensuring a unified and comprehensive view of each customer. By integrating AI-powered analytics, CDPs allow businesses to segment customers based on behavior, preferences, and engagement patterns, facilitating hyper-personalized marketing campaigns that resonate with individual users. Real-time insights generated by CDPs empower marketers to adjust strategies dynamically, optimize customer interactions, and enhance user engagement, all while ensuring efficiency and accuracy in decision-making. Furthermore, CDPs play a crucial role in predictive marketing by analyzing past customer interactions to forecast future behaviors, helping businesses anticipate needs and tailor their offerings accordingly. As data privacy regulations such as GDPR and CCPA become more stringent, CDPs also assist in maintaining compliance by implementing secure data storage, consent management, and transparency in customer data usage. The integration of CDPs with AI not only streamlines marketing operations but also enhances customer experience, builds trust, and drives long-term brand loyalty by delivering relevant, data-driven, and highly personalized marketing efforts at scale.

6.2 How CDPs Facilitate the Consolidation of Customer Data from Various Sources

One of the major advantages of CDPs is their ability to integrate data from multiple sources to create a unified customer profile. These sources include website interactions, mobile app usage, social media engagements, CRM systems, email marketing platforms, and offline transactions (Wirtz, Tuzovic, & Kuppelwieser, 2014). By consolidating customer data, CDPs eliminate data silos, ensuring that marketing and sales teams have a comprehensive and consistent view of customer behaviours and preferences. Additionally, CDPs employ AI-powered identity resolution techniques to match data across different touchpoints, recognizing the same customer even if they engage with a brand through multiple devices or platforms (Erevelles, Fukawa, & Swayne, 2016).

6.3 Strategies for Utilizing CDPs to Create Personalized Marketing Experiences

Businesses can leverage CDPs to implement highly personalized and data-driven marketing strategies. Predictive segmentation, powered by AI, enables marketers to categorize customers into specific groups based on behavioural patterns and purchasing history (Wedel & Kannan, 2016). This segmentation allows companies to tailor messaging, product recommendations, and promotional offers based on customer preferences. Additionally, CDPs facilitate real-time marketing automation, allowing brands to deliver dynamic content via personalized emails, chatbots, and targeted advertisements (Delen & Demirkan, 2013). A prime example is Netflix, which utilizes AI-driven CDPs to personalize movie and TV show recommendations based on user behaviour, leading to increased engagement and customer satisfaction (Patil, 2024). Furthermore, CDPs improve customer retention strategies by tracking churn signals and automating proactive engagement campaigns, ensuring that at-risk customers receive personalized offers before they disengage Smith, A. and Jones, B. (2023).

Figure 1. AI – Driven Customer Data Processing Pipeline

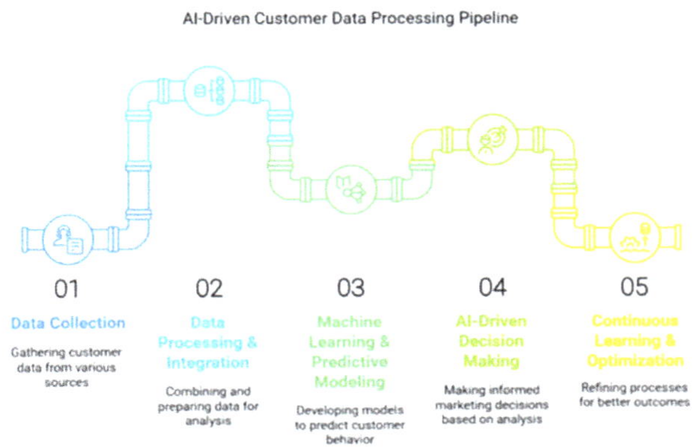

Figure 1 illustrates how AI processes customer data from multiple sources, integrating machine learning to generate predictive insights and optimize marketing strategies. In today's data-driven marketing landscape, businesses collect vast amounts of customer data from various touchpoints, including website interactions, mobile applications, social media engagements, transactional records, IoT sensors, and CRM systems. However, raw data alone is not valuable unless it is effectively processed and analyzed. AI-driven data processing pipelines automate this transformation, ensuring that businesses can extract meaningful insights from unstructured datasets. The process begins with data collection, where AI gathers customer information in real-time from multiple sources, such as user activity on websites, purchase history, social media sentiments, and offline interactions. This raw data is then passed through data processing and integration, where AI-powered algorithms clean, categorize, and standardize it to ensure consistency and accuracy. Customer Data Platforms (CDPs) play a crucial role at this stage, consolidating disparate datasets and creating unified customer profiles that allow for a 360-degree view of consumer behaviour. Once the data is structured, machine learning and predictive modeling come into play, analyzing historical trends and behavioural patterns to forecast future customer actions. AI-powered behavioural analytics enables marketers to segment customers based on interests, demographics, and purchase intent, allowing for hyper-personalized marketing strategies. Predictive sales models identify the likelihood of a customer making a purchase, while sentiment analysis tools assess customer opinions from social media and online reviews to gauge brand perception. These insights feed into the AI-driven decision-making process, where businesses can automate marketing strategies such as dynamic pricing, real-time ad targeting, product recommendations, and personalized email marketing. AI continuously refines these strategies by utilizing feedback loops and real-time performance tracking, ensuring that marketing efforts remain effective and adaptable to changing consumer behaviour. The final stage of the pipeline, continuous learning and optimization, ensures that AI-driven marketing remains dynamic and responsive to emerging trends. AI models are regularly updated using fresh data, allowing businesses to improve predictive accuracy and enhance customer engagement strategies. Techniques such as A/B testing, AI-driven campaign performance analysis, and reinforcement learning help refine marketing messages and improve conversion rates. As shown in Figure 1, AI-driven customer data processing pipelines allow businesses to move beyond traditional marketing approaches, enabling them to engage with consumers in a more targeted, efficient, and data-driven manner. This seamless integration of AI and big data analytics ensures that marketing decisions are not only based on historical insights but also proactively anticipate customer needs, leading to higher retention rates, increased ROI, and improved customer satisfaction.

7. BEHAVIOURAL ANALYTICS: TRANSFORMING DATA INTO CUSTOMER INSIGHTS

7.1 The Role of Behavioural Analytics in Understanding Customer Journeys

Behavioural analytics is the practice of analyzing how customers interact with digital platforms to gain insights into their decision-making processes and preferences. Unlike traditional analytics, which focus primarily on demographic data, behavioural analytics examines user actions, engagement levels, and patterns to predict future behaviour (Chen, Chiang, & Storey, 2012). Businesses use this data to map customer journeys, identifying key touchpoints where customers engage with their brand (Erevelles et al., 2016). This deeper understanding allows companies to optimize marketing strategies, reduce friction in the customer experience, and enhance conversion rates. For example, Amazon tracks browsing history, product clicks, and time spent on pages to refine its recommendation algorithms and boost sales (Patil, 2024).

7.2 Techniques for Tracking and Analyzing Customer Behaviour Across Digital Touchpoints

Companies employ various techniques to track and analyze customer behaviour across multiple platforms. Heatmaps and session recordings help businesses understand how users navigate websites and identify obstacles that may hinder conversions (Davenport & Ronanki, 2018). AI-driven sentiment analysis examines customer reviews, social media comments, and chatbot interactions to gauge public perception of a brand (Rahaman, 2024). Additionally, funnel analysis tracks how users progress through the sales journey, pinpointing where they drop off and optimizing touchpoints accordingly (Keikhosrokiani, 2024). Clickstream analysis, another powerful tool, examines user navigation patterns across a website, helping marketers refine content placement and UI/UX design (Latifi, 2024). By integrating these techniques, businesses gain a comprehensive view of customer behaviour, allowing them to craft more targeted marketing strategies.

7.3 Practical Applications of Behavioural Analytics in Enhancing Customer Engagement and Retention

Behavioural analytics plays a crucial role in enhancing customer engagement, personalization, and retention strategies. Businesses use behavioural insights to deliver hyper-personalized experiences, such as customized email campaigns, dynamic product recommendations, and targeted discounts (Wirtz et al., 2014). E-commerce brands like Shopify leverage behavioural analytics to send abandoned cart reminders, recovering lost sales. Similarly, Spotify analyzes listening behaviour to create personalized playlists and music suggestions, keeping users engaged and reducing churn (Patil, 2024). Furthermore, behavioural analytics enhances customer service automation, enabling chatbots to respond with relevant solutions based on past interactions Smith, A. and Jones, B. (2023).These practical applications ensure that brands remain proactive in anticipating customer needs and maintaining long-term relationships.

8. PREDICTIVE ANALYTICS: ANTICIPATING CUSTOMER NEEDS

8.1 Exploring Predictive Analytics and Its Importance in Marketing Strategies

Predictive analytics is an AI-powered approach that uses historical data, statistical algorithms, and machine learning techniques to anticipate future customer behaviours and market trends (Wedel & Kannan, 2016). By identifying patterns in past consumer interactions, businesses can make data-driven marketing decisions, such as predicting demand, optimizing pricing strategies, and enhancing customer retention efforts (Chen et al., 2012). Predictive analytics helps businesses reduce marketing inefficiencies, ensuring that resources are allocated toward the most promising prospects (Erevelles et al., 2016). A practical example includes email marketing automation, where predictive analytics determines the best time to send emails based on customer activity patterns .

Table 3. Predictive Analytics Tools for AI-Optimized Marketing

Tool	Primary Function
Google Analytics	Web traffic insights, predictive audience targeting
IBM Watson	AI-driven customer segmentation and sentiment analysis
Salesforce Einstein	Predictive CRM analytics and customer lifecycle management
Adobe Sensei	AI-powered creative automation and personalized content recommendations
Amazon SageMaker	Machine learning model development for demand forecasting

The table 3 highlights the critical role of predictive analytics in AI-driven marketing by showcasing the leading AI-powered tools that help businesses anticipate customer needs, optimize engagement, and allocate marketing budgets more effectively. Predictive analytics leverages machine learning algorithms and data-driven insights to identify patterns in consumer behaviour, allowing companies to make informed marketing decisions with greater accuracy. By analyzing vast amounts of historical and real-time data, these tools enable businesses to forecast demand, segment customers based on behavioural trends, and personalize marketing efforts to maximize customer engagement. AI-powered predictive analytics tools, such as Google Analytics, IBM Watson, and Salesforce Einstein, specialize in key areas like audience targeting, sentiment analysis, and predictive CRM, providing businesses with actionable insights that improve decision-making. These technologies empower organizations to refine ad placements, automate personalized recommendations, and optimize customer interactions, leading to improved conversion rates and higher return on investment. Additionally, predictive analytics helps businesses enhance customer retention strategies by identifying at-risk customers and proactively engaging them with tailored offers or content. As AI continues to advance, predictive analytics tools will become even more sophisticated, enabling marketers to deliver more relevant, data-driven campaigns while improving overall marketing performance.

8.2 Tools and Technologies That Enable Predictive Modeling

Several advanced AI-powered tools facilitate predictive modeling in marketing. Google Analytics and IBM Watson use machine learning to analyze website traffic, predict user behaviour, and suggest marketing optimizations (Latifi, 2024). Salesforce Einstein and Adobe Sensei provide AI-driven insights into customer preferences, enabling businesses to deliver targeted content (Rahaman, 2024). Additionally, Amazon SageMaker helps companies build and deploy predictive models for demand forecasting and pricing strategies (Keikhosrokiani, 2024). These tools automate customer segmentation, conversion probability analysis, and personalized content recommendations, making predictive analytics a cornerstone of AI-driven marketing.

As shown in Figure 2, predictive analytics follows a structured process, where AI-driven analysis extracts patterns from historical customer data to anticipate purchasing behaviour and optimize marketing campaigns. Predictive analytics plays a crucial role in modern marketing strategies, enabling businesses to shift from reactive decision-making to proactive, data-driven engagement. This process begins with data input and collection, where AI gathers information from multiple sources such as historical purchase data, website clickstream behaviours, social media engagement, and competitor market trends. These datasets serve as the foundation for AI-driven analysis, where machine learning algorithms identify patterns, detect emerging trends, and predict customer intent and purchasing likelihood. Using these insights, AI generates predictive marketing recommendations that fuel personalized advertising, tailored content suggestions, and dynamic customer engagement strategies. For example, AI-powered systems can recommend products based on individual browsing history, optimize ad placements in real-time, and enhance customer retention efforts through predictive churn models. Once implemented, these predictive insights guide campaign execution and performance monitoring, ensuring that marketing strategies remain highly adaptive and data-optimized. AI systems automatically adjust ad spend, refine messaging, and optimize targeting based on real-time campaign performance data. The final stage, continuous learning and strategy refinement, ensures that AI models evolve as new consumer behaviours emerge. AI-driven marketing strategies undergo constant optimization, with models adapting to market shifts, retraining for accuracy improvements, and refining targeting parameters to maximize ROI. Predictive analytics is a game-changer in marketing, allowing businesses to forecast trends, enhance personalization, and optimize marketing investments with data-backed precision.

Figure 2. AI-Powered Predictive Analytics Workflow in Marketing

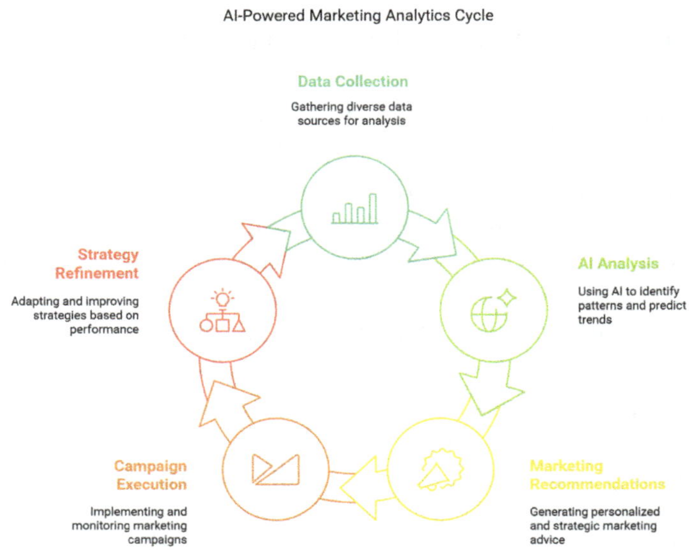

8.3 Examples of Businesses That Successfully Implemented Predictive Analytics to Improve ROI

Several industry leaders have successfully integrated predictive analytics into their marketing strategies. Walmart uses predictive analytics to optimize inventory management, reducing stock shortages and improving operational efficiency (Davenport & Ronanki, 2018). Netflix leverages AI-driven predictive models to recommend content, increasing user engagement and retention. Starbucks uses predictive analytics to personalize customer offers, resulting in higher conversion rates and increased loyalty. These success stories demonstrate how predictive analytics enhances marketing ROI, customer satisfaction, and business growth.

9. CASE STUDIES OF SUCCESSFUL DATA-DRIVEN MARKETING

9.1 Real-World Examples from Various Industries (Retail, E-Commerce, Finance)

The implementation of AI-driven, data-driven marketing strategies has revolutionized multiple industries, optimizing customer engagement, improving decision-making, and enhancing business performance. In the retail sector, Walmart has leveraged AI-powered predictive analytics to optimize its inventory management and supply chain. By analyzing historical purchasing data, real-time customer demand, and market trends, Walmart ensures that products are stocked efficiently across different locations (Davenport & Ronanki, 2018). This AI-driven forecasting system has significantly reduced out-of-stock situations, minimized operational costs, and improved customer satisfaction. The e-commerce industry has also greatly benefited from data-driven marketing strategies. Amazon, for instance, utilizes AI-based recommendation engines to personalize shopping experiences. By analyzing customer purchase history, browsing behaviour, and product preferences, Amazon generates tailored product recommendations, increasing customer engagement and sales (Patil, 2024). AI-powered dynamic pricing algorithms further enhance Amazon's competitiveness by adjusting product prices in real-time based on demand, inventory levels, and competitor pricing strategies (Erevelles, Fukawa, & Swayne, 2016). In the finance industry, JPMorgan Chase employs AI-powered chatbots and predictive analytics to improve customer experience and fraud detection. The bank's chatbot, COIN, processes legal documents and customer queries using natural language processing (NLP), significantly reducing manual workload and improving operational efficiency (Rahaman, 2024). Additionally, JPMorgan's AI-driven fraud detection systems analyze transaction patterns to identify suspicious activities in real time, ensuring better financial security for customers (Keikhosrokiani, 2024).

These examples highlight how AI-driven marketing strategies enhance efficiency, personalization, and customer retention across different industries, leading to improved business performance and customer satisfaction.

Natural Language Processing (NLP) is revolutionizing the financial industry by enabling the extraction of valuable insights from unstructured data like news and social media. Techniques such as sentiment analysis and transformers are increasingly applied in areas like algorithmic trading and fraud detection (Jagdale & Deshmukh, 2025).

9.2 Lessons Learned and Best Practices for Implementing AI-Driven Marketing Strategies

The successful adoption of AI-driven marketing strategies requires businesses to embrace best practices that ensure efficient execution and long-term sustainability. One key lesson is the importance of data quality and integration. Companies must invest in Customer Data Platforms (CDPs) and data management tools to consolidate information from various touchpoints, ensuring accurate insights and real-time decision-making (Latifi, 2024). Another best practice is continuous AI model training and optimization. AI-driven marketing is most effective when machine learning models are regularly updated to reflect changing consumer behaviours and market conditions (Wedel & Kannan, 2016). Businesses should establish AI feedback loops to refine their predictive algorithms over time. Moreover, organizations must prioritize ethical AI implementation. Ensuring data privacy compliance, minimizing algorithmic bias, and maintaining transparency in AI-driven decisions fosters consumer trust and strengthens brand reputation Smith, A. and Jones, B. (2023). Fairness-aware AI models should be developed to prevent discriminatory marketing practices (Davenport & Ronanki, 2018).

Lastly, successful AI-driven marketing strategies emphasize personalization at scale. Companies should leverage AI for automated customer segmentation, hyper-personalized recommendations, and real-time engagement strategies to enhance user experiences and boost conversion rates.

9.3 Metrics for Measuring Success and Impact on Business Growth

Measuring the success of AI-driven marketing strategies requires a combination of quantitative and qualitative performance indicators. Key metrics include:

- Customer Engagement Metrics: Businesses track click-through rates (CTR), bounce rates, and time spent on pages to evaluate how well AI-driven marketing campaigns capture customer interest.
- Conversion Rates: The effectiveness of personalized recommendations, targeted advertisements, and AI-powered email marketing is assessed through conversion rates (Erevelles et al., 2016).
- Return on Investment (ROI): Companies analyze the profitability of AI-driven campaigns by comparing marketing spend to generated revenue (Delen & Demirkan, 2013).

- Customer Retention and Churn Rate: AI models predict churn risk, allowing businesses to implement retention strategies and improve customer loyalty (Keikhosrokiani, 2024).
- Predictive Accuracy of AI Models: Businesses monitor the accuracy of AI-driven forecasts, such as demand predictions, sentiment analysis, and customer behaviour modeling (Rahaman, 2024).
- Sentiment Analysis Scores: NLP-based AI tools measure customer sentiment on social media and review platforms, providing insights into brand perception (Latifi, 2024).
- By systematically tracking these metrics, businesses can optimize AI-driven marketing strategies, enhance personalization efforts, and drive sustainable business growth.

10. ETHICAL CONSIDERATIONS IN AI AND DATA USAGE

10.1 The Importance of Ethical Data Practices in Marketing

As AI-driven marketing becomes more sophisticated, businesses must prioritize ethical data practices to maintain consumer trust and regulatory compliance. Ethical AI ensures that customer data is collected, processed, and utilized responsibly, preventing manipulative marketing tactics and discriminatory decision-making Smith, A. and Jones, B. (2023). With increasing concerns about data privacy violations, AI bias, and lack of transparency, companies must establish clear ethical guidelines for AI deployment in marketing. Moreover, ethical data practices enhance customer-brand relationships. A study found that 76% of consumers are more likely to engage with brands that prioritize data transparency and ethical AI usage (Keikhosrokiani, 2024). By implementing privacy-first policies, businesses can build trust, foster loyalty, and reduce legal risks associated with AI-driven marketing (Latifi, 2024).

Figure 3. Hierarchical Model of Ethical AI Governance

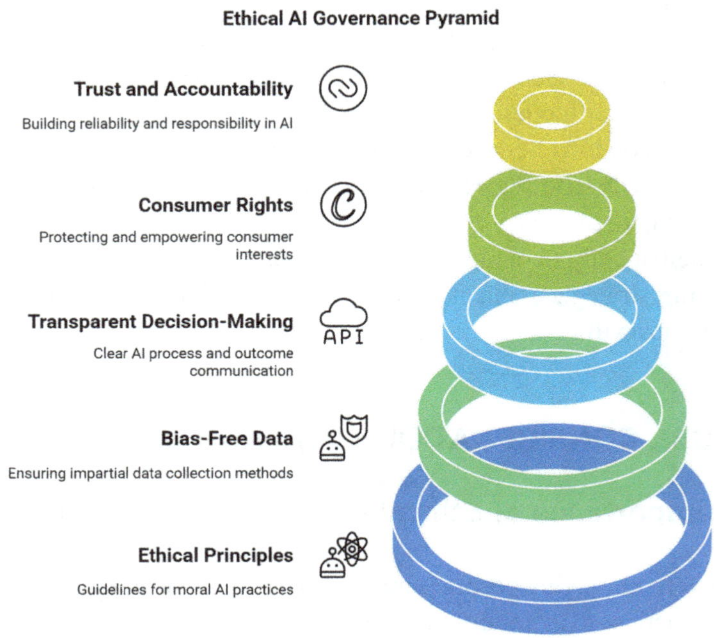

Figure 3 presents a Hierarchical Model of Ethical AI Governance, outlining the necessary steps for maintaining fairness, transparency, and compliance in AI-driven marketing strategies. As AI adoption in marketing continues to grow, so do concerns related to data privacy, algorithmic bias, and transparency. Ethical AI governance ensures that marketing technologies are fair, accountable, and consumer-centric, protecting user rights while maintaining the integrity of AI-driven decision-making. The framework begins with AI development and deployment, where businesses must ensure that data collection practices are bias-free, model training follows ethical principles, and AI implementations comply with global data protection regulations such as GDPR and CCPA. Transparent AI decision-making is another critical component, requiring businesses to adopt explainable AI (XAI) models that allow consumers to understand how AI-driven recommendations and automated marketing decisions are made. To address concerns about algorithmic bias, organizations must implement bias detection and mitigation strategies, such as diverse training datasets, fairness-aware AI models, and ongoing audits to monitor discrimination risks. The framework also prioritizes consumer rights and data control, ensuring that users have opt-in/opt-out choices, access to AI decision explanations, and the ability to modify or delete their personal data upon request. The final stage of the framework, continuous AI ethics evaluation, emphasizes regular updates to AI policies based on emerging regulatory requirements, ongoing bias monitoring, and incorporating consumer feedback to enhance AI transparency. Ethical AI governance is essential for building trust, ensuring regulatory compliance, and fostering long-term customer relationships in AI-driven marketing. By prioritizing responsible AI practices, businesses can leverage AI's transformative power while upholding ethical standards and consumer rights.

10.2 Addressing Concerns Related to Data Privacy, Bias, and Transparency

Three major ethical concerns in AI-driven marketing are data privacy, algorithmic bias, and transparency.

Data Privacy: Many consumers worry about how their personal data is collected, stored, and shared (Wirtz et al., 2014). Companies must comply with data protection regulations like GDPR and CCPA, ensuring that customers have control over their personal data (Rahaman, 2024). AI-driven systems should incorporate privacy-by-design principles, minimizing data exposure risks (Erevelles et al., 2016).

Algorithmic Bias: AI models can reinforce existing biases if trained on unrepresentative or skewed datasets (Davenport & Ronanki, 2018). Biased AI can lead to discriminatory marketing practices, disproportionately targeting or excluding certain consumer groups. Companies should employ bias detection tools and diverse training datasets to mitigate algorithmic bias (Patil, 2024).

Transparency and Explainability: AI-driven marketing strategies must be transparent and explainable so that customers understand how decisions are made (Chen et al., 2012). Businesses should implement explainable AI (XAI) techniques, ensuring that AI models provide clear, interpretable justifications for recommendations.

10.3 Guidelines for Responsible Data Usage to Maintain Customer Trust

To ensure ethical AI adoption in marketing, businesses should adhere to the following guidelines:

User Consent and Data Control: Companies must provide opt-in/opt-out options for data collection and allow users to access and delete their data upon request Smith, A. and Jones, B. (2023).

Fair and Inclusive AI Models: AI algorithms should be regularly audited for bias, ensuring fair representation across diverse customer segments (Keikhosrokiani, 2024).

Transparent AI Decision-Making: Businesses should disclose how AI-driven recommendations, ad targeting, and pricing models function (Latifi, 2024).

Compliance with Data Regulations: Organizations must align with global data protection laws to avoid legal repercussions and safeguard consumer privacy.

AI Ethics Committees: Companies should establish internal AI ethics boards to oversee responsible AI deployment in marketing campaigns (Erevelles et al., 2016).

By adhering to these ethical guidelines, businesses can harness the power of AI responsibly, ensuring sustainable and consumer-friendly marketing strategies.

CONCLUSION

As businesses navigate an increasingly data-driven world, the integration of artificial intelligence (AI) with big data analytics presents a transformative opportunity to revolutionize marketing decision-making. The ability to collect, analyse, and leverage vast amounts of customer data in real time has redefined how organizations engage with consumers, optimize campaigns, and drive business growth. AI-powered tools such as predictive analytics, machine learning, and customer data platforms (CDPs) have enabled companies to anticipate customer needs, personalize interactions, and maximize return on investment. By harnessing these advanced technologies, marketers can move beyond traditional intuition-based strategies and embrace a data-driven approach that enhances efficiency and effectiveness.

However, while AI-driven marketing offers significant advantages, it also introduces new challenges, particularly in the areas of data privacy, algorithmic bias, and transparency. Businesses must adopt responsible AI practices, ensuring ethical data usage to maintain consumer trust and comply with evolving regulations. The future of AI in marketing lies in striking a balance between technological advancement and ethical accountability, allowing organizations to innovate while safeguarding customer rights.

This chapter provides a comprehensive understanding of AI-powered marketing strategies, exploring their applications across various industries and highlighting real-world case studies that demonstrate success. By examining the intersection of AI, big data, and behavioural analytics, we aim to equip marketers with actionable insights and best practices for leveraging AI to enhance customer engagement and optimize marketing performance. As the digital landscape continues to evolve, businesses that embrace AI-driven decision-making will gain a competitive edge, positioning themselves as industry leaders in a rapidly changing marketplace.\

REFERENCES

Chen, H., Chiang, R. H., & Storey, V. C. (2012). Business intelligence and analytics: From big data to big impact. *Management Information Systems Quarterly*, *36*(4), 1165–1188. DOI: 10.2307/41703503

Davenport, T. H., & Ronanki, R. (2018). Artificial intelligence for the real world. *Harvard Business Review*, *96*(1), 108–116.

Delen, D., & Demirkan, H. (2013). Data, information, and analytics as services. *Decision Support Systems*, *55*(1), 359–363. DOI: 10.1016/j.dss.2012.05.044

Erevelles, S., Fukawa, N., & Swayne, L. (2016). Big data consumer analytics and the transformation of marketing. *Journal of Business Research*, *69*(2), 897–904. DOI: 10.1016/j.jbusres.2015.07.001

Gandomi, A., & Haider, M. (2015). Beyond the hype: Big data concepts, methods, and analytics. *International Journal of Information Management*, *35*(2), 137–144. DOI: 10.1016/j.ijinfomgt.2014.10.007

Jagdale, R., & Deshmukh, M. (2025). Natural Language Processing in Finance: Techniques, Applications, and Future Directions. In Machine Learning and Modeling Techniques in Financial Data Science (pp. 411-434). IGI Global Scientific Publishing. https://doi.org/DOI: 10.4018/979-8-3693-8186-1.ch016

Jagdale, R. S., Shirsat, V. S., & Deshmukh, S. N. (2019). Sentiment analysis on product reviews using machine learning techniques. In Cognitive Informatics and Soft Computing: Proceeding of CISC 2017 (pp. 639-647). Springer Singapore. https://doi.org/DOI: 10.1007/978-981-13-0617-4_61

Lamplugh, M. (2024). *The AI marketing playbook: Concepts – Methods – Applications*. Mercury Learning and Information.

Latifi, S. (Ed.). (2024). *ITNG 2024: 21st International Conference on Information Technology–New Generations* (Vol. 1456). Springer. ISBN: 978-3031565991

Nkomo, N., & Mupa, M. N. (2024). The impact of artificial intelligence on predictive customer behaviour analytics in e-commerce: A comparative study of traditional and AI-driven models. *Iconic Research and Engineering Journals*, *8*(5), 432–439.

Patil, D. (2024, November 19). *Artificial intelligence for personalized marketing and consumer behaviour analysis: Enhancing engagement and conversion rates. SSRN*. https://doi.org/DOI: 10.2139/ssrn.5057436

Rahaman, S. U. (2024). Real-Time Customer Journey Mapping: Combining AI and Big Data for Precision Marketing. IJLRP-International Journal of Leading Research Publication, 5(7). https://doi.org/g8vkzp

Smith, A., & Jones, B. (2023). Ethical Considerations in AI-Driven Marketing: A Framework for Responsible Personalization. *Journal of Business Ethics*, *174*, 405–421.

Wedel, M., & Kannan, P. K. (2016). Marketing analytics for data-rich environments. *Journal of Marketing*, *80*(6), 97–121. DOI: 10.1509/jm.15.0413

Wirtz, J., Tuzovic, S., & Kuppelwieser, V. (2014). The role of artificial intelligence in service innovation. *Journal of Service Management*, *25*(6), 830–848.

Chapter 4
AI in Content Creation and Management:
Generative AI Focus

Sankareswari Govindarajan
https://orcid.org/0009-0001-8047-8842
Expedia Group, USA

ABSTRACT

As the digital marketing landscape evolves, advertisers and publishers must continually adapt their content creation strategies to remain competitive. This chapter explores effective strategies for content creation, addressing both advertiser and publisher perspectives. We delve into content strategies across various marketing channels, focusing on key aspects such as content marketing, keyword harvesting, ad copy optimization, multilingual content generation, and more. By integrating traditional methods with advanced technologies, this chapter serves as a comprehensive guide for marketers aiming to enhance their content strategies.Recent insights reveal that early adopters of GenAI have been significantly better prepared to leverage its potential. Early adopters are three times more likely to have a fully functioning project planning process with dedicated tools for content marketing. They are also three times more likely to have a formal, analytics-driven approach to balancing content supply and demand and a high level of automation for content fulfillment and distribution.

1. INTRODUCTION

As the demand for high-quality content continues to grow, manual content generation becomes increasingly unsustainable due to its high costs, inconsis-

DOI: 10.4018/979-8-3693-9994-1.ch004

tent quality, and limited scalability. This chapter explores effective strategies for content creation, addressing both advertiser and publisher perspectives. We delve into content strategies across various marketing channels, focusing on key aspects such as content marketing, keyword harvesting, ad copy optimization, multilingual content generation, and more. By integrating traditional methods with advanced technologies, this chapter serves as a comprehensive guide for marketers aiming to enhance their content strategies.

Recent insights from Deloitte (Deloitte Digital, 2025) reveal that early adopters of Generative AI have been significantly better prepared to leverage its potential. For example, early adopters are three times more likely to have a fully functioning project planning process with dedicated tools for content marketing. They are also three times more likely to have a formal, analytics-driven approach to balancing content supply and demand and a high level of automation for content fulfillment and distribution.

Some of the limitations that manual content generation present are around cost to generate content, maintaining consistency and scalability. Content creators have limited exposure to data points, which can lead to bias. While manual efforts cannot be eliminated, automation enhances productivity, encourages out-of-the-box thinking, and increases content volume. Using a balanced approach to enable automation would complement human creativity, enabling higher advertisement posting frequency and improved effectiveness.

In any advertising pipeline advertisers and publishers are the main entities that play a critical role. Advertisers aim to generate revenue through ad spending across various channels. Publishers focus on targeting the right audience to attract more users to their platforms while ensuring steady revenue from advertisers. This objective of this chapter is to provide a comprehensive overview of how machine learning techniques specifically generative AI can be efficiently leveraged for content creation. We will also discuss key performance indicators (KPIs) for validating the effectiveness of these strategies and conclude with a review of ethical considerations to ensure content remains appropriate and non-offensive.

The target audience includes both technical professionals (eg: ML Engineers, Data Scientists, AI Product Managers) and non-technical stakeholders (eg: content strategies, marketing leads, digital creatives) working within or adjacent to marketing teams. The scope spans foundational concepts of generative AI, real-world applications in creative workflows, ethical implications and future directions. We also discuss the challenges present in traditional content pipelines that AI seeks to address such as limited personalization, high production costs, and scalability barriers. With the foundation of content generation laid out, let's dive into the various techniques and models used in generative AI for text-based content creation.

2. CONTENT GENERATION STRATEGIES

In this section we delve into the various content modalities - text, images, videos, audio, and their generation techniques and applications in emails, internet searches, podcasts, and music channels. This section is set in two parts, we will first go over the traditional machine learning techniques for content generation and then we will review the generative AI based techniques.

2.1 Traditional Machine Learning

There is a family of base models that can be used for content generation, let's briefly review them next.

Text Generation: Sequence models like Recurrent Neural Networks (RNNs) (Wikipedia, 2025), Long Short-Term Memory (LSTMs) (Hochreiter & Schmidhuber, 1997), and Gated Recurrent Units (GRUs) play a key role in text generation. Traditional NLP-based text processing tools enable text editing and are used to correct spelling, grammar, and punctuation. In terms of generation, they have been effective in basic text generation or chatbot responses. The limitation of sequence-based models is their inability to capture long-term dependencies. During training, deep learning models capture patterns by constantly reducing the difference between the actual and predicted values. This difference is called the gradient. When learning long sequences, the gradient value becomes smaller, leading to a scenario called vanishing gradient. In evolved models like LSTMs and GRUs, this problem has been addressed using gating mechanisms. However, even these models suffer from forgetting information, and hence generation has not been as effective.

Image and Video Generation: Models like Markov Random Fields (MRFs) (Kindermann & Snell, 1980) and Gaussian Mixture Models (GMMs) (McLachlan & Peel, 2000) have been used for image generation, while Hidden Markov Models (Rabiner, 1989) (HMMs) and Dynamic Time Warping (DTW) (Sakoe & Chiba, 1978) have been used for video analysis or comparison. These models are highly interpretable, computationally efficient, and work effectively with smaller datasets. However, these models are less creative and suffer from the difficulty of generating novel content, and they require careful feature engineering. They generally underperform compared to their generative AI counterparts and are not easily scalable to larger volumes of data.

Tools like Grammarly (Grammarly, 2025) are traditionally known for integrating NLP-based capabilities for text editing. Libraries like PyMRF (PyMRF, 2025) and scikit-learn provide MRF and GMM implementations for basic subtasks like image segmentation. Hmmlearn (hmmlearn, 2025) and dtw-python (dtw-python, 2025) are used for basic video analysis or comparison between sequences but not for generating them. To summarize, traditional techniques can be used for performing basic generation tasks, spell checks, segmentation, and ensuring correctness. However, there are no user-friendly software products or tools for general generation tasks alone.

In the next section let's see how Generative AI has highly influenced the productivity, especially in the content generation space.

2.2 Generative AI

Generative models have significantly outperformed the traditional models for content generation. These models can learn much more complex patterns and generate more realistic and creative content. While technology like internet adoption was a gradual growth and it took decades to reach mass adoption, Generative AI saw an extremely explosive growth and it has only taken years for Generative AI to move from research to widespread public usage. While the technology adaptation for content generation within marketing is still somewhat elusive, it is undeniable that the use of Generative AI in marketing is rapidly increasing. The adaptation has taken varied forms like short-form content, personalized email marketing, etc.

The subsections discuss different type of content: text, image, video and audio. Each of the subsection is organized in a way we will be reviewing the implementation details of the different generative AI models that are currently existent at the time of writing and then we review the solution that are developed ground-up and discuss about the software products that are currently available in the market. Readers can navigate across the chapter accordingly based on their interest.

2.2.1 Text in Advertisement

Text in advertisement can take varied forms like ad copy, product description, email copy - is crucial for encouraging user action. The Large Language Models (a.k.a LLMs) are deep learning models pre-trained on vast datasets. Using transformers, they encode and decode text with self-attention mechanisms to understand context, recognize relationships, and generate coherent text. Studies show LLMs can reduce the time spent drafting initial content by up to 40%.

2.2.1.1 Review of LLM for Text

Text data is sequential and traditional text processing involved sequential data processing architectures RNN, LSTM, GRU. The downside of these architectures however as seen in the earlier section was their inability to remember context and to learn their semantic meaning. Then came the attention mechanism introduced in the

"Attention is all you need" paper (Vaswani et al., 2017). Transformer architecture explained in the paper is based on attention mechanisms.

Transformer model is a neural network that can learn context and meaning by tracking relationships in sequential data. As per Kevin Murphys' PML book "We can think of attention as a soft dictionary look up, in which we compare the query q to each key k_i and then retrieve the corresponding value v_i ." — Chapter 15, p. 513. So, in simple terms, attention can be considered more like a dictionary lookup to retrieve values, however, it allows us to grab values from multiple keys and return their weighted sum for the given query (Yuan Meng, 2025).

Large language models (LLMs) are a class of deep learning architecture based on transformer networks. They are trained on internet-scale datasets with billions of parameters and can read, generate text, and write code. As of this writing, companies like OpenAI, Google, Meta, DeepSeek, and Anthropic are some of the forerunners developing proprietary LLMs. The Llama family of models (Touvron et al., 2024), as well as some DeepSeek models, have been open-sourced, allowing users to repurpose them for their use cases without incurring additional infrastructure costs.

Let us briefly review the LLM architecture. As of this writing, commonly used LLMs are based on the transformer architecture. Input data for these models typically takes the form of embeddings, which are continuous vector representations. A standard architecture consists of encoder and decoder layers. The encoder analyzes and weighs the importance of different input tokens using self-attention or multi-head attention mechanisms. The decoder then generates sequential outputs based on the processed input and previously generated tokens. Most LLMs employ a cross-entropy loss function, comparing the predicted probability distribution of each token to the true distribution, aiming to minimize this difference. Specific architectural details can vary between models.

Stages of training in LLM involve pre-training, finetuning and reinforcement learning. Pre-training requires large volume of data to predict the next word. Model learns semantic and syntactical knowledge of the language during this phase. At the end of this phase, the model will be capable enough to complete sentences but not be able to respond to instructions. For example, for an input "write an ad copy for new line model of cars" the model might not be able to respond creatively. The model hence requires fine-tuning to parse instructions and essential to steer the model in accordance to generate the required response. This is done by using high-quality instruction and response pairs as input for training. The dataset size at this stage is typically smaller compared to pre-training phase. The model now will be able to respond instead of simply generating text. The third and final stage is Reinforcement Learning from Human Feedback (RLHF), purpose of which is like instruction fine-tuning. The stage is required for surpassing human-level performance especially for applications that require creative writing and storytelling.

LLMs can now be used for applications for text generation, summarization and translation. For instance, in the case of text generation, the primary objective of an LLM model would be to predict the next word. Ensuring the prediction falls within the probability of the next token. Two of the commonly used training paradigms are masked language modeling (MLM) (Devlin et al., 2018) and causal language modeling (CLM) (Brown et al., 2020; Radford et al., 2018; Radford et al., 2019).

Masked language modeling predicts a masked token in a sequence, and the model can attend to tokens bidirectionally. This means the model has full access to the tokens on the left and right. Masked language modeling is great for tasks that require a good contextual understanding of an entire sequence. BERT (Devlin et al., 2018) is an example of a masked language model. Causal language modeling predicts the next token in a sequence of tokens, and the model can only attend to tokens on the left. This means the model cannot see future tokens. GPT-2 (Radford et al., 2018) is an example of a causal language model.

To train these models, there are many open-source datasets available online. Especially datasets curated towards product reviews. While there are not many dedicated datasets for advertising, below are few datasets that can be potentially explored.

- Yahoo! Advertising Dataset (Yahoo, 2025): This is a relatively small dataset containing aggregated bid performance data for an advertiser. For a given sequence of keywords, corresponding market analysis data is collected. The dataset size is 845 MB. This dataset can be used for ad copy generation by correlating keywords with their performance metrics.
- OpenAI's WebText Dataset (OpenAI, 2025): OpenAI's WebText dataset is a large collection of text scraped from web pages linked on Reddit, used for training language models like GPT-2. It is considered a high-quality dataset due to user-driven curation on Reddit, providing a better representation of engaging online content compared to indiscriminate web scraping. While not directly related to product advertisements, it can be useful for extracting user sentiment and generating ad copy tailored to user needs.
- Amazon Reviews Dataset (McAuley & Leskovec, 2013): This dataset contains product reviews and metadata from Amazon, including approximately 100 million reviews spanning over a decade. It includes reviews (ratings, text, helpfulness votes), product metadata (descriptions, category information, price, brand, and image features), and co-purchase information (also viewed/ also bought graphs). This data can be used as supplementary input for models generating ad copy.

* prompt – think of prompt as an instruction that you provide to the large language model, in order to get the necessary output generated. Like how model

outputs depend on the quality of the data, output generated by an LLM depends on the quality of the prompt it receives.

2.2.1.2 Building a Custom Ad Copy Generation Tool

Building your own custom text generation tool using open-source LLMs can provide a tailored solution for your specific needs. Here's a step-by-step guide:

Step 1. Open-Source LLM Selection

Start by exploring the Hugging Face Hub, a central repository for pre-trained models. Look for models that are suitable for text generation tasks and are released under open-source licenses. Models like the Llama family are popular choices. Consider factors like model size, language support, and task-specific fine-tuning potential when selecting a model. Download the chosen model and its associated files.

Step 2. Data Preparation

The core of your tool's effectiveness lies in the training data. Gather or create a dataset relevant to your advertising domain. This could involve - ADGIST Dataset, Datasets from platforms like Yelp or TripAdvisor can help your model understand customer sentiment and language patterns. You can also collect data from websites, marketing materials, or customer interactions to create a dataset tailored to your specific needs. Ensure your dataset is clean, diverse, and representative of the types of ads copy you want to generate.

Step 3. Fine-Tuning

Fine-tuning involves adapting the pre-trained LLM to your specific advertising dataset. Use CLM techniques, which are commonly used for text generation, to train the model to predict the next word in a sequence. Experiment with fine-tuning methods like LoRA (Hu et al., 2021), which can efficiently adapt large models with fewer resources. LoRA freezes the pre-trained model weights and injects trainable rank-decomposition matrices into each layer of the Transformer architecture, greatly reducing the number of trainable parameters for downstream tasks.

Step 4. User Interface and Integration

Create a user-friendly interface for interacting with your model. Tools like Streamlit (Streamlit, 2025) can simplify the process of building a chatbot-style interface, allowing users to input prompts and receive generated ad copy. You can also create an API to integrate the model into existing marketing workflows or applications.

Step 5. Orchestration with LangChain

Use a framework like LangChain to orchestrate the various steps of your workflow. LangChain (LangChain, 2025) can help with data loading and processing advertising dataset, prompt engineering by creating effective prompts for the LLM and model chaining by combining different LLM components or tools to create more complex workflows

Step 6. Prompt Engineering and Testing:

Craft effective prompts that guide the LLM to generate the desired ad copy. Consider factors like product/service description, target audience, desired tone and style (e.g., humorous, professional, persuasive), keywords to improve ad relevance. Test different prompts and fine-tuning methods to optimize the quality of the generated ad copy.

Step 7. Enhancing with Retrieval Augmented Generation (RAG):

Models' knowledge can be enhanced with domain specific information using techniques like Retrieval Augmented Generation (RAG) (Lewis et al., 2020). Train the LLM on a dataset containing domain-specific captions. Implement a RAG system that retrieves relevant information from the knowledge base based on the user's prompt and provides it to the LLM. This allows the model to generate more targeted and customized ad copy.

Step 8. Deployment and Monitoring:

Deploy your tool in a cloud environment or on a local server. Continuously monitor the performance of your tool and adjust as needed. Collect user feedback to identify areas for improvement.

This approach allows content generators to generate highly targeted and customized ad copy for each car model, improving the effectiveness of their marketing campaigns.

2.2.1.3 Text Generation Software and Platforms

Companies have already invested in large scale infrastructures to make their existing text editing tools more intelligent using large language models.

Some of the forerunners are Jasper, Copy.ai, Grammarly, Inc, Surfer and their tools Jasper (Jasper, 2025), Copy.ai (Copy.ai, 2025), GrammarlyGO (Grammarly, 2025), and SurferSEO (SurferSEO, 2025), are powered by large language models (LLMs) to support features beyond editing. These tools can now enable personalization, text composition, rewriting texts and can help with ideation. Table 1 provides a brief overview of the tool capabilities and the corresponding audience.

Table 1. Text generation tools currently available in market

Tool	Capability	Target Audience
Jasper	AI-powered content generation for blogs, ad copies, emails, and more. Offers templates and tone control.	Marketers, content creators, and businesses seeking scalable content generation.
Copy.ai	Quick text generation for ad copies, social media captions, and product descriptions. Focused on ease of use.	Small businesses, social media managers, and entrepreneurs.
GrammarlyGO	AI-enhanced writing assistant for editing, grammar correction, and generating concise, professional text.	Professionals, students, and writers improving clarity and correctness.
SurferSEO	Combines AI-generated text with SEO optimization tools, focusing on keyword usage and ranking.	Content strategists, SEO specialists, and digital marketers.

Text generation goes beyond simply putting the words together, text generation specifically for marketing must be more communicative and relative to the user whom it is targeting. The generated text must have a clear objective, understand the target audience, adjust to the different conventions and style guidelines on different platforms. To have a better reach, ad copies generated should be scaled out to target audiences from different regions. Multilingual text generation must go beyond simple text translation, including adapting text to cultural nuances, preferences to target locale. Transcreation of text is essential to convey the same message while evoking the same emotions pertaining to a specific location. To streamline multilingual content generation, there are more tools available in the market in addition to the products tabulated above. DeepL Translator (DeepL, 2025), Google Cloud Translation AI (Google Cloud, 2025), Lokalise (Lokalise, 2025), Jasper, Copy.ai now are available with integrated user-friendly capability.

2.2.2 Infographics - Images and Videos in Advertisement

Human brains process visual information faster than text, making infographics an effective medium for conveying messages. Content generation has been made possible using a class of models called VLMs. VLM (Vision Language Models) can employ any of the techniques utilizing variational autoencoder, autoregressive models, GANs or diffusion models. These generators have the capacity to create original, realistic visuals based on textual input provided in natural language. What makes them particularly remarkable is their ability to fuse styles, concepts, and attributes to fabricate artistic and contextually relevant imagery.

Human eyes can interpret visual information quickly, given this fact image-based advertising has been more effective even with traditional advertising. Platforms like YouTube and streaming services like HBO, Netflix are common channels for video marketing. Content creators can benefit from tools like Synthesia and Pictory, which facilitate video generation for engaging audiences.

2.2.2.1 Review of Infographics Techniques

Below we will discuss some of the popular image and video generation techniques at a high level.

Neural Style Transfer

Neural Style Transfer (Gatys, Ecker, & Bethge, 2015) is the technique of blending style from one image into another image keeping its content intact. The only change is the style configurations of the image to give an artistic touch to your image. The technique uses a pre-trained Convolutional Neural Network (CNN) (Krizhevsky, Sutskever, & Hinton, 2012) to blend the style of one image with the content of another.

It works by using two loss functions content loss and style loss. Content loss ensures the generated image preserves the content of the original image. Style loss ensures the generated image adopts the style (textures, patterns) of the style image. These two losses are combined into a single formula, allowing users to control the relative importance of content and style in the final output. NST requires the image whose content you want to retain and the image whose style you want to transfer as input. The initial image that will be iteratively modified to achieve the desired style transfer. In essence, NST leverages the CNN's learned feature representations to extract and recombine style and content from different images, creating a novel and artistic synthesis.

NST can be useful for creating visually striking and unique ads. By transferring the visual style of a user's preferred art or photos to product advertisements NST can be a powerful tool for personalizing the ads as well.

Generative Adversarial Network (GAN)

The goal of generative modeling is to autonomously identify patterns in input data, enabling the model to produce new examples that feasibly resemble the original dataset. Generative Adversarial Networks (Goodfellow et al., 2014) is a machine learning model that consists of two neural networks competing against each other – a generator, a discriminator. The generator takes random noise as input and tries to produce data that looks like the training data. The discriminator attempts to classify data as either real data from the original dataset or fake data that is generated by the generator. Some of the most popular GAN formulations are to transform an image from one domain to another using modified GAN models like CycleGAN (Zhu, Park, Isola, & Efros, 2017), generating an image from a textual description text-to-image and generating very high-resolution images and many more.

Like NSTs, GANs can also be used for style transfer, ad personalization, dynamic video generation. GANs offer a more versatile and powerful approach when it comes to content generation in advertising compared to NST.

Diffusion models

Diffusion Model (Ho, Jain, & Abbeel, 2020) consists of a forward process a.k.a diffusion process, in which data, generally an image is progressively noised, and a reverse process or reverse diffusion process, in which noise is transformed back into a sample from the target distribution. The backbone of such a diffusion process can be either a transformer or a non-transformer-based model. Traditionally the process is usually implemented using a U-Net (Ronneberger, Fischer, & Brox, 2015) based architecture and currently there is a growing trend to use transformers as backbone and DiTs models (Peebles & Xie, 2023) are used.

Now that we have reviewed the different techniques, let's briefly see how these are applicable for image and video generation

2.2.2.2 Infographics Generation Pipeline for Advertisement

Image Generation

Most of the current image generation are based on diffusion-based models. Different variations of generating images could involve either generating images from a given text or generating images from similar images. The above two variations differ in the fact that the input that are used for generating the images could either be a text or image. In this part we will review the steps to host your own model for generating image. If you are interested to explore generating images by hosting your own version of model, follow the below steps,

Choose the model of your choice that are available on platforms like Hugging Face. Popularly available Vision-Language Models (VLMs) like Midjourney, DALL-E 2 and Stable Diffusion (Rombach et al., 2022) generate visuals based on textual input. Some of the factors to consider during model selection are budget, creative control, image style.

Some of the popular advertising specific datasets that are available open source are below,

- LAION (LAION, 2025): LAION is a non-profit organization that has been instrumental in making data reusable and accessible for machine learning. These projects specifically focus on curating datasets for text-to-image models including Stable Diffusion and Imagen. There are multiple projects apart from the 400M dataset, users can leverage the dataset specific to the use case. The datasets are hosted on open-source platforms like Hugging Face
- Googles' Conceptual Captions (Google AI Research, 2025): A large-scale dataset of images with descriptive captions. The dataset caters to a varied range of applications including image captioning, image retrieval, visual question answering, text-to-image synthesis. The dataset consists of approximately 3.3M images annotated with captions providing rich descriptions for advertisers to enable tasks like contextual understanding, semantic matching, etc.
- COCO (COCO Consortium, 2025): COCO short for Common Objects in Context is a large-scale object detection, segmentation and context recognition dataset. These datasets are available for access via FiftyOne an open-source tool that allows for easy access, development, visualization and evaluation for computer vision modeling. COCO dataset comprises of approximately 220k labeled images with multiple captions per image. What sets these datasets apart is that it also contains images of everyday scenes with multiple objects and annotations
- AdImageNet (PeterBrendan, 2025): Available on Hugging Face this is a small dataset with approximately 10k samples allowing users to perform text generation, augmentation. As the name goes by this dataset specifically targets the advertising domain and supports the growth of advertising technologies outside of the giant players like Google and Meta.

It is also worth to ensure these datasets are not biased and are free of NSFW content. Alternatively, the user can also create custom datasets by carefully collecting images and captioning them manually by creating embedding codes for specific concepts based on user brand logo, a particular product or a specific style. Models can also be fine-tuned on a specific subject to create highly personalized and unique images. Models like ControlNet (Zhang, Agrawala, & Li, 2023) can be utilized to guide the generation process with additional information, such as sketches, depth maps, or human poses, giving more precise control over the final output. In addition to this, the image models can also be fine-tuned using LoRA and RAG as discussed in Step 3 under section 2.2.1.2

Video Generation

Unlike image generation, video generation is a relatively new area. There is an added complication when it comes to video generation with respect to considering the temporal dimension as well. Video models are computationally complex and requires modification to the existing architectures such as incorporating temporal convolutions, specialized attention mechanism, etc.

Nevertheless, generative models like Sora released by OpenAI (OpenAI, 2025a), RunwayML (RunwayML, 2025), Pika Labs (Pika Labs, 2025) developed based on diffusion, GAN or NST technique as explained in section 2.2.2.1 have proven efficient for video generation. This opens new creative possibilities for filmmakers, storytellers and marketers.

2.2.2.3 Infographics Generation Software and Platforms

Infographic generation tools empower users to create visually engaging and informative graphics with ease. These platforms offer a range of features, from simple drag-and-drop interfaces to advanced data visualization tools, catering to both novice and experienced designers. They often provide access to a vast library of templates, stock images, and illustrations, streamlining the design process and enabling users to quickly create professional-looking infographics for various purposes, including marketing, education, and presentations. Table 2 outlines different infographics tools that are currently available in the market.

Table 2. Comparison across different infographics generation tools

Tool	Capability	Target Audience
Canva (Canva, 2025)	Provides a user-friendly drag-and-drop interface, vast library of templates, stock photos, and illustrations. Highly customized designs are limited.	Marketers, educators, students, social media managers, small businesses.
Visme (Visme, 2025)	Powerful features for data visualization, animations, and interactive elements. Requires a steeper learning curve compared to Canva.	Businesses, marketers and educators who need more advanced features and customization.
Venngage (Venngage, 2025)	Focuses on data-driven infographics, strong analytics features to track performance. But fewer design elements compared to Canva.	Marketers and businesses who prioritize data visualization and performance tracking.
Piktochart (Piktochart, 2025)	Wide range of templates, good for creating professional-looking infographics. The tool can be more expensive than some alternatives.	Businesses, educators and non-profits who need a balance of design flexibility and affordability.
Adobe Creative Cloud Express (Adobe, 2025)	Integrated with Adobe ecosystem, offers powerful design tools, and AI-powered features. This can have a steeper learning curve for beginners.	Designers who are familiar with Adobe products and require advanced design capabilities.
Easel.ly (Easel.ly, 2025)	Simple and intuitive interface, great for beginners. Fewer advanced features and customization options compared to some competitors.	Educators, students who need a basic and easy-to-use tool for creating simple infographics.
Infogram (Infogram, 2025)	Strong focus on data visualization, interactive features, and integrations with other tools. Can be more expensive for advanced features.	Businesses, data analysts who need to create interactive and data-rich infographics.

2.2.3 Audio

Audio remains an underexplored channel we will very briefly touch base on these models in this section. With the user base listening to podcasts on the rise, podcasts and music streaming platforms like Pandora, Spotify represent opportunities for content creators to engage audiences more efficiently.

Text to audio models enabling audio content production from textual prompts, employ techniques such as Tokenization, Quantization and Vectorization to represent and manipulate audio data. Future advancements in AI-driven audio content tools could revolutionize this space. In this section let's dive into two new variations of generative models that can be useful for auto generating audio data as below.

2.2.3.1 Audio Generation Techniques

Below we discuss two techniques that forms the basis for audio generation,

Autoregressive models

Autoregressive models (Neal, 1990) generate sequential data by predicting the next element based on previous inputs, making them well-suited for time-series tasks such as financial forecasting, weather prediction, and natural language processing. Since audio is inherently sequential, autoregressive models effectively model sound patterns by analyzing past waveforms to predict future samples, ensuring continuity and coherence in generated speech or music. Examples include WaveNet, which synthesizes high-quality speech by processing raw waveforms, and transformer-based models, which refine sequential dependencies using self-attention. These models capture intricate temporal dependencies, making them crucial for realistic and contextually aware audio generation.

Variational autoencoders (VAEs)

A Variational Autoencoder (VAE) (Kingma & Welling, 2013) is a generative model that learns to encode input data into a lower-dimensional latent space and then reconstruct it. Unlike traditional autoencoders, VAEs introduce probabilistic encoding by mapping inputs to a distribution (mean and variance) rather than a fixed point. This enables controlled sampling from the latent space, allowing for smooth interpolation between data points. The model consists of an encoder that compresses input into a latent representation, a decoder that reconstructs data from this representation, and a loss function combining reconstruction loss and a KL-divergence term to ensure latent space continuity. VAEs are widely used in tasks like image and audio synthesis due to their ability to generate diverse and coherent outputs.

2.2.3.2 Challenges in Audio Generation

Audio generation is inherently complex, unlike text, which follows a structured format, audio is continuous and requires capturing intricate variations in pitch, tone, and volume over time. Speech varies significantly across regions, requiring models to handle one-to-many mappings. A single word may be pronounced differently based on factors like accent, dialect, and speaking style. This variation makes generalization difficult and increases the data diversity needed for training.

Audio data is typically represented as waveforms with two fundamental parameters - time and amplitude. However, these raw waveforms contain vast amounts of information, making direct modeling computationally expensive. Instead, models often transform waveforms into spectrograms or mel-frequency representations to capture frequency variations more efficiently.

Overcoming these challenges requires advanced architectures such as diffusion models, autoregressive models like WaveNet (van den Oord et al., 2016), or generative adversarial networks like MelGAN (Lee, Kim, Kim, & Kwon, 2020), along with self-supervised learning techniques to capture the rich structure of audio effectively. Models like Googles' AudioLM (Borsos et al., 2022), Metas' AudioCraft (Copet et al., 2023), RAVE (Zeghidour, Chou, Zeiler, Zeghidour, & Adi, 2021) are some of generative AI audio models that are currently available.

2.2.3.3 Custom Audio Generation using LLM

Let us consider a scenario how these models can be used for generating a personalized ad for marketing a product in channels like Spotify. Personalized podcast ads based on user playlists raise significant privacy and technical hurdles. While generative models like Google's AudioLM could theoretically be used, practical and ethical concerns currently outweigh the potential benefits. Direct access to user playlist data is restricted, and even with access, careful consideration of user consent and potential creepiness is essential. Technically, training AudioLM on a massive dataset of playlists and corresponding ad scripts would be necessary, and real-time generation poses further challenges.

Hypothetically assuming data access and ethical considerations are addressed, steps like what is outlined under section 2.2.1.2 can be followed for audio generation as well. Currently, a simplified use case is not realistically feasible due to the obstacles discussed in section 2.2.3.2

2.2.3.4 Audio generation software tools and platforms

Nevertheless, there are ready to use software solutions that are available in the market, that can be leveraged for audio generation as seen below in Table 3

Table 3. Features of different audio generation tools

Tool	Capability	Target Audience
ElevenLabs (ElevenLabs, 2025)	AI voice generation, voice cloning, text-to-speech in multiple languages, voice customization.	Podcasters, voice actors, game developers, video creators, businesses needing voiceovers.
Soundraw (Soundraw, 2025)	AI music generation, royalty-free music creation, various genres and moods, song customization.	Content creators, filmmakers, YouTubers, marketers, businesses needing background music.
Amper Music (Jukebox) (OpenAI, 2025b)	AI music composition, custom soundtracks, integration with video and other media, various musical styles.	Filmmakers, game developers, advertisers, businesses needing custom music scores.
Artificial Intelligence Virtual Artist (AIVA, 2025)	AI music composition, focus on emotional and cinematic scores, customizable music parameters.	Filmmakers, game developers, composers seeking AI assistance, those needing evocative soundtracks.

continued on following page

Table 3. Continued

Tool	Capability	Target Audience
Boomy (Boomy, 2025)	AI music generation, simple interface for creating and publishing music, various styles and templates.	Musicians, content creators, individuals wanting to easily create and share music.
Loudly (Loudly, 2025)	AI music generation, customizable music for videos, podcasts, and social media, royalty-free tracks.	Content creators, marketers, podcasters, businesses needing background music for media.

The choice between traditional modeling approach vs leveraging AI enabled software depends upon the individual users' preference. Ready-to-use audio generation software simplifies audio creation by abstracting the complexity of AI modeling. These platforms offer user-friendly interfaces, pre-trained models, and intuitive workflows, requiring no coding or machine learning expertise. They provide access to powerful AI capabilities through cloud-based solutions and subscription models, making audio generation more accessible and affordable. By focusing on user experience and creative output, these tools empower individuals and businesses to easily generate high-quality audio for various purposes, from voiceovers and music to sound effects, without the technical hurdles of building and training their own models.

3. CONTENT GENERATION STRATEGIES ON ADVERTISER END

Advertisers aim to tailor content to user needs despite limited capabilities for user-level personalization. By leveraging historical user data, advertisers can target demographics and psychographics, adjust content tone to include humor, cultural nuances, and local references, enhancing user engagement. Advertisers face challenges in maintaining a consistent narrative while customizing content for different user groups. But nevertheless, by analyzing historical purchase and browsing history patterns are identified and datapoints are segmented based on spend or other similar user characteristics.

Common advertising channels like Email Marketing, Social Media Marketing (SMM) and Search Engine Marketing (SEM) require a multifaceted approach to content creation. The following subsections detail the adaptation of content generation techniques for specific channels.

3.1 Email Marketing

Emails have revolutionized communication by enabling fast, accessible and asynchronous personal and business interactions. They are one of the channels that can be used for efficiently targeting audience based on users' demographic and contextual data.

Marketing via emails can attribute to different stages of a customer journey – create awareness for new products, promote existing products, targeted personalization by creating user segments. Techniques discussed in section 2.2.1 and 2.2.2 can be used for text and image-based generation. Like ad copy, text used in email is called email copy.

Provided the advertisers have taken necessary consent from the user, data containing user transaction or click history, product description, regional references to get the cultural nuance can be used as input for generating the email copy. If user clicks the email, it can be considered as a positive response. It is crucial to ensure the email does not get trashed or spammed manually or auto trigger spam filters.

3.2 Social Media Marketing

Social media platforms like Facebook, Instagram, TikTok and similar platforms offer maximum reach. Key strategies to engage with end users include:

- Infographics and polls to engage users and gather feedback
- Authenticity through behind-the-scenes content showcasing the product life-cycles. This allows the advertisers to connect with consumers by building trust
- Images / short videos highlighting product features, existing user reviews, influencer-based marketing

Social media content can be multimodal – it can be only text based, image + text or video + text. Content can be generated dynamically using the techniques discussed in section 2.2.

Assuming we are an advertiser marketing dental hygiene product to a user who is a frequent traveler. Since we only know the user is a traveler, we'll need to make some educated guesses and use creative approaches. We will assume our traveler is likely concerned about health and hygiene, especially while on the go. So, the user could be focusing on products that need to be portable and easy to use. Let's outline the steps for a multimodal campaign targeting the user with a water flosser, focusing on awareness. We want the traveler to learn about the water flosser and its benefits. Secondary goals might be to drive traffic to a product page or encourage engagement via likes, comments, shares.

Below are some of the multimodal content that we can be dynamically generated,

Text and image generation - Let's say we want an image generated for this user could have a person smiling confidently while holding a small, portable water flosser in an airport lounge or on a scenic overlook. Data for this would be licensed stock photo sites, or ideally, a custom photoshoot. We can use AI image generation tools like Stable Diffusion for flexibility as discussed in the previous section and text generation models can be used for generating comment and hash tag like "Fresh breath, anywhere. Introducing the portable water flosser for travelers. #travelhygiene #oralcare #freshtravels"

Video, audio and text generation – Now, let's see how we can create a short video-based ad along with a text overlay. The ad could be a quick, engaging video demonstrating how easy the water flosser is to use and pack. Show it being used in a hotel room or on a plane. Input data for this could be smartphone video recording, simple video editing software like iMovie or CapCut. Consider animation or motion graphics to highlight product features. Instead of relying on existing audio data, audio generation models like Soundraw or AIVA can be used for adding an upbeat, travel-themed music.

A platform like Instagram or TikTok would be suitable, given the visual nature of the content and the potential for reaching a travel-focused audience. Then we target the users based on demographics / location / hashtag, some of the examples as below,

- Demographics: Age range (likely 25-55), interests which in this case could be travel, adventure, health, wellness, behaviors like frequent travelers, users interested in travel gear
- Location: Target users in areas known for high travel activity areas like airports, major cities
- Hashtags: Use relevant hashtags like #travelhacks, #travelgram, #oralcare, #travelessentials

At the time of writing this book, platforms like Meta Ads Manager (Meta, 2025), LinkedIn Business (LinkedIn, 2025) allows advertisers to create dynamic creatives. Advertisers who meet certain criteria set by the platform can leverage this feature. We can review more on these upcoming sections.

3.3 Search Engine Marketing

These are one of the easiest yet tricky channel for the advertisers to market. Advertising on Search Engine Results Page are also known as Search Engine Advertising and are auction based. They allow the advertiser to directly display paid ads among the search results on different search engines like Google, Bing, Amazon, etc. Advertiser bids on certain keywords relevant to product or service.

To improve the chances of winning the auction and getting their advertisements posted on the website, advertisers can focus on selecting the right keywords and parameters like quality score.

Keyword selection determines which searches display the ads, without proper research to identify the terms, there is a potential to miss out on the target audience. Search engines specifically Google places a heavy emphasis on Quality Score – this is a metric that measures the relevance and quality of ads, keywords and landing pages. It is usually calculated using CTR, Ad relevance and Landing page experience.

Below are some of the SEM strategies that advertisers can achieve using AI,

- **Keyword Harvesting**: This involves researching and identifying high-traffic, relevant keywords to optimize ad targeting. Advertisers use tools like Google Keyword Planner or SEMrush to discover long-tail keywords, monitor trends, and analyze competitor strategies. These insights enable the creation of impactful campaigns that align with user intent and improve search engine rankings.
- **Ad Copy Generation**: Crafting persuasive and targeted ad copy tailored to specific audience segments. This process includes employing AI tools to generate engaging, contextually relevant text that resonates with users and prompts desired actions.
- **Landing Page Personalization**: Tailoring landing pages to reflect keyword strategies and enhance user experience. Landing pages play a pivotal role in converting visitors into customers by offering a seamless and relevant experience. Regular updates to the editorial content on landing pages not only improve Search Engine Results Page (SERP) rankings but also contribute to better quality scores, leading to more efficient ad spend.

    Some of the other key strategies that the advertiser must keep in mind are as follows,

- **Multilingual content generation**: Creating multilingual content is crucial for reaching diverse audiences. Content localization, capturing the cultural nuances enables advertisers to better connect with the users. Tools and techniques discussed in the earlier sections can be leveraged for the same
- **Dynamic content optimization**: Optimizing website landing pages are crucial for converting visitors into customers. This boosts engagement on the website at the same time keeps the content fresh. Website content acts as the products' face, making it a key part of advertising. While complete website overhauls are costly, personalizing the text according to the user preference is

a great way to keep the user engaging. For instance, Stitch Fix's 'Style File,' which analyzes user purchases, highlights individuality and builds trust.

Having explored the advertisers' perspective on content generation, we will now shift our focus to the publisher's role in the advertising ecosystem and how they can leverage generative AI for content optimization.

4. CONTENT GENERATION STRATEGIES ON PUBLISHER END

Publishers serve as critical intermediaries in the advertising ecosystem. By recommending content that aligns with advertiser goals, publishers can help retain advertiser interest and optimize performance. This section we will discuss strategies publishers can adopt to analyze user behavior and preferences, thereby tailoring content recommendations that benefit both advertisers and readers. Since we have covered content specific optimization in the earlier sections, let's review some of the techniques that can indirectly help marketing the product. Common and popular publisher advertiser platforms include – Meta, Google, Snapchat.

Given publishers are the intermediate entity, they will need to cater to enhance both advertiser and user experience. Some of the direct ways publisher can uplift advertiser revenue is via personalization, data driven insights and reporting, creative optimization and testing.

- **Performance Analysis**: Advertisers generate content and provide it to publishers. However, to understand specific user behavior related to the content shared with the publisher, advertisers would require market analysis. Publishers have direct access to the performance of a specific ad campaign in the market. Advertisers can then use these performance-based data to train their model to tailor the content to improve conversion rate and drive revenue.
- **Audience Insights**: Users consent to publishers tracking their website activity. However, publishers often cannot share user information with advertisers. Instead, they can provide aggregated insights, such as user interests, behaviors and demographics. Advertisers can then use these insights to create user groups and generate targeted content.

Compared to an advertiser, publisher has more control on the user experience as they have direct access to the user data. For instance, considering a scenario where a user on a social media platform like Instagram. Instagram as a platform has access to user data at different levels – their preference, their network, their interaction like posts they liked or shared, influencer or product accounts they follow. Now targeting these users with the corresponding ads become straightforward as the publisher also has the advertiser inventory on their end.

Another scenario could be for a given user, the publisher will be able to evaluate and prioritize landing pages of advertisements that have higher conversion. Whenever an advertisement is configured on the publisher platform, there can be multiple landing page options that can be provided. By carefully collecting landing page metrics input like bounce rate, time on page, conversion rate, page load speed, etc. and ad performance input a publisher can develop a machine learning based ranking system to identify the most efficient landing pages.

This way they will be able to ensure their users are directed to high-quality and relevant landing pages, optimize ad placements and prioritize those advertisers. The publisher would also be able to provide feedback to the advertiser to improve their landing page. Advertisers will also be able to generate landing pages dynamically using AI techniques as we have seen in the section above.

As we have seen how publishers can benefit from generative AI, it is essential to evaluate the performance of these models and strategies, which is what we will cover in the next section on metrics and evaluation.

5. METRICS AND EVALUATION

So far, we have understood the techniques that can be used for content generation. To ensure the generated content is efficient meeting the business requirements and has the expected reach to the correct set of users it is crucial to track the performance. In this section we can dive into how to evaluate the models both offline and online metrics. We can also delve into the different variations how the algorithm can be deployed and can be evaluated online.

5.1 Metrics

5.1.1 Offline Metrics

Evaluating the performance of a generative AI content generation system is crucial for understanding its effectiveness and ensuring its alignment with business goals. We need to consider a combination of quantitative and qualitative metrics, spanning various aspects of content generation.

Text Generation Metrics

Text generation metrics (Microsoft, 2025) are required to evaluate how well the generated text be it part of ad copy, email copy, etc. matches the users' query or the intended topic. We have touch because the generated content requires manual review. In addition, these metrics can be useful to evaluate semantic similarity between the words to ensure the intent is captured. Some of the commonly used metrics as below,

- Bilingual Evaluation Understudy (BLEU): Measures the precision of n-grams which are a sequence of words in the generated text compared to the reference text.
- Recall-Oriented Understudy for Gisting Evaluation (ROUGE): Measures the recall of n-grams in the generated text compared to the reference text.
- Jensen-Shannon Divergence (JS-Divergence): Measures the similarity between probability distributions of words or phrases in the generated and reference text.

Infographics Generation Metrics

Infographics metrics help in understanding if the generated image or infographic accurately represents the goal of the campaign and at the same time aligning with the user intent. It also helps us to understand the visual appeal of the generated image or video. In the below sub-sections let's review the commonly used metrics for assessing generated images and videos.

Image Generation Metrics

- Fréchet Inception Distance (FID): Measures the similarity between the distribution of generated images and real images. Lower FID scores indicate better quality and closer similarity to real images. This is widely used for evaluating GANs and other generative models
- Inception Score (IS): Measures the diversity and quality of generated images. Higher IS scores indicate better quality and diversity. Relies on an Inception network for feature extraction
- Peak Signal-to-Noise Ratio (PSNR): Measures the ratio between the maximum possible power of a signal and the power of corrupting noise. Often used for evaluating image denoising and compression.
- Perceptual Quality Metrics: Metrics that try to align with human perception of image quality. These metrics often involve deep learning models trained to predict human ratings

Video Generation Metrics

- Fréchet Video Distance (FVD): Extends FID the metric as seen earlier to the video domain, measuring the similarity between the distribution of generated and real video sequences. Captures both spatial and temporal aspects of video quality

- Temporal Coherence: Measures the smoothness and consistency of motion in the generated video. Evaluates how well the frames flow together
- Video Quality Assessment (VQA) Metrics: Metrics designed to predict human ratings of video quality

It is also important to ensure content consistency across videos and images using human evaluation either in-house or collecting feedback from end users. Diversified human evaluation also helps with standardizing as image and video quality can be subjective. The choice of selection of the most appropriate metrics will depend on the specific task and goals of the task.

Audio Evaluation

In this section let's see how we can evaluate the generated audio to see if it meets the requirements of the prompt. The assessment of audio quality involves checking for clarity and realism, ensuring the absence of any disruptive distortions.

- Signal-to-Noise Ratio (SNR): Measures the ratio of desired signal power to background noise power. A higher SNR generally indicates better audio quality.
- Root Mean Square Error (RMSE): Measures the difference between the generated audio and a reference audio signal. A lower RMSE indicates better similarity and quality.
- Perceptual Evaluation of Speech Quality (PESQ): Specifically designed for evaluating the quality of speech signals. Predicts subjective listening quality scores. Used to assess speech synthesis and enhancement.
- Short-Time Objective Intelligibility (STOI): Predicts the intelligibility of speech signals, particularly in noisy environments. Useful for evaluating speech synthesis and noise reduction algorithms.
- Mel-Cepstral Distortion (MCD): Measures the difference between mel-cepstral coefficients, which are used to represent the spectral envelope of audio signals. Commonly used for evaluating speech synthesis.

By evaluating the offline performance of generative AI models, we can better understand their strengths and weaknesses, which will inform our discussion on online metrics and evaluation.

5.1.2 Online Metrics

The above metrics can be used for evaluating the models offline. Monitoring Key Performance Indicators (KPIs) is essential for understanding how effectively generated content engages users and performs in the market. In the next part let us briefly review some of the key KPIs that are relevant to marketing,

- Click-Through Rate (CTR): Measures the percentage of users who click on the content. Indicated initial engagement.
- Number of Impressions: Measures the number of times the content is displayed. This is especially helpful for an advertiser to track the number of contents that won the auction in the publisher end.
- Engagement (Time on Content): Measures how long users spend interacting with the content. The more time, the better.
- Conversion Rate (CVR): Measures the percentage of users who complete a desired action like purchase or sign-up. Essential for tracking the effectiveness of calls to action.

Tools like Google Analytics provides valuable insights into content performance and user behavior and can enable data-driven decision-making.

In addition to the above metrics, the technical performance of the content generation system can be monitored through system metrics such as: model uptime, reflecting availability, error rate, showing stability, model latency, indicating generation speed, retrieval latency, for data access, throughput, to measure output volume and utilization, to assess resource consumption.

5.2 Testing & Evaluation

Let's say you have been able to successfully roll out the contents generated, and the first iteration is complete, it is important to refresh the content to keep up with the trend, to keep the users engaged, to create awareness of new products. Before every release the contents can be tested to ensure the same. One of the common techniques uses is A/B testing. A/B testing is a powerful method for optimizing content performance. By experimenting with different content formats, headlines, and visuals, advertisers can identify what resonates best with their audience. This section will cover best practices for conducting A/B tests and how the results can inform future content creation efforts.

By understanding how to measure the effectiveness of generative AI in content creation, we can now discuss the ethical considerations and future directions of this technology, ensuring its responsible development and deployment.

6. ETHICAL CONSIDERATIONS

Finally, it is essential to ensure content remains ethical and non-offensive. Automation should be used responsibly to uphold values and avoid harm to target audiences.

- Transparency: While some brands might not explicitly state they use AI, transparency is crucial. If AI is used to generate content that interacts with users, it's important to be upfront about it.
- Human Oversight: AI should be seen as a tool to augment human creativity, not replace it. Human oversight is essential to ensure the quality, accuracy, and brand consistency of AI-generated content.
- Privacy Compliance: In addition to user consent, it is important to follow the regulations set by the government of a country in which the content could potentially be advertised. Compliance regulations such as GDPR and CCPA must be followed.
- Ethical Considerations: Brands must be mindful of the ethical implications of using AI for social media marketing, such as potential biases in AI algorithms and the potential for misuse of AI-generated content. Machine learning is heavily dependent on the data being used. With content generation, it is highly important to prioritize diversity in training datasets. Integrating human moderators as part of a feedback loop and collecting user feedback could help eliminate bias and promote fairness.
- Copyright: Intellectual property infringements have been an ongoing concern, especially with the advent of Generative AI. It is crucial to ensure the necessary copyright transfer or license agreements are in place before using an artist's data for training a model.

Ethical AI is still an active field of research. Companies are finding ways to incorporate organizations that can enforce strict ethical practices within their company. Governments, along with the companies, are actively working together to ensure fairness. At the time of writing this book, the US government, United Nations and European Union have passed regulations to ensure ethical standards are followed. The role of United Nations Educational, Scientific and Cultural Organization (UNESCO) is highly critical for getting countries to agree upon at the global level and there is no one 'pick-and-choose' approach to ethics. (Murugesan, 2025)

In conclusion as we have navigated the complex landscape of generative AI in content creation, it is crucial to remember that this technology has the potential to revolutionize the industry, but only if we prioritize its' ethical development and use.

7. CONCLUSION

Let's conclude by reviewing some of the key points covered in this chapter. With the advent of generative AI, we have seen how content generation has been greatly revolutionized. We have reviewed various techniques, from foundational methods to readily available software solutions in the market. We also explored how different players, publishers and advertisers, in the marketing funnel can potentially leverage these techniques. Resources are available online to educate marketers to optimally leverage machine learning to create content. Links can be found in the reference section below. The field of AI/ML, especially within the Generative AI space, is evolving rapidly. This enables marketers to generate content and enhance their productivity and efficiency.

However, it is essential to remember that this technology is still evolving and its' development and deployment must by guided by ethical considerations. By prioritizing responsible AI development and use, we can unlock the full potential of generative AI in content creation and drive meaningful progress in the industry.

REFERENCES

Adobe. (2025). Adobe Creative Cloud Express. https://www.adobe.com/express/

AIVA. (2025). AIVA: AI Music Composer. https://www.aiva.ai/

Boomy. (2025). Boomy: Create Original Music with AI. https://boomy.com/

Borsos, Z., Weiss, R. J., Gelly, A., Bailleux, B., Romoff, J., Gutkin, A., & Drossos, L. (2022). AudioLM: A Language Modeling Approach to Audio Generation. arXiv preprint arXiv:2201.12789

Brown, T. B., Mann, B., Ryder, N., Subbiah, M., Kaplan, J., Dhariwal, P., Neelakantan, A., Shyam, P., Sastry, G., Askell, A., Agarwal, S., Herbert-Voss, A., Krueger, G., Henighan, T., Narayan, R., Gao, R., Beck, A., Chen, N., Chen, H., . . . Amodei, D. (2020). Language models are few-shot learners. In Advances in neural information processing systems, 1877–1901.

Canva. (2025). Canva: Design Anything. Publish Anywhere. https://www.canva.com/

Cloud, G. (2025). Translation AI. https://cloud.google.com/translate

COCO Consortium. (2025). COCO - Common Objects in Context. https://cocodataset.org/

Copet, J., Kreuk, F., Gatilov, I., Hsu, W.-N., Polyak, A., Ben-yair, E., Rubenstein, Y., Chou, J.-S., Chen, Y.-A., Polyak, A., Hoffmann, T., Zeghidour, H., & Adi, Y. (2023). AudioCraft: A generative audio library for music and audio compression. arXiv preprint arXiv:2308.10467

Copy.ai. (2025). Copy.ai: AI Writing Tools & Content Generator. https://www.copy.ai/

Deep, L. (2025). DeepL Translator: World's best AI translator. https://www.deepl.com/translator

Devlin, J., Chang, M. W., Lee, K., & Toutanova, K. (2018). BERT: Pre-training of deep bidirectional transformers for language understanding. arXiv preprint arXiv:1810.04805.

Digital, D. (2025). Generative AI in Marketing Content Production. https://www.deloittedigital.com/content/dam/digital/us/documents/insights/insights-20240408-genai-in-marketing-content-production-pov.pdf

dtw-python. (2025). dtw-python: Dynamic Time Warping in Python. https://github.com/DynamicTimeWarping/dtw-python

Easelly. (2025). Easel.ly: Create and Share Visual Ideas Online. https://www.easel.ly/

ElevenLabs. (2025). ElevenLabs: AI Speech Software. https://elevenlabs.io/

Gatys, L. A., Ecker, A. S., & Bethge, M. (2015). A neural algorithm of artistic style. arXiv preprint arXiv:1508.06576

Goodfellow, I. J., Pouget-Abadie, J., Mirza, M., Xu, B., Warde-Farley, D., Ozair, S., Courville, A., & Bengio, Y. (2014). Generative adversarial nets. In Advances in neural information processing systems, 2672–2680

Google, A. I. Research. (2025). Conceptual Captions: A Clean Descriptive Captioning Dataset. https://ai.google.com/research/ConceptualCaptions/

Grammarly. (2025). Grammarly: AI-Powered Writing Assistance. https://www.grammarly.com/

hmmlearn. (2025). hmmlearn: Hidden Markov Models in Python. https://hmmlearn.readthedocs.io/en/stable/

Ho, J., Jain, A., & Abbeel, P. (2020). Denoising diffusion probabilistic models. In Advances in neural information processing systems, 6840–6851

Hochreiter, S., & Schmidhuber, J. (1997). Long short-term memory. *Neural Computation*, *9*(8), 1735–1780. PMID: 9377276

Hu, E. J., Shen, Y., Wallis, P., Allen-Zhu, Z., Li, Y., Wang, S., Wang, L., Chen, M., & Chen, W. (2021). LoRA: Low-Rank Adaptation of Large Language Models. arXiv preprint arXiv:2106.09685

Infogram. (2025). Infogram: Create Interactive Charts & Infographics. https://infogram.com/

Kindermann, R., & Snell, J. L. (1980). *Markov random fields and their applications*. American Mathematical Society.

Kingma, D. P., & Welling, M. (2013). Auto-encoding variational bayes. arXiv preprint arXiv:1312.6114

Krizhevsky, A., Sutskever, I., & Hinton, G. E. (2012). Imagenet classification with deep convolutional neural networks. In Advances in neural information processing systems, 1097–1105

Labs, P. (2025). Pika Labs. https://pika.art/

LAION. (2025). LAION Projects. https://laion.ai/projects/

LangChain. (2025). LangChain: Building applications with LLMs through composability. https://www.langchain.com/

Lee, K., Kim, J., Kim, J., & Kwon, O. (2020). MelGAN: Generative adversarial networks for conditional waveform synthesis. In *Proceedings of the 37th International Conference on Machine Learning*, 4187-4196

Lewis, P., Perez, E., Piktus, A., Petroni, F., Karpukhin, V., Goyal, N., Küttler, H., Lewis, M., Yih, W., & Riedel, S. (2020). Retrieval-augmented generation for knowledge-intensive nlp tasks. In Advances in Neural Information Processing Systems, 9459–9474

LinkedIn. (2025). LinkedIn Marketing Solutions. https://business.linkedin.com/marketing-solutions

Lokalise. (2025). Lokalise: Translation Management System. https://lokalise.com/

Loudly. (2025). Loudly: AI Music Generator. https://loudly.com/

McAuley, J., & Leskovec, J. (2013). Hidden factors and hidden topics: understanding rating dimensions with review text. In *Proceedings of the 7th ACM conference on Recommender systems*, 165–172

McLachlan, G. J., & Peel, D. (2000). *Finite mixture models*. John Wiley & Sons.

Meng, Y. (2025). Attention as Dictionary. https://www.yuan-meng.com/posts/attention_as_dict/

Meta. (2025). Meta Ads Manager. https://www.facebook.com/business/ads

Microsoft. (2025). Evaluation metrics. https://learn.microsoft.com/en-us/ai/playbook/technology-guidance/generative-ai/working-with-llms/evaluation/list-of-eval-metrics

Murugesan, S. (2025). Ethical Concerns on AI Content Creation. https://www.computer.org/publications/tech-news/trends/ethical-concerns-on-ai-content-creation

Neal, R. (1990). Connectionist learning of expert systems. *Communications of the ACM*, *33*(3), 42–53.

Open, A. I. (2025). gpt-2-output-dataset. https://github.com/openai/gpt-2-output-dataset

Open, A. I. (2025a). Sora. https://openai.com/sora

Open, A. I. (2025b). Jukebox. https://openai.com/research/jukebox

Peebles, W., & Xie, S. (2023). Scalable diffusion models with transformers. In *International Conference on Machine Learning*, 28133–28156

PeterBrendan. (2025). AdImageNet. https://huggingface.co/datasets/PeterBrendan/AdImageNet

Piktochart. (2025). Piktochart: Visual Content Creation Platform. https://piktochart.com/

PyMRF. (2025). PyMRF: Python Markov Random Fields Library. https://pymrf.github.io/

Rabiner, L. R. (1989). A tutorial on hidden Markov models and selected applications in speech recognition. *Proceedings of the IEEE, 77*(2), 257–286.

Radford, A., Narasimhan, K., Salimans, T., & Sutskever, I. (2018). Improving language understanding by generative pre-training.

Radford, A., Wu, J., Child, R., Luan, D., Amodei, D., & Sutskever, I. (2019). Language models are unsupervised multitask learners. OpenAI blog, 1(8), 9.

Rombach, R., Blattmann, A., Lorenz, D., Esser, P., & Ommer, B. (2022). High-resolution image synthesis with latent diffusion models. In *Proceedings of the IEEE/CVF conference on computer vision and pattern recognition*, 10684–10695

Ronneberger, O., Fischer, P., & Brox, T. (2015). U-net: Convolutional networks for biomedical image segmentation. In *International Conference on Medical image computing and computer-assisted intervention*, 234–241

Runway, M. L. (2025). RunwayML: Everything you need to make anything you want. https://runwayml.com/

Sakoe, H., & Chiba, S. (1978). Dynamic programming algorithm optimization for spoken word recognition. *IEEE Transactions on Acoustics, Speech, and Signal Processing, 26*(1), 43–49.

Soundraw. (2025). Soundraw: AI Music Generator. https://soundraw.io/

Streamlit. (2025). Streamlit: The fastest way to build and share data apps. https://streamlit.io/

Surfer, S. E. O. (2025). SurferSEO: AI Content Optimization & SEO Tools. https://surferseo.com/

Touvron, H., Martin, L., Stone, K., Albert, P., Almahairi, A., Babaei, Y., Bashyal, N., Biswas, S., Lacroix, T., Lavalley, G., & Roux, A. (2024). Llama 3: The Llama 3 Herd of Models. arXiv preprint arXiv:2407.21783 van den Oord, A., Dieleman, S., Zen, H., Simonyan, K., Vinyals, O., Graves, A., Kalchbrenner, N., Senior, A., & Kavukcuoglu, K. (2016). WaveNet: A generative model for raw audio. arXiv preprint arXiv:1609.03499

Vaswani, A., Shazeer, N., Parmar, N., Uszkoreit, J., Jones, L., Gomez, A. N., Kaiser, L., & Polosukhin, I. (2017). Attention is all you need. In Advances in neural information processing systems, 5998–6008

Visme. (2025). Visme: Create Visual Content. https://www.visme.co/

Wikipedia. (2025). Recurrent neural network. https://en.wikipedia.org/wiki/Recurrent_neural_network

Yahoo. (2025). Yahoo Webscope Dataset. https://webscope.sandbox.yahoo.com/

Zeghidour, M., Chou, J.-S., Zeiler, N., Zeghidour, H., & Adi, Y. (2021). RAVE: A variational autoencoder for fast and high-quality neural audio synthesis. In ICASSP 2021-2021 IEEE International Conference on Acoustics, Speech and Signal Processing (ICASSP), 316-320

Zhang, L., Agrawala, R., & Li, B. (2023). Adding conditional control to text-to-image diffusion models. In *Proceedings of the IEEE/CVF International Conference on Computer Vision*, 3827–3837

Zhu, J. Y., Park, T., Isola, P., & Efros, A. A. (2017). Unpaired image-to-image translation using cycle-consistent adversarial networks. In *Proceedings of the IEEE international conference on computer vision*, 2223–2232

Chapter 5
Authenticity in Marketing Strategies:
A Comparison Between Human and AI-Created Promotional Campaigns

Joaquim A. Casaca
https://orcid.org/0000-0002-9588-8983
UNIDCOM/IADE, Universidade Europeia, Portugal

Frederico S. Caetano
https://orcid.org/0009-0000-8930-3961
IADE, Universidade Europeia, Portugal

Luís P. Miguel
https://orcid.org/0000-0002-0722-992X
IADE, Universidade Europeia, Portugal

ABSTRACT

The increasing adoption of Artificial Intelligence (AI) in marketing raises critical questions about the authenticity of AI-generated campaigns compared to those created by humans. Grounded in the theory of authenticity, this study investigates the perceptions of authenticity, emotional resonance, trust, and loyalty in marketing campaigns produced by human marketers versus those generated by AI. The research employed an experimental design with two groups of participants—undergraduate and master's students—who were exposed to either an original Airbnb campaign or an AI-generated version created using Pictory and ChatGPT. A structured questionnaire was used to assess participants' responses to the campaigns. Results reveal that authenticity significantly influences trust in both campaign types, with a

DOI: 10.4018/979-8-3693-9994-1.ch005

stronger effect in AI-generated campaigns. Emotional resonance played a critical role in shaping authenticity perceptions, particularly in human-created campaigns. However, trust did not directly correlate with loyalty in either group.

1. INTRODUCTION

Artificial Intelligence (AI) is reshaping marketing strategies by enhancing personalization, improving customer interactions, and optimizing decision-making processes. AI analyzes large amounts of consumer data through sophisticated algorithms and machine learning models, allowing businesses to create more tailored and dynamic marketing campaigns (Davenport & Ronanki, 2018). AI-driven tools, such as chatbots, predictive analytics, and recommendation systems, offer marketers the ability to deliver real-time, data-backed insights, resulting in improved customer engagement and conversion rates (Kietzmann et al., 2018). Furthermore, AI facilitates automation in various marketing activities, such as content creation, social media management, and customer service, which reduces human workload while increasing efficiency (Chaffey & Ellis-Chadwick, 2019).

Despite these benefits, there are concerns regarding AI's limitations in understanding nuances like cultural sensitivity and emotional intelligence, which are essential for effective marketing (Huang & Rust, 2021). Furthermore, as AI-generated content becomes more prevalent, the authenticity issue in marketing campaigns arises. Consumers may perceive AI-driven marketing efforts as less genuine than human-generated content (Schneider & Woolley, 2010), making it crucial to balance AI innovation and human touch.

Authenticity in marketing is critical for building trust and fostering deeper connections with consumers. In human-created marketing campaigns, authenticity is often achieved through emotional engagement, cultural relevance, and storytelling that resonates with target audiences (Gilmore & Pine, 2007). Consumers appreciate transparency and honesty, valuing campaigns that reflect genuine human experiences. These elements help companies establish long-term loyalty, as customers are more likely to engage with brands they perceive as trustworthy and authentic (Moulard et al., 2015).

The theory of authenticity is rooted in the notion that individuals or entities must remain true to their values, identity, and actions, aligning these elements with external expressions. Authenticity, particularly in the context of consumer behavior and marketing, has become a crucial determinant of how others perceive brands and individuals. Gilmore and Pine (2007) suggest that authenticity is the foundation of meaningful consumer experiences, as consumers seek out products, services, and brands that they view as genuine and transparent. Authenticity conveys trustworthiness, as consumers are more likely to engage with brands that act with integrity and honesty (Moulard et al., 2015).

Within the marketing framework, authenticity involves consistency between a brand's communicated values and actions. When there is alignment between these aspects, consumers are more likely to develop loyalty, as they perceive the brand to be sincere and dependable (Morhart et al., 2015). However, authenticity is not simply about truthfulness; it also encompasses emotional resonance and relevance, as individuals value personal connection and relatability (Leigh et al., 2006). As consumers become more skeptical of commercial motives, the demand for authenticity in brand communication has increased.

However, with the rise of AI-created marketing campaigns, questions about authenticity emerge. While efficient and data-driven, AI-generated content often needs more emotional nuance and cultural awareness in human-created campaigns (Huang & Rust, 2021). Consumers may perceive AI-driven marketing as overly generic or mechanical, which can diminish trust if it lacks personal relevance or seems disingenuous. Research suggests that customers are more critical of AI-generated content, particularly when it comes to brand messages that rely on emotional appeal or ethical values (Schneider & Woolley, 2010). Thus, marketers' challenge lies in blending AI's efficiency with human-created content's emotional depth, ensuring that campaigns are perceived as authentic regardless of origin.

Some studies focus on how AI can optimize marketing communication strategies (Malthouse & Copulsky, 2023; Bormane & Blaus, 2024; Stallone et al., 2024; Wen et al., 2022) or how consumers respond to AI-generated marketing communication (Kirk & Givi, 2025). However, to the best of the authors' knowledge, no study addresses the issue of the authenticity of marketing campaigns created by humans versus those produced by AI through blind proofing.

This study aims to fill the research gap by advancing the understanding of how people evaluate AI-designed marketing communication. Specifically, under the theory of authenticity, one physical experiment examines consumer responses to marketing communication campaigns designed by AI, comparing those created by a human marketer. The aim of this study is to assess how consumer loyalty to a brand is influenced by the authenticity and trustworthiness of marketing communications created by humans compared to those generated by AI. So, the experiment will try to answer the following research question: "Will campaigns created by humans be perceived as more authentic than those created by AI?". To validate this research question, we adopted the following methodology: two promotional campaigns will be used –Airbnb's original "Belong Anywhere" campaign and an AI-generated campaign based on the first one - ensuring that the objectives, target audience, and means of dissemination will be similar for both campaigns. The campaigns will be presented to a group of consumers without revealing the origin of each one (blind experiment). Participants will be asked to rate the campaigns' authenticity, creativity, emotional impact, brand trust, and loyalty (buying propensity).

2. LITERATURE REVIEW

AI is rapidly advanced as a transformative tool in the realm of marketing, enabling brands to engage consumers in more sophisticated and data-driven ways. Its influence in marketing strategies has expanded to areas as diverse as the transportation industry, online retail, banking, travel, among several others (Davenport et al., 2020). By analyzing vast sets of consumer data with intricate algorithms and machine learning models, AI empowers companies business capabilities in various ways: automating business processes and routine tasks through robot process automation techniques such as update customer files; analyze and organize vast volumes of data (Osadchaya et al., 2024) and identify patterns within them that allow them to extract relevant insights and produce, using predictive analytics, personalized and responsive campaigns that align closely with individual consumer preferences; develop cognitive engagement through technology tools such AI driven tools such as natural language chatbots to interact with both employees and customers (Davenport & Ronanki, 2018). This shift has led to the proliferation of AI-powered tools which facilitate a more dynamic and efficient approach to connecting with customers throughout the different stages of the consumer journey (Kietzmann et al., 2018). With the ability to deliver real-time insights, these tools have driven significant improvements in customer engagement, satisfaction, and conversion rates.

While developing strategic marketing planning approaches, AI may also prove to be beneficial in key steps of the process: mechanical AI excels in creating standardized outcomes as it reliably performs repetitive tasks with consistency which is relevant to ensure uniform quality; thinking AI is effective in delivering personalization because of its ability to detect and interpret patterns within large data sets and it is very effective for tailored recommendations such as cross-selling recommendations; and feeling AI supports relational benefits by personalizing interactions based on emotion recognition and it is suited for marketing tasks that require customer interaction and communication, especially when building lasting relationships is crucial, such as in customer service (Huang & Rust, 2020).

AI is also playing a growing role in areas related to content creation, as AI tools can assist with drafting posts, generating ads, or even creating visual content based on analytics and consumer preferences (Chaffey & Ellis-Chadwick, 2019; Wahid et al., 2023), craft personalized campaigns based on the insights it gathers (Davenport & Ronanki, 2018) Moreover, AI helps brands in one of their most important missions, creativity, by being a source of inspiration or ideation or even a repository of success cases that can be the ignition of other ideas (Osadchaya et al., 2024). At the same time, however, the rise of AI-generated marketing introduces new complexities that the academic research is still studying, within different streams, and aims to provide a way to leverage its benefits (Huang & Rust, 2021).

Despite the many benefits and applications, AI also faces limitations which are related to several aspects of its usage. One important issue relates to the struggle with retaining the context while gathering and integrating data, an important aspect when dealing with emotional insights like customer sentiment (Huang & Rust, 2021). Additionally, as the capabilities of recognizing patterns are based on data mapping, its decision-making processes are often opaque and lead to transparency concerns, as they produce results which may be difficult to interpret or justify (Rai, 2020). Although it aims to respond to human emotions, AI does not have human emotions that can genuinely understand and react to feelings and the attempts to simulate this empathy are sometimes perceived as artificial and may lead to disengagement.

2.1 Authenticity

In today's landscape, authenticity has emerged as a cornerstone of successful marketing, serving as a vital element in building consumer trust and loyalty. Authenticity, as it relates to AI-generated creativity, revolves around how consumers perceive content that is created by algorithms instead of humans (Nunes et al., 2021). The use of AI in creative fields like marketing, art, and content production raises questions about whether something generated by a machine can feel "authentic" in the way that human-created content can. As brands strive to create meaningful connections, consumers increasingly demand experiences that resonate as genuine and aligned with their own values (Huang & Rust, 2021).

The concept of authenticity in marketing has created numerous definitions, as research on the topic proliferates (Nunes et al., 2021). Consequently, and despite the agreement on the relevance of the concept, there is no consensus about its definition (Becker et al., 2019). Focusing on authenticity in the context of branding and content, Gilmore and Pine (2007) refer that it involves the alignment between a brand's core values and the public image it projects. Authenticity entails much more than merely adhering to facts; it requires a brand to reflect a consistent, relatable identity that fosters both trustworthiness and emotional engagement. Morhart et al. (2015) focus their approach on how the brand is perceived by consumers as authentic by proposing a definition of brand authenticity as "the extent to which consumers perceive a brand to be faithful and true toward itself and its consumers, and to support consumers being true to themselves." (Morhart et al., 2015, p. 202). Nunes et al. (2021) also take the consumer's view and define authenticity as a "consumer holistic assessment" based on six components, which are consumer judgments:

accuracy, connectedness, integrity, legitimacy, originality, and proficiency. It is the combination of these consumer judgments that determines the authenticity degree of a consumer experience.

The pursuit of authenticity in branding has taken on new dimensions with the advent of AI, a technology that, while powerful in data analysis and consumer interaction, raises significant questions regarding its ability to deliver authentic experiences. While human marketers can intuitively incorporate these nuanced qualities, AI's capacity for emotional intelligence and cultural awareness is more limited (Huang & Rust, 2021), raising concerns that AI-generated content may feel mechanical or generic, potentially lacking the personal touch that many consumers value.

As brands increasingly rely on AI to enhance customer interactions, the authenticity of these engagements can be compromised. Authenticity theory posits that for consumers, the perception of authenticity is based on the consistency, transparency, and genuine values of a brand. Brands must, therefore, communicate in a way that aligns their core values, mission, and actions with their external messaging and consumer interactions.

Moulard et al. (2015) suggest that brands with a "human" identity, those that adopt a relatable, human-like persona, tend to benefit from a more authentic perception. According to their view, authenticity in human brands is built on passion for their craft, they are purpose-driven and have causes that the consumers relate to, they foster a sense of connection with consumers that make them feel heard and are consistent over time as their values and mission does not change over time or opportunity. These factors help brands foster meaningful relationships with consumers. Moulard et al (2021) establish the link between authenticity as driver of consumer trust, suggesting that consumers are more likely to engage with brands they believe are sincere and true to themselves. In that sense, AI-generated content may struggle to establish the same depth of authenticity because it lacks genuine human intention and emotions. Authenticity is inherently human, as it is based on values and emotions which may be difficult for AI to fully replicate.

Recent studies have aimed to understand generative AI's role in creating content for social media, an area where authenticity is crucial to building trust and engagement with followers. Brüns and Meißner (2024) examine how the use of generative AI for content creation impacts perceptions of brand authenticity, analyzing how audiences respond when they discover that a brand's posts are AI-generated rather than created by humans. Their research involved experimental methods where participants were exposed to social media content generated by either AI or humans, with transparent disclosures about the content's origin, and concludes that content generated by AI is often perceived as less authentic than content created by humans. Even when AI produces high-quality, relevant content, consumers tend to rate it as less genuine and trustworthy. On the other hand, as AI technology learns and evolves, at some point it will be almost impossible to detect the differences between a human produce content such as a video and a fake or manipulated one (Maras & Alexandrou, 2019). Based on the above, we formulate the following research hypotheses:

H_1: Authenticity is positively related to brand loyalty

H_2: Authenticity is positively related to brand trust

2.2 Emotional Resonance

As authenticity is explored in the most various contexts, Nunes et al. (2021) mention connectedness as one of its components within the context of a consumption experience. Connectedness refers to the extent of consumers' engagement, to the degree to which a brand helps them feel linked to something larger than themselves, as Leigh et al. (2006) refer regarding the MG car brand and a collective sense of self.

Khanal (2024) refers to this idea of connection as emotional resonance when addressing the economic value of brand authenticity in a study about Tailor Swift as a brand. This emotional resonance relates to the ability the performer has to forge deep emotional connections with her audience. Emotional resonance is amplified by Swift's storytelling, which integrates personal stories and struggles that many fans identify with, creating a strong sense of empathy and belonging. Heath (2009) elaborates on this idea using the term emotional engagement, exploring how television advertising effectively builds strong brands even under conditions of low viewer attention. The author challenges the traditional definitions of engagement, that are tied to cognitive attention and affirms that emotional engagement operates at a subconscious level, meaning it does not rely on the viewer's full attention to create an emotional connection. When applied to the context of TV ads, this emotional engagement is achieved by using emotional elements like visuals, storytelling and music to create a mood that aligns with the brand. This demonstrates that TV's emotional engagement allows brands to connect with audiences on a subconscious level, making it a high-engagement but low-attention medium. Despite receiving less direct attention than print ads, TV excels in fostering emotional connections, which is crucial for developing brand loyalty and strengthening brand perception over time (Heath, 2009).

In segments where the emotional value is predominant part of brand essence, such as luxury brands (Xu & Mehta, 2022), AI-designed products lead to a decreased perceived value and a diminished emotional connection with the product in the absence of a human designer. As luxury products have a significant portion of occasional buyers, an aspirational middle-class that access luxury brands in very special moments (Dubois, 2021), the usage of AI technology as replacement of fashion designers is a concern, since this already large segment buys luxury items mainly for emotional and social reasons. Xu & Mehta (2022) suggest, as a result from their experiments with the brands Louis Vuitton and Burberry, that when a brand's essence is primarily rooted in emotional value, as is typical for luxury fashion brands, the use of an AI-led design process is likely to have a negative impact. However, as functional value is also part of brand essence, the authors conclude that when functional value is significant, as the case of BMW, the negative effect of the using AI technology as a design source is reduced. Thus, the following research hypothesis is stipulated:

H_3: Emotional resonance is positively related to authenticity

2.3 Trust

In the context of experiential marketing, within the several moments of contact between a brand and consumers (Lemon & Verhoef, 2016), brand authenticity results from these interactions and may trigger a favorable disposition towards the brand (Fritz et al., 2017) as it delivers what it promises, and thus generates a sense of trust. As artificial intelligence (AI) systems become increasingly integrated into various aspects of modern life, from autonomous vehicles and medical diagnostics to financial decision-making and customer service, trust emerges as a critical factor shaping their adoption and effectiveness.

Trust is a complex and multidimensional concept that varies across disciplines and contexts, that has found multiple definitions within and across social science disciplines (Laux et al., 2024) often leading to ambiguity in its definition. In the context of technology and institutions, it is commonly understood as a relational process involving vulnerability and uncertainty. Bannister and Connolly (2011) define trust as the willingness of one party to expose themselves to a position of vulnerability towards another party, under conditions of risk and uncertainty about the latter's intentions. This understanding emphasizes that trust is not merely about risk calculation, but about expectation and perception.

The concept of trust refers to both interactions among humans and human and technology interactions, as in the case of AI (Glikson & Woolley, 2020). Chaudhuri and Holbrook (2001) address the concept of brand trust as particularly important in reducing consumers uncertainty and define brand trust as "the willingness of the average consumer to rely on the ability of the brand to perform its stated function." (Chaudhuri & Holbrook, 2001, p. 82). In uncertain environments, trust is perceived as an implicit belief system ensuring that no one exploits the situation, particularly in contexts where rules fail to guarantee that others will behave as expected.

Gilmore and Pine (2007) highlight the close relationship between authenticity and trust, arguing that trust is built on perceived authenticity; authenticity serves as a key driver of trust by aligning an organization's practices and values with consumer expectations and experiences.

Literature assumes that, at some point in the future, AI and its usage of algorithms will allow it to perform many tasks just as well as humans, or even better. However, as trust is an important predictor of technology reliance, a low trust in highly capable technology such as AI may lead to a lower usage (Glikson & Woolley, 2020).

Hoff and Bashir's (2015) exploration of trust in automation technology provides significant insights into how users perceive and interact with outputs from automated systems, including AI. As they recognize the differences between trusting human versus technology, the authors focus user trust of AI tools and highlight output's reliability, transparency and situational context as factors of trust generation. Users need to perceive AI outputs as dependable and aligned with their expectations while retaining the ability to question and validate them, as the "black box" issue still raises concerns about the accuracy of the outputs.

As for the users' trust regarding content built by AI and not by humans, literature attempts to shed some light on how people perceive and respond to different types of content created by computers versus that created by humans in areas such as fashion, music, or arts. Xu & Metha (2022) examine how consumers perceive luxury products that are designed by AI. Luxury brands are traditionally associated with exclusivity, craftsmanship and high emotional value, AI-designed products, on the other hand, are typically viewed as mass-produced or created using algorithms rather than human craftsmanship. The study concludes that consumers associate AI-designed luxury products with lower prestige and reduced exclusivity. This stems from the belief that human creativity is a key element of luxury that AI cannot replicate. Moffat & Kelly (2006) explored how people perceive music composed by computational systems compared to music created by humans. Music composition is a domain where creativity is often linked to emotion, intuition, and human experience, making it an ideal testbed for exploring biases against computational systems. Participants rated music less favorably when they believed it was composed by a computational system. However, when the labels of identification as human or computer-generated music were switched, the preference was to the music labeled as human, demonstrating a clear bias against computational creativity in music. Chamberlain et al. (2018) explored whether people perceive computer-generated art differently from human-created art, investigating how knowledge of the creator (human or machine) impacts aesthetic responses, including appreciation, evaluation, and emotional engagement. The authors conclude that there is a bias favoring human-created art, as participants tended to rate it as more creative and emotionally engaging. In contrast, attributing the artwork to a computer often diminished its perceived aesthetic value. Chiarella et al. (2022) also highlight a negative bias against artwork created by AI when there is prior knowledge about the authorship, identified as "Human" or "AI", that influences aesthetic appreciation of abstract art. Their study also concludes that perception is tied to the contextual framing, as the lower scores of pleasantness attributed to AI identified artwork result from prejudice and not from an unbiased judgement. Chiarella et al. (2022) affirm that "*a priori* cognitive factors also have the power of influencing a person's response in other fields and even undermine his/her feeling of trust" (Chiarella et al., 2022, p.9).

AI creativity products in several fields such as music, arts, even when producing high-quality outputs, are seen as lacking "intentionality" and emotional authenticity, undermining trust in its outputs as genuine works of art. Bias against AI-authorship directly impacted trust in the outputs, illustrating how preconceived notions about authenticity influence trust judgments. So, we formulate the following research hypothesis:

H_4: Trust is positively related to loyalty.

2.4 Brand Loyalty

As consumers are increasingly discerning and value-driven, brand authenticity has emerged as a cornerstone for fostering lasting consumer relationships. Authentic brands, perceived as genuine, transparent, and true to their values, evoke trust and emotional connection, making them more likely to inspire brand loyalty (Napoli et al., 2014; Morhart et al., 2015). Murshed et al. (2023) argue that authenticity is a predictor of loyalty intentions, as these tend to reinforce consumers bonds with the brands of their choice. Therefore, authenticity should be on the core of brand strategic initiatives, fostering the consistency of their messages across all channels. The impact of brand authenticity on loyalty is not merely emotional but also behavioral. Studies such as the one developed by Fritz et al. (2017) demonstrate that consumers who perceive a brand as authentic are more inclined to engage in repeat purchases and advocate for the brand, contributing to its long-term success.

While AI-generated content has the potential to enhance efficiency, its impact on brand loyalty is mediated by how it aligns with consumer expectations of authenticity and emotional engagement.

Brand loyalty continues to be a central topic in contemporary marketing literature, with recent studies emphasizing its multifaceted nature. Parris and Guzmán (2023) argue that traditional definitions of brand loyalty, which were developed at the dawn of internet, primarily focus on repeat purchases or patronage and favorable attitudes, are increasingly inadequate in capturing the multifaceted relationships stakeholders now have with brands. Advancements in technology have expanded the ways stakeholders can express loyalty to a brand, moving beyond mere purchasing to include deeper forms of engagement and relationship-building (Coelho et al., 2019). Parris and Guzmán (2023) propose an evolved definition of brand loyalty as a dynamic, multidimensional relationship that stakeholders develop with a brand. This relationship is exhibited not only through repurchasing but also through engagement, advocacy, and co-creation or co-ownership of the brand, acknowledging that loyalty can manifest in various forms beyond transactional behaviors, reflecting the broader ways in which consumers and other stakeholders interact with brands, particularly in the digital age.

Early interpretations of brand loyalty emphasized a behavioral perspective, primarily focusing on purchasing patterns or the probability of repurchase. However, relying solely on purchasing behavior can provide a misleading representation of loyalty, as it does not account for the underlying reasons for repeat purchases. To address this limitation, the attitudinal aspect of loyalty was introduced, encompassing consumers' psychological predispositions, such as attitudes, preferences, and commitment toward a brand. By integrating these two perspectives, brand loyalty is defined as a deeply held commitment to rebuy or support a brand in the future, irrespective of situational influences (Chaudhuri & Holbrook, 2001).

Following the above, we proposed the following research model in Figure 1:

Figure 1. Research model.

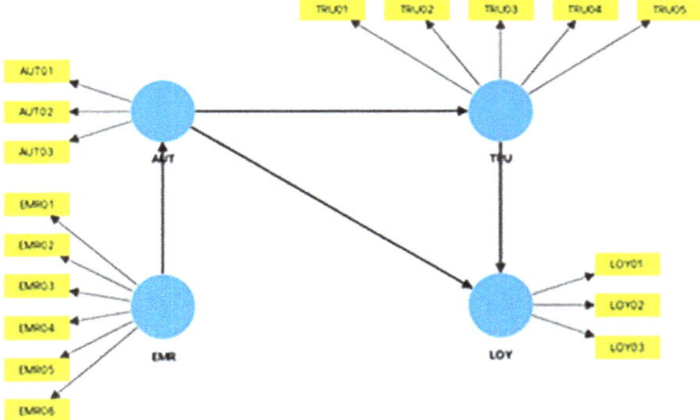

3. RESEARCH METHODOLOGY

3.1 Experimental Design

This study employs an experimental design to explore the perception of authenticity in marketing campaigns, comparing those created by human professionals with those developed using artificial intelligence (AI). To achieve this, two distinct video campaigns were used as stimuli: one based on Airbnb's original "Belong Anywhere" campaign, crafted by human experts, and another produced by an AI tool, Pictory, using a script generated by ChatGPT. The research was conducted with eight classes of undergraduate and master's students from the European University, Portugal. Each class was randomly assigned to view one of the two videos, ensuring no participant was exposed to both. This approach was critical to minimizing bias from direct comparisons and ensuring that each participant's perceptions were formed independently.

The production of the videos was carefully managed to ensure comparability. The human-created video was directly adapted to Airbnb's professional campaign, which was recognized for its skilled craftsmanship and emotive appeal. The AI-generated video was created using Pictory, a platform for automated video production, with a script developed by ChatGPT to simulate the creative process. Both videos were aligned in length, structure, and thematic elements, allowing the study to focus on the core variable of interest: perceived authenticity.

To maintain the integrity of the experiment, a double-blind approach was adopted. Participants were not informed whether the video they watched was created by humans or by AI, and the researchers facilitating the sessions were unaware of which video was being shown in each classroom. This rigorous setup aimed to eliminate potential biases from participants and the researchers and ensures that the outcomes are not influenced by the expectations or behaviors of those involved (Holman et al., 2015). After watching their assigned video, students completed a structured questionnaire to measure perceptions of authenticity, emotional resonance, trust, and loyalty. The questions were based on established scales adapted to the study's context. To ensure the simplicity and efficiency of the data collection instrument, we applied the translation-backward-comparison process (Malhotra, 2010) to the questionnaire.

The final sample consists of 204 valid responses for analysis, with a higher proportion of females (67.6%) compared with males (32.4%), who are aged between 17 and 48 years old ($M = 21.1$; $SD = 3.58$). The students who viewed the original Airbnb campaign video (humans) represent 47.5% of the total sample. The group (artificial intelligence) that viewed the AI-generated video represented 52.5% of the sample.

3.2 Measurement Instruments

The scales perceived authenticity, trust and loyalty were adapted from the study Lee et al. (2024). All items in these scales were rated on a five-point Likert-type scale, rating from (1) strongly disagree to (5) strongly agree. The emotional resonance scale was adapted from Bruhn et al. (2012). All six items were rated on a five-point semantic differential scale (EMR01-EMR06) from 1 (unimportant to me) to 5 (important to me), 1 (of no concern to me) to 5 (of concern to me), 1 (irrelevant to me) to 5 (relevant to me), 1 (means nothing to me) to 5 (means a lot to me), 1 (useless to me) to 5 (useful to me), and 1 (insignificant to me) to 5 (significant to me). The scale description is presented in the annex.

3.4 Data Analysis

3.4.1 Multigroup Analysis

The experiment subjects were divided into two groups: the "human" group, which watched the original Airbnb campaign video, and the " Artificial Intelligence " group, which viewed the video created by the AI tool Pictory.

The multigroup analysis allows to test if pre-defined data groups have significant differences in their group-specific parameter estimates (e.g., path coefficients). We used the bootstrap MGA (Sarstedt et al., 2011) to determine the significance differences between the groups "Human" and "Artificial Intelligence".

3.4.2 Model Estimation and Results Evaluation

This study used partial least squares–structural equation modelling (PLS-SEM). SmartPLS 4 (Ringle et al. 2024) was used to compute the path model and parameter estimation was carried out based on the path weighting scheme (Hair et al., 2017; Henseler et al., 2009).

Following the key arguments for selecting an appropriate method to estimate structural equation models (Hair et al., 2017; Hair, Ringle, et al., 2012; Hair, Sarstedt, Pieper, et al., 2012), we decided to use the PLS-SEM approach for the following reasons: (1) the research goal is to predict the key target constructs and to identify the key "driver" constructs; (2) the structural model is complex; (3) the data are clearly non-normal as evidenced from normality test results; and (5) the latent variable scores are needed in subsequent analyses.

In evaluating and reporting the PLS path modelling results, we follow recent guidelines for PLS-SEM by Becker et al. (2023), Benitez et al. (2019), Hair et al. (2017), Hair, Ringle, et al. (2012) Hair, Sarstedt, Ringle, et al. (2012), Henseler et al. (2016).

4. RESULTS

4.1 Measurement Models

The reflective measurement models must be assessed for their reliability (i.e., the construct measures' indicator reliability and internal consistency reliability) and validity (i.e., convergent and discriminant validity).

The initial step in assessing a reflective measurement model entails examining the indicator loadings. (Table 1). Some indicators have outer loadings less than 0.70 (EMR02 in models M1, M2, and M3, LOY03, TRU01, TRU02, and TRU03 in model M2), which is normal in social science studies (Hulland, 1999). Since the indicators with outer loadings between 0.40 and 0.70 do not enhance the composite reliability or the average variance extracted (AVE) when removed from their respective scales, we retained these indicators in the measurement models (Hair et al., 2017). As a result, we conclude that the indicators in the reflective measurement models demonstrate good reliability levels. Internal consistency reliability is achieved in all three models since almost all Cronbach's Alpha, reliability (ρ_A), and composite reliability (ρ_C) indicators are above 0.70 (Hair et al., 2019). As all AVE values on all models are higher than the critical threshold value of 0.50, we conclude that there is a strong convergent validity.

Table 1. Results of the measurement models.

Latent Variable	Indicators	Convergent Validity			Internal Consistency Reliability		
		Loadings	Indicator Reliability	AVE	Cronbach's Alpha	Reliability ρ_A	Composite Reliability ρ_C
Model 1 (Artificial Intelligence)							
AUT	AUT01	0.760	0.578	0.708	0.791	0.804	0.878
	AUT02	0.894	0.799				
	AUT03	0.864	0.746				
EMR	EMR01	0.793	0.628	0.586	0.849	0.886	0.891
	EMR02	0.443	0.196				
	EMR03	0.794	0.630				
	EMR04	0.771	0.594				
	EMR05	0.867	0.751				
	EMR06	0.846	0.715				
LOY	LOY01	0.811	0.657	0.589	0.654	0.670	0.811
	LOY02	0.782	0.611				
	LOY03	0.705	0.497				

continued on following page

Table 1. Continued

Latent Variable	Indicators	Convergent Validity			Internal Consistency Reliability		
		Loadings	Indicator Reliability	AVE	Cronbach's Alpha	Reliability ρ_A	Composite Reliability ρ_C
TRU	TRU01	0.834	0.695	0.683	0.883	0.894	0.915
	TRU02	0.754	0.568				
	TRU03	0.785	0.616				
	TRU04	0.886	0.784				
	TRU05	0.864	0.746				
Model 2 (Human)							
AUT	AUT01	0.832	0.692	0.654	0.734	0.772	0.849
	AUT02	0.699	0.488				
	AUT03	0.883	0.779				
EMR	EMR01	0.773	0.597	0.617	0.872	0.884	0.905
	EMR02	0.578	0.334				
	EMR03	0.809	0.654				
	EMR04	0.857	0.734				
	EMR05	0.789	0.622				
	EMR06	0.870	0.756				
LOY	LOY01	0.822	0.675	0.602	0.696	0.733	0.819
	LOY02	0.812	0.659				
	LOY03	0.687	0.471				
TRU	TRU01	0.565	0.319	0.433	0.662	0.673	0.788
	TRU02	0.679	0.461				
	TRU03	0.502	0.252				
	TRU04	0.775	0.600				
	TRU05	0.728	0.529				
Model 3 (Complete)							
AUT	AUT01	0.796	0.633	0.708	0.793	0.798	0.879
	AUT02	0.850	0.722				
	AUT03	0.876	0.767				
EMR	EMR01	0.782	0.611	0.603	0.863	0.877	0.899
	EMR02	0.528	0.278				
	EMR03	0.801	0.641				
	EMR04	0.817	0.667				
	EMR05	0.824	0.678				
	EMR06	0.860	0.739				
LOY	LOY01	0.819	0.670	0.600	0.676	0.704	0.817
	LOY02	0.787	0.619				
	LOY03	0.713	0.508				

continued on following page

Table 1. Continued

Latent Variable	Indicators	Convergent Validity			Internal Consistency Reliability		
		Loadings	Indicator Reliability	AVE	Cronbach's Alpha	Reliability ρ_A	Composite Reliability ρ_C
TRU	TRU01	0.771	0.594	0.623	0.848	0.855	0.892
	TRU02	0.755	0.570				
	TRU03	0.724	0.524				
	TRU04	0.855	0.731				
	TRU05	0.834	0.695				

Finally, we assess the discriminant validity using the heterotrait-monotrait (HTMT) criterion (Henseler et al., 2015), and we run a bootstrapping procedure to compute bootstrap confidence intervals with the following parameter settings: 10,000 subsamples, percentile bootstrap as the confidence interval method, one-tailed as test type, and a 0.05 significance level. Almost all HTMT values in the three models (Table 2), like values in the 95% column, are clearly below the conservative threshold of 0.90 (Hair et al., 2021), suggesting good discriminant validity.

Table 2. Heterotrait-monotrait (HTMT) values

	AUT	EMR	LOY	TRU
Model 1 (Artificial Intelligence)				
AUT				
EMR	0.420 [0.259;0.621]			
LOY	0.347 [0.187;0.558]	0.214 [0.157;0.434]		
TRU	0.944 [0.858;1.019]	0.439 [0.242;0.652]	0.180 [0.122;0.398]	
Model 2 (Human)				
AUT				
EMR	0.592 [0.407;0.768]			
LOY	0.416 [0.218;0.687]	0.226 [0.145;0.536]		
TRU	0.810 [0.634;1.011]	0.581 [0.442;0.754]	0.315 [0.213;0.608]	
Model 3 (Complete)				
AUT				

continued on following page

Table 2. Continued

	AUT	EMR	LOY	TRU
EMR	0.499 [0.353;0.636]			
LOY	0.370 [0.221;0.523]	0.198 [0.131;0.386]		
TRU	0.911 [0.832;0.977]	0.473 [0.329;0.613]	0.26 [0.128;0.372]	

Note: The values in the brackets represent the lower and the upper bounds of the 95% one-sided bootstrap confidence interval

In addition, we examined the Fornell-Larcker criterion. Although this criterion is not well-suited to reveal existing discriminant validity issues, any violation of the Fornell-Larcker criterion should be considered strong evidence of a significant discriminant validity problem (. According to Table 3, the square root of the AVE of each construct is higher than the construct's highest correlation with any other construct in the model, indicating that all constructs are valid measures of unique concepts.

Table 3. Fornell-Larcker criterion

	AUT	EMR	LOY	TRU
Model 1 (Artificial Intelligence)				
AUT	0.841			
EMR	0.352	0.766		
LOY	0.258	0.110	0.767	
TRU	0.797	0.383	0.124	0.826
Model 2 (Human)				
AUT	0.809			
EMR	0.481	0.785		
LOY	0.319	0.194	0.776	
TRU	0.587	0.437	0.244	0.658
Model 3 (Complete)				
AUT	0.841			
EMR	0.414	0.777		
LOY	0.284	0.158	0.774	
TRU	0.752	0.401	0.173	0.789

4.2 Structural Model

Following the structural model assessment procedure (Hair et al., 2021), the first step involves assessing the significance and relevance of the structural model relationships (Table 4). The results indicate that the path coefficient TRU → LOY is not statistically significant for the three models, and the path coefficient AUT → LOY is not statistically significant for model 2.

Table 4. Significance testing results of the structural model path coefficients.

	Path coefficient	*t* Values	*p* Values	95% BC confidence interval	Hypothesis supported?
Model 1 (Artificial Intelligence)					
H_1: AUT -> LOY	0.437	2.775	0.006	[0.044;0.696]	YES
H_2: AUT -> TRU	0.797	20.926	0.000	[0.703;0.859]	YES
H_3: EMR -> AUT	0.352	4.808	0.000	[0.209;0.483]	YES
H_4: TRU -> LOY	-0.224	1.247	0.212	[-0.529;0.192]	NO
Model 2 (Human)					
H_1: AUT -> LOY	0.268	2.072	0.038	[-0.058;0.475]	NO
H_2: AUT -> TRU	0.587	10.343	0.000	[0.439;0.675]	YES
H_3: EMR -> AUT	0.481	6.432	0.000	[0.297;0.604]	YES
H_4: TRU -> LOY	0.087	0.688	0.491	[-0.186;0.319]	NO
Model 3 (Complete					

continued on following page

Table 4. Continued

	Path coefficient	*t* Values	*P* Values	95% BC confidence interval	Hypothesis supported?
H_1: AUT -> LOY	0.356	3.536	0.000	[0.136;0.533]	YES
H_2: AUT -> TRU	0.752	21.537	0.000	[0.668;0.810]	YES
H_3: EMR -> AUT	0.414	7.238	0.000	[0.287;0.513]	YES
H_4: TRU -> LOY	-0.095	0.862	0.389	[-0.303;0.125]	NO

Note: BC – Bias Correction

Next, we assess the model's explanatory power. The coefficient of determination (R^2) represents the amount of explained variance of each endogenous latent variable (Hair, Sarstedt, Ringle, et al., 2012). For research on marketing issues, R^2 values of 0.75, 0.50, or 0.25 for endogenous latent variables can, as a rough rule of thumb, be respectively described as substantial, moderate, or weak (Hair et al., 2011, 2013). The results (Table 5) show that all the variables have weak or moderate explanatory power in all models, wherein the variable TRU show higher R^2 values in all models, while the LOY variable presents the lowest R^2 values in all models.

Table 5. The R^2 and Q^2 indicators.

Variable	Model 1 (Artificial Intelligence)		Model 2 (Human)		Model 3 (Complete)	
	R^2	Q^2	R^2	Q^2	R^2	Q^2
AUT	0.124	0.093	0.232	0.199	0.171	0.156
LOY	0.085	0.007	0.107	0.025	0.085	0.020
TRU	0.635	0.115	0.344	0.157	0.566	0.143

The f^2 effect size (Table 6) evaluates the change in the R^2 value when a specified exogenous construct is omitted from the model. According to the threshold values (0.02 – small, 0.15 - medium, 0.35 - large effects, Hair et al., 2019) we conclude that the exogenous constructs AUT and TRU have no effect on LOY in all models. On the other hand, the construct AUT has a large effect on TRU in all models.

Table 6. The f^2 effect size.

Path	Model 1 (Artificial Intelligence)	Model 2 (Human)	Model 3 (Complete)
AUT -> LOY	0.076 ($p = 0.231$)	0.053 ($p = 0.341$)	0.060 ($p = 0.109$)
AUT -> TRU	1.740 ($p < 0.001$)	0.525 ($p = 0.004$)	1.302 ($p < 0.001$)
EMR -> AUT	0.142 ($p = 0.087$)	0.302 ($p = 0.029$)	0.207 ($p = 0.005$)
TRU -> LOY	0.020 ($p = 0.591$)	0.006 ($p = 0.815$)	0.004 ($p = 0.738$)

We used the Q^2 value (Table 5) to assess the model's predictive ability, where $Q^2 > 0$ means that the latent endogenous variables have predictive relevance (Hair et al., 2019). As all Q^2 values are greater than 0, it can be concluded, using the threshold values (0.00 – small, 0.25 - medium, 0.50 – large, Hair et al., 2019), that all the constructs have a medium predictive relevance in all models.

4.3 Multigroup Analysis

To test if the two data groups have significant differences in their path coefficients, we run a bootstrap multigroup analysis (MGA) with the following parameter settings: 10,000 subsamples, bias-corrected and accelerated (BCa) bootstrap as confidence interval method, two-tailed as test type, and a 0.05 significance level.

The bootstrap MGA results (Table 7) show only a significant difference between the "Artificial Intelligence" group and the "Human" group in the path AUT → TRU.

Table 7. Path coefficients – Bootstrap MGA

Path	Difference (Human - AI)	2-tailed (AI - Human) p value
AUT -> LOY	-0.169	0.386
AUT -> TRU	-0.210	0.002*
EMR -> AUT	0.129	0.224
TRU -> LOY	0.312	0.164

Note: * significant at $p < 0.05$

5. DISCUSSION

The main goal of this study is to assess how consumer loyalty to a brand is influenced by the authenticity and trustworthiness of marketing communications created by humans compared to those generated by AI, in a transversal study based on a multigroup analysis ("Artificial Intelligence" and "Human" groups).

Findings for the overall sample revealed that three of the four hypotheses are accepted. The main results indicate that authenticity has a positive and statistically significant effect on loyalty (H1, $\beta = 0.437$, $p = 0.006$) and trust (H2, $\beta = 0.797$, $p < 0.001$). Emotional resonance has a positive effect on authenticity (H3, $\beta = 0.353$, $p < 0.001$). However, the hypothesis that trust has a positive effect on loyalty is not supported (H4, $\beta = -0.224$, $p < 0.212$).

When testing the conceptual model in each group, the findings were similar to the results reported for the overall sample. Nevertheless, for the human group, the hypothesis that authenticity has a positive effect on loyalty is not supported, as the 95% BC confidence interval includes zero.

The data indicated a significant relationship between authenticity and loyalty only in the AI campaigns model (H1 confirmed for model 1). On the other hand, for human campaigns, the relationship was not significant, suggesting that consumers may judge authenticity in human campaigns differently, possibly assuming that authenticity is already present and, therefore, not a decisive factor in generating loyalty. This result contrasts with studies that highlight authenticity as an important predictor of loyalty (Morhart et al., 2015; Napoli et al., 2014). It is possible that, in the case of human campaigns, other emotional or contextual factors more directly influence loyalty, such as the quality of the narrative or the cultural alignment of the campaign. For AI campaigns, authenticity appears to be more decisive in influencing loyalty, aligning with the idea that overcoming biases toward AI can create a more intense response when authenticity is perceived (Chiarella et al., 2022).

The findings confirmed that authenticity is significantly related to trust in both groups, humans and AI (H2 confirmed). This finding reinforces the view of Gilmore and Pine (2007), who identify authenticity as a central component for building trust in brands. However, the impact was more pronounced in AI campaigns, as indicated by multi-group analysis, which revealed a significant difference between the two groups on the AUT -> TRU path. This effect can be interpreted as a reflection of lower expectations towards AI, where the perception of authenticity acts as a redeeming factor. In contrast, in human campaigns, the trust generated by authenticity may be more "normalized" by consumers, as human campaigns are expected to be authentic by default.

Emotional resonance demonstrated a significant impact on the perception of authenticity in both groups (H3 confirmed). However, the effect was stronger for human campaigns, corroborating literature that highlights the ability of human-created campaigns to incorporate emotional and cultural nuances more effectively (Heath, 2009; Nunes et al., 2021). This result reflects the importance of emotional storytelling in creating a sense of genuine connection with consumers. In the case of AI campaigns, although emotional resonance is also significant, the absence of a "human creator" can limit the perception of intentionality, reducing the perceived emotional impact (Huang & Rust, 2021). An important implication is that for AI campaigns, emotional design must be carefully crafted to simulate genuine human connections, while human campaigns can focus on the depth and authenticity of emotions.

Contrary to the prevailing literature, which suggests a positive relationship between trust and loyalty (Chaudhuri & Holbrook, 2001; Gilmore & Pine, 2007), the results indicated that this relationship was not significant in any of the groups (H4 not confirmed). This result can be interpreted in several ways. First, it is possible that trust is a necessary but not sufficient condition for generating loyalty. Other factors, such as brand relevance, the overall consumer experience, or the emotions evoked by the campaign, may be more decisive for loyalty. Furthermore, the lack of a significant relationship may reflect the limitations of the experimental design, where a single exposure to the campaign may not be sufficient to measure a consistent impact on loyalty. As Oliver (1997) suggests, loyalty is built over time and requires repeated and consistent interactions with the brand.

6. CONCLUSION

This study investigated differences in the perception of authenticity, emotional resonance, trust, and loyalty in marketing campaigns created by humans and artificial intelligence (AI). Using an experimental design, two promotional campaigns were compared: an original Airbnb campaign created by humans and an AI-generated campaign based on the first. The results revealed distinct dynamics between the two groups, providing relevant insights for both theory and practice in the field of marketing.

The main findings highlight the importance of authenticity as an essential factor in building trust in marketing campaigns, regardless of their origin. However, in the case of AI-created campaigns, authenticity played a more significant role in influencing loyalty, suggesting that overcoming initial biases about AI may lead to a more robust positive response when authenticity is perceived. On the other hand, human campaigns showed a greater impact from emotional resonance, reinforcing the idea that emotional storytelling and cultural connection are distinctive features of human work in marketing.

The absence of a significant relationship between trust and loyalty in both groups is surprising, indicating that loyalty may be influenced by a more complex combination of factors beyond trust. This result suggests the need to explore more deeply the contextual and emotional elements that contribute to building loyalty in marketing.

This study provides several pertinent practical implications for marketing professionals operating in an increasingly hybrid environment, where advertising campaign creation involves both human and artificial intelligence (AI) agents, such as:

- Strengthen authenticity in AI-generated campaigns:

The results show that authenticity has a greater impact on consumer loyalty when the campaign is created by AI. Therefore, professionals using AI in campaign creation should invest in strategies that enhance transparency, such as explaining how the content was generated, the human role in supervising it, and how consumer data was ethically and personally used.

- Create emotionally resonant narratives even with AI:

Although emotional resonance has a stronger effect in human-created campaigns, it also contributes to authenticity perception in AI campaigns. Professionals should ensure that AI-generated content incorporates storytelling, emotionally appealing visuals and music, simulating genuine human involvement.

- Use AI as a complement to human creativity:

Rather than replacing human creatives, AI can be used to generate initial ideas, analyse trends, or automate repetitive tasks—freeing up time for professionals to develop more engaging and culturally relevant content. The most effective campaigns may emerge from human–AI collaboration, combining analytical efficiency with human empathy and intuition.

- Ethical personalisation as a source of authenticity:

Data-based personalisation must be implemented with ethical care and transparency. Brands should clearly communicate how they use consumer data, respect privacy, and show genuine interest in customers' values, contributing to a perception of authenticity and trust.

- Acknowledge the limits of AI-generated trust:

The trust–loyalty relationship was not significant in either group, indicating that trust alone is not enough to generate repeat behaviour. Professionals should therefore develop integrated loyalty-building strategies, such as rewards programmes, omnichannel experiences, community engagement, or cause marketing, which help consolidate the bond with the brand beyond momentary trust.

- Continuously assess evolving consumer perceptions:

As AI becomes more widespread, perceptions of authenticity in AI-generated content may shift. Professionals should regularly monitor brand perception and consumer acceptance of AI-generated content, adjusting strategies as digital literacy and consumer expectations evolve.

For theory, this study contributes to the literature by demonstrating that the perception of authenticity and its relationships with trust and loyalty differ between campaigns created by humans and AI. These findings challenge universal approaches to authenticity in marketing, suggesting that future theoretical models should consider the origin of campaigns as an important moderating variable.

Finally, the study's limitations point to avenues for future research. Future research could include more diverse samples, explore different sectors and campaign types, and adopt longitudinal approaches to examine how perceptions of authenticity and trust evolve over time. It may be relevant to develop longitudinal studies that seek to mirror the evolution of preference for content generated by AI versus humans, which demonstrate the evolution of AI capabilities in this area, leveling its capabilities with humans or even surpassing it. As AI continues to advance in marketing, understanding how to balance technological efficiency and human connection will be critical to creating campaigns that genuinely resonate with consumers.

In short, this study highlights the relevance of authenticity in contemporary marketing and offers a starting point for deeper reflections on how to integrate the advantages of AI and the unique qualities of human creativity to maximize the impact of promotional campaigns.

ACKNOWLEDGMENT

We would like to express gratitude to the Editor and the Arbitrators. They offered extremely valuable suggestions for improvements. The first author receives financial support from UNIDCOM/IADE, Design and Communication Research Unit (UIDB/00711/2020) + (UIDP/00711/2020), funded by national funds through FCT- Fundação para a Ciência e a Tecnologia.

REFERENCES

Bannister, F., & Connolly, R. (2011). Trust and transformational government: A proposed framework for research. *Government Information Quarterly*, *28*(2), 137–147. DOI: 10.1016/j.giq.2010.06.010

Becker, J.-M., Cheah, J.-H., Gholamzade, R., Ringle, C. M., & Sarstedt, M. (2023). PLS-SEM's most wanted guidance. *International Journal of Contemporary Hospitality Management*, *35*(1), 321–346. DOI: 10.1108/IJCHM-04-2022-0474

Becker, M., Wiegand, N., & Reinartz, W. J. (2019). Does it pay to be real? Understanding authenticity in TV advertising. *Journal of Marketing*, *83*(1), 24–50. DOI: 10.1177/0022242918815880

Benitez, J., Henseler, J., Castillo, A., & Schuberth, F. (2019). How to perform and report an impactful analysis using partial least squares: Guidelines for confirmatory and explanatory IS research. *Information & Management*, *103168*. Advance online publication. DOI: 10.1016/j.im.2019.05.003

Bormane, S., & Blaus, E. (2024). Artificial intelligence in the context of digital marketing communication. *Frontiers in Communication*, *9*, 1411226.

Bruhn, M., Schoenmüller, V., Schäfer, D., & Heinrich, D. (2012). Brand Authenticity: Towards a Deeper Understanding of Its Conceptualization and Measurement. *Advances in Consumer Research. Association for Consumer Research (U. S.)*, *40*, 567–576.

Brüns, J. D., & Meißner, M. (2024). Do you create your content yourself? Using generative artificial intelligence for social media content creation diminishes perceived brand authenticity. *Journal of Retailing and Consumer Services*, *79*, 103790. DOI: 10.1016/j.jretconser.2024.103790

Chaffey, D., & Ellis-Chadwick, F. (2019). *Digital Marketing: Strategy, Implementation and Practice*. Pearson Education.

Chamberlain, R., Mullin, C., Scheerlinck, B., & Wagemans, J. (2018). Putting the art in artificial: Aesthetic responses to computer-generated art. *Psychology of Aesthetics, Creativity, and the Arts, 12*(2), 177. DOI: 10.1037/aca0000136.supp

Chaudhuri, A., & Holbrook, M. B. (2001). The chain of effects from brand trust and brand affect to brand performance: The role of brand loyalty. *Journal of Marketing, 65*(2), 81–93. DOI: 10.1509/jmkg.65.2.81.18255

Chiarella, S. G., Torromino, G., Gagliardi, D. M., Rossi, D., Babiloni, F., & Cartocci, G. (2022). Investigating the negative bias towards artificial intelligence: Effects of prior assignment of AI-authorship on the aesthetic appreciation of abstract paintings. *Computers in Human Behavior, 137*, 107406. DOI: 10.1016/j.chb.2022.107406

Coelho, A., Bairrada, C., & Peres, F. (2019). Brand communities' relational outcomes, through brand love. *Journal of Product and Brand Management, 28*(2), 154–165. DOI: 10.1108/JPBM-09-2017-1593

Davenport, T., Guha, A., Grewal, D., & Bressgott, T. (2020). How artificial intelligence will change the future of marketing. *Journal of the Academy of Marketing Science, 48*, 24–42. DOI: 10.1007/s11747-019-00696-0

Davenport, T. H., & Ronanki, R. (2018). Artificial intelligence for the real world. *Harvard Business Review, 96*(1), 108–116.

Dubois, D., Jung, S., & Ordabayeva, N. (2021). The psychology of luxury consumption. *Current Opinion in Psychology, 39*, 82–87. DOI: 10.1016/j.copsyc.2020.07.011

Fritz, K., Schoenmueller, V., & Bruhn, M. (2017). Authenticity in branding–exploring antecedents and consequences of brand authenticity. *European Journal of Marketing, 51*(2), 324–348. DOI: 10.1108/EJM-10-2014-0633

Gilmore, J. H., & Pine, B. J. (2007). *Authenticity: What Consumers Really Want*. Harvard Business Press.

Glikson, E., & Woolley, A. W. (2020). Human trust in artificial intelligence: Review of empirical research. *The Academy of Management Annals, 14*(2), 627–660. DOI: 10.5465/annals.2018.0057

Hair, J. F., Hult, G. T. M., Ringle, C. M., & Sarstedt, M. (2017). *A Primer on Partial Least Squares Structural Equation Modeling (PLS-SEM)* (2nd ed.). Sage.

Hair, J. F., Hult, G. T. M., Ringle, C. M., & Sarstedt, M. (2021). *A Primer on Partial Least Squares Structural Equation Modeling (PLS-SEM)* (3rd ed.). Sage.

Hair, J. F., Ringle, C. M., & Sarstedt, M. (2011). PLS-SEM: Indeed a Silver Bullet. *Journal of Marketing Theory and Practice*, *19*(2), 139–152. DOI: 10.2753/MTP1069-6679190202

Hair, J. F., Ringle, C. M., & Sarstedt, M. (2012). Partial Least Squares: The Better Approach to Structural Equation Modeling? *Long Range Planning*, *45*(5–6), 312–319. DOI: 10.1016/j.lrp.2012.09.011

Hair, J. F., Ringle, C. M., & Sarstedt, M. (2013). Partial Least Squares Structural Equation Modeling: Rigorous Applications, Better Results and Higher Acceptance. *Long Range Planning*, *46*(1–2), 1–12. DOI: 10.1016/j.lrp.2013.01.001

Hair, J. F., Risher, J. J., Sarstedt, M., & Ringle, C. M. (2019). When to use and how to report the results of PLS-SEM. *European Business Review*, *31*(1), 2–24. DOI: 10.1108/EBR-11-2018-0203

Hair, J. F., Sarstedt, M., Pieper, T. M., & Ringle, C. M. (2012). The Use of Partial Least Squares Structural Equation Modeling in Strategic Management Research: A Review of Past Practices and Recommendations for Future Applications. *Long Range Planning*, *45*(5–6), 320–340. DOI: 10.1016/j.lrp.2012.09.008

Hair, J. F., Sarstedt, M., Ringle, C. M., & Mena, J. A. (2012). An assessment of the use of partial least squares structural equation modeling in marketing research. *Journal of the Academy of Marketing Science*, *40*(3), 414–433. DOI: 10.1007/s11747-011-0261-6

Heath, R. (2009). Emotional engagement: How television builds big brands at low attention. *Journal of Advertising Research*, *49*(1), 62–73. DOI: 10.2501/S0021849909090060

Henseler, J., Hubona, G., & Ray, P. A. (2016). Using PLS path modeling in new technology research: Updated guidelines. *Industrial Management & Data Systems*, *116*(1), 2–20. DOI: 10.1108/IMDS-09-2015-0382

Henseler, J., Ringle, C. M., & Sarstedt, M. (2015). A new criterion for assessing discriminant validity in variance-based structural equation modeling. *Journal of the Academy of Marketing Science*, *43*(1), 115–135. DOI: 10.1007/s11747-014-0403-8

Henseler, J., Ringle, C. M., & Sinkovics, R. R. (2009). The use of partial least squares path modeling in international marketing. In Sinkovics, R. R., & Ghauri, P. N. (Eds.), *Advances in International Marketing* (Vol. 20, pp. 277–319). Emerald Group Publishing Limited., DOI: 10.1108/S1474-7979(2009)0000020014

Hoff, K. A., & Bashir, M. (2015). Trust in automation: Integrating empirical evidence on factors that influence trust. *Human Factors*, *57*(3), 407–434. DOI: 10.1177/0018720814547570

Holman, L., Head, M., Lanfear, R., & Jennions, M. (2015). Evidence of Experimental Bias in the Life Sciences: Why We Need Blind Data Recording. *PLoS Biology*, *13*. Advance online publication. DOI: 10.1371/journal.pbio.1002190

Huang, M. H., & Rust, R. T. (2021). A strategic framework for artificial intelligence in marketing. *Journal of the Academy of Marketing Science*, *49*(1), 30–50. DOI: 10.1007/s11747-020-00749-9

Hulland, J. (1999). Use of partial least squares (PLS) in strategic management research: A review of four recent studies. *Strategic Management Journal*, *20*(2), 195–204. DOI: 10.1002/(SICI)1097-0266(199902)20:2<195:AID-SMJ13>3.0.CO;2-7

Khanal, K. (2024). Taylor Swift's Branding Strategy: The Economics of Authenticity. In *Compelling Storytelling Narratives for Sustainable Branding* (pp. 230-243). IGI Global. https://doi.org/DOI: 10.4018/979-8-3693-3326-6.ch012

Kietzmann, J., Paschen, J., & Treen, E. (2018). Artificial Intelligence in Advertising How Marketers Can Leverage Artificial Intelligence Along the Consumer Journey. *Journal of Advertising Research*, *58*(3), 263–267. DOI: 10.2501/JAR-2018-035

Kirk, C. P., & Givi, J. (2025). The AI-authorship effect: Understanding authenticity, moral disgust, and consumer responses to AI-generated marketing communications. *Journal of Business Research*, *186*, 114984.

Laux, J., Wachter, S., & Mittelstadt, B. (2024). Trustworthy artificial intelligence and the European Union AI act: On the conflation of trustworthiness and acceptability of risk. *Regulation & Governance*, *18*(1), 3–32. DOI: 10.1111/rego.12512

Lee, H., Shin, M., Yang, J., & Chock, T. M. (2024). Virtual Influencers vs. Human Influencers in the Context of Influencer Marketing: The Moderating Role of Machine Heuristic on Perceived Authenticity of Influencers. *International Journal of Human-Computer Interaction*, •••, 1–18. DOI: 10.1080/10447318.2024.2374100

Leigh, T. W., Peters, C., & Shelton, J. (2006). The consumer quest for authenticity: The multiplicity of meanings within the MG subculture of consumption. *Journal of the Academy of Marketing Science*, *34*(4), 481–493. DOI: 10.1177/0092070306288403

Lemon, K. N., & Verhoef, P. C. (2016). Understanding customer experience throughout the customer journey. *Journal of Marketing*, *80*(6), 69–96. DOI: 10.1509/jm.15.0420

Malhotra, N. K. (2010). *Marketing Research—An Applied Orientation (6a ed.)* (6.[a]). Prentice Hall.

Malthouse, E., & Copulsky, J. (2023). Artificial intelligence ecosystems for marketing communications. *International Journal of Advertising*, *42*(1), 128–140.

Maras, M. H., & Alexandrou, A. (2019). Determining authenticity of video evidence in the age of artificial intelligence and in the wake of Deepfake videos. *The International Journal of Evidence & Proof*, *23*(3), 255–262. DOI: 10.1177/1365712718807226

Moffat, D. C. D. C., & Kelly, M. (2006). An investigation into people's bias against computational creativity in music composition. *Assessment*, *13*(11), 1–8.

Morhart, F. M., Malär, L., Guèvremont, A., Girardin, F., & Grohmann, B. (2015). Brand authenticity: An integrative framework and measurement scale. *Journal of Consumer Psychology*, *25*(2), 200–218. DOI: 10.1016/j.jcps.2014.11.006

Moulard, J. G., Garrity, C. P., & Rice, D. H. (2015). What makes a human brand authentic? Identifying the antecedents of celebrity authenticity. *Psychology and Marketing*, *32*(2), 173–186. DOI: 10.1002/mar.20771

Moulard, J. G., Raggio, R. D., & Folse, J. A. G. (2021). Disentangling the meanings of brand authenticity: The entity-referent correspondence framework of authenticity. *Journal of the Academy of Marketing Science*, *49*(1), 96–118. DOI: 10.1007/s11747-020-00735-1

Napoli, J., Dickinson, S. J., Beverland, M. B., & Farrelly, F. (2014). Measuring consumer-based brand authenticity. *Journal of Business Research*, *67*(6), 1090–1098. DOI: 10.1016/j.jbusres.2013.06.001

Nunes, J. C., Ordanini, A., & Giambastiani, G. (2021). The concept of authenticity: What it means to consumers. *Journal of Marketing*, *85*(4), 1–20. DOI: 10.1177/0022242921997081

Osadchaya, E., Marder, B., Yule, J. A., Yau, A., Lavertu, L., Stylos, N., Oliver, S., Angell, R., Regt, A. D., Gao, L., Qi, K., Zhang, W. Z., Zhang, Y., & AlRabiah, S. (2024). To ChatGPT, or not to ChatGPT: Navigating the paradoxes of generative AI in the advertising industry. *Business Horizons*. Advance online publication. DOI: 10.1016/j.bushor.2024.05.002

Parris, D. L., & Guzmán, F. (2023). Evolving brand boundaries and expectations: Looking back on brand equity, brand loyalty, and brand image research to move forward. *Journal of Product and Brand Management*, *32*(2), 191–234. DOI: 10.1108/JPBM-06-2021-3528

Rai, A. (2020). Explainable AI: From black box to glass box. *Journal of the Academy of Marketing Science*, *48*, 137–141. DOI: 10.1007/s11747-019-00710-5

Ringle, C. M., Wende, S., & Becker, J.-M. (2024). SmartPLS 4. Bönningstedt: SmartPLS. Retrieved from https://www.smartpls.com

Sarstedt, M., Henseler, J., & Ringle, C. M. (2011). Multigroup Analysis in Partial Least Squares (PLS) Path Modeling: Alternative Methods and Empirical Results. In Sarstedt, M., Schwaiger, M., & Taylor, C. R. (Eds.), *Advances in International Marketing* (Vol. 22, pp. 195–218). Emerald Group Publishing Limited., DOI: 10.1108/S1474-7979(2011)0000022012

Schneider, D. M., & Woolley, S. M. (2010). Discrimination of communication vocalizations by single neurons and groups of neurons in the auditory midbrain. *Journal of Neurophysiology*, *103*(6), 3248–3265.

Stallone, A., Selva, J., Cordrie, L., Faenza, L., Michelini, A., & Lauciani, V. (2024). ProbShakemap v1. 0: a Python toolbox propagating source uncertainty to ground motion prediction for urgent computing applications. *Authorea Preprints*.

Wahid, R., Mero, J., & Ritala, P. (2023). Written by ChatGPT, illustrated by Midjourney: Generative AI for content marketing. *Asia Pacific Journal of Marketing and Logistics*, *35*(8), 1813–1822. DOI: 10.1108/APJML-10-2023-994

Wen, Q., Zhou, T., Zhang, C., Chen, W., Ma, Z., Yan, J., & Sun, L. (2022). Transformers in time series: A survey. *arXiv preprint arXiv:2202.07125*.

ADDITIONAL READING

Alzoubi, H. M., Mushtaq, S., Joghee, S., Shameem, B., Al Kurdi, B., & Hamadneh, S. (2025). Unveiling the Role of Artificial Intelligence: Navigating Personalized Content Marketing, Customer Engagement, and Commitment with Data Transparency and Security. *International Review of Management and Marketing*, *15*(2), 343–355. DOI: 10.32479/irmm.18499

Gomes, S., Lopes, J. M., & Nogueira, E. (2025). Anthropomorphism in artificial intelligence: A game-changer for brand marketing. *Future Business Journal*, *11*(1), 1–15. DOI: 10.1186/s43093-025-00423-y

Hagtvedt, L. P., Harvey, S., Demir-Caliskan, O., & Hagtvedt, H. (2025). Bright and Dark Imagining: How Creators Navigate Moral Consequences of Developing Ideas for Artificial Intelligence. *Academy of Management Journal*, *68*(1), 19–49. DOI: 10.5465/amj.2022.0850

Mahmoudian, H. (2021). Ethics and data governance in marketing analytics and artificial intelligence. *Applied Marketing Analytics*, *7*(1), 17–22. DOI: 10.69554/gznh7571

Mgiba, F. M. (2020). Artificial intelligence, marketing management, and ethics : their effect on customer loyalty intentions : a conceptual study. *The Retail and Marketing Review*, *16*(2), 18–35.

Mircea, V.-A. (2024). About Ethics, Marketing And Artificial Intelligence In Business. *Manager (University of Bucharest, Faculty of Business & Administration)*, *39*(1), 39–48.

Pagani, M., & Wind, Y. (2025). Unlocking Marketing Creativity Using Artificial Intelligence. *Journal of Interactive Marketing*, *60*(1), 1–24. DOI: 10.1177/10949968241265855

Vindytia, M., & Balqiah, T. E. (2024). AI Marketing Impact on Consumer Behavior: An SOR Model Analysis of Online Food Delivery Services. *JDM: Jurnal Dinamika Manajemen*, *15*(2), 215–228.

Yoldaş, E. N., & Ayci, A. (2024). The Role of Artificial Intelligence in Integrated Marketing Communication: An Evaluation of ChatGPT. *Pamukkale University Journal of Business Research / Pamukkale Üniversitesi İşletme Araştırmaları Dergisi*, *11*(2), 611–637. https://doi.org/DOI: 10.47097/piar.1562412

KEY TERMS AND DEFINITIONS

Artificial Intelligence: Artificial Intelligence refers to computer systems designed to simulate human intelligence, performing tasks such as learning, reasoning, problem-solving, perception, and decision-making autonomously or with minimal human intervention.

Artificial Intelligence-Designed Marketing Communication: Artificial Intelligence-designed marketing communication refers to promotional content or interactions developed or optimized by AI systems, using data analytics, algorithms, and machine learning to personalize messages, predict consumer responses, automate content creation, and enhance engagement and effectiveness.

Brand Authenticity: Brand authenticity refers to consumers' perception of a brand as genuine, transparent, honest, consistent in its messaging and actions, and aligned with its declared values and identity, fostering consumer trust and emotional connection.

Brand Loyalty: Brand loyalty is the consumer's consistent preference and commitment to repeatedly purchase or engage with a particular brand over competitors, driven by positive experiences, perceived value, emotional attachment, or satisfaction.

Brand Trust: Brand trust is the confidence and reliability consumers attribute to a brand based on its consistent ability to fulfil promises, provide quality products or services, demonstrate transparency, and act ethically and responsibly over time.

Ethical Personalization: Ethical personalization involves tailoring marketing practices and customer experiences using consumer data and technology responsibly, transparently, and respectfully, ensuring informed consent, data privacy, fairness, and consumer autonomy, thereby fostering trust and mitigating risks of manipulation or exploitation.

Personalization: Personalization is the strategic customization of marketing communications, products, services, or experiences based on individual consumer preferences, behaviours, characteristics, or historical interactions, aiming to increase relevance, engagement, satisfaction, and loyalty.

Theory of Authenticity: The theory of authenticity posits that consumers seek genuine and credible experiences, products, or brands that align with their beliefs, values, and identity. Authenticity influences consumer attitudes, satisfaction, loyalty, and emotional connections, particularly in contexts of perceived commercialization or superficiality.

APPENDIX

Constructs and Items

Perceived Authenticity (AUT)

AUT01 - The campaign 'Belong Everywhere' from Airbnb is genuine.
AUT02 - The campaign 'Belong Everywhere' from Airbnb seems real to me.
AUT03 - The campaign 'Belong Everywhere' from Airbnb is authentic

Emotional Resonance (EMR)

EMR01 - Unimportant to me / important to me
EMR02 - Of no concern to me / of concern to me
EMR03 - Irrelevant to me / relevant to me
EMR04 - Means nothing to me / means a lot to me
EMR05 - Useless to me / useful to me
EMR06 - Insignificant to me / significant to me

Trust (TRU)

TRU01 - I am confident in the campaign 'Belong Everywhere' from Airbnb
TRU02: The campaign 'Belong Everywhere' from Airbnb provides security
TRU03: The campaign 'Belong Everywhere' from Airbnb has integrity
TRU04: The campaign 'Belong Everywhere' from Airbnb is reliable
TRU05 - I can trust the campaign 'Belong Everywhere' from Airbnb

Loyalty (LOY)

LOY01 - When I intend to use Airbnb service, I ignore competing brands
LOY02 - If Airbnb service is unavailable, I will postpone the use
LOY03 - If I don't use the Airbnb service, I won't use another one

Chapter 6
A Comprehensive Literature Review on the Influence of Artificial Intelligence on Consumer Engagement and Brand Loyalty in Digital Marketing

Albérico Travassos Rosário
https://orcid.org/0000-0003-4793-4110
GOVCOPP, Escola Superior de Ciências Empresariais, Instituto Politécnico de Setúbal, Portugal

Rui Nunes Cruz
https://orcid.org/0000-0002-5773-6049
UNIDCOM-IADE, Universidade Europeia, Portugal

ABSTRACT

This literature review synthesizes key findings from recent studies examining the impact of artificial intelligence (AI) technologies on consumer engagement, brand loyalty, and digital marketing strategies. Utilizing frameworks such as affordance theory, social identity theory, and delegation theory, these studies reveal how AI influences brand perception, consumer trust, and purchase behavior across various sectors, including finance, retail, and tourism. The review highlights how specific AI features, such as anthropomorphism, interactivity, and personalization, enhance

DOI: 10.4018/979-8-3693-9994-1.ch006

user experience, fostering brand identification and loyalty. However, ethical concerns regarding data privacy, customer manipulation, and authenticity are also noted as challenges within the AI-driven marketing landscape. By consolidating these insights, this review provides a theoretical and practical foundation for future research on AI's role in consumer behavior and offers strategic considerations for marketing professionals in the digital age

INTRODUCTION

The rapid advancement of artificial intelligence (AI) has transformed industries globally, positioning it as the foundation of innovation in the digital age. According to the National Qualifications Register's (n.d.) report, the global AI market was estimated at US $119.78 billion in 2022 and is projected to reach US $1,591.03 billion by 2030, growing at a CAGR of 38.1%, as shown in Figure 1. In addition, AI is projected to contribute approximately US $15.7 trillion by 2030. This AI potential has led to its significant adoption in numerous industries and sectors, including marketing. For instance, Motamedi (2024) found that AI's capabilities have revolutionized business operations in marketing, from automating mundane tasks to driving sophisticated predictive analytics. Traditional marketing approaches are increasingly being augmented or replaced by AI-driven strategies that leverage big data, machine learning, and natural language processing. This transformation is especially evident in digital marketing, where AI technologies enable marketers to personalize consumer interactions at scale, optimize campaigns, and enhance decision-making processes (Gans, 2023). These advancements redefine how businesses communicate with their audience and elevate the overall efficiency and effectiveness of marketing efforts.

Consumer engagement and brand loyalty have emerged within digital marketing as critical determinants of long-term business success. Consumer engagement refers to the interactions between a brand and its audience that build meaningful relationships (Chen et al., 2022). Brand loyalty reflects a customer's consistent preference and commitment to a specific brand over its competitors (Rane, 2023). Customer engagement and brand loyalty are pivotal for achieving sustainable growth, increasing customer retention, and driving revenue. However, the competitive nature of the digital landscape demands innovative strategies to capture and maintain consumer attention (Bag et al., 2022). AI is a powerful tool for marketers to create highly personalized and immersive experiences, thus reshaping how engagement and loyalty are cultivated in the digital era.

AI influences consumer engagement through its ability to analyze vast amounts of consumer data, predict preferences, and deliver tailored content across multiple channels. For instance, AI-driven algorithms in recommendation engines, chatbots, and predictive analytics allow brands to interact with consumers in a personalized and immediate manner (Suraña-Sánchez & Aramendia-Muneta, 2024). This level of customization strengthens the emotional connection between brands and consumers, resulting in higher engagement levels. Similarly, AI enhances brand loyalty by enabling seamless and consistent customer experiences, predictive retention strategies, and reward programs tailored to individual behaviors (Ziakis & Vlachopoulou, 2023). As consumers increasingly value convenience, personalization, and relevance, AI's role in addressing these demands becomes central to a brand's ability to build enduring relationships. This literature review examines AI's technological capabilities and strategic applications in digital marketing and their consequent impacts on consumer engagement and brand loyalty.

METHODOLOGICAL APPROACH

This study employs the PRISMA 2020 framework and a systematic bibliometric literature review to examine the influence of AI on consumer engagement and brand loyalty in digital marketing. According to Haddaway et al. (2022), the PRISMA guidelines ensure methodological transparency, reproducibility, and objectivity and reduce the risk of bias. On the other hand, the bibliometric literature review approach helped identify thematic patterns and trends in the literature.

The search process began with identifying specific keywords to capture the scope of the research. The primary terms “Artificial Intelligence” and “Marketing” were initially chosen to explore AI applications in marketing. These were expanded with additional terms such as “Digital Marketing,” “Consumer Engagement,” and “Brand Loyalty” to narrow the search to literature explicitly addressing AI's role in digital marketing and its impact on building consumer relationships and loyalty. This comprehensive approach ensured that the final selection included publications relevant to the study's focus.

The Scopus database was selected for this review due to its extensive coverage of peer-reviewed literature across diverse fields. Baas et al. (2020, p.377) describe Scopus as one of the “largest curated abstract and citation databases.” In addition, this database provides comprehensive indexing of high-quality publications, from books and scientific journals to conference proceedings. This makes it an ideal resource for exploring interdisciplinary topics such as AI and marketing. Its advanced search functionalities also facilitate precise results filtering to align with the study's objectives.

The Scopus database served as the primary tool for identifying and selecting relevant materials, adhering to the methodologies outlined by Rosário et al.,

(2020,2021)andRosário and Dias (2024). The platform maintains exceptional data quality through the oversight of its independent Content Selection and Advisory Board, which applies rigorous selection criteria and conducts regular re-evaluations.

In contrast to traditional literature reviews, the Systematic Bibliometric Literature Review (LRSB) method offers a more structured and in-depth exploration of a specific research domain, as emphasized by Rosário et al., (2020,2021) and Rosário and Dias (2024). This approach prioritizes a refined selection process to include only studies that are directly pertinent to the research question. Moreover, it establishes a transparent audit trail, allowing readers to critically assess the methodology, findings, and overall quality of the selected studies.

The LRSB methodology employs a meticulous protocol to screen and select sources, ensuring data reliability and relevance. This protocol is systematically organized into three phases and six distinct steps, as illustrated in Table 1 and detailed by Rosário et al., (2020,2021) and ; Rosário and Dias (2024).

Table 1. Process of systematic LRSB.

Fase	Step	Description
Exploration	Step 1	formulating the research problem
	Step 2	searching for appropriate literature
	Step 3	critical appraisal of the selected studies
	Step 4	data synthesis from individual sources
Interpretation	Step 5	reporting findings and recommendations
Communication	Step 6	Presentation of the LRSB report

Source: adapted *Rosário et al., (2020,2021) and Rosário and Dias (2024).*

The researchers utilized the Scopus database to identify and select reliable sources, widely acknowledged by the academic and scientific community. However, a notable limitation of this study is its exclusive reliance on the Scopus database, excluding other academic and scientific databases. Additionally, the search was confined to publications available up to December 2024. The search strategy prioritized peer-reviewed academic and scientific works to ensure the credibility and rigour of the selected materials.Parte superior do formulário

The literature search was conducted using a tiered query system within the Scopus database. The initial query, TITLE-ABS-KEY "Artificial Intelligence," retrieved 613,931 documents. Adding the keyword "Marketing" refined the results to 4,899 documents. To narrow the focus further, TITLE-ABS-KEY "Digital Marketing" was incorporated, and the query was limited to the exact keywords "Consumer Behavior" and "Brand Loyalty," resulting in 106 relevant documents. These documents were screened using inclusion criteria such as relevance to consumer engagement and brand loyalty, peer-reviewed status, and publication in English. Exclusion criteria ensured a curated selection, including a lack of focus on digital marketing contexts and duplicates.

Specific inclusion and exclusion criteria were established to guarantee the relevance and rigour of the documents analyzed in the final report (Table 2). The researchers included only peer-reviewed journal articles that explored the intersection of marketing strategy and brand development. To maintain a focused dataset, publications outside the fields of business, marketing, or branding were excluded. This systematic selection process ensured that the final set of literature was of high quality and closely aligned with the study's objectives. A detailed summary of the search process is provided in Table 2.

Table 2. Screening Methodology.

<table>
<tr><th>Database Scopus</th><th>Screening</th><th>Publications</th></tr>
<tr><td>Meta-search</td><td>Keyword: Artificial Intelligence</td><td>613,931</td></tr>
<tr><td>First Inclusion Criterion</td><td>Keyword: Artificial Intelligence, Marketing</td><td>4,899</td></tr>
<tr><td>Second Inclusion Criteria</td><td>Keyword: Artificial Intelligence, Marketing
Exact Keyword: Consumer Behavior</td><td rowspan="2">106</td></tr>
<tr><td>Screening</td><td>Keyword: Artificial Intelligence, Marketing
Exact Keyword: Consumer Behavior
Until December 2024</td></tr>
</table>

Source: own elaboration

Content and thematic analysis methods were employed to identify, evaluate, and present the range of documents, following the framework established by Rosário et al., (2020,2021) and Rosário and Dias (2024). Rigorous selection criteria were applied to ensure the inclusion of only high-quality and relevant academic sources. The researchers focused on studies specifically addressing luxury brands and consumer behavior. Eligibility was determined based on the studies' alignment with the research topic, methodological rigor, and publication in peer-reviewed journals (refer to Figure 1).

Figure 1. PRISMA 2020 flow diagram for the systematic literature search.

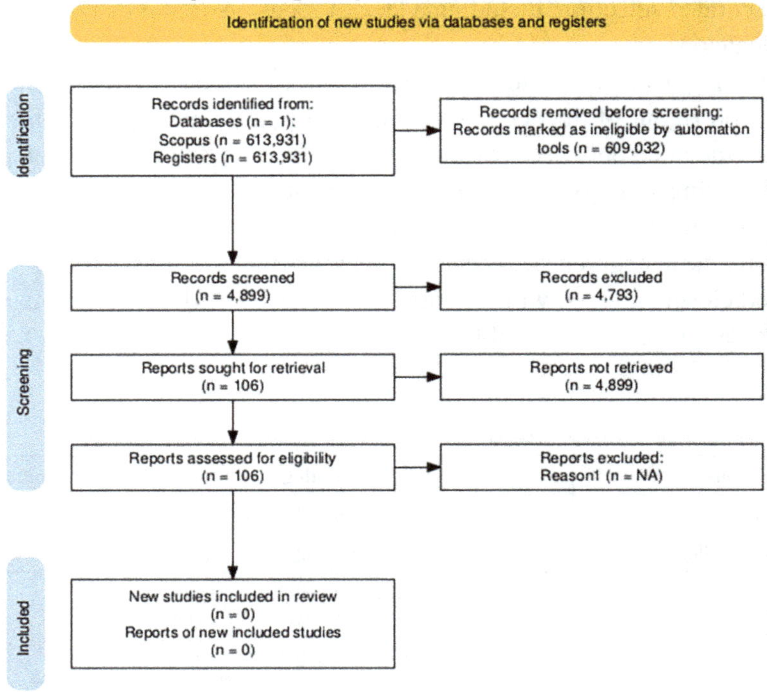

A total of 106 scientific and academic documents indexed in Scopus were analyzed using a blend of narrative and bibliometric approaches, as outlined by Rosário et al., (2020,2021); Rosário and Dias (2024). These methodologies were employed to thoroughly examine the content of the documents and identify recurring themes closely aligned with the research questions.

Of the 106 documents selected, 40 were journals, 39 were conference proceedings, 25 were book series, and 2 were books.

PUBLICATION DISTRIBUTION

Peer-reviewed articles on a Comprehensive Literature Review on the Influence of Artificial Intelligence on Consumer Engagement and Brand Loyalty in Digital Marketing, December 2024. The year 2024 has the highest number of peer-reviewed publications, reaching 26. Figure 2 summarises the peer-reviewed literature published until December 2024.

Figure 2. Documents by year

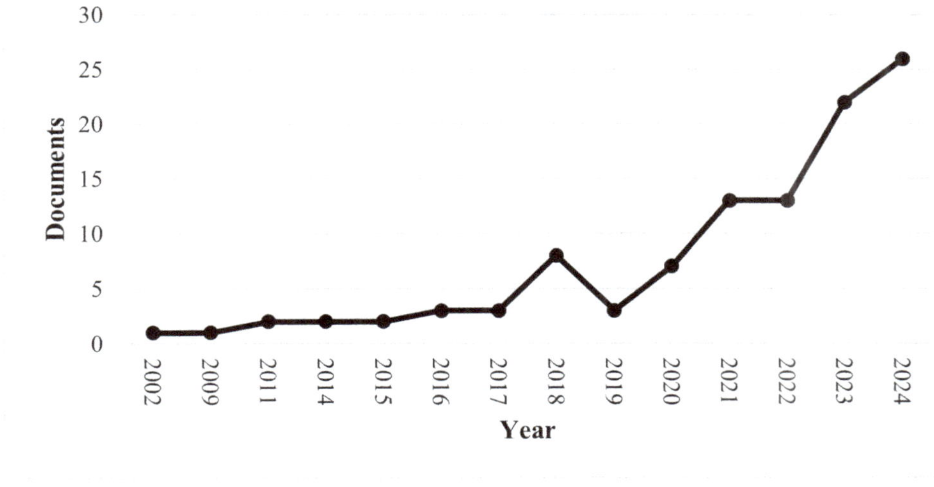

Figure 3 displays the countries exhibiting the highest levels of scientific output in specific research areas, with particular emphasis on India, China, the USA, and Indonesia, which boast the most significant number of publications.

Figure 3. Scientific production by country.

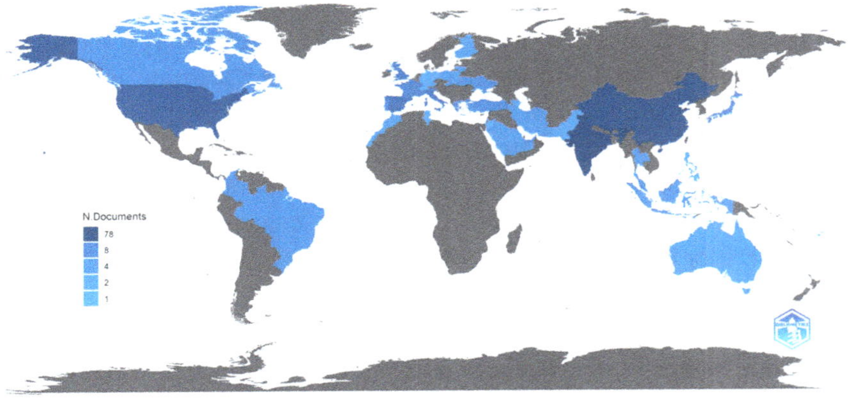

Table 3 and Figure 3 visually illustrate the top 10 nations making notable scientific contributions in the examined domains. This investigation aims to identify countries that prioritise studying luxury brands and their consumption.

Table 3. Top 10 countries by number of publications.

Country	Number of Publications
INDIA	78
CHINA	54
USA	38
SPAIN	18
ITALY	12
UK	12
FRANCE	10
GREECE	8
JAPAN	8
PORTUGAL	7

Source: own elaboration

The publications were sorted out as follows: Lecture Notes In Computer Science Including Subseries Lecture Notes In Artificial Intelligence And Lecture Notes In Bioinformatics (6); ACM International Conference Proceeding Series (5); Lecture Notes In Networks And Systems (4); Lecture Notes In Electrical Engineering (3); with 2 documents (Technological Forecasting And Social Change; Studies In Computational Intelligence; Smart Innovation Systems And Technologies; International Journal Of Information Management; IEEE Access; Electronic Commerce Research; Advances In Intelligent Systems And Computing; 2023 International Conference On Sustainable Emerging Innovations In Engineering And Technology Icseiet 2023; and the remaining publications with 1 document. The subject areas covered by the 106 scientific or academic documents were Computer Science (70); Engineering (38); Business, Management and Accounting (22); Decision Sciences (20); Mathematics (19); Economics, Econometrics and Finance (9); Social Sciences (8); Psychology (7); Energy (7); Physics and Astronomy (6); Materials Science (6); Medicine (5); Agricultural and Biological Sciences (4); Multidisciplinary (3); Environmental Science (3); Neuroscience (2); Chemical Engineering (2); Earth and Planetary Sciences (1); Biochemistry, Genetics and Molecular Biology (1); and Arts and Humanities (1).

The most quoted article was "Setting the future of digital and social media marketing research: Perspectives and research propositions" by Dwivedi et al. (2021), with 986 quotes published in the International Journal of Information Management 5,780 (SJR), the best quartile (Q1), and with H index (177). In this article, "This article brings together the collective insight from several leading experts on issues relating to digital and social media marketing."

In Figure 4, we can analyse citation changes for documents published up to December 2024. The period ≤2014-2024 shows a positive net growth in citations with an R2 of 7%, reaching 711 in 2024.

Figure 4. Evolution of citations between ≤2014 and 2024.

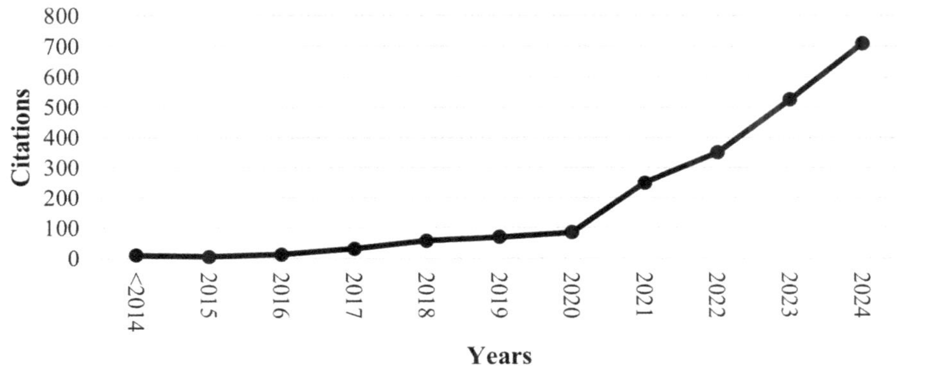

The h-index measures the productivity and impact of published works by identifying the highest number of articles each has received at least an equal number of citations. Nineteen of the documents considered for the h-index received at least 19 citations.

Citations of all scientific and academic documents from the period ≤2014 to December 2024, with a total of 2,153 citations; of the 106 documents, 34 were not cited. Using the main keywords "A Comprehensive Literature Review on the Influence of Artificial Intelligence on Consumer Engagement and Brand Loyalty in Digital Marketing," the bibliometric analysis revealed key indicators of the evolving landscape of scientific and academic information within the documents, as shown in Figure 5. The researchers derived these insights using VOSviewer scientific software, focusing specifically on the primary search terms: "Artificial Intelligence", "Marketing" and "Consumer Behavior".

Figure 5. Network of all keywords

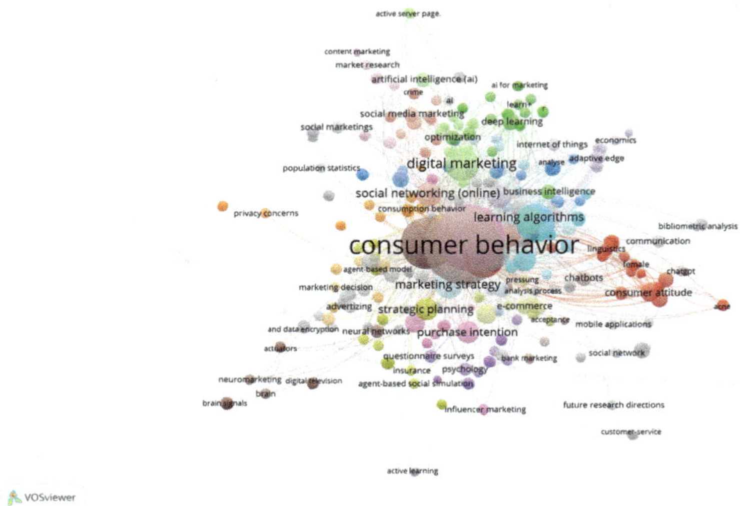

This study builds on a thorough review of scientific and academic literature exploring the Influence of Artificial Intelligence on Consumer Engagement and Brand Loyalty in Digital Marketing.

The focus of the three-field plot is in the middle field. AU stands for the author, meaning the focus is on the top author (the main concern), associated with the CR as cited reference, and DE as authors keyword.

To analyze how the different authors' keywords connect in the papers, we developed a Sankey diagram in Bibliometrix, shown in Figure 6.

Figure 6. Three fields plot analysis (AU=authors, CR=references, DE=authors keywords)

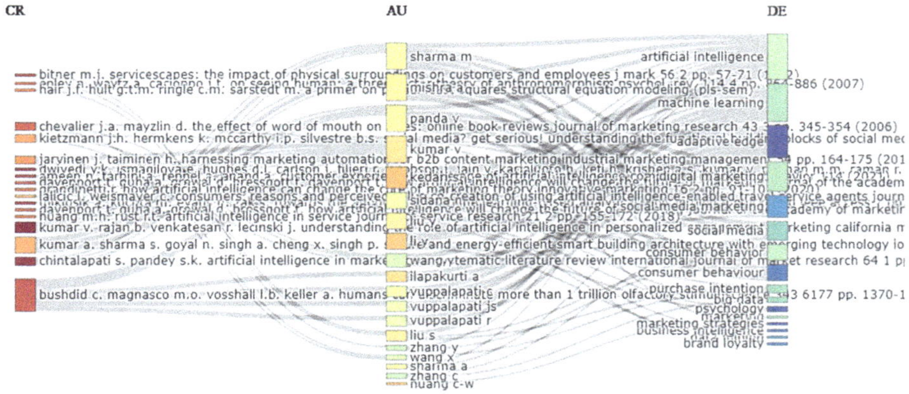

In the Sankey diagram, the size of the boxes is proportional to the frequency of the theme's occurrences. The flows connect each box, showing the theme's evolution traces. The thicker the connecting line, the greater the connection between the two themes (Xiao et al., 2022). Figure 6 shows that the keywords most commonly used are "Artificial intelligence" (incoming flow count: 11; outgoing flow count: 0) and "machine learning" (incoming flow count: 7; outgoing flow count: 0), which are linked mainly to the most cited references.

Figure 7 provides a detailed examination of the interrelated keywords, highlighting the connections between critical terms across the academic articles. This analysis helps identify the topics covered in these studies and offers valuable insights into potential avenues for future research. Furthermore, Figure 8 illustrates a substantial number of co-citations and units, enhancing the analysis of the cited references and supporting the overall findings.

Figure 7. Network of Linked Keywords

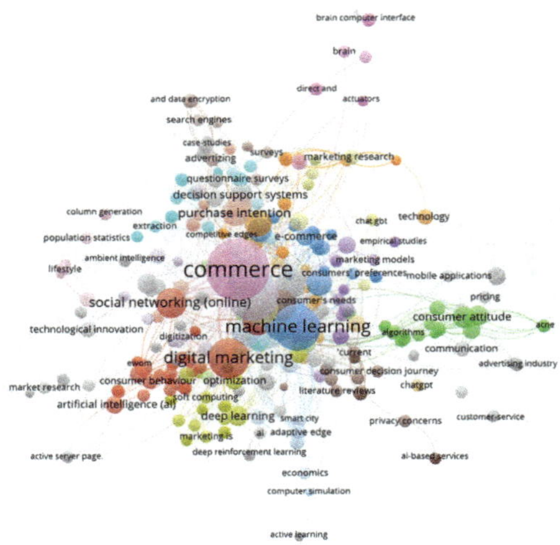

Figure 8. Network of co-citation

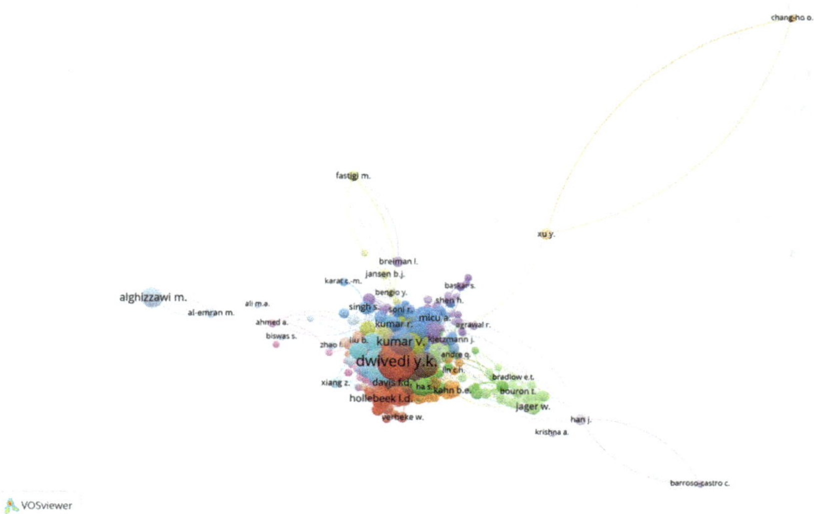

THEORETICAL PERSPECTIVES

AI has been widely adopted in digital marketing to enhance operational efficiency and improve the effectiveness of marketing strategies. This innovation empowers marketers to deliver highly personalized and context-aware interactions, influencing consumer engagement and brand loyalty (Ramirez et al., 2022). For instance, AI capabilities enable brands to create deeper connections and more dynamic interactions with their audiences through targeted marketing strategies. In addition, AI has reshaped the concept of brand loyalty by allowing companies to leverage AI-driven tools to create tailored loyalty programs, anticipate consumer needs, and ensure consistent, high-quality experiences across digital platforms (Ilapakurti et al., 2018b; Gkikas & Theodoridis, 2022). This literature review section explores existing research on how AI has transformed digital marketing practices, focusing on its impact on consumer engagement and brand loyalty.

Defining Key Concepts

Artificial Intelligence

Artificial intelligence (AI) is the simulation of human intelligence by machines and computer systems, enabling them to perform tasks that typically require cognitive functions such as learning, reasoning, problem-solving, and decision-making. Chintalapati and Pandey (2022, p.39) define this innovation as the "science and engineering of making intelligent machines, especially intelligent computer programs." Although AI involves understanding human intelligence and using computers to carry out similar tasks, the authors explain that it does not have to limit itself to biologically observable methods. The core of AI lies in its ability to process vast amounts of data, identify patterns, and adapt its operations based on new information, often with minimal human intervention (Gupta et al., 2024; Kaponis & Maragoudakis, 2022). AI technologies encompass various methodologies, including machine learning (ML), natural language processing (NLP), computer vision, and neural networks, each tailored to specific applications. These capabilities have found practical uses in areas ranging from healthcare diagnostics and autonomous vehicles to financial forecasting and marketing (Lu & Boutilier, 2015). AI's evolution from rule-based systems to advanced deep learning frameworks has significantly enhanced its capacity to tackle complex tasks, making it a cornerstone of technological innovation in the modern era.

One of the defining characteristics of AI is its capacity for personalization and predictive analytics. Through machine learning algorithms, AI systems can analyze consumer behavior, predict future trends, and provide insights that help businesses make data-driven decisions (Meepung & Kannikar, 2022). For example, recommendation engines in e-commerce platforms use AI to suggest products based on user preferences, purchase history, and browsing patterns. Similarly, AI-powered chatbots provide instantaneous customer support, mimicking human interaction to enhance user satisfaction (Mittal et al., 2023; Olan et al., 2024). These applications have had profound implications for digital marketing, where AI is used as a strategic tool to optimize campaigns, improve customer targeting, and deliver personalized experiences at scale. As businesses continue to leverage AI's potential, its influence on reshaping industries and consumer experiences grows increasingly significant, warranting deeper exploration into its role and impact.

Digital Marketing

Digital marketing refers to the use of digital channels, technologies, and platforms to promote products, services, and brands to consumers. It encompasses multiple activities, including search engine optimization (SEO), social media marketing, email campaigns, content marketing, and paid advertising, aiming to engage audiences and drive measurable outcomes (Patil et al., 2024; Jayashree et al., 2022). Unlike traditional marketing, digital marketing leverages data analytics and technology to deliver personalized, real-time consumer interactions. This personalization is facilitated by tracking tools and algorithms that gather insights into consumer behavior, enabling marketers to create targeted strategies that resonate with specific demographics (Siva Balan & Kalpana, 2023). In recent years, the emergence and adoption of smartphones, high-speed internet, and social media platforms have expanded the reach and significance of digital marketing, making it a foundational component of modern business strategies.

Digital marketing significantly relies on interactivity and engagement. Unlike one-way communication methods in traditional advertising, digital marketing enables two-way interactions, allowing consumers to actively participate in shaping their experiences with brands (Wang & Wang, 2022). Technologies such as AI, machine learning, and predictive analytics have further enhanced digital marketing by providing tools to automate processes, optimize campaigns, and deliver dynamic, personalized content (Vinaykarthik, 2022; Ziakis & Vlachopoulou, 2023). For instance, platforms like Google Ads and Meta Ads utilize AI algorithms to maximize the relevance of advertisements shown to users. Similarly, email marketing platforms use AI to predict the best times to send messages, resulting in higher engagement rates (Albinali & Hamdan, 2021). As digital marketing evolves, its integration with advanced technologies such as artificial intelligence continues to redefine how brands build relationships with consumers and establish lasting loyalty.

Consumer Engagement

Consumer engagement is a multifaceted concept encompassing consumers' interactions, emotions, and cognitive involvement with a brand or product. At its core, consumer engagement represents their level of involvement toward a brand (Ilapakurti et al., 2018a). This perspective is reflected in Srivastava et al.'s (2023, p.1) definition of customer engagement: "customer's behavior that has a brand or firm focus beyond purchase, which has resulted from motivational drivers of cognitive, emotional, and behavioral activities." This can result in various behaviors, such as participation in social media, engagement with brand-related content, and communication with the brand through customer service or feedback. Thus, consumer engagement is seen as an emotional and psychological connection that drives consumers to form positive relationships with brands (Fernández-Rovira et al., 2021; Zhuang et al., 2018). Effective consumer engagement has become increasingly important in digital marketing, where brands compete for consumer attention in an oversaturated market (Vij et al., 2024). The rise of digital channels, including social media, mobile applications, and personalized websites, has provided brands with numerous opportunities to create deeper engagement through interactive content, personalized messaging, and consistent communication.

Traditionally, consumer engagement was driven largely by consumer experiences, product quality, and the brand's ability to meet consumer needs. Today, it involves more dynamic and multifaceted interactions, especially in the digital environment (Vij et al., 2024). Consumer engagement now also includes creating meaningful and personalized experiences that resonate with individuals on a deeper level, allowing brands to foster loyalty and increase retention. While traditional forms of engagement, such as word-of-mouth and customer reviews, are still valuable, modern engagement strategies have expanded into digital spaces where consumers can engage directly with a brand's content, share feedback, and participate in virtual communities (Wang et al., 2023; Suzuki et al., 2018). The importance of engagement lies in its ability to encourage repeat behavior and build emotional connections that make consumers more likely to advocate for the brand and maintain a long-term relationship.

Consumer engagement is a crucial part of successful digital marketing. According to Srivastava et al. (2023), digital consumer engagement (DCE) can be classified into three levels: cognitive, affective, and behavioral, as shown in Figure 4. Cognitive engagement is driven by factors such as attention, absorption, and informativeness. These reflect how well consumers focus on and process content, often influenced by interactive and vivid media that capture their interest and deliver valuable information (Sleiman et al., 2024). Affective engagement builds on emotional connections fueled by enjoyment and entertainment. It reflects how much consumers emotionally resonate with content, whether through humor, storytelling, or an overall positive experience that strengthens their bond with the brand (Sun, 2023). Behavioral engagement relates to action-oriented interactions such as sharing, learning, and endorsing. This level reflects consumers' willingness to participate actively in brand-related activities, extending their engagement into visible and impactful behaviors (Figure 9) (Srivastava et al., 2023). These forms of engagement lead to meaningful outcomes, including brand equity, customer loyalty, trust, and commitment. It also drives key behaviors such as word-of-mouth recommendations, continued product use, and repurchase intentions, ultimately contributing to long-term brand success.

Figure 9. Antecedents, divers, and outcomes of DCE

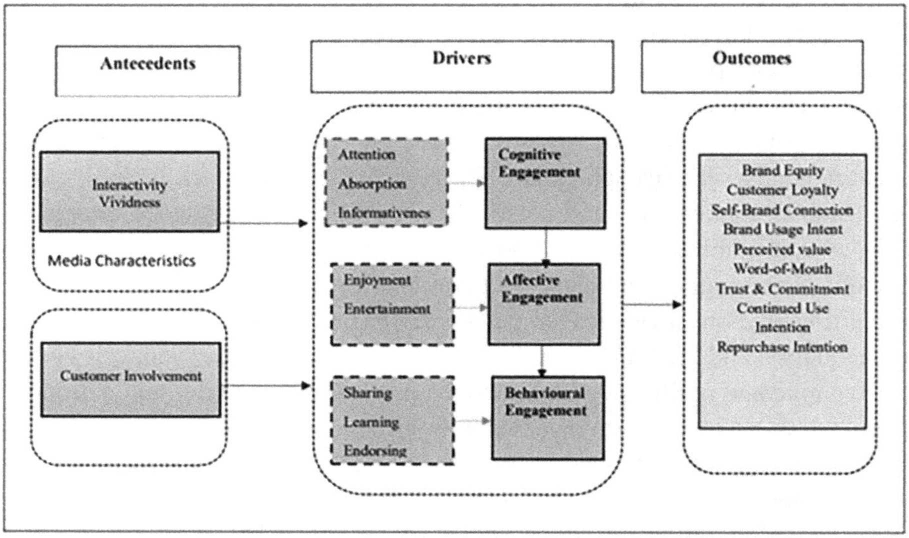

(Srivastava et al., 2023)

Brand Loyalty

Brand loyalty refers to a consumer's consistent preference for one brand over others. It is often exhibited through repeat purchases, brand advocacy, and an emotional attachment to the brand (Vieira et al., 2023; Biswas & Sanyal, 2019). Brand loyalty is essential for business success since loyal customers tend to have a higher lifetime value and are less sensitive to price changes or competitor offers. Brand loyalty goes beyond simple satisfaction; it reflects a deep-seated trust and commitment to a brand, influencing consumers' decision-making processes even in the face of alternatives (Li & You, 2021; Abdelkader, 2023). Loyalty is often seen as a long-term outcome of positive consumer experiences and is built over time through consistent delivery of value, quality, and emotional resonance with the consumer (Bacilieri, 2019). It is integral to digital marketing because loyal customers generate repeat sales and contribute to free promotion through word-of-mouth recommendations.

Theoretical Frameworks

Multiple theoretical frameworks can be used to explain the impact of AI technologies on consumer engagement and brand loyalty in digital marketing. These frameworks offer valuable insights into how AI shapes consumer behavior, brand interactions, and overall marketing strategies (Laszkiewicz & Kalinska-Kula, 2023). This section discusses three key theories, including affordance theory, social identity theory, and delegation theory, and their relevance to understanding AI's transformative role in digital marketing.

Affordance Theory

American ecological physiologist James J. Gibson pioneered the affordance theory. Wang et al. (2018, p.56) define it as "the possibilities for action." This theoretical framework focuses on the opportunities and constraints provided by technological features and their interaction with users' perceptions and actions. It highlights how users perceive actionable possibilities (affordances) that technology offers based on its design. In AI-driven marketing, affordances such as interactivity, personalization, and automation create new ways for consumers to engage with brands (Wu et al., 2024). For instance, chatbots afford real-time communication, while recommendation systems afford tailored product suggestions, fostering deeper consumer engagement (Yang et al., 2020). Understanding these affordances enables marketers to predict and adapt to shifting consumer preferences, ensuring sustained engagement. Therefore, affordance theory helps explain why certain AI features resonate with consumers, making them more likely to interact with and form emotional connections to brands.

Social Identity Theory

Social identity theory explores how individuals derive part of their identity from membership in social groups, including brand communities. Davis et al. (2019) explain that participating in collective activities through networks and relationships helps people create emotional attachments and identities. Therefore, this theory is used in marketing to understand how consumers identify with brands that align with their self-concept or social aspirations (Kothari & Mani, 2024; Ling & Che, 2021). AI technologies enhance this identification process by enabling personalized experiences that reflect consumers' preferences, values, and behaviors. For example, AI-powered tools can curate content reinforcing a consumer's association with a brand's community, increasing loyalty and engagement (Liu et al., 2023). They facilitate stronger identification between consumers and brands, reinforcing brand loyalty through social connection. Marketers targeting niche audiences can leverage AI tools to create a sense of exclusivity within brand communities. This would strengthen the consumer-brand bond, ultimately driving engagement and loyalty.

Delegation Theory

Delegation theory examines how individuals delegate tasks and decisions to external agents or technologies to achieve desired outcomes efficiently. Cooter and Gilbert (2022) identify delegation as a way to save the delegator's time, resources, efforts, energy, and concentration while ensuring the desired purposes are achieved. Consumers use AI tools to delegate decision-making to tools such as virtual assistants, robo-advisors, and predictive analytics systems (Rohden & Espartel, 2024; Saraiva Gonçalves et al., 2020). These technologies simplify decision-making by analyzing vast data and providing optimized recommendations. As a result, such delegation introduces a layer of cognitive ease for consumers since AI minimizes the mental effort required in complex decision-making scenarios. For brands, this represents a critical touchpoint to build consumer trust by ensuring that delegated decisions align with customer expectations and preferences. In addition, this delegation creates opportunities for marketers to influence consumer choices and establish trust by delivering reliable and effective solutions (Ricci et al., 2015). Understanding delegation theory helps explain why consumers are willing to rely on AI tools in their interactions with brands, ultimately impacting engagement and loyalty.

AI's Influence on Customer Engagement

AI provides tools that influence how brands engage their customers. For instance, Perez-Vega et al. (2021) found that marketers leverage AI tools to segment social media users, allowing for more targeted messaging. As a result, this has led to increased customer engagement, ultimately improving the selling processes and boosting sales. This section explores other common ways in which AI influences customer engagement:

AI-Powered Interaction

AI-powered interaction has redefined how brands engage with consumers by providing seamless, efficient, and highly personalized experiences. Tools such as chatbots and recommendation engines serve as front-line agents capable of delivering real-time assistance and tailored content (Dong, 2023; Kachamas, 2016). These systems address consumer queries and enhance engagement by predicting preferences and curating relevant options. AI-powered tools create a dynamic, responsive environment that meets consumer expectations for immediacy and convenience by automating repetitive tasks and ensuring 24/7 availability (Said et al., 2002). This level of engagement creates a deeper connection between consumers and brands, building the foundation for sustained interaction and loyalty.

Anthropomorphism in AI

Integrating anthropomorphic elements into AI systems leverages human-like attributes to establish emotional connections with consumers. These AI entities, such as virtual assistants or chatbots, create a sense of familiarity and relatability by mimicking human behaviors, speech, and expressions (Salles et al., 2020; Mueller, 2020). Anthropomorphism can enhance trust and comfort, encouraging consumers to interact more freely with brands. Placani (2024) explains that this emotional engagement is particularly impactful in environments where consumers seek personalized attention, as human-like AI creates an illusion of understanding and empathy (Li & Suh, 2021). Blending technology with human-like characteristics allows brands to use anthropomorphism to make their AI systems approachable and engaging, thus strengthening consumer-brand relationships.

Interactivity and Customization

AI drives interactivity and customization by tailoring experiences to individual preferences, enabling deeper consumer engagement. AI identifies unique user preferences and behaviors through data-driven insights, creating highly personalized interactions (Poornima et al., 2024). For example, content personalization, such as customized advertisements, recommendations, or interactive chat interfaces, creates a sense of individual importance and relevance (Armutcu et al., 2024). According to Imanova and Imanova (2021), interactivity ensures consumers remain actively involved with the brand, while customization ensures the content delivered resonates with their specific needs. This synergistic approach enhances user satisfaction and keeps consumers engaged over time.

Real-Time Responsiveness

Real-time responsiveness facilitated by AI significantly enhances consumer engagement by delivering immediate solutions and services. AI systems like chatbots or customer support platforms can process queries, complaints, or purchase requests in real time, eliminating delays (Fukui & Tabata, 2024). This instantaneous interaction meets the growing consumer demand for quick problem resolution and seamless experiences. Moreover, Papavasileiou and Tsadiras (2011) explain that real-time AI capabilities enable brands to adapt to dynamic consumer needs through live recommendations, inventory updates, or transactional assistance (Lei et al., 2020; Davis & Jin, 2024). The ability to provide prompt responses builds trust and satisfaction, ensuring consumers feel valued and prioritized in their engagement with the brand.

Virtual and Augmented Reality Experiences

Virtual and augmented reality (VR/AR) AI-powered experiences create immersive and engaging interactions. These innovations have revolutionized traditional marketing approaches by allowing consumers to explore products, services, or environments in highly interactive ways, such as virtually trying on clothing or experiencing a virtual property tour (Chica et al., 2023; Zaveri & Amin, 2019). AI enhances these experiences by integrating features like voice commands, real-time customization, and tailored recommendations based on user behavior. AI-powered VR/AR combines sensory engagement with advanced interactivity to support a stronger emotional connection between consumers and brands (Egieya et al., 2023; Wedel et al., 2020). This practice drives deeper levels of engagement and enhances the overall consumer experience.

Consumer Trust and Brand Perception

AI influences consumer trust and brand perception by enabling brands to offer consistent, transparent, and efficient interactions. Features like AI-driven chatbots and personalized recommendations enhance reliability and authenticity since consumers feel their needs are being met thoughtfully and promptly (Ltifi, 2023; Yao, 2021). Furthermore, Alizadeh and Nazarpour Kashani (2024) indicate that the ethical application of AI in data privacy and security establishes trust, reinforcing positive brand perception. When brands utilize AI responsibly, consumers are more likely to perceive them as innovative, competent, and customer-focused (Vyas, 2024). This alignment of trust and perception directly contributes to more engaged consumers who feel confident in their relationship with the brand.

Personalized Customer Journeys

AI enhances personalized customer journeys by continuously adapting interactions based on consumer behavior, preferences, and needs. Through advanced analytics, AI tracks each step of the customer lifecycle, offering tailored recommendations, reminders, and offers at optimal times (Santos & Gonçalves, 2021; Manca et al., 2018). This personalization ensures that every touchpoint aligns with individual expectations, creating a smooth and rewarding experience. As a result, AI facilitates deeper engagement and loyalty by understanding consumer preferences on a granular level (Yu & Huang, 2021). Personalized journeys make consumers feel valued and encourage repeated interaction, strengthening their connection to the brand over time (Vázquez et al., 2014). This targeted approach maximizes satisfaction and drives sustained engagement.

AI's Influence on Brand Loyalty

Digital marketers use AI to create marketing and consumer engagement strategies that promote brand loyalty. For instance, Li and You (2021) found that big data and machine learning algorithms can be used to extract valuable insights used to measure brand loyalty. Such insights can then be applied in decision-making and strategizing to improve customer relationships and trust. This section summarizes other findings on the various ways marketers can use AI to improve brand loyalty:

Personalization and Loyalty

AI-driven personalization delivers individualized experiences that resonate with consumers. AI tools facilitate the analysis of behavioral and demographic data, which is then used to customize interactions, product recommendations, and marketing messages to align with specific consumer preferences (Banik et al., 2024; Sachar et al., 2022). This tailored approach makes customers feel valued and understood, enhancing their emotional connection to the brand. When consumers consistently experience relevant and meaningful interactions, they are more likely to develop a sense of loyalty (Ifekanandu et al., 2023). Personalization results in repeat purchases and reinforces trust, ensuring consumers view the brand as attentive and aligned with their needs.

AI in Loyalty Programs

AI transforms traditional loyalty programs by enabling adaptive strategies that better cater to consumer behavior and preferences. Kushnarevych and Kollárová (2024) indicate that AI can identify trends through real-time data analysis, predict rewards that resonate with customers, and personalize program offerings. For instance, AI-driven loyalty programs can provide individualized discounts, tier upgrades, or reward recommendations based on past purchases and engagement patterns (Meftah et al., 2024). In addition, Menidjel et al. (2022) found that AI streamlines the program experience, offering automated points tracking, reminders, and reward redemptions. These enhancements ensure that loyalty programs remain engaging and relevant, encouraging long-term consumer commitment and enhancing the brand's overall value proposition.

Predictive Analytics for Loyalty

Predictive analytics empowers brands to proactively strengthen loyalty by anticipating consumer needs and preferences. Using advanced AI algorithms, brands can analyze historical data to predict future behaviors, such as product interests, preferred engagement channels, and potential churn risks (Shukla et al., 2024). Brands acting on these insights can implement targeted strategies to keep consumers engaged, such as offering personalized discounts or preemptive support (Peng et al., 2020; Tian et al., 2018). This forward-looking approach enhances the consumer experience and reinforces trust and satisfaction since customers feel the brand understands their unique needs (Zuo et al., 2017). Predictive analytics thus serves as a critical tool for cultivating lasting loyalty.

Customer Retention Strategies

AI significantly enhances customer retention strategies by identifying patterns indicative of disengagement and implementing timely interventions. For instance, AI identifies at-risk customers and triggers proactive retention efforts by analyzing consumer data, such as declining purchase frequency or reduced engagement (Al-ghizzawi, 2024). Brands can then deploy targeted campaigns, offering incentives like discounts, exclusive offers, or personalized outreach to rekindle interest. AI also allows for continuous monitoring and adaptation of retention strategies, ensuring they remain effective in dynamic market conditions (Banytė et al., 2024). This proactive approach reduces churn and reinforces consumer trust and satisfaction since consumers perceive the brand as attentive to their needs (Chatterjee et al., 2024; Wang et al., 2023). Retention strategies powered by AI ensure sustained consumer loyalty.

Feedback Loops

AI facilitates robust feedback loops by automating the collection, analysis, and implementation of consumer insights. Using tools like sentiment analysis, customer reviews, and surveys, AI categorizes feedback to identify emerging trends, pinpoint satisfaction drivers, and highlight areas for improvement (Aydin & Silahtaroglu, 2021; Sanchez-Nunez et al., 2020). Unlike traditional feedback mechanisms, AI processes vast amounts of data in real time, enabling brands to respond quickly to consumer concerns (Dwivedi et al., 2021). For example, AI can detect a recurring issue in product reviews and recommend corrective actions, ensuring consumers see their input as valued (Exenberger & Bucko, 2020). Brands demonstrate responsiveness and reliability by actively incorporating feedback into product or service enhancements, strengthening consumer trust and long-term loyalty.

Brand Differentiation

AI empowers brands to differentiate themselves in competitive markets by delivering unique, innovative consumer experiences. Brands can leverage AI-driven technologies, such as hyper-personalization, immersive virtual assistants, or real-time dynamic pricing, to create distinctive offerings that captivate consumers (Chen et al., 2024; Sivarethinamohan, 2023). For instance, a retail brand might use AI to provide a fully personalized shopping experience, including tailored recommendations and curated content (Su, 2018). This level of customization enhances consumer satisfaction and sets the brand apart as a leader in innovation (Gao, 2023). Differentiation through AI solidifies a brand's reputation as forward-thinking and consumer-focused, which appeals to modern audiences and fosters lasting loyalty in an increasingly competitive business environment.

Consistency Across Channels

AI enhances brand loyalty by ensuring a consistent experience across multiple consumer touchpoints. With the growing importance of omnichannel marketing, brands must provide a unified experience whether consumers interact via websites, mobile apps, social media, or in-store (Sharma et al., 2017). Zehmakan (2021) explains that AI technologies like machine learning and natural language processing enable brands to deliver consistent messaging, offers, and customer support across all platforms. They can utilize AI to track consumer behavior across channels to maintain interaction continuity (Shameem et al., 2023). This ensures that customers receive personalized experiences regardless of the platform they engage with. The consistency enhances the customer experience and reinforces brand reliability, building trust and deepening consumer loyalty over time.

Ethical Considerations Associated with AI Use in Digital Marketing

The rapid integration of AI in digital marketing presents numerous opportunities for innovation and enhanced brand loyalty and consumer engagement. However, Su et al. (2023) indicate that its widespread use also raises critical ethical concerns that marketers and businesses must address. For instance, deploying AI technologies in consumer interactions, data collection, and personalization often intersects with fundamental ethical principles such as privacy, autonomy, and transparency. This section explores three primary ethical challenges that emerge from using AI in digital marketing: data privacy, customer manipulation, and authenticity.

Data Privacy

Data privacy is one of the critical ethical concerns surrounding AI in digital marketing. AI relies heavily on vast consumer data to personalize experiences, predict behaviors, and optimize marketing strategies (Benjelloun & Kabak, 2024). This data can include sensitive personal information such as browsing habits, purchasing history, and location tracking. While this data allows brands to deliver tailored content and improve customer engagement, it also creates significant privacy risks (Li et al., 2016; Moreno-Sandoval et al., 2018). Consumers may be unaware of the extent to which their personal information is being collected, stored, and analyzed, leading to concerns about unauthorized access and misuse of their data. In addition, breaches in data security or the use of data without explicit consent can lead to legal and reputational repercussions for companies (Buhas et al., 2024). As data collection practices grow more invasive, the ethical dilemma of balancing personalized marketing with consumer privacy remains a persistent issue. This creates distrust between consumers and brands.

Customer Manipulation

AI technologies in digital marketing can potentially influence consumer behavior in ways that raise ethical concerns about manipulation. By leveraging predictive analytics, machine learning, and personalized targeting, AI can identify vulnerabilities in consumer decision-making (Taqwa et al., 2016). These can then be used to subtly guide them toward taking specific actions, such as purchasing or engaging with a certain brand (Cheredniakova et al., 2021). While this is a standard practice in digital marketing, the ethical challenge arises when AI manipulates consumers into making decisions that may not be in their best interest. For example, AI can target vulnerable populations with ads for products not aligned with their needs or financial situation, or it can create a sense of urgency by exploiting consumers' emotional triggers, such as using scarcity tactics to drive impulsive buying (Liciotti et al., 2017). This type of manipulation undermines consumer autonomy by exploiting personal data and emotional responses to influence decisions without the consumer's full awareness or consent (Kumar et al., 2024; Majeed & Kim, 2024). As AI systems become more sophisticated, the line between persuasive marketing and unethical manipulation continues to blur, making it a key concern for businesses and regulators.

Authenticity

Another ethical challenge associated with AI in digital marketing is the issue of authenticity. As AI-driven tools, such as chatbots, virtual assistants, and AI-generated content, become more prevalent, there is growing concern over the authenticity of consumer interactions with brands (Pedersen & Ritter, 2024; Pilone et al., 2023). AI can create the illusion of human-like engagement, but these interactions may not reflect the true values or intentions of the brand. For example, when a chatbot is programmed to provide overly polished or overly empathetic responses, consumers may feel deceived into thinking they are communicating with a real person who understands their needs when in fact they are interacting with a machine (Kirk & Givi, 2025). This lack of transparency can erode trust since consumers may feel manipulated or misled by AI-driven content.

Using AI to generate content such as reviews or testimonials raises questions about the authenticity of brand communications. If consumers cannot distinguish between human-generated and AI-generated content, it becomes difficult for them to assess the credibility of the information they encounter (Wei et al., 2020; Qazi et al., 2014). This situation can lead to potential distrust in the brand. The ethical concern in this regard is whether brands are honest and transparent about using AI and maintaining genuine connections with their audience.

CONCLUSION

The use of artificial intelligence (AI) in digital marketing has revolutionized how brands interact with consumers, offering personalized, dynamic, and highly responsive engagement strategies. As AI continues to evolve, its integration into digital marketing practices has facilitated more efficient consumer targeting, enhanced personalization, and deeper insights into consumer behavior. Key technologies like chatbots, recommendation engines, and predictive analytics have transformed customer interactions by providing tailored experiences that support connections between consumers and brands. AI's ability to engage consumers in real time and through interactive, customized experiences has significantly increased customer engagement. This allows brands to create personalized journeys that align closely with individual consumer preferences. In addition, AI-driven innovations, such as anthropomorphism in AI systems, have enabled brands to humanize their digital interactions, building emotional connections and enhancing consumer trust.

As AI reshapes consumer engagement, it has also profoundly impacted brand loyalty. For instance, AI's capacity for personalization extends to loyalty programs, where it allows businesses to offer individualized rewards and anticipate consumer needs. Predictive analytics further strengthens brand loyalty by enabling companies to foresee customer behavior and proactively address their needs, thus enhancing retention. AI-driven feedback loops and consistency across multiple channels ensure that brands maintain a cohesive relationship with their consumers. These activities ensure continued loyalty through reliable and personalized experiences. Moreover, AI's role in differentiating brands through tailored marketing and loyalty strategies further solidifies consumer commitment to specific brands, reinforcing long-term relationships.

However, the rapid adoption of AI in digital marketing comes with significant ethical considerations that require careful attention. For instance, data privacy remains a primary concern. The collection of vast amounts of personal data for AI-powered targeting raises issues of consumer consent and security. AI also introduces the potential for customer manipulation, where consumers may be subtly influenced toward decisions that are not in their best interest. This challenges ethical boundaries in marketing. The authenticity of AI-driven interactions is another ethical issue. Brands may use AI to create misleading impressions of human engagement, potentially eroding consumer trust. Addressing these ethical challenges is crucial for ensuring that AI is used responsibly and transparently in digital marketing.

The influence of Artificial Intelligence on consumer engagement and brand loyalty in digital marketing has been extensively researched, revealing multifaceted impacts across personalization, predictive analytics, and interactive user experiences.

Key Contributions to Theory and Practice: (i) Personalized Marketing Strategies - AI-driven tools like recommendation engines and chatbots enable brands to provide tailored content and adaptive suggestions, enhancing consumer satisfaction and brand loyalty; (ii) Predictive Analytics for Loyalty Programs - Predictive modeling powered by AI improves the efficiency of loyalty programs by identifying customer retention patterns and designing targeted incentives. This results in higher engagement and long-term brand commitment; (iii) Enhanced Consumer Interaction - Chatbots and AI-based customer service agents, such as those using generative AI models like ChatGPT, provide 24/7 support, fostering deeper consumer trust and repeat interactions; AI in Social Media Marketing - AI's role in managing social media campaigns, including sentiment analysis and targeted advertisements, helps brands engage consumers more effectively, building a strong brand equity foundation; (iv) Customer Trust and Brand Loyalty - Studies highlight trust as a critical mediator between AI-driven engagement strategies and brand loyalty. The implementation of transparent and ethical AI systems further strengthens customer relationships; (v) Multichannel AI Strategies - Integrating AI across various marketing channels (email, mobile apps, social media) optimizes outreach, creating cohesive customer experiences that reinforce loyalty; (vi) Impact on Sales Dynamics - AI applications in personalized promotions and real-time offers increase sales efficiency and customer retention rates, particularly in highly competitive digital marketplaces; (vii) Challenges and Ethical Considerations - Ethical use of AI, including transparency in algorithmic decisions, is essential for sustaining consumer trust and loyalty in the long term. Studies emphasize the need for responsible AI deployment in marketing practices.

These findings highlight that while AI significantly enhances consumer engagement and brand loyalty, successful implementation requires balancing technological innovation with ethical and strategic considerations.

The future directions for investigating the influence of Artificial Intelligence (AI) on consumer engagement and brand loyalty in digital marketing span across technological, behavioral, and ethical dimensions: (i) Developing AI models capable of creating ultra-personalized experiences by integrating cross-platform data, such as real-time behavioral inputs, wearable tech data, and geolocation insights. Investigating how AI-driven systems can adapt to changes in consumer preferences over time to maintain relevance and loyalty; (ii) Exploring the role of emotion-recognition technologies in understanding consumer sentiments and their impact on brand loyalty. Behavioral Predictive Modeling: Examining how AI can predict shifts in consumer moods and preferences to tailor engagement strategies accordingly; (iii) Investigating how AI can enhance loyalty programs through gamification strategies, such as real-time progress updates, tailored rewards, and predictive leveling systems. Sustainability of Gamified Loyalty: Exploring whether AI-enabled gamification maintains long-term loyalty or merely generates short-term engagement spikes.

By examining these areas, researchers can better understand and harness the potential of AI in digital marketing to foster long-term, meaningful consumer relationships while addressing ethical and societal challenges.

ACKNOWLEDGEMENT

We want to express gratitude to the Editor and the Arbitrators. They offered precious suggestions or improvements. The GOVCOPP Research Center of the University of Aveiro and UNIDCOM supported the authors.

REFERENCES

Abdelkader, O. A. (2023). ChatGPT's influence on customer experience in digital marketing: Investigating the moderating roles. Heliyon, 9(8 C7 - e18770). https://doi.org/DOI: 10.1016/j.heliyon.2023.e18770

Albinali, E. A., & Hamdan, A. (2021). *The Implementation of artificial intelligence in social media marketing and its impact on consumer behavior: evidence from Bahrain*. Lecture Notes in Networks and Systems., DOI: 10.1007/978-3-030-69221-6_58

Alghizzawi, M. (2024). A review of the Chat GBT technology role in marketing research. In *Studies in Big Data* (Vol. 144, pp. 497–507). Springer Science and Business Media Deutschland GmbH., DOI: 10.1007/978-3-031-52280-2_31

Alizadeh, H., & Nazarpour Kashani, H. (2024). The impact of perceived experience with ChatGPT on online consumers' information searching behavior: An empirical study of Iranian college students. *Asia Pacific Journal of Marketing and Logistics*. Advance online publication. DOI: 10.1108/APJML-02-2024-0140

Armutcu, B., Tan, A., Ho, S. P. S., Chow, M. Y. C., & Gleason, K. C. (2024). The effect of bank artificial intelligence on consumer purchase intentions. *Kybernetes*. Advance online publication. DOI: 10.1108/K-01-2024-0145

Aydin, G., & Silahtaroglu, G. (2021). Insights into mobile health application market via a content analysis of marketplace data with machine learning. PLoS ONE, 16(1 January C7 - e0244302). https://doi.org/DOI: 10.1371/journal.pone.0244302

Baas, J., Schotten, M., Plume, A., Côté, G., & Karimi, R. (2020). Scopus as a curated, high-quality bibliometric data source for academic research in quantitative science studies. *Quantitative Science Studies*, *1*(1), 377–386. DOI: 10.1162/qss_a_00019

Bacilieri, C. (2019). Online insurance and locus of control. *Micro and Macro Marketing*, (3), 591–607. DOI: 10.1431/95044

Bag, S., Srivastava, G., Bashir, M. M. A., Kumari, S., Giannakis, M., & Chowdhury, A. H. (2022). Journey of customers in this digital era: Understanding the role of artificial intelligence technologies in user engagement and conversion. *Benchmarking*, *29*(7), 2074–2098. DOI: 10.1108/BIJ-07-2021-0415

Banik, B., Banik, S., & Annee, R. R. (2024). AI-driven strategies for enhancing customer loyalty and engagement through personalization and predictive analytics. *International Journal of Machine Learning Research in Cybersecurity and Artificial Intelligence*, *15*(1), 416–447. http://ijmlrcai.com/index.php/Journal/article/view/133/124

Banytė, J., Lindžiuvienė, J., & Dargytė, G. (2024). *What factors determine the consumer acceptance of AI-based services? the case of Lithuanian consumers*. Smart Innovation, Systems and Technologies.

Benjelloun, A., & Kabak, S. (2024). *Ethical challenges and managerial implications of artificial intelligence in digital marketing*. Lecture Notes in Networks and Systems.

Biswas, B., & Sanyal, M. K. (2019). Soft intelligence approaches for selecting products in online market. Proceedings of the 9th International Conference On Cloud Computing, Data Science and Engineering, Confluence 2019 C7 – 8776921.

Buhas, V., Ponomarenko, I., Buhas, N., & Hulak, H. (2024). Cybersecurity Role in AI-Powered Digital Marketing. *CEUR Workshop Proceedings*.

Chatterjee, J., Guha Neogi, S., & Saraswat, S. (2024). *Consumer perspectives for purchase intentions of online pharmacy products using generative artificial intelligence*. Lecture Notes in Networks and Systems.

Chen, J., Zhang, Y., & Wu, Y. (2024). The impact of differential pricing subject on consumer behavior. BMC Psychology, 12(1 C7 - 431). https://doi.org/DOI: 10.1186/s40359-024-01928-x

Chen, Y., Prentice, C., Weaven, S., & Hisao, A. (2022). The influence of customer trust and artificial intelligence on customer engagement and loyalty–The case of the home-sharing industry. *Frontiers in Psychology*, *13*, 912339. DOI: 10.3389/fpsyg.2022.912339 PMID: 35992434

Cheredniakova, A., Lobodenko, L., & Lychagina, I. (2021). A Study of advertising content in digital communications: the experience of applying neuromarketing and traditional techniques. Proceedings of the 2021 Communication Strategies in Digital Society Seminar, ComSDS 2021 C7 - 9422887.

Chica, M., Cordon, O., Robles, J. F., Garrido, A., Mingot, J., & Damas, S. (2023). Zio: an artificial intelligence digital twin to build virtual markets. Proceedings - 2023 IEEE Conference on Artificial Intelligence, CAI 2023, Chintalapati, S., & Pandey, S. K. (2022). Artificial intelligence in marketing: A systematic literature review. *International Journal of Market Research, 64*(1), 38–68. DOI: 10.1177/14707853211018428

Cooter, R. D., & Gilbert, M. (2022). Theory of delegation. In *Public Law and Economics* (pp. 265–304). Academic., DOI: 10.1093/oso/9780197655870.003.0008

Davis, J. L., Love, T. P., & Fares, P. (2019). Collective social identity: Synthesizing identity theory and social identity theory using digital data. *Social Psychology Quarterly, 82*(3), 254–273. DOI: 10.1177/0190272519851025

Davis, N., & Jin, J. (2024). Beyond code: Consumer response to chatbots. *Current Opinion in Psychology, 58*, C7–C101841. DOI: 10.1016/j.copsyc.2024.101841 PMID: 38981369

Dong, H. (2023). Research Progress and Review on Service Interaction between Intelligent Service Robots and Customers. Proceedings - 2023 International Conference on Service Robotics, ICoSR 2023, Dwivedi, Y. K., Ismagilova, E., Hughes, D. L., Carlson, J., Filieri, R., Jacobson, J.,...Wang, Y. (2021). Setting the future of digital and social media marketing research: Perspectives and research propositions. *International Journal of Information Management, 59*, C7–C102168. DOI: 10.1016/j.ijinfomgt.2020.102168

Egieya, Z. E., Ewuga, S. K., Adegbite, A. O., & Oke, T. T. (2023). The role of virtual and augmented reality in modern marketing: A critical review. *Computer Science & IT Research Journal, 4*(3), 244–272. DOI: 10.51594/csitrj.v4i3.660

Exenberger, E., & Bucko, J. (2020). Analysis of Online Consumer Behavior - Design of CRISP-DM Process Model. *AGRIS On-Line Papers in Economics and Informatics, 12*(3), 13–22. DOI: 10.7160/AOL.2020.120302

Fernández-Rovira, C., Álvarez Valdés, J., Molleví, G., & Nicolas-Sans, R. (2021). The digital transformation of business. Towards the datafication of the relationship with customers. *Technological Forecasting and Social Change, 162*, C7–C120339. DOI: 10.1016/j.techfore.2020.120339

Fukui, Y., & Tabata, T. (2024). Prediction of Consumer Purchases in a Session on an EC Site Considering the Variety of Past Browsing. Lecture Notes in Computer Science (including subseries Lecture Notes in Artificial Intelligence and Lecture Notes in Bioinformatics), Gans, J. S. (2023). Artificial intelligence adoption in a competitive market. *Economica, 90*(358), 690–705. DOI: 10.1111/ecca.12458

Gao, X. (2023). KNN-based Precision Marketing Data Mining Algorithm for E-business Platform. Proceedings - 2023 International Conference on Networking, Informatics and Computing, ICNETIC 2023.

Gkikas, D. C., & Theodoridis, P. K. (2022). AI in Consumer Behavior. In Learning and Analytics in Intelligent Systems (Vol. 22, pp. 147-176). Springer Nature. https://doi.org/DOI: 10.1007/978-3-030-80571-5_10

Gupta, R., Umang, P., & Gupta, S. (2024). *Artificial Intelligence and Its Application in Marketing*. Lecture Notes in Mechanical Engineering.

Haddaway, N. R., Page, M. J., Pritchard, C. C., & McGuinness, L. A. (2022). PRISMA2020: An R package and Shiny app for producing PRISMA 2020-compliant flow diagrams, with interactivity for optimised digital transparency and Open Synthesis. *Campbell Systematic Reviews*, *18*(2), e1230. DOI: 10.1002/cl2.1230 PMID: 36911350

Ifekanandu, C. C., Anene, J. N., Iloka, C. B., & Ewuzie, C. O. (2023). Influence of artificial intelligence (AI) on customer experience and loyalty: Mediating role of personalization. *Journal of Data Acquisition and Processing*, *38*(3), 1936. DOI: 10.5281/zenodo.98549423

Ilapakurti, A., Vuppalapati, J. S., Kedari, S., Vuppalapati, R., & Vuppalapati, C. (2018a). Adaptive edge analytics for creating memorable customer experience and venue brand engagement, a scented case for Smart Cities. 2017 IEEE SmartWorld Ubiquitous Intelligence and Computing, Advanced and Trusted Computed, Scalable Computing and Communications, Cloud and Big Data Computing, Internet of People and Smart City Innovation SmartWorld/SCALCOM/UIC/ATC/CBDCom/IOP/SCI 2017 - Conference Proceedings.

Ilapakurti, A., Vuppalapati, J. S., Kedari, S., Vuppalapati, R., & Vuppalapati, C. (2018b). *AI infused fragrance systems for creating memorable customer experience and venue brand engagement*. Advances in Intelligent Systems and Computing.

Imanova, G. E., & Imanova, G. (2021). Digital Marketing Technologies Selection Under Z-Environment. Advances in Intelligent Systems and Computing, Jayashree, S., Sidana, N., Pham, L. T., Kunju, L. M., Ratnavalli, B., & Gangodkar, D. (2022). The Progressive Role of Machine learning in Enhancing the Effectiveness of Digital Marketing in Emerging Economies. 2022 2nd International Conference on Advance Computing and Innovative Technologies in Engineering, ICACITE 2022.

Kachamas, P. (2016). Shaping interactive marketing communication (IMC) through social media analytics and modelling. Lecture Notes in Computer Science (including subseries Lecture Notes in Artificial Intelligence and Lecture Notes in Bioinformatics), Kaponis, A., & Maragoudakis, M. (2022). Data Analysis in Digital Marketing using Machine learning and Artificial Intelligence Techniques, Ethical and Legal Dimensions, State of the Art. ACM International Conference Proceeding Series C7 – 15.

Kirk, C. P., & Givi, J. (2025). The AI-authorship effect: Understanding authenticity, moral disgust, and consumer responses to AI-generated marketing communications. *Journal of Business Research*, *186*, 114984.

Kothari, B., & Mani, A. P. (2024). AI-enabled identification of consumer's purchase intention with a practical implementation through analysis of review comments in real time. Multidisciplinary Science Journal, 6(11 C7 - e2024244). https://doi.org/ DOI: 10.31893/multiscience.2024244

Kumar, V., Ashraf, A. R., & Nadeem, W. (2024). AI-powered marketing: What, where, and how? *International Journal of Information Management*, *77*, C7–C102783. DOI: 10.1016/j.ijinfomgt.2024.102783

Kushnarevych, A., & Kollárová, D. (2024, September). The Possibilities of Artificial Intelligence Usage in Loyalty Programs. In *European Conference on Innovation and Entrepreneurship* (Vol. 19, No. 1, pp. 384-390).

Laszkiewicz, A., & Kalinska-Kula, M. (2023). Virtual influencers as an emerging marketing theory: A systematic literature review. *International Journal of Consumer Studies*, *47*(6), 2479–2494. DOI: 10.1111/ijcs.12956

Lei, W., Yikai, Y., Jiehui, Z., & Xiaoyi, W. (2020). Predicting consumer behavior in the perspective of consumer neuroscience: Status, challenge, and future. *Guanli Gongcheng Xuebao*, *34*(6), 1–12. DOI: 10.13587/j.cnki.jieem.2020.06.001

Li, M., & Suh, A. (2021, January). Machinelike or humanlike? A literature review of anthropomorphism in AI-enabled technology. In 54th Hawaii international conference on system sciences (HICSS 2021) (pp. 4053-4062).

Li, Y., Murali, P., Shao, N., & Sheopuri, A. (2016). Applying Data Mining Techniques to Direct Marketing: Challenges and Solutions. Proceedings - 15th IEEE International Conference on Data Mining Workshop, ICDMW 2015 C7 – 7395688.

Li, Y., & You, C. (2021). Brand Loyalty Measurement Model Based on Machine Learning Clustering Algorithm. *Journal of Physics: Conference Series*.

Liciotti, D., Frontoni, E., Mancini, A., & Zingaretti, P. (2017). Pervasive system for consumer behaviour analysis in retail environments. Lecture Notes in Computer Science (including subseries Lecture Notes in Artificial Intelligence and Lecture Notes in Bioinformatics).

Ling, C. Y., & Che, H. Y. (2021). A study on the establishing data on consumer behavior and lifestyle of singles. *ACM International Conference Proceeding Series*.

Liu, S., Aw, E. C. X., Tan, G. W. H., & Ooi, K. B. (2023). Virtual Influencers as the Next Generation of Influencer Marketing: Identifying Antecedents and Consequences. In Studies in Computational Intelligence (Vol. 1128, pp. 23-39). Springer Science and Business Media Deutschland GmbH. https://doi.org/DOI: 10.1007/978-3-031-48397-4_2

Ltifi, M. (2023). Impact of the E-brand on the Consumer's E-trust, Reliance and Resistance Towards the Chatbot. In Springer Series in Design and Innovation (Vol. 32, pp. 267-292). Springer Nature. https://doi.org/DOI: 10.1007/978-3-031-35385-7_16

Lu, T., & Boutilier, C. (2015). Value-directed compression of large-scale assignment problems. *Proceedings of the National Conference on Artificial Intelligence*.

Majeed, S., & Kim, W. G. (2024). Antecedents and consequences of conceptualizing online hyperconnected brand selection. *Journal of Consumer Marketing*, *41*(3), 328–339. DOI: 10.1108/JCM-08-2023-6193

Manca, F., D'Uggento, A. M., & Convertini, N. (2018). Customer segmentation through multiple correspondence analysis. 2018 110th AEIT International Annual Conference, AEIT 2018 C7 - 8577279, Meepung, T., & Kannikar, P. (2022). Artificial Intelligence for Digital Business Performance. 7th International Conference on Digital Arts, Media and Technology, DAMT 2022 and 5th ECTI Northern Section Conference on Electrical, Electronics, Computer and Telecommunications Engineering, NCON 2022, Meftah, M., Ounacer, S., & Azzouazi, M. (2024). Enhancing Customer Engagement in Loyalty Programs Through AI-Powered Market Basket Prediction Using Machine Learning Algorithms. In Engineering Applications of Artificial Intelligence (pp. 319-338). Cham: Springer Nature Switzerland.

Menidjel, C., Hollebeek, L. D., Leppiman, A., & Riivits-Arkonsuo, I. (2022). Role of AI in enhancing customer engagement, loyalty and loyalty programme performance. In *Handbook of Research on Customer Loyalty* (pp. 316–331). Edward Elgar Publishing.

Mittal, T., Dhiman, A., Singh, V. V., Gupta, A. K., & Kedia, N. (2023). Delving The Role Of Artificial Intelligence-Driven Advertisements On Purchase Intention Of Omnichannel Customers Using SEM. 2023 4th International Conference on Computation, Automation and Knowledge Management, ICCAKM 2023, Moreno-Sandoval, L. G., Sánchez-Barriga, C., Buitrago, K. E., Pomares-Quimbaya, A., & Garcia, J. C. (2018). Spanish Twitter data used as a source of information about consumer food choice. Lecture Notes in Computer Science (including subseries Lecture Notes in Artificial Intelligence and Lecture Notes in Bioinformatics), Motamedi, R. (2024). Integrating Artificial Intelligence and Multichannel Marketing Strategies: Impacts on Consumer Engagement and Brand Loyalty. Business, Marketing, and Finance Open, 1(5), 1-14. https://doi.org/DOI: 10.1111/ijcs.13027

Mueller, S. T. (2020). Cognitive anthropomorphism of AI: How humans and computers classify images. *Ergonomics in Design*, *28*(3), 12–19.

National Qualifications Register. (n.d.). Evidence of need for skilling in the areas of artificial intelligence and machine learning. https://nqr.gov.in/sites/default/files/Annexure%20B_Evidence%20of%20Need.pdf

Olan, F., Suklan, J., Arakpogun, E. O., & Robson, A. (2024). Advancing Consumer Behavior: The Role of Artificial Intelligence Technologies and Knowledge Sharing. *IEEE Transactions on Engineering Management*, *71*, 13227–13239. DOI: 10.1109/TEM.2021.3083536

Papavasileiou, V., & Tsadiras, A. (2011). Time variations of association rules in market basket analysis. *IFIP Advances in Information and Communication Technology*.

Patil, B., Ashok, P., & Chirputkar, A. (2024). Artificial Intelligence Powered Paradigm Shift: Revolutionizing Digital Marketing. 4th International Conference on Innovative Practices in Technology and Management 2024, ICIPTM 2024

Pedersen, C. L., & Ritter, T. (2024). Digital authenticity: Towards a research agenda for the AI-driven fifth phase of digitalization in business-to-business marketing. *Industrial Marketing Management*, *123*, 162–172. DOI: 10.1016/j.indmarman.2024.10.005

Peng, C. C., Wang, Y. Z., & Huang, C. W. (2020). Artificial-Neural-Network-Based Consumer Behavior Prediction: A Survey. 2nd IEEE Eurasia Conference on Biomedical Engineering, Healthcare and Sustainability 2020, ECBIOS 2020 C7 - 9203699

Perez-Vega, R., Kaartemo, V., Lages, C. R., Razavi, N. B., & Männistö, J. (2021). Reshaping the contexts of online customer engagement behavior via artificial intelligence: A conceptual framework. *Journal of Business Research*, *129*, 902–910.

Pilone, V., Di Pasquale, A., & Stasi, A. (2023). Consumer Preferences for Craft Beer by Means of Artificial Intelligence: Are Italian Producers Doing Well? Beverages, 9(1 C7 - 26). https://doi.org/DOI: 10.3390/beverages9010026

Placani, A. (2024). Anthropomorphism in AI: Hype and fallacy. *AI and Ethics*, •••, 1–8. DOI: 10.1007/s43681-024-00419-4

Poornima, N., Sridharan, C., Pavithra, A., Narendiran, R., Vijay, B., & Neelesh, V. S. (2024). Recommender Systems for Personalized Business Marketing: Employing Artificial Intelligence and Business Intelligence in Machine Learning Techniques. Lecture Notes in Electrical Engineering, Qazi, A., Raj, R. G., Tahir, M., Cambria, E., & Syed, K. B. S. (2014). Enhancing business intelligence by means of suggestive reviews. *TheScientificWorldJournal, 2014*, C7–C879323. DOI: 10.1155/2014/879323

Ramirez, M., Khalil, M. A., Can, J., & George, K. (2022). Classification of 'Like' and 'Dislike' Decisions from EEG and fNIRS Signals Using a LSTM Based Deep Learning Network. 2022 IEEE World AI IoT Congress, AIIoT 2022

Rane, N. (2023). Enhancing customer loyalty through Artificial Intelligence (AI), Internet of Things (IoT), and Big Data technologies: improving customer satisfaction, engagement, relationship, and experience. Internet of Things (IoT), and Big Data Technologies: Improving Customer Satisfaction, Engagement, Relationship, and Experience (October 13, 2023). http://dx.doi.org/DOI: 10.2139/ssrn.4616051

Ricci, F., Shapira, B., & Rokach, L. (2015). *Recommender systems handbook* (2nd ed.). Springer US., DOI: 10.1007/978-1-4899-7637-6

Rohden, S. F., & Espartel, L. B. (2024). Consumer reactions to technology in retail: Choice uncertainty and reduced perceived control in decisions assisted by recommendation agents. *Electronic Commerce Research*, *24*(2), 901–923. DOI: 10.1007/s10660-024-09808-7

Rosário, A., & Dias, J. (2024). Exploring the Landscape of Smart Tourism: A Systematic Bibliometric Review of Internet of Things Literature. *Administrative Sciences*, *14*(22), 22. DOI: 10.3390/admsci14020022

Rosário, A., Moreira, C., & Macedo, P. (2021). Competitive dynamics of strategic groups in the Portuguese banking Industry, Cuadernos de Gestión, 21(2), 1-15. ISSN: 1131-6837. DOI: <ALIGNMENT.qj></ALIGNMENT>10.5295/cdg.180975ac

Rosário, A. T., Fernandes, F., Raimundo, R. G., & Cruz, R. N. (2021). Determinants of Nascent Entrepreneurship Development. In Carrizo Moreira, A., & Dantas, J. G. (Eds.), *Handbook of Research on Nascent Entrepreneurship and Creating New Ventures* (pp. 172–193). IGI Global., DOI: 10.4018/978-1-7998-4826-4.ch008

Sachar, M., Xiong, M., & Lee, K. C. (2022). Consumer preferences of top-rated over-the-counter acne treatment products: A cohort study. *Archives of Dermatological Research, 314*(8), 815–821. DOI: 10.1007/s00403-021-02230-1 PMID: 33866436

Said, L. B., Bouron, T., & Drogoul, A. (2002). Agent-based interaction analysis of consumer behavior. *Proceedings of the International Conference on Autonomous Agents.*

Salles, A., Evers, K., & Farisco, M. (2020). Anthropomorphism in AI. *AJOB Neuroscience, 11*(2), 88–95. DOI: 10.1080/21507740.2020.1740350 PMID: 32228388

Sanchez-Nunez, P., Cobo, M. J., Heras-Pedrosa, C. D. L., Pelaez, J. I., & Herrera-Viedma, E. (2020). Opinion Mining, Sentiment Analysis and Emotion Understanding in Advertising: A Bibliometric Analysis. IEEE Access, 8 C7 - 9141266, 134563-134576. https://doi.org/DOI: 10.1109/ACCESS.2020.3009482

Santos, S., & Gonçalves, H. M. (2021). The consumer decision journey: A literature review of the foundational models and theories and a future perspective. *Technological Forecasting and Social Change, 173*, C7–C121117. DOI: 10.1016/j.techfore.2021.121117

Saraiva Gonçalves, C., Souza Carneiro, J. D. D., Abadia Reis Rocha, R., & Carvalho de Rezende, D. (2020). The impact of varying educational intervention on consumer understanding and attitude toward reducing sodium in food: Implications for marketing strategies. Journal of Sensory Studies, 35(2 C7 - e12558). https://doi.org/DOI: 10.1111/joss.12558

Shameem, A., Ramachandran, K. K., Sharma, A., Singh, R., Selvaraj, F. J., & Manoharan, G. (2023). The Rising Importance of AI in Boosting the Efficiency of Online Advertising in Developing Countries. 2023 3rd International Conference on Advance Computing and Innovative Technologies in Engineering, ICACITE 2023.

Sharma, S., Sharma, A., Sharma, Y., & Bhatia, M. (2017). Recommender system using hybrid approach. Proceeding - IEEE International Conference on Computing, Communication and Automation, ICCCA 2016 C7 - 7813722

Shukla, R. P., Juneja, D., & Monga, S. (2024). *Predictive Analytics in Marketing Using Artificial Intelligence*. Lecture Notes in Networks and Systems.

Siva Balan, R. V., & Kalpana, P. (2023). The role of big data in predicting consumer behavior. In *Big Data: A Road-Map for Successful Digital Marketing* (pp. 111–132). Nova Science Publishers, Inc.

Sivarethinamohan, R. (2023). Exploring the Transformation of digital tourism: trends, impacts, and future prospects. *2023 International Conference on Digital Applications, Transformation and Economy, ICDATE 2023.*

Sleiman, R., Nguyen, Q. T., Lacaze, S., Tran, K. P., & Thomassey, S. (2024). Evaluating the sales potential of new products using machine learning techniques and data collected from mobile applications. *International Journal of Clothing Science and Technology*, *36*(3), 454–473. DOI: 10.1108/IJCST-07-2023-0099

Srivastava, R., Gupta, P., Kumar, H., & Tuli, N. (2023). Digital customer engagement: A systematic literature review and research agenda. *Australian Journal of Management*. Advance online publication. DOI: 10.1177/03128962231177096

Su, Q. (2018). Research on influencing factors of consumer behavior based on Wechat Stores. *ACM International Conference Proceeding Series*

Su, Y., Wang, E., & Berthon, P. (2023). Ethical Marketing AI? A Structured Literature Review of the Ethical Challenges Posed by Artificial Intelligence in the Domains of Marketing and Consumer Behavior. *Proceedings of the Annual Hawaii International Conference on System Sciences*

Sun, L. L. (2023). *Analysis of E-Commerce Live Broadcast Marketing Strategy Based on Big Data Algorithm*. Lecture Notes in Electrical Engineering.

Suraña-Sánchez, C., & Aramendia-Muneta, M. E. (2024). Impact of artificial intelligence on customer engagement and advertising engagement: A review and future research agenda. *International Journal of Consumer Studies*, *48*(2), e13027. DOI: 10.1111/ijcs.13027

Suzuki, R., Ishino, Y., & Takahashi, S. (2018). Characterization of consumers' behavior in medical insurance market with agent parameters' Estimation process using Bayesian network. Lecture Notes in Computer Science (including subseries Lecture Notes in Artificial Intelligence and Lecture Notes in Bioinformatics).

Taqwa, T., Suhendra, A., Hermita, M., & Darmayantie, A. (2016). Implementation of Naïve Bayes method for product purchasing decision using neural impulse actuator in neuromarketing. Proceedings of 2015 International Conference on Information and Communication Technology and Systems, ICTS 2015 C7 – 7379882.

Tian, J., Zhang, Y., & Zhang, C. (2018). Predicting consumer variety-seeking through weather data analytics. *Electronic Commerce Research and Applications*, *28*, 194–207. DOI: 10.1016/j.elerap.2018.02.001

Vázquez, S., Muñoz-García, T., Campanella, I., Poch, M., Fisas, B., Bel, N., & Andreu, G. (2014). A classification of user-generated content into consumer decision journey stages. *Neural Networks*, *58*, 68–81. DOI: 10.1016/j.neunet.2014.05.026 PMID: 24996448

Vieira, M., Santos, V., & Bacalhau, L. M. (2023). *Systematic Literature Review—Factors of Loyalty and Acceptance in Voice Commerce*. Smart Innovation, Systems and Technologies.

Vij, M., Vij, A., Kumar, P., & Shameem, B. (2024). Impact of AI-Driven Customer Insights on Brand Engagement and Loyalty in Tourism Marketing. *2nd International Conference on Cyber Resilience, ICCR 2024*

Vinaykarthik, B. C. (2022). Design of Artificial Intelligence (AI) based User Experience Websites for E-commerce Application and Future of Digital Marketing. 3rd International Conference on Smart Electronics and Communication, ICOSEC 2022 - Proceedings

Vyas, A. M. (2024). Exploring the Impact of 'Emotion-Recognition-AI' on Consumer Trust and Satisfaction. 2024 IEEE International Students' *Conference on Electrical, Electronics and Computer Science, SCEECS 2024*.

Wang, C., Liu, Y., & Zhou, H. (2023). Consumer Consumption Behavioral Model for Business Intelligence Using Artificial Intelligence. *Journal of the Knowledge Economy*. Advance online publication. DOI: 10.1007/s13132-023-01391-w

Wang, H., Wang, J., & Tang, Q. (2018). A review of application of affordance theory in information systems. *Journal of Service Science and Management*, *11*(1), 56–70. DOI: 10.4236/jssm.2018.111006

Wang, W., Li, B., Luo, X., & Wang, X. (2023). Deep Reinforcement Learning for Sequential Targeting. *Management Science*, *69*(9), 5439–5460. DOI: 10.1287/mnsc.2022.4621

Wang, Y., & Wang, H. (2022). *Reinventing the Wheel of Marketing: Assessing the Impact of Artificial Intelligence (AI) on Digital Marketing and Consumer Buying Behavior*. Lecture Notes in Electrical Engineering.

Wedel, M., Bigné, E., & Zhang, J. (2020). Virtual and augmented reality: Advancing research in consumer marketing. *International Journal of Research in Marketing*, *37*(3), 443–465.

Wei, C. S., Hsu, P. Y., Huang, C. W., Cheng, M. S., & Prassida, G. F. (2020). Devising a Cross-Domain Model to Detect Fake Review Comments. *Communications in Computer and Information Science*.

Wu, W., Wang, X., & Zhang, Y. (2024). Determinants and Effects of Digital Marketing Tools: An Affordance Lens. *SSRN*. https://dx.doi.org/DOI: 10.2139/ssrn.4827567

Xiao, Z., Qin, Y., Xu, Z., Antucheviciene, J., & Zavadskas, E. K. (2022). The Journal Buildings: A Bibliometric Analysis (2011–2021). [Academic]. *Buildings (Basel, Switzerland)*, *12*(1), 37–52. DOI: 10.3390/ buildings12010037

Yang, Y., Liu, S., Li, Y., & Jia, J. (2020). Big data marketing: Review and prospect. Xitong Gongcheng Lilun yu Shijian. *Xitong Gongcheng Lilun Yu Shijian*, *40*(8), 2150–2158. DOI: 10.12011/1000-6788-2020-1187-09

Yao, S. (2021). Method and Research of E-commerce Consumers' Purchasing Behavior Forecast and Analysis Based on Machine Learning. *ACM International Conference Proceeding Series*

Yu, X., & Huang, Y. C. (2021). Research on the consumption of different user populations. *ACM International Conference Proceeding Series*

Zaveri, B., & Amin, P. (2019). Augmented and virtual reality: Future of marketing trends. *MANTHAN: Journal of Commerce and Management*, *6*(1), 16–25.

Zehmakan, A. N. (2021). Majority opinion diffusion in social networks: an adversarial approach. *35th AAAI Conference on Artificial Intelligence, AAAI 2021*.

Zhuang, Y., Li, X., Sun, Y., & He, X. (2018). A correlation-aware ml-knn algorithm for customer value modeling in online shopping. Lecture Notes in Computer Science (including subseries Lecture Notes in Artificial Intelligence and Lecture Notes in Bioinformatics)

Ziakis, C., & Vlachopoulou, M. (2023). Artificial intelligence in digital marketing: Insights from a comprehensive review. *Information (Basel)*, *14*(12), 664. DOI: 10.3390/info14120664

Ziakis, C., & Vlachopoulou, M. (2023). Artificial Intelligence in Digital Marketing: Insights from a Comprehensive Review. Information (Switzerland), 14(12 C7 - 664). https://doi.org/DOI: 10.3390/info14120664

Zuo, Y., Yada, K., & Ali, A. B. M. S. (2017). Prediction of Consumer Purchasing in a Grocery Store Using Machine Learning Techniques. Proceedings - Asia-Pacific World Congress on Computer Science and Engineering 2016 and Asia-Pacific World Congress on Engineering 2016, APWC on CSE/APWCE 2016 C7 – 7941935

ADDITIONAL READING

Beccalli, E., Elliot, V., & Virili, F. (2020). *Artificial Intelligence and Ethics in Portfolio Management.* In *Springer Proceedings in Business and Economics*, 19-30. DOI: DOI: 10.1007/978-3-030-47355-6_2

Han, R., Lam, H. K. S., Zhan, Y., Wang, Y., Dwivedi, Y. K., & Tan, K. (2021). Artificial intelligence in business-to-business marketing: A bibliometric analysis of current research status, development, and future directions. *Industrial Management & Data Systems*, *121*(10), 2467–2497. DOI: 10.1108/imds-05-2021-0300

Hermann, E. (2021). Leveraging Artificial Intelligence in Marketing for Social Good—An Ethical Perspective. *Journal of Business Ethics*, •••, 1–19. DOI: 10.1007/s10551-021-04843-y PMID: 34054170

Mogaji, E., Soetan, T. O., & Kieu, T. (2020). The implications of artificial intelligence on the digital marketing of financial services to vulnerable customers. *Australasian Marketing Journal*, *29*(3), 235–242. DOI: 10.1016/j.ausmj.2020.05.003

Saura, J. R., Ribeiro-Soriano, D., & Palacios-Marqués, D. (2021). Setting B2B digital marketing in artificial intelligence-based CRMs: A review and directions for future research. *Industrial Marketing Management*, *98*, 161–178. DOI: 10.1016/J.INDMARMAN.2021.08.006

Shaik, M. (2023). Impact of artificial intelligence on marketing. *East Asian Journal of Multidisciplinary Research*, *2*(3). Advance online publication. DOI: 10.55927/eajmr.v2i3.3112

Stone, M., Aravopoulou, E., Ekinci, Y., Evans, G., Hobbs, M., Labib, A., Laughlin, P., & Machtynger, L. (2020). Artificial intelligence (AI) in strategic marketing decision-making: A research agenda. *The Bottom Line (New York, N.Y.)*, *33*(3), 183–200. DOI: 10.1108/bl-03-2020-0022

Vaio, A. D., Palladino, R., Hassan, R., & Escobar, O. (2020). Artificial intelligence and business models in the sustainable development goals perspective: A systematic literature review. *Journal of Business Research*, *121*, 283–314. DOI: 10.1016/J.JBUSRES.2020.08.019

Yadav, A., & Sondhi, H. (2023). *Systematic Literature Review on Sustainable Marketing and Artificial Intelligence. 2023 10th International Conference on Computing for Sustainable Global Development (INDIACom)*, 583-588. DOI: N/A. Link

KEY TERMS AND DEFINITIONS

Artificial Intelligence: is a set of technologies that enable computers to perform various advanced functions, including the ability to see, understand, and translate spoken and written language, analyse data, make recommendations, and more.

Brand Loyalty: refers to a consumer's enduring positive attitude towards a familiar brand and their commitment to consistently purchasing the brand's products and/or services despite any shortcomings, competitor actions, or shifts in the market environment.

Chatbots: a computer program that simulates husimulation with an end user.

Customer Engagement: is the way a company creates a relationship with its customer base to foster brand loyalty and awareness.

Data Analytics: converts raw data into actionable insights.

Data-Driven: a strategic concept that can be applied to any business.

Ethical: is the philosophical study of moral phenomena.

Machine Learning: is a field of study in artificial intelligence concerned with the development and study of statistical algorithms that can learn from data and generalize to unseen data, and thus perform tasks without explicit instructions.

Natural Language Processing: speech recognition, text classification, natural-language understanding, and natural-language generation.

Search Engine Optimization: is the set of strategies to enhance and improve a website's positioning on organic results pages, disregarding sponsored links on search engines, generating conversions, be they a lead, a purchase, a form submission, scheduling an appointment, or others.

Social Identity Theory: is the feeling of an individual to fit in (belong) to a specific social group (segments, categories).

Chapter 7
Artificial Intelligence in Online Travel Agencies:
Perspectives of Consumers, Channel Managers, and Accommodation Managers

Gorete Dinis
https://orcid.org/0000-0002-5484-022X
Polytechnic Institute of Portalegre, Portugal

Márcia Marat Grilo
https://orcid.org/0000-0002-4592-0973
Polytechnic Institute of Portalegre, Portugal

Ana Vieira
Polytechnic Institute of Portalegre, Portugal

Ana Margarida Silva
Polytechnic Institute of Portalegre, Portugal

ABSTRACT

OTAs have increasingly adopted advanced technologies to deliver more personalized and efficient services. In Portugal, where tourism plays a crucial economic role, this technological shift presents an opportunity to enhance competitiveness and offer customers a more distinctive experience. This study examines the use and future perceptions of technology and artificial intelligence in the tourism, with a particular focus on the accommodation platforms, exploring perspectives from both consumers and companies, namely channel managers, short-term rental management companies, and accommodation owner. A mixed-methods approach was employed,

DOI: 10.4018/979-8-3693-9994-1.ch007

enabling the collection of both quantitative and qualitative results, which reveal a predisposition from both individuals and companies to adopt artificial intelligence, along with high expectations for the future, although some concerns persist, particularly regarding the lack of human contact.

INTRODUCTION

Tourism is undergoing a transformation driven by technology and artificial intelligence (AI). With increasing competitiveness and evolving consumer demands, tourism companies are continually seeking innovative ways to enhance customer experience and optimize their operations. Platforms such as Booking.com, Airbnb, and other Online Travel Agencies (OTAs) have embraced advanced technologies to deliver more personalized and efficient services. In Portugal, where tourism is a crucial sector, this transformation represents an opportunity to increase competitiveness and provide better customer experiences. The evolution of tourism in Portugal and the growing adoption of digital technologies position OTAs and channel managers strategically for sector transformation. AI, through personalization and automation, empowers tourism companies to optimize processes and proactively respond to customer needs, shaping the sector's future.

This chapter analyzes the perspectives of consumers and businesses in Portugal regarding technology and AI in the tourism sector, with a particular focus on accommodation platforms. The study adopts a mixed-methods approach, combining quantitative and qualitative research, enabling an in-depth analysis of tourism companies' and customers' perceptions and practices. Semi-structured interviews were conducted with accommodation management companies, accommodation owners, and channel managers, while surveys were applied to individuals residing in Portugal during December 2024 and January 2025.

The first part of the chapter focuses on literature review, particularly on digital transformation and artificial intelligence in the context of OTAs dedicated to accommodation. The methodology used for the study is then described in more detail, followed by a report and discussion of the research findings, highlighting their implications for future research.

LITERATURE REVIEW

Digital Transformation in OTAs

Buhalis (2003), a pioneer in the concept of eTourism, highlighted that information technologies have profoundly transformed tourism management by promoting process digitization and facilitating access to tourism services. The tourism sector, which relies heavily on personalized experiences and human interaction, has increasingly recognized digital technologies as valuable assets for gaining a competitive advantage. However, their integration poses significant challenges, making digital transformation a critical necessity in the setor (Youssofi et al., 2024)

According to Verhoef et al. (2021), digital transformation involves the strategic use of digital technologies to reshape business operations and enhance value propositions for customers. They define digital transformation as a change in how a company employs digital technologies to develop a new digital business model that creates and appropriates more value for the enterprise. The authors emphasize the importance of conducting a thorough evaluation of all business processes during this transformation, stressing the need for a redesign that prioritizes improving customer experience, adding value, ensuring scalability, and strategically optimizing operations.

In the ongoing digital transformation, numerous technological advancements have significantly reshaped the tourism sector. Giannoni et al. (2021) identify OTAs as a major driver of this transformation, offering consumers access to a wide array of travel products, such as airline tickets (e.g., Kayak, Opodo) and accommodation (e.g., Booking.com, Expedia, Tripadvisor), from diverse suppliers. According to Boteva (2023), OTAs, as third-party platforms facilitating the booking of services like flights, accommodations, and car rentals, marked a turning point in the late 1990s by revolutionizing the travel industry's distribution model.

Over time, booking platforms such as Booking.com, Hotels.com, and Airbnb have not only streamlined the reservation process but also transformed the hospitality sector. Cheng et al. (2020) emphasize that platforms like Airbnb, that connect travelers with hosts who offer accommodations, and Uber, link passengers with drivers providing transportation services, offer tourists affordable options and enable more authentic local experiences. From the perspective of suppliers, these platforms enhance sales, create new marketing opportunities, and add value to their offerings (Giannoni et al., 2021)

Platform technologies, such as those underpinning OTAs, provide the digital infrastructure that facilitates direct interactions between consumers and providers, enabling resource exchange and value co-creation. These platforms empower users to access goods and services offered by peers, fostering community and trust while bypassing traditional intermediaries. There are several motivations that lead tourists to use OTA platforms, in Sharma (2024) opinion the key motivating factors are the ease of use, the ability to plan customized travel holidays, access to online travel reviews, availability of comprehensive travel information, and the best deals on holiday travel packages. However, as Ndaguba and Van Zyl (2023) affirmed, the active participation of users depends on the platform's availability and functionality, with user feedback mechanisms playing a critical role in engagement and continuous improvement after the platform's launch. Moreover, Boteva (2023), and Guo et al. (2024) argue that the integration of online platforms, smartphones, and applications has been revolutionary in redefining how tourists plan and book their trips. These tools serve as critical bridges between service providers and consumers, enabling direct and seamless interactions and fundamentally transforming trip planning.

Tourism suppliers, such as hotels, have access to numerous sources or platforms through which they can receive bookings (Boteva, 2023). These platforms, primarily electronic, function as hotel distribution channels, enabling hotels to sell their rooms to customers worldwide. On one hand, these distribution channels serve as the mechanisms that facilitate the transfer of bookings to hotels. On the other hand, they act as the means of communicating information about room availability, pricing, and details about the hotel and its services. Due to this bidirectional relationship, distribution channels are vital tools that can quickly adapt to market dynamics, meeting the needs of both the industry and end consumers (Boteva, 2023).

Electronic channels are diverse, however, Boteva (2023) highlights that OTAs (Online Travel Agencies) account for more than two-thirds of hotel bookings, meaning that the majority of bookings are made primarily through OTAs. The same applies to other accommodation providers, such as short-term rentals, which have various competing online platforms to choose from, at the international (e.g., Airbnb and Booking.com), European, national, or local level (Giannoni et al., 2021). In the European OTA market, Booking.com is the largest player, with a relative market share of 70.6% as of 2021, holding the top position among leading online travel companies globally. Following on the list are Airbnb, Trip.com, and Expedia. Airbnb has proven its global dominance as the most widely used platform for alternative accommodations (Ndaguba & Van Zyl, 2023).

OTAs offer several advantages over direct channels, particularly in terms of marketing, where their leadership capacity and significant investment in digital marketing stand out. This allows them to appear frequently at the top of users' search results. Moreover, an OTA's marketing campaign is typically much larger than that of individual hotels, helping them attract significantly more traffic to their websites and potentially convert some of that traffic into hotel bookings (Boteva, 2023).

Hoteliers widely adopt multichannel distribution as a strategy, and it has proven to be an effective practice for enhancing profitability within the accommodation sector. They utilize a combination of physical and virtual distribution channels to increase visibility and improve competitiveness, ensuring a broader audience reach and staying ahead in a competitive market. Similarly, some hosts on home-sharing platforms are likely to adopt a similar approach to enhance their performance (Giannoni et al., 2021). In a study conducted the authors involving a sample of 3,916 hosts in the Corsican short-term rental market in 2017, all present on the Airbnb platform, it was concluded that more than half of the hosts engage in multichannel distribution. However, the tendency to use different distribution channels depends significantly on the host's level of professionalization. Professional hosts tend to mimic the behavior of hospitality firms to improve their economic performance, while non-professional hosts (small hosts) demonstrate a willingness to optimize their occupancy rates through channel diversification. The authors also found that a large proportion of the host population shows weak attachment to the platform, suggesting limited platform retention capabilities.

Building a successful distribution strategy in the accommodation subsector requires finding the right balance among all the channels used (Boteva, 2023). Deciding which channel is best suited for a hotel depends on various factors, such as the overall value of the hotel room, room size, geographic location, customer segments, affiliation with a branded chain, OTA commissions, and digital marketing costs (Boteva, 2023). Moreover, the choice of digital channels and the decision to adopt a multichannel distribution strategy depend on the level of knowledge and professionalism of the person responsible for marketing. This is why hosts, particularly in the short-term rental market, often turn to management firms or agents, which are individuals or groups responsible for managing three or more properties (Deng & Ravichandran, 2020). These management firms or agents play a crucial role in managing and optimizing short-term rental properties, enhancing the facilities, revenue, and occupancy rates. Their expertise also ensures that accommodations meet the expectations of travelers and comply with local regulations (Ndaguba & van Zyl, 2023).Hosts managed by professional firms are less likely to exit the short-term rental market compared to those managed by non-professional hosts.

Choosing the right distribution strategy and the most suitable channels or platforms is a complex decision that depends on various factors of different natures. However, the technological component of distribution systems should be a priority for these companies. In this context, it is essential for OTAs, channel managers, management firms, or agents to incorporate advanced technologies, such as Artificial Intelligence (AI), to stay aligned with the ongoing expansion and transformations in the tourism sector.

According to Chiu et al. (2021), traditional booking systems have limitations, with one of the most prominent being their inability to cater to the specific preferences of travelers. Moreover, by applying a one-size-fits-all approach, these systems fail, from an economic perspective, to maximize utility for both providers and consumers.

The adoption of AI is, therefore, crucial to overcoming these limitations, enabling more effective personalization, price optimization, and a customer experience that is better aligned with expectations, which is an essential requirement in the dynamic and competitive accommodation subsector. (Guo et al., 2024).

In summary, tourism suppliers have been among the pioneers in adopting new technologies. These technologies have played a crucial role in improving operational processes and guiding the strategic decisions of these businesses. However, the growing demands of increasingly sophisticated consumers, coupled with the rising number of distribution intermediaries in the accommodation sector, pose significant challenges—particularly for small and medium-sized accommodation providers. Many of these businesses lack the technical expertise and financial resources needed to adopt and integrate advanced technological innovations, such as artificial intelligence.

Artificial Intelligence in OTAs

Research on AI in the hospitality and tourism industry demonstrates a clear growing trend. While the first study on this topic was published in 1991, it was only after 2018 that the number of publications and citations increased significantly, garnering substantial attention from the academic community (Kong et al, 2023). An analysis of research spanning from 1984 to 2021 indicates that the predominant focus of AI studies in hospitality and tourism has been on big data and machine learning (Knani et al., 2022). However, a recent systematic review of AI-related studies in hospitality, published between 2021 and 2023, reveals a shift in thematic emphasis, with service robots and voice assistants emerging as primary areas of interest (Law et al., 2024). According to Kong et al. (2023), research on AI in this field can be categorized into four main clusters: AI technologies, technology acceptance, consumer perception, and future trends. Despite these advancements, studies on AI in tourism and hospitality are still in their early stages, revealing significant potential for further exploration. To the best of our knowledge, no research has yet analyzed the use of AI in OTAs from the perspectives of users, channel managers, and short-term rental managers. Therefore, we believe that the originality of our study lies in addressing this gap.

AI, defined as the ability of machines to simulate human intelligence processes such as learning and decision-making, is at the core of innovations aimed at personalizing, automating, and optimizing tourism services. The central concept revolves around leveraging technological tools to deliver more efficient and tailored experiences, meeting the growing demands of modern consumers. According to Choi and Kim (2024), AI systems consist of software or hardware designed to achieve complex goals by perceiving their environment through data acquisition, interpreting information, generating knowledge, and determining the best actions to accomplish the given objectives.

AI has emerged as a transformative force within the tourism industry, reshaping various facets of travel and hospitality (Nam et al., 2021). The integration of AI into the sector is characterized by its diverse applications, which contribute significantly to enhanced operational efficiency, personalized customer experiences, and overall industry growth. A significant application of AI in tourism is in customer service and engagement. AI-driven tools, such as chatbots and virtual assistants, offer 24/7 support, helping travelers in real-time with inquiries, bookings, and personalized recommendations (Bouchareb, 2023). Ivanov and Webster (2019) examine the impact of chatbots in the hospitality industry, explaining how these automated systems enhance customer service by providing rapid and continuous responses, available at all times. In addition to optimizing resources and reducing operational costs, chatbots deliver an efficient service tailored to the user's needs, ensuring a more seamless and personalized experience.

According to a study conducted by Euromonitor International, several leading travel companies began integrating generative artificial intelligence technologies into their services. For example, Expedia partnered with OpenAI to launch a ChatGPT-based trip planning feature in its iOS app, as well as a plug-in for ChatGPT Plus users, offering personalised recommendations and booking support. Other platforms, such as Kayak, OpenTable, TripAdvisor, GetYourGuide, and Klook, also adopted ChatGPT plug-ins. Trip.com integrated ChatGPT into its AI assistant, TripGen, to provide real-time support for itinerary planning and travel suggestions. (Bremner, 2023)

Tourists interact with a wide array of AI-driven systems, including QR codes, automatic translation, chatbots, and voice assistants (Sousa et al., 2024). Additionally, advanced technologies such as machine learning, predictive analytics, recommendation systems, and data analysis tools enable the processing of vast datasets to predict tourist preferences and offer personalized suggestions, enriching the customer journey. In the hospitality sector, AI-powered solutions, including self-service kiosks, smart room systems, and automated chatbots, have demonstrated their potential to streamline hotel operations by expediting check-ins and check-outs, optimizing resource management, and providing individualized guest experiences. Increasingly, hotels are also adopting generative AI to enhance customer service and automate repetitive tasks (Bremner, 2023). To fully leverage these technologies, it is essential that AI solutions are tailored to the specific characteristics and operational needs of each hotel (Arceta et al., 2024).

In this context, Marriott International introduced Alexa for Hospitality, a system that includes basic Alexa features such as internet searches and music playback, but also offers functionalities specifically designed for the hospitality sector, including adjusting room temperature, ordering room service, and facilitating virtual check-out. In addition, the company adopted technologies such as facial recognition for check-in, has developed its own chatbot system, and, in a hotel in Belgium, implemented a concierge robot. Digital concierge services have also been integrated by Hilton International Hotels, aiming to enhance the customer experience (Štilić et al., 2023).

As evidenced by Guo et al. (2024), intelligent booking systems in the tourism and hotel industry, powered by AI and machine learning, enable the creation of hyper-personalized travel recommendations that significantly enhance user experiences and drive greater engagement. This ensures that each user's journey, from the initial booking to the conclusion of the trip, is seamless, enjoyable, and memorable. On the other hand, stakeholders, by offering customized suggestions tailored to individual preferences and contextual factors, can boost user satisfaction, build stronger loyalty, and encourage repeat bookings. AI adoption is a challenge for many companies, due to organizational resistance and the need to adapt to new technological processes, however, the successful implementation of these technologies leads to significant gains in operational efficiency and customer satisfaction.

According to a study conducted by Sousa et al. (2024), AI systems are increasingly utilized across five key areas of tourism activities, namely entertainment (62.7%), catering (56.5%), accommodation (55.8%), tourist attractions (54.6%), and transportation (50%). On the other hand, activities such as tour guiding (33.1%), tour operations (26.2%), and travel agencies (23.5%) are the areas where AI is used the least. Regarding the stages of the travel journey where AI systems are used, 38.1% of respondents report using AI "before the trip", while 33.8% utilize it "during the trip". However, an even larger proportion (47.3%) reported using AI "at all stages of the trip", while only 1.5% explicitly mentioned using AI "after the trip". Respondents also expressed an increased likelihood of using AI more frequently in activities directly related to travel planning or those designed to facilitate and optimize the tourist experience. These activities include "language translation" (74.6%), "map/navigation systems" (68.8%), "itinerary planning" (66.5%), and "making travel reservations" (56.2%). The growing propensity to adopt AI in these areas reflects its increasing relevance in enhancing the travel experience.

The authors highlight the perceived benefits of AI significantly outweigh its drawbacks, with its use generally induces positive emotions among users. According to their study, AI systems contribute to increased operational efficiency, cost reduction, and enhanced visitor satisfaction by meeting the modern demand for convenience and personalization. Additionally, AI's ability to reduce operational and maintenance costs facilitates the development of innovative business models, supporting long-term growth. Therefore, investments in AI technologies are vital for enhancing customer experiences, improving operational efficiencies, and fostering the evolution of dynamic and sustainable business strategies (Ansari et al., 2022; Siddik et al., 2025).

Despite these benefits, the adoption of AI in tourism and hospitality faces significant challenges. High implementation costs, technical complexities, and the necessity for staff training represent key barriers that must be addressed to optimize the benefits of AI and ensure its sustainable integration (Arceta et al., 2024). Moreover, as noted by Murphy et al. (2019), there is a risk of depersonalization when digital interactions replace human contact. These authors emphasize the importance of humanizing automated processes to ensure that the customer experience remains meaningful without compromising emotional engagement. Buhalis (2020) reinforces this perspective, highlighting additional challenges such as privacy and data protection, which are essential for maintaining customer trust, as well as the continued need for human connection in service encounters.

Some authors have examined the regulatory and ethical considerations surrounding AI implementation in tourism. For instance, Hermann (2022) addresses the ethical and security challenges associated with AI use in the sector and proposes best practice recommendations for tourism marketers, AI developers, and policymakers to mitigate the most significant ethical issues related to AI deployment. In line with these concerns, Sharma et al. (2021) emphasize the need to transform AI from a "black box" to a "glass box" by applying explainable machine learning techniques. Their study illustrates how greater transparency in AI systems can enhance user trust and support ethical decision-making in the hospitality sector. By making the decision-making process of AI models more interpretable, hospitality professionals can gain meaningful customer insights, improve service personalization, and ensure more responsible use of data.

When analyzing the practices adopted, controversies arise regarding the real impact of AI on customer satisfaction and maintaining a close relationship, which is traditionally valued in the tourism sector. While advanced systems allow for highly tailored suggestions and greater efficiency, they also raise concerns about the loss of human touch and the risk of turning the travel experience into a purely data-driven process.

Helgemeir & Cenzano (2019) concluded that OTAs are the sector most affected by AI. Experts have identified OTAs as the most important field of AI application, followed by the hotel sector, aviation, and tourism destinations. The growing adoption of advanced technologies, such as artificial intelligence and machine learning, by OTAs has significantly transformed the hospitality and tourism setor, enhancing the booking experience for travelers and optimizing service delivery for suppliers (Car et al., 2024). According to the authors, various AI-driven features are already integrated into OTA platforms, which have invested in AI to offer personalized recommendations and enhance customer experiences (Boteva, D., 2023), as well as to enhance operations in order to stay competitive in the ever-changing digital age (Vinod, 2016). Alarcón-del-Amo and Rialp-Criado (2021) analyze the role of personalization algorithms in the context of OTAs and verified that machine learning allows offers to be tailored to each customer's specific preferences. Through machine learning algorithms, these platforms can collect and process large volumes of user behavior data, anticipating needs and customizing offers. This ability to personalize is one of the major advantages provided by AI, fostering customer loyalty and increasing competitiveness in the tourism market.

Sousa et al. (2024) highlight that AI is widely embraced by the surveyed tourists and plays a pivotal role in tourism marketing. It functions both as a research tool for exploring destinations and tourism products and as a communication tool that enables personalized tourist experiences. Kotler et al. (2024) emphasize that the future of marketing strategies lies in the ability to create immersive and tailored experiences. AI facilitates increasingly targeted interactions, delivering services customized to individual needs and strengthening the bond between brands and consumers. Kotler et al. (2024) states that digital marketing is becoming more of an information-based battle than a sales-force battle, underscoring the critical role of personalization and data-driven approaches in digital marketing. This focus on personalization not only enhances customer satisfaction but also boosts brand loyalty and drives commercial success (Brenner, 2021). The integration of advanced technologies, such as AI, into digital marketing is essential for developing strategies that genuinely resonate with consumers, offering unique and customized experiences that solidify the connection between brands and their customers (Kotler et al., 2024; Norton, 2019; Genadinik, 2020).

However, the adoption of artificial intelligence in management systems also presents several challenges for tourism service providers. These include high initial implementation costs and the need for ongoing maintenance and regular system updates (Sinha et al., 2021). In accommodation access systems, issues such as privacy, security, and ethical considerations must be carefully addressed and managed. Furthermore, the automation of certain tasks introduces additional barriers, such as the requirement for specialized technical skills and potential employee resistance to change. Chatbots and virtual assistants, while widely used in the hospitality sector to provide efficient customer service, also face inherent limitations, including the need for extensive data training, the risk of technical failures, and a reduced ability to interpret complex or nuanced requests, as well as a lack of emotional intelligence. These limitations become operational and experiential challenges that require careful management, as they can undermine customer trust and emotional connection, potentially leading to consumer resistance to their use. (Vinnakota et al.,2023).

In summary, AI in the tourism sector goes beyond task automation, playing a strategic role in creating value for businesses and consumers. Personalization, data analysis, and automation converge to deliver an optimized customer experience, proactively addressing market demands. Despite its evident advantages, challenges related to humanizing services and protecting user data remain critical areas of focus. Moreover, digital transformation not only enhances operational processes but also creates opportunities for more immersive and personalized marketing. At the same time, it underscores the need to balance technological efficiency with the humanization of interactions, ensuring that the benefits of AI are fully leveraged without compromising the quality of service provided.

Despite this growing body of work, little research has explored AI adoption, especially from the perspectives of users, channel managers, and short-term rental . OTAs have been identified as the segment most affected by AI innovations (Helgemeir & Cenzano, 2019), driven by the integration of advanced tools such as personalization algorithms, recommendation systems, and AI-powered chatbots (Boteva, 2023; Alarcón-del-Amo & Rialp-Criado, 2021). These technologies enhance booking experiences, tailor services to individual preferences, and improve platform competitiveness. However, the literature lacks a structured understanding of how these systems are adopted, implemented, and perceived within the accommodation sector. This gap highlights the relevance and originality of the present study, which aims to investigate the evolving role of AI in tourism and its implications for stakeholders across the accommodation ecosystem, as well as from the consumer perspective.

METHODS

The objective of the study is to analyze the use and the effect of AI in tourism, namely in OTAs (accommodation platforms), especially in terms of digital marketing, from the perspective of consumers, channel managers, and professionals. This research employed a mixed methodology, quantitative and qualitative, which resulted in two distinct samples. The use of mixed methodologies allows the researcher to have a broader and deeper view of the phenomenon under study, thus being recommended and widely used in fields of knowledge such as tourism.

For the qualitative approach, semi-structured interviews were constructed. According to Veal (2018), this is an appropriate method when the population is small. The questions were prepared in advance, with attention given to include open-ended responses so that the interviewee has more freedom in their answers. The quantitative approach was conducted through a survey, with questions appropriate for the target audience, mostly closed-ended, with simple and easy-to-understand language.

Thus, in the study, the opinions of OTA customers (Sample A) were obtained through questionnaires about their profile, usage habits, and perception of AI use in OTAs, namely chatbots and personalization engines (Annex A); and, on the other hand, professionals involved in accommodation management, mainly short-term rental and channel managers (Sample B) shared their experiences in implementing AI tools through semi-structured interviews (Annex B). This approach allowed for capturing not only the perception of end users but also the perspective of those who manage and integrate technology into their daily operations.

The distribution and dissemination of the data collection instruments occurred simultaneously, during the period from December to January 2025. The interviews were sent by invitation via email to 8 channel managers, and 48 professional accommodation managers operating in the Portuguese market. A total of 7 interviews were validated. In Table 1 is illustrated the interview focus and the participants. Regarding the questionnaires, they were created on Google Forms and distributed through social media and direct contacts via WhatsApp. The responses from 89 respondents were validated. The data is analyzed with SPSS 27.0.

Table 1. Interview focus, Participants, and Interview date

Interview Focus	Organization/ Participant	Date
- Interviewee profile - Company profile - Utilization and impact of AI in daily operations, company management, and customer experience - Challenges and obstacles in implementing AI tools within the company - Effects of AI on customer satisfaction, optimization of digital marketing strategies, and the company's competitiveness - Future perceptions of the impact of AI tools in digital marketing and the future of AI within the company	- Accommodation management company, located in Lisbon (I1) - Accommodation management company, located in Portalegre (I2) - Channel Manager (I3) - Accommodation management company, located in Porto (I4) - Accommodation owner, Portalegre (I5) - Accommodation management company, located in Portalegre (I6) - Accommodation management company, located in Évora (I7)	December 2024

Source: Own elaboration

ANALYSIS AND DISCUSSION OF RESULTS

The sample of this study is divided into two distinct groups. The first (Sample A) includes clients of booking platforms (OTAs) such as Booking.com and Airbnb, who responded to a questionnaire about their sociodemographic profile and habits in using technological tools. The respondents are predominantly female (73%), aged between 35 and 54 years (76%), with education levels corresponding to secondary education and higher education, particularly bachelor's degrees (69%), and monthly net incomes mostly ranging between €1,000 and €1,999 (58%). These participants work in diverse professions, such as administration and management (19%), education and training (11%), and public services and administration (29%), residing mainly in the municipalities of Portalegre (67%), Lisbon (4%), Campo Maior (2%), and Aveiro (2%).

Of the respondents, 90% indicated regularly using OTAs. According to Table 2, which identifies the OTAs most frequently used by respondents, Booking.com was the most mentioned OTA, accounting for approximately 67% of the responses, followed by Airbnb (19.1%) and Hotels.com (6.2%). Other OTAs, provided as response options, were mentioned by very few individuals. Most of the respondents (78%) indicated that they use OTAs a few times a year, however, 75% mentioned that they have never interacted with chatbots or virtual assistants when booking accommodations.

When asked whether the recommendations made by the platforms matched their preferences and needs, 65% responded affirmatively, with 56% of the respondent's expressing satisfaction with the recommendations.

Table 2. OTAs most used by respondents

OTAs	**Nº**	**%**
Booking.com	139	66,5
Airbnb	40	19,1
Hotels.com	13	6,2
Expedia	3	1,4
Trip.com	7	3,3
Agoda	4	1,9
Lastminute.com	1	0,5
VRBO	2	1,0
Total	**209**	**100**

Source: Own elaboration

The individuals' perceptions of their interaction with OTAs highlight positive aspects, such as suggestions of competitive prices (21%), quick responses (20%), and ease of use (18%), while also revealing negative aspects, including limited responses (28%) and a lack of more human interactions (37%)(Table 3), these findings are aligning with the conclusions of Murphy et al. (2019) regarding the need to balance digital efficiency with emotional proximity

Table 3. Positive and negative aspects of users' interaction with OTAs

Positive aspects	%	Negative aspects	%
Suggestions of competitive prices	21	Lack of human interaction	37
Quick answer	20	Limited responses	28
Ease of use	18	Difficulty in understanding the system	4
Efficiency in the booking process	16	Recommendation errors	4
Personalization of the experience	4	Privacy problems	2
Missing	21	Missing	25
Total	**100**	**Total**	**100**

Source: own elaboration

When asked about their opinion on how AI could enhance their experience when booking accommodations on these OTAs, respondents emphasized the need for AI to become more humanized, provide personalized suggestions tailored to each user's needs, offer greater ease of use, improve visual access to accommodations, enable voice-based booking, and optimize price comparisons across different platforms.

Regarding the types of AI-related features or technologies they would like to see implemented in the future on such platforms, the respondents who answered this question suggested greater interaction between platforms, more reliable and personalized recommendations, improved ease and speed of use, features that enhance safety and trust, voice technology, virtual reality, suggestions that align strictly with the user's profile, as well as increased interaction and humanization of the platforms.

The second group (Sample B) consists of four females and three males, aged 25-34 (1 participant), 35-44 (4 participants), and 45-54 (2 participants). All interviewees hold higher education degrees, with six having postgraduate or master's degrees and one holding a bachelor's degree. Among the participants, five are CEOs, one is a manager, and another is a marketing assistant. For confidentiality reasons, the names of the companies where the participants work cannot be disclosed.

Relatively to the companies where the interviewees work, it was found that five are micro-enterprises (up to 9 employees), one is a small enterprise (10 to 49 employees), and another is medium-sized (50 to 249 employees). The companies are located in Portalegre (3), Lisbon (2), Évora (1), and Porto (1), and they emerged in the market between 2014 and 2022. One interviewee works at a channel manager company, one is an individual accommodation owner, and four work for professional accommodation management companies.

When asked whether their company uses any AI-based tools, four interviewees responded negatively, while three responded positively. This indicates that some companies still refrain from adopting AI solutions, preferring to maintain human contact as a differentiation strategy. The companies that do use AI-based tools primarily utilize data analysis tools or CRM platforms with predictive algorithms to adjust pricing, manage marketing campaigns, and enhance operational efficiency.

Regarding the impact of AI tools on daily operations, I1 states that AI has had a "strong impact on price management, reporting, and marketing." I2 mentions that it "optimizes data analysis," and I3 emphasizes the impact on "price automation and dynamic tariff updates." In terms of customer experience impact, I1 highlights that AI "has contributed to customer contact (owner/guest), although we have stepped back from using chatbots, as we found that the impact they were having on customers was more negative than positive, and people still prefer contact with humans." I2 points out that AI "optimizes response time," while I3 notes that it "provides reservations with real-time adjusted prices." Regarding the impact on company management, I1 indicates that "the tools have contributed to marketing, revenue management, and report creation." I2 mentions that "it reduces the time spent on repetitive tasks and has been especially helpful in marketing and report creation," while I3 states that "it helps with occupancy forecasting and optimizes response time."

In terms of optimizing digital marketing strategies and increasing the company's competitiveness, I1 and I2 mentioned that the tools have assisted in the creation of advertisements, operation, and marketing management. I2 further added that "marketing campaigns have led to an increase in direct bookings," while I3 stated that "it allowed for customer segmentation based on purchasing behavior and the direction of more effective campaigns." Additionally, "the dynamic pricing system has boosted sales."

Regarding the question raised about the main challenges faced in implementing AI tools, four interviewees mentioned costs (I1, I2, I7, I4), I3 also highlighted team training, I5 mentioned "Organisational resistance" and I6 emphasized "the company's effective profitability without losing the necessary human factor for the business." Associated with the challenges are also the interviewees' responses regarding the biggest obstacles in using AI for service personalization. three of the interviewees pointed out "implementation costs", I2 mentioned "limitations in understanding preferences," I3 referred to "lack of integration between booking systems and marketing platforms," I4 highlighted "mechanization of services and depersonalization towards the customer," and I5, in addition to costs, added "the lack of skilled labor in technology".

Regarding the technologies or tools that could have the greatest impact on Digital Marketing, I2 mentions "data analysis tools and marketing automation, social media, and intelligent advertising platforms". For I3, these are "marketing automation tools and natural language chatbots", and in I5´s opinion, they are "augmented reality, virtual reality, chatbots, and digital kiosks".

When asked whether they believe AI replaces or complements human contact with clients, all interviewees, except I4, consider AI to be a complement to human interaction. I3 was the only one who mentioned having "observed specific improvements in operations or customer satisfaction with the use of AI.

The interviewees were asked about their views on the future of AI applied to their sector, and only I4 mentioned that "they had no intention of using AI in the company, as we focus on personalizing our services." in contrast, I5 stated that AI integration is "mandatory". Regarding this matter, I1 pointed out, "we are paying attention to the development and use of new tools. We observe that many new AI technologies for image and video appear daily, but they haven't really influenced the company's daily operations." I2 believes that AI will be "essential for optimizing operations and offering increasingly personalized experiences," and I3 stated, "we believe it can be very beneficial for streamlining bookings and improving customer service."

Several issues emerge from sample B that warrant reflection In general, the interviewees highlights the growing role of technology in daily management but also points out challenges related to implementation costs, team training, and the need to preserve the human component in customer service. When properly implemented, AI offers competitive advantages, greater personalization of offerings, and significant benefits for digital marketing strategies.

The discussion also highlights specific problems, such as the difficulty of integrating booking platforms with CRM systems, the need for financial resources to support innovation, and the variability in customer acceptance, which is sometimes divided between valuing digital speed and preferring the human warmth of face-to-face service. This tension reflects the current state of the market, which balances evident benefits in terms of profitability, competitiveness, and agility with the perception that AI cannot fully replace human empathy.

To face the identified challenges, a balanced approach that promotes the coexistence of technology and humanization is recommended. OTAs and accommodation companies should continue to invest in AI tools for data analysis optimization, price management, and digital marketing, but without neglecting close contact. Team training and careful integration of systems are key steps to ensure that service remains personalized and empathetic. In this sense, maintaining human support lines and providing the possibility of direct contact with real operators can serve as a valuable complement to chatbots. Additionally, strengthening privacy and data security policies is essential to maintaining customer trust. The use of visual elements can help illustrate improvements or practical solutions in terms of interfaces, but clarity in communication and ease of navigation should be prioritized to facilitate adoption by different user profiles.

The study's results allow for the anticipation of future research paths, particularly regarding the development of AI capable of interpreting emotions and tones of voice, bringing automated solutions even closer to human dynamics. Given the current pace of innovation, it is expected that new forms of AI application will emerge, focusing on predictive analysis of trends and customer preferences, the complete automation of certain stages of the booking process, and integration with augmented or virtual reality to provide immersive tours of accommodations even before booking.

Based on the presented results, accommodation managers and OTAs should adopt a balanced approach that integrates the potential of artificial intelligence tools with the humanization of customer service. To this end, it is essential to invest in team training, ensuring the proper integration of AI systems with booking platforms and CRM to optimize service personalization and efficiency without compromising direct and empathetic consumer contact. Maintaining human support channels complementary to chatbots could enhance user satisfaction and trust. Additionally, organizations should strengthen privacy and data security policies to safeguard consumer trust. Personalized contact with guests should also be promoted, using technology as support for human service rather than as a substitute. Meanwhile, owners of small and medium-sized accommodations should adopt accessible technological solutions that improve visibility and competitiveness, such as the use of multichannel distribution and AI-based management platforms to optimize occupancy and pricing.

CONCLUSION

This study aimed to gather the opinion of portuguese individuals regarding the use of AI in OTAs and the perception from companies, namely channel managers and accommodation management companies, about the use, impact, and future prospects of AI in this sector. The lack of studies focusing on OTAs and their growing role as a hub for consumers in tourism, accompanying the entire booking process from the planning stage to post-trip, motivated the development of this study. The adoption of a mixed methodology, with semi-structured interviews and questionnaires, was key to achieving the study's objectives and reaching the target population.

The results of the empirical study show that tourism companies in Portugal, particularly those in accommodation subsector, have gradually embraced AI technologies, not only to automate processes but also to improve marketing strategies and customer experience on platforms such as Booking.com and Airbnb. These results point to a path where efficiency and personalization driven by AI coexist with the need to maintain a human touch in customer interactions. As observed, the successful implementation of these technologies requires careful planning, investment in training, and an awareness that the human factor remains crucial to ensure user satisfaction. This balanced approach, which combines technological innovation with close and empathetic customer service, is essential for the future of digital tourism and for the competitiveness of Portuguese companies in the global market.

It is also concluded that there are concerns about the lack of integration between different systems and the perception that not all customers feel comfortable dealing with fully automated interfaces. The interviewee that mentioned scaling back on the use of chatbots highlights customers' preference for more personal contact, confirming the hybrid nature of the trend that combines greater technological adoption with caution in customer relationships.

Although the combination of methods provides greater robustness in drawing conclusions, the study presents as a limitation the geographic representation of responses, particularly from OTA users, which reduces the representativeness of the data, and the difficulty in obtaining information through interviews, as some companies were either unavailable or reluctant to share details about their operations.

The future points to platforms that continuously learn from user behavior, adapting offerings in real-time, which reinforces the importance of ethical and practical reflection on data collection and usage. At the same time, there remain opportunities for research on balancing the adoption of chatbots with maintaining close service, as well as understanding customers' emotional responses when receiving recommendations or interacting with virtual assistants. This context encourages the exploration of new tools and business models, fostering a broader perspective on the impact of AI in tourism, including the ongoing evaluation of customer satisfaction and the analysis of potential collaboration opportunities between major platforms and small businesses in the sector.

REFERENCES

Ansari, N., Tyagi, S., Mehrwal, N., Rastogi, N., Chibber, S., Memoria, M., Kumar, R., & Gupta, A. (2022). A Critical Insight into the Impact of Technology in Transformation of Tourist Business into Smart Tourism, *2022 International Conference on Machine Learning, Big Data, Cloud and Parallel Computing (COM-IT-CON)*, pp. 832-837, Faridabad, India. https://doi: DOI: 10.1109/COM-IT-CON54601.2022.9850779

Arceta, N., Montero, M., & Quilitis, J. (2024). Adaptation and Effectiveness of Artificial Technology Used by Selected Hotels in Quezon City. *International Journal of Tourism and Hospitality*, *4*(2), 27–46. DOI: 10.51483/IJTH.4.2.2024.27-46

Boteva, D. (2023). Advantages and Disadvantages of OTAs in the Distribution System of a Seaside Holiday Hotels. *Izvestia Journal of the Union of Scientists - Varna. Economic Sciences Series*, *12*(1), 239–250. DOI: 10.56065/IJUSV-ESS/2023.12.1.239

Bouchareb, N. (2023). The Role of Artificial Intelligence in Improving Hotels Property Management Systems. *International Journal of Economic Performance*, *06*(02), 554–567.

Bremner, C. (2023). Revolutionising Travel: ChatGPT and Generative AI Usher in New Era of Automation. *Euromonitor International*. https://www.euromonitor.com/article/revolutionising-travel-chatgpt-and-generative-ai-usher-in-new-era-of-automation?utm_campaign=&utm_content=&utm_medium=Organic&utm_source=linkedin

Brenner, M. (2021). *The Age of Personalization: Digital Marketing Strategies for the Modern Consumer*. Wiley.

Buhalis, D. (2003). *eTourism: Information technology for strategic tourism management*. Pearson Education. https://doi.org/DOI: 10.13140/2.1.2274.0804

Buhalis, D. (2020). Technology in tourism-from information communication technologies to eTourism and smart tourism towards ambient intelligence tourism: A perspective article. *Tourism Review*, *75*(1), 267–272. DOI: 10.1108/TR-06-2019-0258

Car, T., Šuman, S., & Kliman, A. (2024). Customer Booking Habits and Attitudes Towards AI-Powered Features in Online Travel Agencies. *International Journal of Advances in Computer Science and Technology*, *13*(9), 111–117. DOI: 10.30534/ijacst/2024/021392024

Cheng, M., Mackenzie, S. H., & Degarege, G. A. (2020). Airbnb impacts on host communities in a tourism destination: An exploratory study of stakeholder perspectives in Queenstown, New Zealand. *Journal of Sustainable Tourism*, *30*(5), 1122–1140. DOI: 10.1080/09669582.2020.1802469

Chiu, M. C., Huang, J. H., Gupta, S., & Akman, G. (2021). Developing a personalized recommendation system in a smart product service system based on unsupervised learning model. *Computers in Industry*, *128*, 103421. DOI: 10.1016/j.compind.2021.103421

Choi, Y., & Kim, D. (2024). Artificial Intelligence in The Tourism Industry: Current Trends and Future Outlook. *International Journal on Advanced Science, Engineering and Information Technology*, *14*(6). Advance online publication. DOI: 10.18517/ijaseit.14.6.20452

Deng, C., & Ravichandran, T. R. (2020). To smile or not? The effect of facial expression on servisse demand in sharing economy platforms. *AMCIS 2020 Proceedings*. 15. https://aisel.aisnet.org/amcis2020/virtual_communities/virtual_communities/15

Genadinik, A. (2020). *Digital Marketing: An Essential Guide to Marketing in the Digital World*. Business Expert Press.

Giannoni, S., Brunstein, D., Guéniot, F., & Jouve, J. (2021). Multichannel distribution strategy of Airbnb hosts. *Annals of Tourism Research Empirical Insights*, *2*(1). Advance online publication. DOI: 10.1016/j.annale.2021.100017

Guo, Q, & Mu, L& Lou. (2024). S. Revolutionizing travel experiences: An in-depth analysis of intelligent booking systems and behavioral patterns. *Intelligent Decision Technologies*, *18*(2), 1477–1494. DOI: 10.3233/IDT-230625

Helgemeir, T., & Cenzano, C. H. (2019). Artificial intelligence in tourism software solutions: Opportunities and challenges until 2024. In K. Jain, S. Sangle, R. Gupta, J. Persis, & M. R. (Eds.), *Managing Technology for Inclusive and Sustainable Growth - 28th International Conference for the International Association of Management of Technology, IAMOT 2019* (pp. 134-142). Excel India Publishers.

Hermann, E. (2022). Leveraging artificial intelligence in marketing for social good—An ethical perspective. *Journal of Business Ethics*, *179*, 43–61. DOI: 10.1007/s10551-021-04843-y PMID: 34054170

Ivanov, S., & Webster, C. (2019). Conceptual Framework of the Use of Robots, Artificial Intelligence and Service Automation in Travel, Tourism, and Hospitality Companies, Ivanov, S. and Webster, C. (Ed.) *Robots, Artificial Intelligence, and Service Automation in Travel, Tourism and Hospitality* (pp. 7-37). Emerald Publishing Limited. https://doi.org/DOI: 10.1108/978-1-78756-687-320191001

Knani, M., Echchakoui, S., & Ladhari, R. (2022). Artificial intelligence in tourism and hospitality: Bibliometric analysis and research agenda. *International Journal of Hospitality Management*, *107*, 103317. DOI: 10.1016/j.ijhm.2022.103317

Kong, H., Wang, K., Qiu, X., Cheung, C., & Bu, N. (2023). 30 years of artificial intelligence (AI) research relating to the hospitality and tourism industry. *International Journal of Contemporary Hospitality Management*, *35*(6), 2157–2177. DOI: 10.1108/IJCHM-03-2022-0354

Kotler, P., Kartajaya, H., & Setiawan, I. (2024). *Marketing 6.0: O Futuro é Imersivo*. Actual Editora.

Law, R., Lin, K., Ye, H., & Fong, D. (2024). Artificial intelligence research in hospitality: A stateof- the-art review and future directions. *International Journal of Contemporary Hospitality Management*, *36*(6). Advance online publication. DOI: 10.1108/IJCHM-02-2023-0189

Murphy, J., Gretzel, U., & Pesonen, J. (2019). Marketing Robot Services in Hospitality and Tourism. *Journal of Hospitality and Tourism Technology*, *10*(1), 73–86. DOI: 10.1080/10548408.2019.1571983

Nam, K., Dutt, C., Chathoth, P., Daghfous, A., & Khan, M. (2021). The adoption of artificial intelligence and robotics in the hotel industry: Prospects and challenges. *Electronic Markets*, *31*(3), 553–574. DOI: 10.1007/s12525-020-00442-3

Ndaguba, E. A., & Van Zyl, C. (2023). Exploring bibliometric evidence of Airbnb's influence on urban destinations: Emotional solidarity, Airbnb supply, moral economy and digital future. *International Journal of Tourism Cities*, *9*(4), 894–922. DOI: 10.1108/IJTC-03-2023-0056

Norton, D. (2019). *Personalization in Marketing*. Kogan Page Publishers.

Sharma, A. (2024). Online Travel Agency (OTA) Platform Usage in the AI Era. *International Journal of Information Management Sciences*, *8*(1), 31–63. https://ijims.org/index.php/home/article/view/86

Sharma, R., Kumar, A., & Chuah, C. (2021). Turning the blackbox into a glassbox: An explainable machine learning approach for understanding hospitality customer. *International Journal of Information Management Data Insights*, *1*(2), 100050.

Siddik, A. Forid, Md. Yong, L. Du, A & Goodell, J. (2025). Artificial intelligence as a catalyst for sustainable tourism growth and economic cycles. *Technological Forecasting and Social Change, 210*, 123875. DOI: 10.1016/j.techfore.2024.123875

Sinha, M., Fukey, L. N., & Sinha, A. (2021). Artificial Intelligence and Internet of Things readiness: inclination for hotels to support a sustainable environment. In *Cognitive Computing for Human-Robot Interaction* (pp. 327–353). Academic Press.

Sousa, A., Cardoso, P., & Dias, F. (2024). The Use of Artificial Intelligence Systems in Tourism and Hospitality: The Tourists' Perspective. *Administrative Sciences, 14*(165), 1–23.

Štilić, A., Nicić, M., & Puška, A. (2023). Check-In to the Future: Exploring the Impact of Contemporary Information Technologies and Artificial Intelligence on the Hotel Industry. *The Business of Tourism, 31*, 5–17. DOI: 10.5937/turpos0-43739

Veal, A. J. (2018). *Research Methods for Leisure and Tourism*. Pearson.

Verhoef, P. C., Broekhuizen, T., Bart, Y., Bhattacharya, A., Qi Dong, J., Fabian, N., & Haenlein, M. (2021). Digital transformation: A multidisciplinary reflection and research agenda. *Journal of Business Research, 122*, 889–901. DOI: 10.1016/j.jbusres.2019.09.022

Vinnakota, S., Mohan, M. D., Boda, J., Sekuini, J., Mustafa, M., & Madala, H. (2023). Leveraging artificial intelligence in the hospitality industry: Opportunities and challenges. *Asian Journal of Social Science and Management Technology, 5*(3), 201–210.

Vinod, B. (2016). Big Data in the travel marketplace. *Journal of Revenue and Pricing Management, 15*(5), 352–359. DOI: 10.1057/rpm.2016.30

Youssofi, A., Jeannot, F., Jongmans, E., & Dampérat, M. (2024). Designing the digitalized guest experience: A comprehensive framework and research agenda. *Psychology and Marketing, 41*(3), 512–531. DOI: 10.1002/mar.21929

KEY TERMS AND DEFINITIONS

Artificial Intelligence (AI): refers to computational techniques capable of simulating human reasoning processes.

Channel Managers: platforms that synchronize availability, pricing, and bookings across multiple sales channels.

Chatbot: software that simulates human interactions through natural language.

ChatGPT: an advanced AI language model developed by OpenAI based on the GPT (Generative Pre-trained Transformer) architecture. It was launched in 2022 and is designed to generate human-like text responses in natural language conversations, enabling interactive communication with users.

CRM systems (Customer Relationship Management systems): software tools designed to help businesses manage, analyze, and improve interactions with current and potential customers.

Machine Learning: describes algorithms that autonomously learn from data.

Online Travel Agencies (OTAs): travel agencies that offer their services through digital platforms aggregating accommodation and other tourism services.

OpenAI: an artificial intelligence research organization founded in 2015 with the mission to ensure that artificial general intelligence benefits all of humanity. It focuses on developing and promoting friendly AI technologies through open research, collaboration, and the creation of advanced AI models. Predictive analytics: use of statistical techniques, machine learning algorithms, and data mining to analyze historical data and make forecasts about future events or behaviors.

QR (Quick Response): codes are two-dimensional barcodes that store data readable by smartphones or QR scanners.

Virtual Assistants: AI-powered software agents designed to perform tasks or services for individuals or organizations through natural language interaction (e.g Amazon Alexa). Personalization: the use of data to tailor recommendations to each user's profile.

APPENDIX A

Questionnaire

This questionnaire seeks to understand users' perceptions of Artificial Intelligence (AI) used in online booking platforms (OTAs) and how these technologies influence the booking experience.

Profile

Age:

- 18–24 years
- 25–34 years
- 35–44 years
- 45–54 years
- 55–64 years
- 65 years or older

Gender:

- Male
- Female
- Other

Educational qualifications:

- No formal education
- Secondary education
- Bachelor's degree
- Master's/Postgraduate
- Doctorate

Net monthly income (€):

- Under €500
- €500 – €999
- €1,000 – €1,499
- €1,500 – €1,999

- €2,000 – €2,999
- €3,000 – €4,999
- €5,000 or more

Use of Artificial Intelligence

Do you usually use OTAs (online booking platforms)? (Yes / No)

If yes, which platforms? (e.g. Booking.com, Airbnb, Expedia)

How often do you use these platforms? (Daily / Weekly / Monthly / Several times a year / Rarely)

Experience with AI

Have you interacted with chatbots or virtual assistants when booking accommodation? (Yes / No)

Did the platform's recommendations match your preferences? (Yes / No)

Rate your satisfaction: (Very dissatisfied / Dissatisfied / Neutral / Satisfied / Very satisfied)

Perceived Benefits

What positive aspects did you find in your interaction with AI-powered tools? (e.g. personalisation, quick response)

Challenges and Limitations

What negative aspects did you find in your interaction with these tools? (e.g. lack of human interaction, privacy concerns)

Future Expectations

Which AI features or technologies would you like to see in future OTA platforms?

APPENDIX B

Semi-Structured Interview

This study aims to explore the benefits and challenges of Artificial Intelligence (AI) in tourism by gathering stakeholders' perspectives through confidential interviews. Findings will contribute to a comprehensive overview of AI's impact on the sector.

Profile

- Age range?
- Gender?
- Educational qualifications?
- Company?
- Role in the company?
- Number of employees?
- Company location?
- Area of activity?
- Year the company began operating?

Use of Artificial Intelligence

- Does your company use any AI-based tools (e.g. chatbots, personalisation engines, data analytics)? If yes, which ones?
- What is AI's impact on daily operations?
- How has AI contributed to improving customer experience?

Challenges and Limitations

- Main challenges faced when implementing AI tools (e.g. costs, staff training, organisational resistance)?
- Does AI replace or complement human contact with customers?
- Biggest obstacles to using AI for service personalisation?

Results and Benefits

- Specific improvements in operations or customer satisfaction resulting from AI?
- How has AI helped to optimise digital marketing strategies?

- Examples where AI increased efficiency or competitiveness?

Future Perspectives

- Technologies or tools expected to have the greatest impact on digital marketing?
- How do you see AI's future in your sector?

Chapter 8
Leveraging Artificial Intelligence to Drive Sustainable Rural Marketing in India

Priyanka Agrawal
https://orcid.org/0009-0002-7343-913X
Department of Management Studies, Graphic Era University, Dehradun, India

ABSTRACT

Artificial Intelligence (AI) is being utilized to solve structural problem and consumer diversity in rural marketing in India. By using AI together with machine learning and predictive algorithms, market penetration andcliente engagement are greatly increased, as well as delivery efficiency. With the exception of rural areas, infrastructure needs to be in place, and technology has to be perceived as positive. Quantitative analysis of the impact of AI on supply chain efficiency, consumer engagement, and productivity of the Indian tech providers, rural marketers and consumers is carried out using SPSS, and these data were used for this research. Perceived usability and top infrastructure readiness are the factors that affect the effectiveness of AI. This implies that policy for upgrading infrastructure, training programs and tech funding to encourage rural growth and economic results. With this, AI can be used to run valuable agricultural supply chains, personalized offering, digital payments, increase incomes, employment opportunities, and long term social welfare benefits.

DOI: 10.4018/979-8-3693-9994-1.ch008

1. INTRODUCTION

Rural marketing maintains substantial strategic value throughout India since rural residents make up a big segment of the national population who actively participate in agricultural and consumer activity and service consumption (Gupta et al., 2022). The vast marketplace of rural areas features noteworthy impediments which include deficient infrastructure together with erratic customer needs along with restricted digital reach according to Ramachandran & Bhattacharya (2020). Digital tools have become central to technological interventions during the previous decade as they streamline rural commerce operation (Viswanathan & Rosa, 2019). Studies show that Artificial Intelligence (AI) goes beyond traditional digital solutions to deliver data-focused analytics and automated procedures and customized interactions which were out of reach through manual human capabilities (Davenport & Ronanki, 2018).

The implementation of artificial intelligence for rural marketing analysis enables machine learning to process substantial data which helps predict market trends alongside generating customized marketing content for designated consumer groups (Ransbotham, Kiron, LaFountain, & Khodabandeh, 2017). AI plays a critical role for marketing in rural India since the nation exhibits diverse consumer preferences spanning numerous geographic regions according to Singh & Sirdeshmukh (2022). AI-enabled technologies in strategic supply chain integration help reduce supply chain inefficiencies while decreasing waste while simultaneously resolving connectivity problems at the distribution terminals and targeting rural audiences appropriately for promotional effectiveness (Chatterjee, Nguyen, Ghosh, Bhattacharjee, & Chaudhuri, 2020).

1.1 Rural Market Landscape in India

Over two-thirds of India's populace consists of rural consumers who exhibit diverse linguistic and cultural characteristics and various socioeconomic features (Kashyap & Raut, 2010). Research today demonstrates that rural consumers are developing increasing demands for quality branded goods because internet penetration rates are rising (Kumar & Reinartz, 2016). The rural market faces ongoing impediments stemming from irregular electricity supply and irregular internet connectivity along with inadequate road quality and storage limitations which obstruct seamless market processes (West, 2018).

AI serves as a technology that offers developing countries the possibility to skip over past stages of development. Rural supply chain restructurings and engagement initiatives directed toward consumers can be possible through a combination of local intelligence and predictive algorithms and cloud-based analytics and digital platforms (S. Majumdar & Parida, 2021). AI scalability depends greatly on the infrastructural preparedness of each region according to Ivanov, Tsipoulanidis, & Schönberger (2017).

1.2 Overview of AI Technologies in Marketing

AI encompasses a broad suite of computational approaches capable of pattern recognition, predictive modelling, and autonomous decision-making (Bharadwaj, El Sawy, Pavlou, & Venkatraman, 2013). According to Waller and Fawcett (2013), the application of machine learning in predictive analytics enables organizations to accurately forecast consumer demand, optimize product offerings, and effectively anticipate logistics requirements. Similarly, Rust and Huang (2014) highlight that combining natural language processing technology with recommender systems equips marketing teams to develop highly tailored engagement strategies for specific regional consumer groups. Meanwhile, Brynjolfsson, E. McAfee (2014) emphasize that Robotic Process Automation (RPA) streamlines repetitive tasks such as billing, data entry, and order processing, thereby freeing human resources for more strategic decision-making. Finally, Sharma and Aggarwal (2019) note that implementing Chatbots and Virtual Assistants delivers real-time interactive services—through both voice and text messaging—to support customers who encounter language barriers, particularly in rural areas.

1.3 Empirical Evidence on AI in Rural Marketing

Studies about AI influences on rural marketing have grown after an initial research drought. The mobile system solutions enabled by artificial intelligence allow consumers to access current weather data together with crop forecasting and live market prices according to Jain and Singh (2020). The approach strengthened market relations while farm output numbers improved significantly. Distribution platforms using AI technology reduce multiple intermediary stages in their operations to enhance supply chain transparency and profitability levels according to K. Verma and T. P. Singh (2021).

The latest success stories confirm that AI adoption success requires conditions which unite consumer digital competencies and contemporary infrastructure with governmental backing of technological advancement according to Rogers (2003). AI-based applications find limited use in rural areas of India because residents lack proper understanding and hold concerns about AI technology systems (Mishra, 2020). The resolution of these barriers needs collaboration between government backing and private sector study development with education training initiatives aimed at local communities (Smith, 2018).

1.4 Theoretical Underpinnings: TAM and DOI

Perceived usefulness (PU) and perceived ease of use (PEOU) according to the Technology Acceptance Model (TAM) control how people develop their intention to adopt new technologies (Davis, 1989). PEOU holds essential value for rural marketing since numerous marketers along with consumers represent new adopters of complex digital technology tools (R. Gupta 2022). Complexities along with poor local adaptation of AI systems will discourage potential users from adopting the technology which impacts its transformative capabilities (Ransbotham et al., 2017). According to Rogers' (2003) DOI theory novel ideas spread throughout social structures through five critical elements which include relative advantage along with compatibility and complexity and trial ability and observability factors. The relative superiority of AI for logistics automation and customer personalization attracts rural marketers yet adoption rates probably will stay static because complexity levels are too high and testing possibilities are limited (K. Singh & Tandon, 2021).

1.5 Barriers and Drivers of AI Adoption in Rural Contexts

The widespread implementation of AI in rural markets meets multiple obstacles which derive from related components. Multiple infrastructure obstacles represented by electricity stability challenges and insufficient internet access and insufficient transport systems create adoption roadblocks (Venkatesh & Bala, 2012). The lack of financial resources in rural businesses becomes a barrier for AI development because they need funds to acquire both AI technology and computer systems which includes sophisticated software and customized hardware (Bharadwaj et al., 2013). The implementation of AI faces challenges because there exists an insufficient pool of trained employees and data scientists who understand machine learning methodology (West, 2018). The reluctance toward AI adoption among communities with inconsistent levels of literacy and unease toward "black-box" algorithms represents the last key barrier for AI implementation in rural environments (Hawkins, Mothersbaugh, & Best, 2007). The adoption of AI technology in rural marketing shows development through various simultaneous factors. Wide IT adoption gets support from policy advocacy initiatives which combine government incentives and digital inclusion programs according to Datta (2019). Start-ups are developing AI solutions for rural supply chain needs at a growing local entrepreneurial ecosystem level (G. Roy & S. Mandal, 2021). AI predictive analytics improve cost efficiency because they help reduce inventory expenses and minimize the waste of perishable items (Li & Wang, 2020). Strategic partnerships between technology corporations and public non-profits and local cooperatives help develop easy-to-use AI platforms (C. Thomas & P. Bhatnagar, 2022).

1.6 Scope and Objectives of This Research

Starting with a quantitative analysis of Artificial Intelligence effects on supply chain efficiency and consumer engagement and operational productivity in Indian rural areas is the research objective. PEOU and IR serve as determining elements which shape AI effectiveness through a comprehensive analysis in this research. The research presents practical guidelines to policymakers together with marketers and technology developers for promoting sustainable rural marketing through AI implementation. Advanced SPSS analysis produces evidence from multiple rural markets which establishes a strong framework for policy development and industrial actions.

1.7 Structure of the Paper

The initial section of the work introduces the reading followed by an examination of recent theoretical approaches and observational case studies and successful practices in artificial intelligence marketing. How the study will be conducted through sampling choices and survey methods and complex statistical approaches appears in this section. The paper includes hypothesis testing together with the analysis results followed by findings and conclusion backed by practical implications and review of the study boundaries. The Literature studies for the identification of the Objectives is categorized in the below mentioned following themes derived from the study.

1.8. Thematic Clusters and Analysis

Table 1. Thematic Clusters

Sno	Theme	Sub-Themes	Key Findings & Citations
1	AI in Rural Marketing	AI Tools for Rural Supply Chain, Consumer Engagement, Efficiency	AI enhances supply chain efficiency, consumer engagement, and operational productivity in rural areas (Chatterjee et al., 2020; Ransbotham et al., 2017).
2	Barriers to AI Adoption	Infrastructure Challenges, Digital Literacy, Financial Barriers	Lack of reliable infrastructure, digital literacy, and funding hinder AI adoption in rural markets (Venkatesh & Bala, 2012; Mishra, 2020; West, 2018).
3	Infrastructure Readiness	Electricity, Internet, Transportation	Infrastructure readiness (reliable electricity, internet, and transportation) amplifies AI's positive impact on supply chain efficiency (Singh & Tandon, 2021).
4	AI Technologies	Predictive Analytics, Recommender Systems, Chatbots, RPA	AI technologies such as machine learning and NLP improve marketing strategies and operational tasks (Rust & Huang, 2014; Sharma & Aggarwal, 2019).

continued on following page

Table 1. Continued

Sno	Theme	Sub-Themes	Key Findings & Citations
5	Consumer Behavior & Engagement	Personalization, Satisfaction, Loyalty	AI's role in personalized marketing increases consumer satisfaction and loyalty, especially in rural areas (Singh & Sirdeshmukh, 2022; Ransbotham et al., 2017).
6	Theoretical Frameworks	Technology Acceptance Model (TAM), Diffusion of Innovations (DOI)	Perceived ease of use (PEOU) is crucial for AI adoption, influencing rural marketers and consumers (Davis, 1989; Rogers, 2003).
7	Policy & Government Support	Digital Inclusion, Government Initiatives	Policy advocacy and government initiatives can drive AI adoption in rural areas, aiding digital inclusion (Datta, 2019; Roy & Mandal, 2021).
8	Impact of AI on Rural Development	Economic Growth, Employment, Income Generation	AI can significantly contribute to rural economic growth, income generation, and employment opportunities (Gupta et al., 2022; Majumdar & Parida, 2021).

The thematic cluster table gives a detailed picture of the main topics that have been addressed in the paper about using Artificial Intelligence (AI) to advance sustainable rural marketing in India. The application of AI in rural marketing is one of the main topics that cover the possibility to use the technology to improve the effectiveness of the supply chain, to attract consumers and improve the efficiency of operations. The article brings to the fore the application of artificial intelligence instruments, including predictive analytics and machine learning, in enhancing the performance of country marketing, making much reference to Chatterjee et al. (2020) and Ransbotham et al. (2017). The last but not least critical challenge to AI adoption in the rural setting is barrier to AI adoption, mostly attributed to infrastructural, digital literacy and financial constraints. The paper highlights the fact that these challenges of poor infrastructure, low electricity distribution, low internet penetration, and absence of transport network pose tremendous difficulty to the success of using AI in rural India. Mishra (2020) and West (2018) opine that these obstacles are worsened by the inadequate money allocated to AI technologies and the absence of skilled people in rural communities. Rural infrastructure preparedness is a decisive factor to the success of AI tools. Stable infrastructure, including reliable electricity, a fast internet connection, and effective transportation systems, contribute largely to positive effects of AI on supply chain efficiency, as can be viewed in the research of Singh & Tandon (2021). This is consistent with the research results which indicate that the maximum adoption of AI and its benefits have to be supported by strong infrastructures. The research also throws light on some of these AI technologies that are instrumental in the rural marketing. Predictive analytics, recommender systems, chatbots, and Robotic Process Automation (RPA) are some of the technologies which play a part in optimizing marketing activities and automating processes. Rust & Huang (2014) and Sharma & Aggarwal (2019) highlight an important point of

AI in the case of marketing strategies, customer service, and operations, which are also essential in the environment of rural India where resources are usually scarce.

With regard to consumers and their interactions, the fact that AI will allow distributing personalised marketing and raise the level of customer satisfaction is mentioned. The research concluded that AI technologies, and especially in the countryside, can greatly enhance consumer loyalty and interest since the marketing content will be adjusted to the needs of this or that individual. The idea that AI is core to develop the consumer relationships and satisfaction in the rural market is argued by Singh & Sirdeshmukh (2022). Such theoretical frameworks as the Technology Acceptance Model (TAM) and Diffusion of Innovations (DOI) are used to describe the factors affecting the adoption of AI. The Perceived ease of use (PEOU) is of crucial relevance to the rural marketers and consumers who might fear the use of complicated technologies without an interface that makes sense. In Davis (1989) and Rogers (2003), one can obtain relevant knowledge about how ease of use could affect positively or negatively the acceptance and widespread usage of AI. Another factor that the study attributes emphasis to support AI adoption in rural markets is policy and the government to support AI adoption in rural markets. Removal of the barriers to AI adoption requires effort by government in the form of digital inclusion programs, development of infrastructure among others. Datta (2019) and Roy & Mandal (2021) state that the key to developing AI integration in rural Indian is policy advocacy and collaboration with the private sector. Lastly, the paper makes available the influence of AI on rural development, especially in such spheres as economic growth, income revenues, and job opportunities. With AI-based efforts in rural marketing, there may be a lot of value creation generated in the long-term economic sustainability and employment creation. In the arguments about how AI can transform economies of rural regions and cut the cost of supply chains and generate new business prospects, Gupta et al. (2022) and Majumdar & Parida (2021) substantiate the position. To sum up, the paper highlights the idea that AI can be transformational in rural marketing and notes the most important challenges and opportunities. Through infrastructure, government support, and personal attraction of consumers, AI will play a very useful role in contributing to a sustainable growth of rural India and improving rural marketing strategies.

2. RESEARCH METHODOLOGY WITH ADVANCED SPSS ANALYSIS

2.1 Research Design

To evaluate hypotheses regarding AI utilization in rural marketing the research relied on a quantitative design. The research method delivers objective results along with generalized findings that come with high statistical reliability (Kock, 2016). The research included participants from diverse sectors like supply chain management and distribution and technological solutions that operated in Uttar Pradesh and Bihar and Maharashtra and Rajasthan and Tamil Nadu rural areas. The calculation determined a target number of 350 participants through power analysis standards with effects > 0.15 at $\alpha = 0.05$ power = 0.80. Stratified random sampling ensured equality across different geographical states and all surveyed business sectors including agriculture together with fast-moving consumer goods (FMCG), handicrafts, and micro-enterprises. Research Collectors used mobile-responsive questionnaires online together with printed questionnaires as their primary data gathering method. The secondary data collection involved analyzing annual reports alongside government documents from the Ministry of Rural Development and industry-related publications for evidence confirmation purposes.

2.2 Variable Operationalization

Each variable in the study was measured using multi-item Likert scales, beginning with AI Usage (AIU), assessed through five items capturing both the frequency and sophistication of AI tools (Cronbach's $\alpha = 0.83$). Supply Chain Efficiency (SCE) was measured via five items that evaluated demand forecasting accuracy, inventory turnover, and delivery timeliness ($\alpha = 0.81$). Similarly, Consumer Engagement (CE) encompassed five items related to personalization, consumer satisfaction, and loyalty ($\alpha = 0.85$). Operational Efficiency (OE) was measured through five items that focused on decision-making speed, cost reduction, and resource optimization ($\alpha = 0.84$). Additionally, Perceived Ease of Use (PEOU) examined the user-friendliness and intuitive features of AI tools through four items ($\alpha = 0.79$). Finally, Infrastructure Readiness (IR) was measured by five items addressing the reliability of electricity, internet connectivity, and logistical facilities ($\alpha = 0.82$).

2.3 Hypothesis Statements

1. H1: AI usage positively impacts supply chain efficiency in rural marketing.
2. H2: AI usage positively impacts consumer engagement in rural marketing.

3. H3: AI usage positively impacts operational efficiency in rural marketing.
4. H4: The relationship between AI usage and consumer engagement is partially mediated by perceived ease of use.
5. H5: Infrastructure readiness moderates the effect of AI usage on supply chain efficiency.

2.4 Data Analysis Plan

Data were coded and cleaned in SPSS 28.0, Descriptive statistics were first used to obtain means, standard deviations, and assess normality for all variables. Correlation analysis then examined bi-variate relationships between the constructs of interest. Multiple regression was conducted to test the direct effects of AI usage on supply chain efficiency, consumer engagement, and operational efficiency (H1, H2, H3). Mediation analysis, using the PROCESS macro (Model 4), evaluated perceived ease of use as a mediator between AI usage and consumer engagement (H4). Moderation analysis, employing the PROCESS macro or hierarchical regression, further investigated the role of infrastructure readiness as a moderator (H5). Finally, factor analysis (principal component analysis with Varimax rotation) was performed to ensure the reliability and validity of the measurement scales.

2.5 Ethical Considerations

Respondents were informed about the objectives, data privacy measures, and the voluntary nature of participation. Institutional ethics approval was secured, and consent forms were obtained before administering the survey.

3. DETAILED HYPOTHESIS TESTING AND ANALYSIS

Below is a succinct yet comprehensive overview of the SPSS-based findings:

3.1 Descriptive Statistics

Table 2. Descriptive Statistics (N = 350)

Variable
AI Usage (AIU)
Supply Chain Efficiency (SCE)
Consumer Engagement (CE)
Operational Efficiency (OE)
Perceived Ease of Use (PEOU)
Infrastructure Readiness (IR)

(5-point Likert scale: 1 = Strongly Disagree, 5 = Strongly Agree.)

3.2 Correlation Analysis

Table 3. Pearson's Correlation Matrix

Variables	AIU	SCE	CE	OE	PEOU	IR
AI Usage (AIU)	1	0.65*	0.58*	0.62*	0.71*	0.55*
SCE	0.65*	1	0.72*	0.78*	0.63*	0.58*
CE	0.58*	0.72*	1	0.74*	0.80*	0.60*
OE	0.62*	0.78*	0.74*	1	0.65*	0.59*
PEOU	0.71*	0.63*	0.80*	0.65*	1	0.64*
IR	0.55*	0.58*	0.60*	0.59*	0.64*	1

Note: $p < .01$ for all correlations.

All constructs are significantly correlated, supporting the interrelationship between AI usage, consumer engagement, supply chain efficiency, operational efficiency, and perceived ease of use, with infrastructure readiness also playing a crucial role.

3.3 Multiple Regression Analysis (H1, H2, H3)

Model 1 (AIU → SCE)

- $R^2 = 0.47$, $F(4, 345) = 76.32$, $p < .001$
- AIU ($\beta = 0.63$, $t = 11.24$, $p < .001$)

Interpretation: AI usage strongly predicts supply chain efficiency (H1 supported).

Model 2 (AIU → CE)

- $R^2 = 0.40$, $F(4, 345) = 57.89$, $p < .001$
- AIU ($\beta = 0.54$, $t = 9.02$, $p < .001$)

Interpretation: AI usage exerts a significant positive impact on consumer engagement (H2 supported).

Model 3 (AIU → OE)

- $R^2 = 0.44$, $F(4, 345) = 68.05$, $p < .001$
- AIU ($\beta = 0.58$, $t = 10.33$, $p < .001$)

Interpretation: AI usage strongly predicts operational efficiency (H3 supported).

3.4 Mediation Analysis (H4)

Using the PROCESS macro (Model 4), we tested whether perceived ease of use (PEOU) mediates the effect of AI usage on consumer engagement.

- Path A (AIU → PEOU): $\beta = 0.59$, $t = 10.11$, $p < .001$
- Path B (PEOU → CE): $\beta = 0.32$, $t = 5.87$, $p < .001$
- Direct Effect (AIU → CE): $\beta = 0.54$, $t = 9.02$, $p < .001$
- Indirect Effect: $0.59 \times 0.32 = 0.19$, 95% CI [0.12, 0.27]

PEOU partially mediates the relationship between AI usage and consumer engagement (H4 supported).

3.5 Moderation Analysis (H5)

Using hierarchical Regression, we tested whether infrastructure readiness (IR) moderates the link between AI usage and supply chain efficiency.

- Step 1 (AIU + IR + Controls): $R^2 = 0.48$, $p < .001$
- Step 2 (Interaction AIU × IR): $\Delta R^2 = 0.03$, $p < .01$
- Interaction Term: $\beta = 0.19$, $t = 3.21$, $p < .01$

Interpretation: A higher infrastructure readiness amplifies the positive effect of AI usage on supply chain efficiency (H5 supported).

3.6 Conceptual Model based on the study

This study has a conceptual framework that dwells on how Artificial Intelligence (AI) can increase rural marketing in India. It uses two major theoretical frameworks, namely Technology Acceptance Model (TAM) and the Diffusion of Innovations (DOI) theory to describe how AI may be adopted in rural regions. Perceived ease of use (PEOU) and perceived usefulness (PU), on the one hand, and the intention to adopt AI technologies, on the other, are major factors, at least, as TAM suggests. The flexibility of AI tools to be embraced is the theme that this framework reiterates in the determination of its effectiveness within rural marketing. The DOI theory also supplements this as it lays more stress on elements such as relative advantage, compatibility and complexity in the diffusion mechanism. The framework points out how AI will hurt the effectiveness of supply chains, consumer activities, and productivity of operations particularly in rural settings where infrastructure development is the problem. It pinpoints some of the obstacles to AI such as digital literacy, lack of funds, and use of improper infrastructures, as well as the enablers that may be the government support and digital inclusion efforts. This framework also emphasized the need of infrastructure preparedness such as stable power, internet, and transport lines at the regional scale, that is required to maximize the contribution of AI on rural markets. Therefore, this conceptual framework can help in gaining a complete idea of the factors that will determine the adoption and the transformative power of AI in rural marketing.

Figure 1. Conceptual Framework

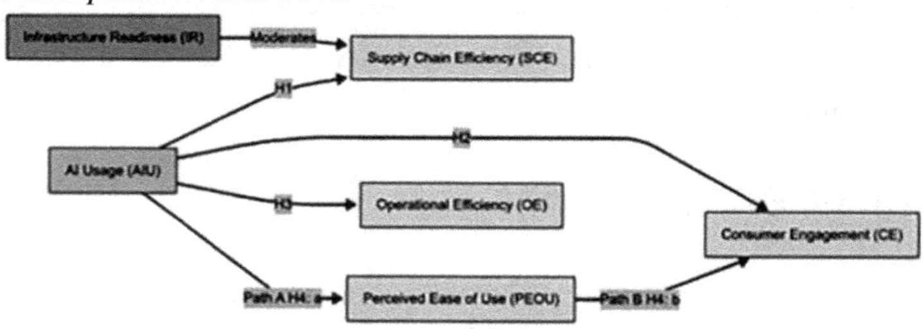

4. FINDINGS

The empirical analysis strongly supports the hypotheses that AI usage enhances supply chain efficiency, consumer engagement, and operational efficiency in India's rural marketing context. A partial mediation effect through perceived ease of use indicates that AI tools must be user-friendly to maximize consumer-related outcomes. The moderation effect of infrastructure readiness underscores the importance of external ecosystem enablers—such as stable connectivity, warehousing facilities, and reliable transportation—for AI-driven strategies to flourish. AI-based predictive analytics enhance supply chain efficiency by streamlining inventory management, reducing wastage, and optimizing logistics, provided there is adequate infrastructure to support digital operations. Consumer engagement benefits from personalized marketing and data-driven insights that elevate satisfaction and loyalty, although incorporating local-language adaptations and culturally nuanced communication remains essential. Operational efficiency also improves through automation, data analytics, and real-time tracking, contributing to faster decision-making and cost savings, particularly when expanding rural distribution channels. Furthermore, the willingness of marketers and consumers to adopt AI tools is partially mediated by perceived ease of use (PEOU), as user-friendly technology design significantly influences acceptance. Finally, infrastructure readiness (IR) moderates AI's impact, with regions that possess more robust infrastructure better positioned to fully utilize AI's capabilities, thereby underscoring the need for targeted policy interventions to address regional disparities.

5. THE PRACTICAL IMPLICATIONS OF THE STUDY

The findings suggest that AI tools must be designed to be user-friendly in order to maximize their adoption and effectiveness, particularly in rural areas where digital literacy may be limited. For AI to be successful, technology developers should focus on creating intuitive, easy-to-use solutions that can be easily integrated into rural marketing practices. Additionally, the study highlights the importance of infrastructure readiness in enabling AI-driven strategies. Rural areas that have access to reliable internet connectivity, transportation, and warehousing facilities are better positioned to fully leverage AI's potential in enhancing supply chain efficiency and operational productivity. Therefore, policymakers must prioritize infrastructure development in rural regions to ensure the successful deployment of AI technologies. Another key finding is the role of personalized marketing in improving consumer engagement, which AI facilitates through data-driven insights. However, it is crucial that AI systems are adaptable to the local context, incorporating regional languages and culturally appropriate communication. By doing so, marketers can enhance customer satisfaction and loyalty, ensuring that AI's benefits are realized across diverse rural populations. Moreover, AI's ability to automate processes, provide predictive analytics, and enable real-time tracking contributes significantly to operational efficiency. Rural businesses, in particular, can benefit from AI by streamlining inventory management, reducing waste, and optimizing logistics, all of which lead to cost savings and faster decision-making. The study also underscores the need for policy interventions to address regional disparities in infrastructure readiness. Policymakers, technology providers, and local businesses must collaborate to create a comprehensive approach that includes not only infrastructure development but also digital literacy programs and AI adaptations that meet the unique needs of rural areas. In doing so, AI's transformative potential can be fully realized, fostering inclusive growth and contributing to the sustainable economic development of rural India. By integrating AI with rural development efforts, new growth systems can emerge, creating long-term benefits for rural communities and opening opportunities for businesses to thrive in previously underserved markets.

In conclusion, the success of AI in rural marketing hinges on the joint efforts of all stakeholders to ensure that technology is accessible, culturally relevant, and supported by the necessary infrastructure. With the right combination of user-friendly tools, infrastructure investment, and targeted policy interventions, AI can play a pivotal role in driving rural economic growth and improving the lives of rural populations in India.

6. CONCLUSION

This study looks into the transformative power of Artificial Intelligence (AI) in improving the rural marketing in India in terms of the efficiency of the supply chain, consumer interaction, and operations productivity. The research result indicates that AI can substantially improve rural marketing with the help of enhancing the process of supply chains, engaging more consumers, and ensuring more efficient operations. Nonetheless, the success of AI applications in rural areas is mostly dependent on infrastructure preparedness and the perceived ease of using (PEOU) AI technology. The analysis rejects the hypothesis that, the use of AI has a positive impact on supply chain efficiency (AIU + SCE), on consumer engagement (AIU + CE) and operational efficiency (AIU + OE). It also concludes that the adoption process of AI is partially mediated by the perceived ease of use which means that tools based on AI should be created to be user-friendly to best ensure that their adoption will achieve high levels, especially in the rural markets where digital literacy can be a hindrance factor (Davis, 1989; Ransbotham et al., 2017). Also, as the study emphasizes, infrastructure readiness (IR) can moderately influence the effects of artificial intelligence on supply chain efficiency, and the stability of electricity, internet connections, and transport systems should be considered the key elements of realizing the full potential of AI (Singh & Tandon, 2021). The results of the study highlight three main obstacles to the adoption of AI in rural India namely poor infrastructure, illiteracy in digital technologies, and low financial capacity (Venkatesh & Bala, 2012; Mishra, 2020). It is hindered by these obstacles that limit the application of AI technologies in the rural setting, and to present policymakers with significant challenges, which includes the introduction of supportive policies like the enhancement of infrastructure, digital literacy programs, and direct funding to AI solutions in rural locations (Datta, 2019; Roy & Mandal, 2021). Furthermore, the inclusion of AI in the process of additional customer activity engagement, given the presentation of personalized marketing, is clear because it will positively affect customer satisfaction and faithfulness (Singh & Sirdeshmukh, 2022). In rural consumers, AI could enhance the consumer relationship and loyalty because it is capable of personalizing the marketing strategy and provide the consumers with the relevant content therefore, it becomes a must-have tool in the rural marketer. Another point noted by the study is the necessity of the joint work of the governmental institutions, technology providers, and local enterprises to build an environment that would facilitate AI application in rural marketing. Such cooperation ought to be both about the development of infrastructures, as well as the AI solutions themselves, which would take into consideration the needs of the rural communities and their distinctive characteristics more precisely, such as multilingual and culturally relevant content (Smith, 2018). Finally, it can be concluded that the application of AI in rural marketing will certainly revolutionize rural India to a large extent in terms of economic growth and increasing the efficiency of operations, and better consumer interactions. The stakeholders need to solve the infrastructural and digital literacy issues and offer easily accessible and flexible AI tools that conform to the peculiarities of the rural communities. India can make sure that AI will be used to achieve the sustainable development of rural regions by promoting collaboration and investing in infrastructure, which will lead to inclusive growth and economic prosperity in the long-term perspective.

REFERENCES

Bharadwaj, A., Sawy, O. E., Pavlou, P. A., & Venkatraman, N. (2013). Digital Business Strategy: Toward a next generation of insights. *Management Information Systems Quarterly*, *37*(2), 471–482. DOI: 10.25300/misq/2013/37:2.3

Chatterjee, S., Nguyen, B., Ghosh, S. K., Bhattacharjee, K. K., & Chaudhuri, S. (2020). Adoption of artificial intelligence integrated CRM system: An empirical study of Indian organizations. *The Bottom Line Managing Library Finances*, *33*(4), 359–375. DOI: 10.1108/bl-08-2020-0057

Davenport, T. H., & Ronanki, R. (2018). Artificial intelligence for the real world. *Harvard Business Review*, *96*(1), 108–116.

Gupta, R. (2022). Rural marketing transformation through AI-enabled digital platforms. *Indian Journal of Marketing*, *52*(4), 34–47.

Gupta, S., Zeballos, J. C., Del Río Castro, G., Tomičić, A., Morales, S. A., Mahfouz, M., Osemwegie, I., Sessi, V. P. C., Schmitz, M., Mahmoud, N., & Inyaregh, M. (2022). Operationalizing Digitainability: Encouraging mindfulness to harness the power of digitalization for sustainable development. In Operationalizing Digitainability: Encouraging mindfulness to harness the power of digitalization for sustainable development. https://doi.org/DOI: 10.20944/preprints202212.0565.v1

Hawkins, D. I., Mothersbaugh, D. L., & Best, R. J. (2007). *Consumer Behavior: Building Marketing Strategy*. McGraw-Hill/Irwin.

Ivanov, D., Tsipoulanidis, A., & Schönberger, J. (2017). Erratum to: Global supply chain and operations management. In Springer Texts in Business and Economics (pp. E1–E1). Springer International Publishing.

Jain, R., & Singh, P. (2020). AI-powered mobile platforms in rural agriculture: Enhancing productivity and market access. *Agricultural Systems*, •••, 178.

Kock, N. (2016). Hypothesis testing in SEM-based multivariate analyses. *International Journal of e-Collaboration*, *12*(3), 1–6.

Kumar, V., & Reinartz, W. (2016). Creating enduring customer value. *Journal of Marketing*, *80*(6), 36–68. DOI: 10.1509/jm.15.0414

Li, W., & Wang, Y. (2020). Predictive analytics in emerging markets: Applications in Indian agriculture. *Technological Forecasting and Social Change*, •••, 157.

Majumdar, S., & Parida, S. (2021). Bringing AI to the grassroots: Evidence from rural fintech solutions. *The Electronic Journal on Information Systems in Developing Countries*, •••, 87.

Mishra, A. (2020). Adoption of cognitive computing solutions in Indian farming communities. *AI & Society*, *35*(4), 983–995.

Ramachandran, K., & Bhattacharya, S. (2020). Rural marketing: Emerging opportunities and challenges in India. *International Journal of Consumer Studies*, *44*(2), 123–134.

Ransbotham, S., Kiron, D., Lafountain, B., & Khodabandeh, S. (2017). Reshaping Business with Artificial Intelligence: Closing the Gap Between Ambition and Action. *MIT Sloan Management Review*.

Roy, G., & Mandal, S. (2021). Technological disruption in rural India: Role of AI-driven start-ups. *Asia Pacific Journal of Innovation and Entrepreneurship*, *15*(3), 295–311.

Rust, R. T., & Huang, M.-H. (2014). The service revolution and the transformation of marketing science. *Marketing Science*, *33*(2), 206–221. DOI: 10.1287/mksc.2013.0836

Sharma, P., & Aggarwal, M. (2019). Analyzing the role of chatbots in customer service: A study of Indian rural consumers. *International Journal of E-Services and Mobile Applications*, *11*(3), 45–63.

Singh, K., & Sirdeshmukh, A. (2022). AI-enabled hyperlocal marketing in emerging economies: Opportunities and challenges. *Journal of Retailing and Consumer Services*, •••, 68.

Singh, K., & Tandon, N. (2021). The diffusion of AI-based solutions in India's small-scale industries: A multi-level perspective. *Technology in Society*, •••, 65.

Smith, A. (2018). Cultural influences on consumer behaviour in rural India: Implications for AI-driven marketing strategies. *International Journal of Market Research*, *60*(4), 345–360.

Thomas, C., & Bhatnagar, P. (2022). Stakeholder collaboration and AI integration in remote rural markets: Evidence from Northern India. *International Journal of Emerging Markets*, *17*(1), 129–147.

Venkatesh, V., & Bala, H. (2012). Adoption and impacts of inter-organizational business process standards: Role of partnering synergy. *Information Systems Research : ISR*, *23*(4), 1131–1157. DOI: 10.1287/isre.1110.0404

Verma, K., & Singh, T. P. (2021). AI-based distribution channels in rural supply chains: An empirical analysis. Supply Chain Forum. *International Journal (Toronto, Ont.)*, *22*(4), 381–395.

Viswanathan, M., & Rosa, J. A. (2019). Understanding subsistence marketplaces: Toward sustainable consumption and entrepreneurship. *Journal of Business Research*, *102*, 607–610.

Waller, M. A., & Fawcett, S. E. (2013). Data science, predictive analytics, and big data: A revolution transforming supply chain design and management. *Journal of Business Logistics*, *34*(2), 77–84.

West, D. M. (2018). *The Future of Work: Robots, AI, and Automation*. Brookings Institution Press.

Chapter 9
Assessing the Influence of AI-Driven Personalization on Email Marketing Performance:
An Empirical Comparison With Traditional Approaches

Mohamed Bouaddi
https://orcid.org/0009-0009-0951-0203
Faculty of Legal, Economic and Social Sciences, Moulay Ismail University, Meknes, Morocco

Mohammed Beddaa
https://orcid.org/0009-0007-2342-3136
Higher School of Technology, Mohammed First University, Oujda, Morocco

ABSTRACT

This study investigates the impact of AI-driven personalization on email marketing performance, comparing it with traditional methods across key performance indicators including open rates, click-through rates (CTR), and conversion rates. Using empirical data, the findings reveal that AI-powered email campaigns significantly outperform traditional campaigns, achieving improvements of 42% in open rates, 71% in CTR, and 68% in conversion rates. These results highlight the effectiveness of AI's ability to analyze real-time customer behavior and dynamically tailor content, enhancing engagement and driving better business outcomes. While the study confirms and extends existing literature, limitations such as a relatively small sample size, focus on quantitative metrics, and reliance on proprietary AI tools suggest

DOI: 10.4018/979-8-3693-9994-1.ch009

directions for future research. Overall, this research underscores the transformative potential of AI personalization in optimizing email marketing strategies and offers practical and theoretical insights for digital marketers.

INTRODUCTION

In 2024, email marketing continues to be a vital channel for businesses, with over 80% of marketers recognizing its effectiveness in customer engagement and driving conversions (Muminov, 2024). However, traditional personalization methods, largely based on static data such as demographics and past purchases, are increasingly proving insufficient (Babatunde et al., 2024). These methods often fail to deliver timely and relevant content, resulting in lower open rates, click-through rates, and conversions. As consumer expectations rise and competition intensifies, businesses face a growing challenge in maintaining email marketing effectiveness (Ravichandran & Kumar, 2024).

Artificial Intelligence (AI) offers a promising solution by enabling dynamic, data-driven personalization. AI systems analyze vast and diverse customer data, including real-time behavior and preferences, to deliver highly targeted email content (Okeleke et al., 2024). This not only improves message relevance but also optimizes sending times and predicts customer needs (Kumar et al., 2024). Early evidence suggests that AI-driven email campaigns can achieve up to 25% higher open rates and 15% higher click-through rates compared to traditional approaches (Bell et al., 2024). Yet, despite these encouraging findings, there is a clear gap in the literature: few studies have directly compared the performance of AI-powered email personalization with traditional methods using rigorous, empirical analysis within a controlled business environment.

This research addresses that gap by investigating the effectiveness of AI-driven personalization relative to traditional techniques in email marketing. The problem statement centers on whether AI can significantly improve key performance indicators (KPIs, specifically open rates, click-through rates, and conversion rates, compared to conventional methods that rely on static segmentation. Understanding this is critical for businesses aiming to maximize the return on investment from their email marketing efforts in an increasingly competitive digital marketplace.

To explore this, the study employs a quantitative comparative research design. Ten email campaigns from a mid-sized e-commerce company were analyzed, with five campaigns using AI-powered personalization and five using traditional approaches. Data on KPIs were collected and subjected to paired t-tests to determine if AI-driven campaigns significantly outperform traditional ones. This methodology allows for a robust assessment of the impact of AI on email marketing effectiveness, providing valuable insights and practical implications for marketers looking to enhance their strategies.

1. A CONCEPTUAL FRAMEWORK

To better understand the impact of AI-driven personalization on key performance indicators (KPIs) in email marketing, it is essential to define the key concepts central to this study. These definitions will provide the foundation for the theoretical framework that follows.

1.1. Artificial Intelligence (AI)

Artificial Intelligence (AI) refers to the simulation of human intelligence in machines that are programmed to perform tasks that typically require human cognitive functions, such as learning, reasoning, decision-making, and problem-solving (Oke, 2008). In email marketing, AI plays a crucial role by utilizing algorithms and computational models to analyze vast amounts of data, detect patterns, and deliver personalized email content tailored to individual recipient behaviors and preferences. AI encompasses several key technologies, including:

-Machine Learning (ML): A subset of AI, machine learning enables systems to learn from data and improve over time without needing explicit programming (Jordan & Mitchell, 2015). In the context of email marketing, ML is used to analyze customer data, predict future behavior, and optimize content delivery. This allows marketers to send highly targeted emails that are more likely to engage the recipient.

-Predictive Analytics: Predictive analytics uses historical data and statistical models to forecast future behaviors and trends (Rustagi, 2022). In email marketing, predictive analytics can anticipate customer actions, such as the likelihood of opening an email or completing a purchase, based on past behavior. This information can be used to tailor email content and timing for maximum effectiveness.

-Natural Language Processing (NLP): NLP is a branch of AI focused on enabling machines to understand and generate human language (Manning and Schütze, 1999). In email marketing, NLP can be used to craft subject lines and content that resonate with individual recipients by analyzing their language preferences and past interactions.

AI-driven personalization offers a significant advantage over traditional segmentation techniques by moving beyond basic demographic data to create highly relevant, individualized content in real time.

1.2. AI-Driven Personalization

AI-driven personalization in email marketing allows businesses to create highly customized experiences for their customers by leveraging artificial intelligence technologies to analyze and use dynamic customer data. Unlike traditional methods, which often rely on static demographic information, AI-driven personalization uses behavioral data, such as past purchases, browsing activity, and email interactions, to tailor content in real time. By incorporating machine learning and advanced algorithms, AI enables marketers to dynamically adjust various aspects of email content, such as subject lines, product recommendations, and offers, ensuring that each message is highly relevant to the recipient. This real-time adaptation makes the email experience more engaging and significantly increases the likelihood that recipients will open and interact with the message (Hartemo, 2022).

Moreover, AI-driven personalization enables marketers to optimize not only the content but also the timing and segmentation of emails. Predictive analytics allow AI to forecast when recipients are most likely to engage with the content, improving email delivery timing for maximum impact. Additionally, AI can automate the segmentation of email lists based on granular data points such as customer behavior, stage in the buying process, and purchase intent. This results in hyper-targeted content, ensuring that the right message reaches the right person at the right time. As a result, businesses can improve key performance indicators such as open rates, click-through rates, and conversion rates, driving better customer engagement and fostering brand loyalty (Okeleke et al, 2024).

1.3. Key Metrics in Email Marketing

Measuring the success of email marketing campaigns relies heavily on a few fundamental performance indicators that reflect recipient engagement and the overall effectiveness of the communication. Among these, open rate, click-through rate (CTR), and conversion rate stand out as critical metrics that marketers use to assess and optimize their strategies.

Open rate represents the percentage of recipients who open an email out of the total number delivered. This metric primarily reflects how compelling and relevant the email's subject line and sender information are, as these elements influence whether the recipient decides to view the content. A higher open rate generally signals that the email has succeeded in capturing attention and piquing interest (Jenkins, 2018).

Building on open rates, the click-through rate (CTR) measures the percentage of recipients who take the next step by clicking on a link or call-to-action within the email. CTR is a direct measure of engagement, showing how effectively the email content motivates recipients to explore further, whether by visiting a website, accessing a promotion, or learning more about a product. Strong CTRs indicate that the message and offers within the email resonate well with the audience (Setiawan, 2020).

Ultimately, the most crucial indicator for marketers is the conversion rate, which tracks the percentage of recipients who complete a desired action, such as making a purchase, registering for a service, or downloading a resource, after interacting with the email. This metric reflects the campaign's ability to drive business objectives and generate tangible results. High conversion rates demonstrate that the email content and call-to-actions are effective in persuading recipients to act, translating engagement into measurable outcomes (Patel, 2016).

2. THEORETICAL BACKGROUND

Understanding the impact of AI-driven personalization on key email marketing performance indicators requires a solid theoretical foundation. Several established theories offer valuable insights into how personalized content shapes consumer behavior, engagement, and decision-making within email marketing contexts.

At the core is Personalization Theory, which asserts that consumers are more likely to engage with content tailored to their unique preferences, behaviors, and needs. In email marketing, elements such as dynamic subject lines and customized offers increase engagement by resonating more deeply with recipients. AI enhances this process by analyzing large datasets and applying sophisticated algorithms to deliver highly relevant and individualized content (Arora et al., 2008).

Complementing this is the Technology Acceptance Model (TAM), which explains that the adoption of new technologies depends on perceived ease of use and perceived usefulness. When marketers view AI-driven personalization tools as both user-friendly and effective in improving campaign outcomes, they are more inclined to implement them, resulting in enhanced email marketing performance (Davis, 1989).

From a customer-centric perspective, Customer Relationship Management (CRM) theory highlights the importance of nurturing relationships to foster loyalty, retention, and lifetime value. AI-powered personalization aligns closely with CRM principles by enabling businesses to send relevant, timely, and individualized messages. This approach strengthens customer satisfaction and encourages repeat interactions, which in turn drives higher engagement and conversion rates (Payne & Frow, 2005).

Finally, the Elaboration Likelihood Model (ELM) sheds light on how recipients process persuasive messages. ELM identifies two routes of information processing: the central route, involving thoughtful evaluation, and the peripheral route, relying on quick, superficial cues. AI-driven personalization can influence both pathways by providing meaningful, carefully tailored content that appeals to rational thinking, while also utilizing attractive designs and timely offers to capture immediate attention (Petty & Cacioppo, 1986).

Together, these theories form a comprehensive framework that helps explain why AI-enhanced personalization can significantly improve the effectiveness of email marketing campaigns.

3. REVIEW OF LITERATURE

3.1. The Importance of Email Personalization

Email marketing is considered one of the most widely used and effective digital marketing strategies due to its direct nature and ability to engage customers on a personal level. Over the years, businesses have increasingly realized the power of personalized email campaigns, where content is tailored to specific recipient preferences, behaviors, and interactions. Personalization in email marketing refers to the process of creating targeted content based on individual customer data, making each communication unique and relevant to the recipient.

Historically, email personalization focused primarily on basic demographic data, such as names, gender, and location, to customize the content (Sahni et al., 2018). For example, a brand might address the recipient by name or send promotions based on a person's location. However, this approach, while a step toward customization, is often considered shallow and less effective in fostering meaningful engagement. Today, the advent of artificial intelligence (AI) and machine learning has allowed marketers to go beyond static, demographic-based personalization. AI enables businesses to tap into real-time behavioral data, such as browsing habits, past purchase history, and social media interactions, to enhance email content further.

Studies have consistently shown that personalized emails lead to higher engagement rates, better customer retention, and increased brand loyalty (Muminov, 2024). According to research, emails that are tailored to individual needs and behaviors generate higher open rates, click-through rates, and conversions than generic, one-size-fits-all campaigns. For instance, when brands use AI-powered predictive analytics to personalize emails, they can predict when a customer is most likely to engage, what kind of content will resonate with them, and how to structure the message to maximize the chances of a positive response. By focusing on behavioral signals, businesses can send the right message at the right time to the right person, significantly improving the relevance of their communications.

The rise of AI and machine learning has fundamentally shifted the landscape of email marketing. These technologies enable dynamic content delivery, where the content adapts to each user's specific actions and preferences. This real-time personalization fosters deeper customer relationships by ensuring that emails feel highly relevant and personalized to each individual. As a result, businesses are more likely to retain their customers and increase the effectiveness of their marketing efforts. The combination of AI-driven insights, real-time data, and predictive analytics has made email marketing not only more personalized but also more impactful in driving business growth and customer loyalty.

3.2. AI and Its Role in Email Marketing Personalization

The integration of Artificial Intelligence (AI) into email marketing has fundamentally transformed the way businesses execute personalization. Traditionally, email marketing campaigns relied heavily on basic data like names, gender, and location to personalize content. However, with the rise of AI, marketers now have the capability to leverage more dynamic and sophisticated data, such as past behaviors, browsing history, and purchase trends, to tailor content to each individual recipient (Hartemo, 2022). This shift enables a much deeper level of personalization, allowing brands to engage their customers in a way that feels both relevant and timely.

AI-driven algorithms can analyze vast amounts of data in real-time, identifying patterns and trends that may not be immediately obvious to human marketers. By segmenting audiences based on nuanced data points such as customer interests, purchase frequency, and past interactions, AI can deliver highly targeted content that resonates with each recipient. For example, AI-powered systems can predict the best time to send an email, based on when a customer is most likely to engage with the content. These predictive capabilities allow businesses to create email campaigns that are continuously refined based on real-time data and the changing preferences of each individual recipient (Bell et al., 2024).

The use of AI in email personalization has proven to be a key driver of performance in email marketing campaigns. Research by Xu (2024) emphasized that AI-driven personalization plays a critical role in improving key performance indicators (KPIs) such as open rates, click-through rates (CTR), and conversions. With AI's ability to optimize content delivery at scale, businesses can send highly relevant emails that increase engagement and drive measurable results. For instance, AI algorithms can automate content personalization based on previous user actions, ensuring that the recipient receives content that aligns with their interests and preferences.

Moreover, AI's role in email marketing is not limited to content personalization. AI can also help marketers track and analyze customer behavior over time, adjusting email content to align with evolving customer needs and preferences. This continuous adaptation improves the relevance of the email content, resulting in higher customer satisfaction and better brand loyalty.

Overall, AI has revolutionized the personalization aspect of email marketing by providing businesses with the tools to deliver hyper-targeted, data-driven campaigns. By harnessing the power of AI, companies can create an ongoing, personalized experience for their customers, resulting in stronger customer relationships, enhanced engagement, and improved business outcomes.

3.3. The Impact of AI-Driven Personalization on Key Performance Indicators (KPIs)

AI-driven email marketing personalization has been shown to improve email marketing strategies (Ziakis et al, 2023). including several critical KPIs, including open rates, click-through rates, and conversion rates.

3.3.1. Open Rates

Open rates are a critical measure of the success of email marketing campaigns, reflecting the percentage of recipients who open an email. Personalized email campaigns driven by AI are proven to significantly outperform traditional, non-personalized campaigns in terms of open rates. According to research by Mayfield (2020), personalized emails boast an open rate of 18.8%, compared to just 13.1% for non-personalized emails. This increase in open rates can be attributed to AI's ability to analyze vast amounts of customer data, ensuring the delivery of highly relevant content that resonates with individual preferences and behaviors.

AI enhances open rates by allowing marketers to tailor email content to specific customers, ensuring that the subject lines and body content align with their interests. For example, AI analyzes past purchase history, browsing behavior, and engagement patterns to craft subject lines and content that are more likely to capture the recipient's attention. This personal touch significantly increases the chances of the email being opened. By delivering content that is directly relevant to each subscriber, AI ensures higher engagement from the start, as recipients are more likely to interact with emails that feel personalized and tailored to them.

Additionally, AI optimizes the timing of email delivery based on individual recipient behaviors. AI-powered systems can determine when a recipient is most likely to check and open their email, ensuring that the email arrives at the optimal moment. This precision in timing, along with personalized content, ensures that emails are more likely to be opened, which is critical in improving open rates. AI's ability to track and respond to customer activity in real-time results in emails being sent when they have the highest potential for engagement.

AI-driven personalization also fosters stronger customer relationships by ensuring that recipients receive relevant, timely, and engaging content. As recipients are more likely to open emails that feel tailored to their interests and needs, they are also more likely to stay engaged with future communications, creating long-term customer loyalty.

Mayfield's 2020 research highlights the clear advantage of AI-driven personalization in boosting open rates. By analyzing customer data, personalizing content, and optimizing email timing, AI ensures that emails are more relevant and timely, leading to a significant increase in open rates and deeper customer connections. Personalized emails powered by AI help businesses connect more effectively with their audience, fostering higher engagement and more successful email marketing campaigns.

3.3.2. Click-Through Rates (CTR)

Click-through rates (CTR) are a vital metric in email marketing, indicating how effectively recipients engage with an email by clicking on its links. AI-driven personalization has become a game-changer in boosting CTR by delivering dynamic, highly relevant content tailored to individual recipients' preferences and behaviors. This personalization ensures that email content resonates with the recipient, leading to higher engagement and more clicks.

AI boosts CTR by leveraging customer data such as past interactions, purchase history, and browsing behavior to create content that matches each subscriber's interests. For instance, if a customer frequently browses a particular product category, AI can send tailored email content featuring similar products or promotions, increasing the likelihood of a click. This targeted approach ensures that email recipients are more likely to engage with content that directly meets their needs and preferences. The more personalized and relevant the content, the greater the chance of driving clicks.

According to Atanasovska's study, marketers who implemented AI for email personalization saw a significant 41% increase in revenue and a 13.44% increase in CTRs. This underscores how AI-powered personalization can substantially enhance engagement and drive greater interaction with email campaigns. By focusing on delivering relevant content based on recipient behavior, AI ensures that emails are not only opened but also acted upon, leading to higher CTRs.

In addition to tailoring content, AI's predictive capabilities play a crucial role in optimizing CTRs. AI can analyze past customer behaviors to predict future actions and send emails at the most opportune times. For example, if AI identifies that a customer has frequently clicked on discounts or promotions in past campaigns, it can predict that similar offers will encourage future clicks. This proactive approach ensures that emails are sent at the right time with content that is most likely to drive clicks, further improving CTRs.

AI also enables dynamic content delivery, meaning that email content can be adjusted based on recipient interactions in real-time. If a recipient clicks on specific product categories, AI can adjust future emails to display more content related to those categories, maintaining relevance and further increasing the likelihood of clicks. By continuously personalizing the content based on recipient behavior, AI-driven campaigns foster higher CTRs and more meaningful engagement.

Overall, Atanasovska (2022) highlights the transformative impact of AI-driven personalization on email marketing. By analyzing customer data, predicting behaviors, and dynamically adjusting content, AI helps businesses deliver more engaging, relevant, and timely emails. This results in a 13.44% increase in CTRs and substantial revenue growth, demonstrating the power of AI to drive engagement and conversions in email marketing campaigns.

3.3.3. Conversion Rates

Open rates are a critical metric in email marketing, reflecting the percentage of recipients who open a given email. A 2023 study by Baldwin highlighted that AI-driven email marketing significantly improves open rates, offering businesses an advanced way to optimize their email campaigns and engage with customers more effectively.

AI enhances open rates primarily by personalizing email subject lines and content to better resonate with individual recipients. By analyzing vast amounts of customer data, including past behaviors, preferences, and engagement patterns, AI can create compelling and tailored subject lines that are more likely to grab the recipient's attention. Personalized subject lines, such as those that incorporate the recipient's name or past interactions, have been shown to increase open rates as customers are more likely to engage with content that feels relevant to them (Baldwin, 2023).

Furthermore, AI optimizes the timing and frequency of email delivery to maximize open rates. AI algorithms analyze when a customer is most likely to check their email, tailoring delivery times based on each recipient's behavior. By sending emails at the optimal time for engagement, businesses can ensure higher open rates, as recipients are more likely to open emails when they receive them during periods of high activity (Baldwin, 2023).

AI's ability to segment audiences based on detailed customer insights also plays a significant role in boosting open rates. By categorizing recipients into groups based on interests, behavior, or demographic factors, AI enables businesses to send highly relevant emails to each group, leading to more engaging subject lines and content. The more relevant an email is to the recipient, the more likely they are to open it (Baldwin, 2023).

3.4. AI-Driven vs. Traditional Email Personalization: A Comparative Analysis

The evolution of email marketing has been significantly impacted by the integration of Artificial Intelligence (AI), which has transformed how businesses approach personalization. A comparative analysis between traditional email personalization and AI-driven methods demonstrates the stark differences in effectiveness, with AI offering clear advantages in targeting, relevancy, and engagement.

Traditional email personalization generally involves segmenting audiences based on broad, static criteria such as demographics (e.g., age, location, or gender) and past purchase behaviors. These methods allow marketers to personalize emails by addressing recipients by their names or sending them content relevant to a generalized group. However, this approach falls short of delivering truly personalized experiences. The content in these emails is static and does not adapt to real-time changes in customer preferences, behavior, or interests. As a result, recipients may feel that the content is less relevant or timely, which can lead to lower open rates and reduced engagement. In this traditional framework, personalization lacks the depth required to make each customer feel uniquely catered to, resulting in missed opportunities to increase conversions.

In contrast, AI-driven email personalization moves beyond basic demographic segmentation by leveraging advanced technologies to analyze large volumes of customer data. AI systems track a variety of signals such as browsing history, previous interactions with emails, purchasing patterns, and even customer engagement on other platforms. Through machine learning algorithms, AI is capable of predicting future customer behaviors and personalizing content in real time. For example, AI can suggest products that a customer is likely to purchase based on recent searches or past purchases, tailoring each email to the recipient's evolving interests. This dynamic personalization enhances the relevance and timeliness of the content, making the email far more engaging and likely to drive action.

As Nkembuh (2024) notes, AI-powered personalization significantly boosts communication effectiveness, leading to higher audience engagement and improved conversion rates. By predicting and reacting to individual customer behavior, AI ensures that the right message reaches the right person at the right time. This level of personalization simply cannot be replicated with traditional methods, which rely on static and limited data.

AI offers several clear advantages over traditional personalization techniques. As highlighted by Kumar and al. (2024), AI enables marketers to efficiently gather and analyze detailed customer insights, leading to more precise targeting and strategic decision-making. With AI, businesses can send highly personalized content that resonates with customers on a large scale, adjusting the timing, frequency, and message to each recipient's preferences. Moreover, AI's predictive capabilities allow businesses to anticipate future customer needs, ensuring that email content is always aligned with what the recipient is most likely to engage with next.

One of the most significant benefits of AI is its ability to continuously learn and adapt. AI-driven systems analyze customer interactions in real-time, refining their predictions and ensuring that email content remains relevant and timely. This ongoing optimization leads to stronger connections with customers, fostering higher open rates and click-through rates. Studies by Nkembuh (2024) and Kumar and al. (2024) demonstrate that AI-powered campaigns consistently outperform traditional campaigns, with significant increases in both engagement and conversion metrics.

3.5. Research Gap and Hypothesis Development

Despite growing recognition that AI-driven personalization has transformed email marketing by enhancing key performance indicators such as open rates, click-through rates (CTR), and conversion rates (Mayfield, 2020; Atanasovska, 2022; Baldwin, 2023), existing research remains fragmented and incomplete. Most studies either focus narrowly on individual KPIs or rely on qualitative insights without employing rigorous, quantitative comparative analysis between AI-powered and traditional email marketing strategies. This gap is critical because marketers lack integrated, data-driven benchmarks that comprehensively evaluate AI's effectiveness across the entire customer engagement funnel. Moreover, while statistical significance is often reported, few studies address the practical relevance of AI's impact through effect size measurements, leaving the true magnitude of benefits unclear. This research is particularly urgent now, given the rapid advancement and adoption of AI technologies amid increasing competition in digital marketing; establishing a robust, empirical framework to quantify AI-driven personalization's comprehensive value is essential for guiding strategic investment and optimizing email marketing effectiveness. In response to these gaps, this study proposes the following hypotheses to empirically evaluate the performance of AI-driven email personalization versus traditional methods:

-**Hypothesis 1 (H1):** AI-driven email personalization will lead to significantly higher open rates compared to traditional email personalization methods.

-Hypothesis 2 (H2): AI-driven email personalization will result in significantly higher click-through rates (CTR) than traditional email personalization methods.
-Hypothesis 3 (H3): AI-driven email personalization will result in significantly higher conversion rates compared to traditional email personalization methods.

These hypotheses are grounded in the theoretical and practical literature on AI-enabled marketing and are designed to provide a data-driven foundation for benchmarking AI personalization effectiveness in real-world email campaigns.

These hypotheses are based on the premise that AI's ability to process large datasets, predict customer behavior, and deliver real-time, individualized content is likely to improve the relevance of email communications, thereby leading to improved engagement and conversion metrics. If confirmed, the results of our study will provide empirical evidence supporting the effectiveness of AI in optimizing email marketing strategies.

Based on the review of literature and the hypotheses that we have presented, the following conceptual framework could be concluded:

Figure 1. The conceptual Model of our Research

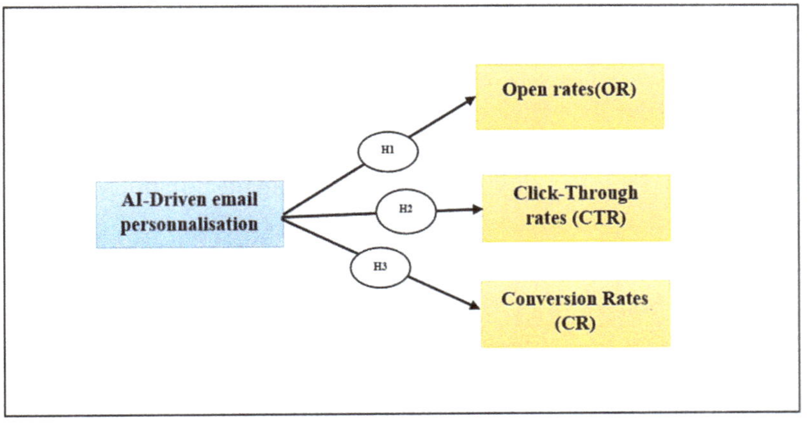

Source: Authors, 2024.

4. RESEARCH METHODOLOGY

The research design for this study employed a quantitative comparative approach to evaluate the effectiveness of AI-driven personalization in email marketing. This approach was selected to allow a direct comparison between AI-powered and traditional email marketing strategies, based on measurable key performance indicators (KPIs). The analysis focused on 10 email marketing campaigns conducted by a mid-sized e-commerce company, split evenly between five campaigns utilizing AI-driven personalization techniques and five campaigns using traditional methods.

To investigate the differences in performance between these two groups, paired t-tests were conducted, focusing on three critical KPIs: open rates, click-through rates, and conversion rates. This statistical method was chosen to ensure a controlled comparison within the same company context, enabling the study to empirically determine whether AI-driven personalization significantly enhances these metrics compared to traditional approaches.

The AI-powered campaigns leveraged machine learning algorithms and predictive analytics to dynamically tailor email content according to customer behaviors, preferences, and past interactions. In contrast, traditional campaigns relied on manual segmentation using static demographic information such as age, location, and purchase history. By collecting and comparing KPIs from each campaign, the study aimed to assess the relative effectiveness of these personalization methods in driving customer engagement and conversions.

Data analysis was performed using IBM SPSS Statistics (version 28), which facilitated both the normality assessment of the dataset and the execution of paired t-tests. The Shapiro-Wilk test confirmed that the data followed a normal distribution, validating the appropriateness of using paired t-tests for comparison. The paired t-tests then compared the open rates, click-through rates, and conversion rates between AI-powered and traditional campaigns, with statistical significance determined at the $p < 0.05$ level. This rigorous analytical process ensured the reliability of the findings regarding the impact of AI-driven personalization on email marketing performance.

5. RESULTS

5.1. Open Rates

AI-powered email campaigns demonstrated a significant advantage in terms of open rates, achieving an average of 27% compared to 19% for traditional campaigns. A paired t-test confirmed the statistical significance of this difference with a t-value of 4.231 (df = 24) and a p-value of 0.001. The standard deviations were 4.2% for AI-driven emails and 3.1% for traditional ones (see Table 1 and Figure 2).

Table 1. Comparison of Average Open Rates (%) Between AI-Powered and Traditional Email Campaigns

Group	Average Open Rate	Standard Deviation	p-value
AI-powered	27%	4.2%	0.001
Traditional	19%	3.1%	

Source: Results of the study, 2024.

Figure 2. Open Rates Comparison

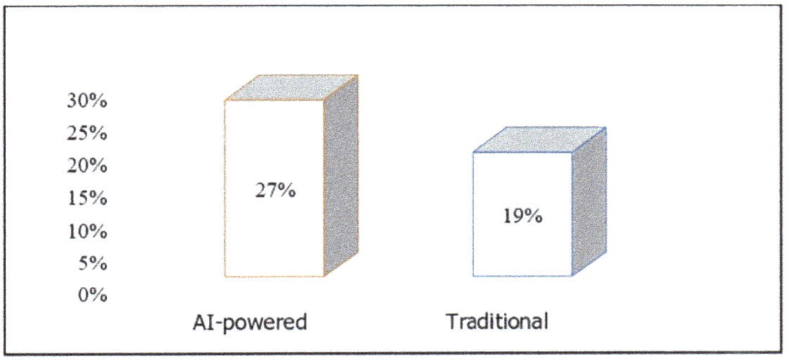

Source: Results of the study, 2024.

Beyond statistical significance, the effect size for this difference is large, with Cohen's d ≈ 1.44, indicating that AI-powered personalization has a very strong impact on increasing open rates. This suggests that AI's optimization of subject lines, send times, and recipient segmentation substantially enhances email visibility and user attention at the first point of contact. The result not only supports the theoretical benefits of AI but also provides a concrete benchmark for its practical value in improving the top-of-funnel performance.

5.2. Click-Through Rates (CTR)

Click-through performance also favored AI-powered campaigns, with an average CTR of 6.5%, significantly higher than the 3.8% recorded for traditional emails. The paired t-test yielded a t-value of 3.872 and a p-value of 0.002, confirming the reliability of this result. The standard deviations were 1.2% and 0.9% for the AI and traditional groups, respectively (see Table 2 and Figure 3).

Table 2. Comparison of Average Click-Through Rates (%) Between AI-Powered and Traditional Email Campaigns

Group	Average CTR	Standard Deviation	p-value
AI-powered	6.5%	1.2%	0.002
Traditional	3.8%	0.9%	

Source: Results of the study, 2024.

Figure 3. Click-Through Rates Comparison

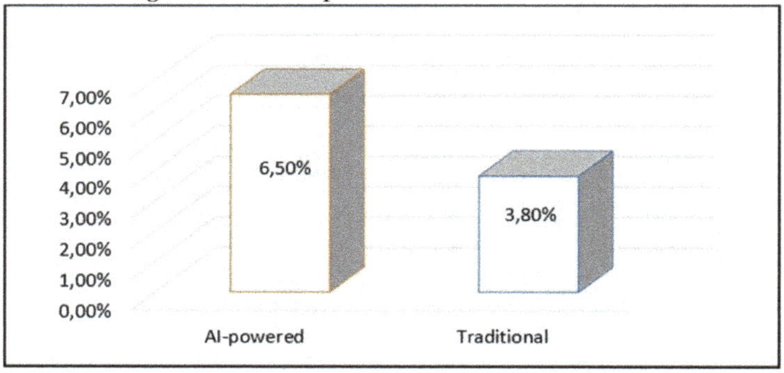

Source: Results of the study, 2024.

The effect size for this difference is also large, with Cohen's d ≈ 1.26, indicating a substantial improvement in user engagement through AI personalization. This finding supports the idea that real-time behavioral data and AI-generated content recommendations significantly increase the likelihood that users will interact with the email beyond simply opening it. It highlights AI's role in creating highly relevant content that motivates clicks and deeper engagement.

5.3. Conversion Rates

Conversion rates, the ultimate goal of most email marketing campaigns, also showed notable improvement with AI-driven personalization. The AI group achieved an average conversion rate of 4.2%, compared to 2.5% for the traditional group (Table 3; Figure 4). A paired t-test revealed this difference to be statistically significant, with a t-value of 2.162 and a p-value of 0.03. Standard deviations were 0.8% for the AI group and 0.6% for the traditional group, as shown in Table 3.

Table 3. Comparison of Average Conversion Rates (%) Between AI-Powered and Traditional Email Campaigns

Group	Average Conversion Rate	Standard Deviation	p-value
AI-powered	4.2%	0.8%	0.03
Traditional	2.5%	0.6%	

Source: Results of the study, 2024.

Figure 4. Conversion Rates Comparison

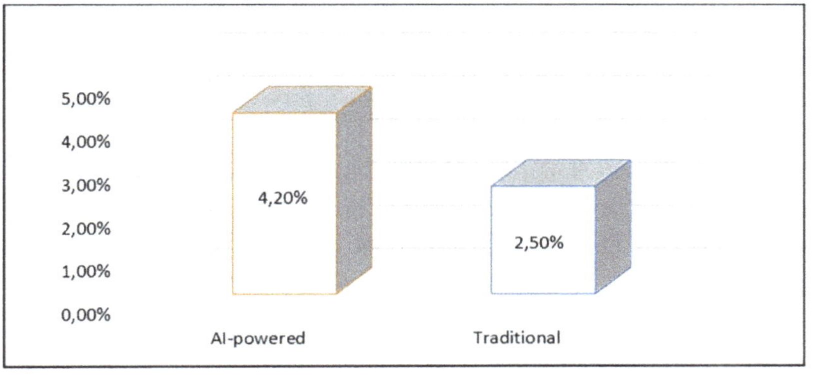

Source: Results of the study, 2024.

Although the effect size here is more moderate (Cohen's d $\approx$ 0.76), it still represents a meaningful improvement in driving actual customer action. This result suggests that AI personalization not only enhances user interaction but also contributes to business outcomes such as purchases or sign-ups. The smaller effect size, compared to open and click-through rates, may indicate the influence of external factors, such as landing page design, pricing, or product relevance, that also affect conversion rates and lie beyond the email content itself.

Across all three KPIs, open rate, CTR, and conversion rate, AI-powered personalization consistently outperformed traditional methods, not only with statistically significant results but also with moderate to large effect sizes. These findings provide robust empirical evidence supporting the use of AI in optimizing email marketing campaigns across the full customer engagement funnel.

5.4. Testing of the Validity of Hypotheses

The statistical results from this study offer strong empirical support for all three research hypotheses regarding the impact of AI-driven personalization in email marketing. The analysis not only confirms statistically significant differences between AI-powered and traditional email campaigns across all key performance indicators (KPIs), open rates, click-through rates (CTR), and conversion rates, but also highlights the magnitude of these differences through effect size calculations, providing both academic and practical relevance.

For Hypothesis 1, which posited that AI-driven email personalization would lead to significantly higher open rates, the data showed a clear advantage for AI-powered campaigns, with an average open rate of 27% compared to 19% for traditional ones. A paired t-test yielded a p-value of 0.001, well below the significance threshold of 0.05. More importantly, the effect size (Cohen's d $\approx$ 1.44) indicates a large and meaningful difference. This suggests that AI's optimization capabilities, such as adaptive subject lines, send-time optimization, and segmentation based on real-time behavioral data, substantially enhance email visibility and appeal, resulting in more recipients opening the emails.

For Hypothesis 2, which predicted higher click-through rates with AI-driven personalization, the results again strongly supported the hypothesis. AI-powered emails achieved an average CTR of 6.5%, significantly higher than the 3.8% observed for traditional campaigns. The statistical test produced a p-value of 0.002 and a large effect size (Cohen's d $\approx$ 1.26). This underscores the ability of AI to generate more compelling, personalized content and calls to action that align closely with recipient interests and online behavior. It demonstrates that personalization powered by AI does more than attract attention, it drives users to interact further with the content.

Hypothesis 3 focused on conversion rates, the most outcome-oriented KPI. AI-driven campaigns achieved an average conversion rate of 4.2%, compared to 2.5% for traditional emails. The paired t-test indicated statistical significance with a p-value of 0.03. Although the effect size here (Cohen's d $\approx$ 0.76) is moderate rather than large, it still represents a meaningful improvement. This suggests that AI-driven personalization not only boosts engagement but also helps convert that engagement into tangible business results, such as purchases or subscriptions. However, the slightly smaller effect size compared to open and click-through rates may also reflect external factors beyond email content itself, such as website experience, product pricing, or checkout process.

Globally, the results across all three hypotheses consistently favor AI-driven email personalization. Not only are the differences statistically significant, but the effect sizes indicate strong and practical improvements, especially in the earlier stages of the customer engagement funnel. These findings suggest that AI does not just marginally improve marketing performance, it offers a strategic advantage by enabling more responsive, relevant, and engaging communication. Therefore, the adoption of AI in email marketing appears to be a necessary evolution for businesses aiming to enhance digital campaign effectiveness.

6. DISCUSSION OF RESULTS

The findings of this study provide strong empirical evidence that AI-driven personalization significantly outperforms traditional email marketing methods in terms of key performance indicators (KPIs): open rates, click-through rates (CTR), and conversion rates. These results are consistent with trends observed in prior literature, but also go beyond previous studies by presenting higher quantitative outcomes, suggesting that advanced AI-based strategies may offer greater efficiency and effectiveness.

Regarding open rates, AI-powered email campaigns in this study achieved an average open rate of 27%, compared to 19% for traditional methods, an absolute increase of 8 percentage points and a relative improvement of approximately 42%. This result is statistically significant, with a p-value of 0.001. This aligns with findings from Mayfield (2020), who reported that personalized emails achieved open rates of 18.8% versus 13.1% for non-personalized emails (a 43% relative increase). Furthermore, Baldwin (2023) emphasized the importance of timing and subject line optimization, both of which are enhanced by AI. The present results reinforce this, as AI's ability to analyze vast datasets and optimize email timing and relevance plays a key role in boosting open rates beyond benchmarks previously reported.

In terms of click-through rates, AI-personalized campaigns demonstrated a clear advantage, achieving an average CTR of 6.5% compared to 3.8% for traditional campaigns, a 71% relative increase, with statistical significance ($p = 0.002$). This result substantially exceeds that of Atanasovska (2022), who observed a 13.44% improvement in CTRs after implementing AI in email marketing. Similarly, research by Zipdo (2024) indicated an average increase in CTR of about 35% with AI use. The higher CTR observed in this study suggests that the AI application here was particularly effective, likely due to its use of real-time behavioral data and personalized recommendations. Bell et al. (2024) also highlighted AI's role in micro-segmenting audiences and dynamically tailoring email content to match user preferences, an approach that aligns closely with the present study's methodology and outcomes.

As for conversion rates, the AI-driven campaigns achieved an average of 4.2%, compared to 2.5% for traditional approaches, an increase of 68%, with a p-value of 0.03. This finding confirms the third hypothesis and is supported by Ziakis et al. (2023), who found that AI-based personalization improved conversions by targeting users more precisely at the right time with relevant content. However, the increase reported here surpasses the 19-25% improvements commonly cited in the literature, indicating that real-time AI adaptation and behavioral prediction may significantly boost conversions when well-implemented.

These comparative results clearly demonstrate that AI-driven methods not only surpass traditional personalization strategies but also exceed the average improvements documented in previous studies. Traditional email marketing largely relies on static data such as demographics or historical purchases, which often fail to capture evolving customer preferences. In contrast, AI leverages dynamic data and real-time behavior to continuously refine content, ensuring that each message is timely, relevant, and aligned with the user's current interests. This ability to adapt and optimize in real time is a fundamental advantage that traditional methods cannot match.

From a practical standpoint, these findings carry significant implications for businesses seeking to improve their email marketing performance. The consistent improvements in open rates (+42%), CTR (+71%), and conversion rates (+68%) make a compelling case for investing in AI-driven email marketing tools. These tools can help businesses personalize communications at scale, deliver relevant content, and enhance customer engagement, ultimately leading to stronger customer relationships and better return on investment.

Moreover, as AI technologies continue to evolve, the depth and precision of personalization are likely to increase even further. Businesses that adopt these tools early will gain a competitive edge by offering highly tailored experiences that traditional segmentation techniques cannot replicate. This study not only validates existing research but also advances the literature by providing higher-than-average performance results, illustrating the transformative potential of AI in digital marketing.

Beyond the clear practical benefits, this study offers meaningful theoretical contributions to the field of digital marketing and AI personalization research. Firstly, it advances understanding of how AI-driven personalization mechanisms function in dynamic consumer environments by empirically validating the role of real-time data analysis and adaptive learning in enhancing email marketing outcomes. Unlike traditional personalization models that rely on static segmentation, this research demonstrates that AI's ability to continuously update user profiles and predict behavior deepens the theoretical framework around customer engagement and decision-making processes.

Moreover, by quantitatively comparing AI-driven personalization with traditional methods across multiple KPIs, this study provides robust evidence supporting the theoretical proposition that hyper-personalization, enabled by machine learning algorithms, substantially alters the efficacy of digital communication channels. This insight contributes to consumer behavior theories by highlighting how evolving personalization strategies influence attention, interest, and conversion in marketing communications. Finally, the research integrates concepts from information processing theory and AI-driven recommendation systems, suggesting new avenues for exploring how algorithmic content tailoring impacts user cognitive responses and purchasing decisions, thus broadening the theoretical landscape for future AI marketing research.

This research contributes important insights to the existing body of knowledge by showing that AI-driven email personalization leads to significantly better performance across all major KPIs. The quantitative improvements observed here highlight the effectiveness of AI in creating more relevant, timely, and engaging marketing messages, offering clear strategic advantages to organizations aiming to optimize their email campaigns.

7. RECOMMENDATIONS

Based on the findings of this study, the following recommendations are proposed for businesses and marketers looking to optimize their email marketing strategies using AI-driven personalization:

Invest in AI-Powered Email Marketing Platforms

Businesses should consider adopting AI-powered email marketing platforms that integrate machine learning algorithms to personalize content dynamically. These platforms can analyze vast amounts of customer data in real-time, enabling the delivery of highly tailored emails that improve engagement and conversion rates. By leveraging AI's ability to process user behavior, preferences, and past interactions, companies can ensure that their emails are relevant and timely, thereby increasing open rates, click-through rates, and ultimately conversions.

Utilize Real-Time Data for Personalization

AI-driven campaigns are most effective when they use real-time data to tailor email content to recipients' current behaviors and interests. Marketers should focus on collecting and utilizing data from customer interactions, such as website visits, past purchases, email opens, and clicks. This data can help AI systems refine the content of emails in real-time, ensuring that offers, product recommendations, and promotions are always aligned with the recipient's most recent actions and preferences.

Segment Audiences Dynamically

Rather than relying on static customer segments (e.g., based solely on demographics or past purchases), businesses should leverage AI to create dynamic audience segments that evolve based on customer behavior and engagement patterns. AI can segment audiences by analyzing how users engage with previous emails, which products or content they view, and their response to specific offers. By continuously updating these segments, businesses can ensure that they are sending the most relevant messages to each customer, further enhancing engagement and conversions.

Focus on Continuous Testing and Optimization

While AI-powered email campaigns offer significant advantages, it is important for businesses to regularly test and optimize their campaigns. This includes A/B testing of subject lines, content, and call-to-action (CTA) elements to determine what resonates best with different segments. AI can assist in these tests by quickly analyzing results and suggesting changes that improve performance. Regular optimization ensures that campaigns remain effective and adaptable to changes in customer behavior and market trends.

Prioritize Timely and Context-Aware Content

AI's ability to analyze user behavior in real-time enables the delivery of timely and contextually relevant content. Marketers should prioritize strategies that send emails at the most opportune moments, such as when a user is most likely to engage based on past activity or time of day. For example, sending personalized recommendations based on a recent website visit or a special offer during a customer's birthday month can dramatically increase the likelihood of engagement and conversion. Context-aware content leads to stronger customer relationships and higher satisfaction rates.

Leverage AI for Advanced Personalization Beyond Email

While email is a crucial marketing channel, AI's potential for personalization extends beyond just email campaigns. Businesses should consider expanding their use of AI to personalize other touchpoints, such as website content, social media ads, and push notifications. By maintaining consistent and cohesive personalized experiences across all customer interactions, businesses can improve overall customer satisfaction and increase the likelihood of conversions across channels.

Monitor and Respond to Customer Feedback

Incorporating customer feedback into AI-driven campaigns can further enhance personalization. AI tools can analyze customer feedback, including responses to surveys, product reviews, and social media interactions, to refine email content. Marketers should monitor customer sentiment and use this information to adjust email strategies, ensuring that content remains aligned with customer preferences and expectations.

Educate Marketing Teams on AI Integration

The successful implementation of AI-driven email campaigns requires collaboration between data scientists, marketers, and content creators. Businesses should invest in educating their marketing teams on the fundamentals of AI and its integration into email marketing strategies. By fostering a better understanding of how AI can be used to enhance personalization, marketers will be better equipped to develop strategies that leverage AI's full potential.

Consider Ethical Implications of AI-Driven Personalization

While AI offers significant benefits in terms of personalization, businesses should also be mindful of privacy concerns and ethical considerations. It is crucial to ensure transparency with customers regarding data collection and usage practices, and to provide options for customers to manage their preferences and consent to personalized communications. Striking the right balance between personalization and privacy will help build trust and maintain positive customer relationships.

Measure and Track Key Performance Indicators (KPIs)

Finally, businesses should consistently measure and track the performance of AI-driven email campaigns using key performance indicators (KPIs) such as open rates, CTR, conversion rates, and ROI. Regular analysis of these metrics will allow businesses to gauge the effectiveness of their AI-driven email strategies and identify areas for further improvement. By continually refining campaigns based on performance data, businesses can ensure that they are maximizing the value of their email marketing efforts.

Incorporating AI into email marketing strategies is no longer a luxury but a necessity for businesses aiming to stay competitive in a fast-paced digital landscape. By focusing on personalization, data-driven insights, and continuous optimization, businesses can unlock the full potential of AI to drive higher engagement, improved conversions, and stronger customer relationships. The recommendations provided above offer actionable steps for marketers looking to implement AI-powered email campaigns and maximize their return on investment.

CONCLUSION

This study provides compelling evidence that AI-driven personalization significantly enhances email marketing performance compared to traditional methods. The results show substantial improvements across key performance indicators, open rates, click-through rates, and conversion rates, with increases of 42%, 71%, and 68%, respectively. These findings not only confirm but also extend prior research by demonstrating that advanced AI techniques, leveraging real-time behavioral data and adaptive learning, deliver superior relevance and timing, thereby driving higher engagement and conversions.

Despite these promising outcomes, the study has some limitations. First, the sample size was relatively small, which may limit the statistical power and the generalizability of the findings, In addition, the data was collected from a specific industry and may not be fully generalizable across all sectors or email marketing contexts. Moreover, the study focused primarily on quantitative metrics and did not explore qualitative factors such as customer satisfaction or brand perception, which may also be influenced by AI personalization. The reliance on proprietary AI tools also limits transparency around the specific algorithms and processes involved, which could affect reproducibility.

Looking forward, future research could address these limitations by examining AI-driven personalization across diverse industries and incorporating customer experience metrics to provide a more holistic assessment. Moreover, as AI technologies continue to evolve rapidly, there is an opportunity to explore emerging techniques such as explainable AI and ethical personalization to ensure transparency and build consumer trust. Investigating long-term effects of AI personalization on customer loyalty and brand equity also presents valuable directions for further study.

In summary, this study highlights the transformative potential of AI in email marketing, providing actionable insights for businesses aiming to optimize engagement and conversions. By addressing current limitations and exploring new perspectives, future work can further advance understanding of AI's role in shaping the future of personalized digital marketing.

REFERENCES

Arora, N., Dreze, X., Ghose, A., Hess, J., Iyengar, R., Jing, B., Joshi, Y., Kumar, V., Lurie, N., Neslin, S., Sajeesh, S., Su, M., Syam, N., Thomas, J., & Zhang, Z. (2008). Putting one-to-one marketing to work: Personalization, customization, and choice. *Journal of Marketing*, *72*(5), 50–68. DOI: 10.1509/jmkg.72.5.50

Atanasovska, G. (2022). The importance of click rates in your email marketing campaign. Bento. Retrieved from https://bentonow.com/posts/click-rates

Babatunde, S. O., Odejide, O. A., Edunjobi, T. E., & Ogundipe, D. O. (2024). The role of AI in marketing personalization: A theoretical exploration of consumer engagement strategies. *International Journal of Management & Entrepreneurship Research*, *6*(3), 936–949. DOI: 10.51594/ijmer.v6i3.964

Baldwin, C. (2023).AI email marketing: Transforming engagement, personalization, and ROI for the future. Insider. Retrieved from https://useinsider.com/ai-email-marketing

Bell, C., Olukemi, A., & Broklyn, P. (2024). AI-driven personalization in digital marketing: Effectiveness and ethical considerations. https://doi.org/DOI: 10.20944/preprints202408.0023.v1

Davis, F., & Davis, F. (1989). Perceived usefulness, perceived ease of use, and user acceptance of information technology. *Management Information Systems Quarterly*, *13*, 319–339. DOI: 10.2307/249008

Hartemo, M. (2022). Conversions on the rise - modernizing e-mail marketing practices by utilizing volunteered data. *Journal of Research in Interactive Marketing*, *16*(4), 585–600. DOI: 10.1108/JRIM-03-2021-0090

Jenkins, L. (2018). How to increase email open rates? HubSpot Blog. Retrieved from https://blog.hubspot.com/marketing/increase-email-open-rates

Kumar, V., Ashraf, A. R., & Nadeem, W. (2024). AI-powered marketing: What, where, and how? *International Journal of Information Management*, *77*, 1–24. DOI: 10.1016/j.ijinfomgt.2024.102783

Manning, C. D., & Schütze, H. (1999). *Foundations of statistical natural language processing*. MIT Press.

Mayfield, E. (2020). AI-driven email marketing: Boosting open rates and conversions. Navigate the Channel. Retrieved from https://www.navigatethechannel.com/ai-driven-email-marketing

Muminov, H. (2024). Personalization in email marketing: How to increase open rates and engagement. *European Journal of Artificial Intelligence and Digital Economy, 1*, 36–41. DOI: 10.61796/jaide.v1i8.885

Muminov, H. (2024). Personalization in email marketing: How to increase open rates and engagement. *Journal of Artificial Intelligence and Digital Economy, 1*(8), 36–41. DOI: 10.61796/jaide.v1i8.885

Nkembuh, N. (2024). Beyond algorithms: A comprehensive analysis of AI-driven personalization in strategic communications. *Journal of Computer and Communications, 12*, 112–131. DOI: 10.4236/jcc.2024.1210009

Oke, S. (2008). A literature review on artificial intelligence. *International Journal of Information and Management Sciences, 19*, 535–570.

Okeleke, P. A., Ajiga, D., Folorunsho, S., & Ezeigweneme, C. (2024). Predictive analytics for market trends using AI: A study in consumer behavior. *International Journal of Engineering Research Updates, 7*(1), 37–49. DOI: 10.53430/ijeru.2024.7.1.0032

Patel, N. (2016). The ultimate guide to conversion rate optimization. Neil Patel Blog. Retrieved from https://neilpatel.com/blog/conversion-rate-optimization/

Payne, A., & Frow, P. (2005). A strategic framework for customer relationship management. *Journal of Marketing, 69*, 167–176. DOI: 10.1509/jmkg.2005.69.4.167

Petty, R., & Cacioppo, J. (1986). The elaboration likelihood model of persuasion. *Advances in Experimental Social Psychology, 19*, 123–205. DOI: 10.1016/S0065-2601(08)60214-2

Ravichandran, M. R., & Kumar, K. (2024). The effectiveness of email marketing for engaging customers. International Journal of Research Publication and Reviews. Retrieved from http://www.ijrpr.com

Rustagi, M., & Goel, N. (2022). Predictive analytics: A study of its advantages and applications. IARS'. *International Research Journal, 12*(1), 60–63.

Sahni, N., Wheeler, S., & Chintagunta, P. (2018). Personalization in email marketing: The role of noninformative advertising content. *Marketing Science, 37*, 1–23. DOI: 10.1287/mksc.2017.1066

Setiawan, I., & Purba, H. (2020). A systematic literature review of key performance indicators (KPIs) implementation. *Journal of Industrial Engineering and Management, 1*, 200–208. DOI: 10.7777/jiemar.v1i3.79

Xu, S. (2024). Exploring the impact of personalization in artificial intelligence on digital marketing: Performance evaluation. *Journal of Innovation and Development*, *8*(1), 41–44. DOI: 10.54097/tht8d457

Ziakis, C., & Vlachopoulou, M. (2023). Artificial intelligence in digital marketing: Insights from a comprehensive review. *Information (Basel)*, *14*, 1–30. DOI: 10.3390/info14120664

Compilation of References

Abbasi, R., & Esmaili, M. (2024). Identifying the applications of artificial intelligence in online marketing. In *Smart and Sustainable Interactive Marketing* (pp. 32–54). IGI Global., DOI: 10.4018/979-8-3693-1339-8.ch003

Abdalla, A. A., Bhat, M. A., Tiwari, C. K., Khan, S. T., & Wedajo, A. D. (2024). Exploring ChatGPT adoption among business and management students through the lens of diffusion of Innovation Theory. *Computers and Education: Artificial Intelligence*, *7*, 100257. DOI: 10.1016/j.caeai.2024.100257

Abdelkader, O. A. (2023). ChatGPT's influence on customer experience in digital marketing: Investigating the moderating roles. Heliyon, 9(8 C7 - e18770). https://doi.org/DOI: 10.1016/j.heliyon.2023.e18770

Abdulla, A., & Hussain, O. B. (2024). AI-enabled business process optimization and digital marketing. *2024 IEEE International Conference on Interdisciplinary Approaches in Technology and Management for Social Innovation, IATMSI 2024.*

Abebe, R., Adamic, L. A., & Kleinberg, J. (2018). Mitigating overexposure in viral marketing. *32nd AAAI Conference on Artificial Intelligence, AAAI 2018.*

Adi Pratama, R., Auliya Khadija, M., Noviana Paradhita, A., & Nurharjadmo, W. (2024). AI-Driven Predictive Analytics to Enhance Digital Marketing Strategies in Domain and Hosting Business. *2024 International Conference on Data Science and Its Applications, ICoDSA 2024.*

Adobe. (2025). Adobe Creative Cloud Express. https://www.adobe.com/express/

Advantages and Disadvantages of Artificial Intelligence in Digital Marketing. (2024, August 5). Dentsu. https://www.dentsu.com/id/en/insights/our-blog/artificial-intelligence-in-digital-marketing

Agrawal, V., Kaswan, K. S., & Kumar, S. (2024). An optimised deep learning model for fast and accurate brain tumour segmentation. *AIP Conference Proceedings.*

AI in Digital Marketing - The Ultimate Guide. (n.d.). Digital Marketing Institute........ . . . https://digitalmarketinginstitute.com/blog/ai-in-digital-marketing-the-ultimate-guide#

AIVA. (2025). AIVA: AI Music Composer. https://www.aiva.ai/

Al Khaldy, M. A., Al-Obaydi, B. A. A., & al Shari, A. J. (2023). The Impact of Predictive Analytics and AI on Digital Marketing Strategy and ROI. In *Studies in Big Data* (Vol. 136, pp. 367–379). Springer Science and Business Media Deutschland GmbH., DOI: 10.1007/978-3-031-42455-7_31

Alammal, A. H., & Al Mubarak, M. (2023). Artificial Intelligence in Marketing: Concerns and Solutions. In Internet of Things (Vol. Part F1270, pp. 101–113). Springer Science and Business Media Deutschland GmbH. https://doi.org/DOI: 10.1007/978-3-031-35525-7_7

Alawadh, H. M., Alabrah, A., Meraj, T., & Rauf, H. T. (2023). Discourse analysis-based credibility checks to online reviews using deep learning-based discourse markers. *Computer Speech & Language*, *78*, C7–C101450. DOI: 10.1016/j.csl.2022.101450

Albán Bartra, C., Alcántara Sánchez, D., & Sagástegui Cruz, J. (2021). Sports Marketing and Its Relationship in the Value Creation for the Customers of Sports Center, Trujillo, 2019. Advances in Intelligent Systems and Computing.

Albinali, E. A., & Hamdan, A. (2021). *The Implementation of artificial intelligence in social media marketing and its impact on consumer behavior: evidence from Bahrain*. Lecture Notes in Networks and Systems., DOI: 10.1007/978-3-030-69221-6_58

Alizadeh, H., & Nazarpour Kashani, H. (2024). The impact of perceived experience with ChatGPT on online consumers' information searching behavior: An empirical study of Iranian college students. *Asia Pacific Journal of Marketing and Logistics*. Advance online publication. DOI: 10.1108/APJML-02-2024-0140

Ansari, N., Tyagi, S., Mehrwal, N., Rastogi, N., Chibber, S., Memoria, M., Kumar, R., & Gupta, A. (2022). A Critical Insight into the Impact of Technology in Transformation of Tourist Business into Smart Tourism, *2022 International Conference on Machine Learning, Big Data, Cloud and Parallel Computing (COM-IT-CON)*, pp. 832-837, Faridabad, India. https://doi: DOI: 10.1109/COM-IT-CON54601.2022.9850779

Antonyuk, S. (2024, March 21). *All about Netflix Artificial Intelligence: the Truth behind Personalized Content*. Litslink. https://litslink.com/blog/all-about-netflix-artificial-intelligence-the-truth-behind-personalized-content

Arceta, N., Montero, M., & Quilitis, J. (2024). Adaptation and Effectiveness of Artificial Technology Used by Selected Hotels in Quezon City. *International Journal of Tourism and Hospitality*, *4*(2), 27–46. DOI: 10.51483/IJTH.4.2.2024.27-46

Armutcu, B., Tan, A., Ho, S. P. S., Chow, M. Y. C., & Gleason, K. C. (2024). The effect of bank artificial intelligence on consumer purchase intentions. *Kybernetes*. Advance online publication. DOI: 10.1108/K-01-2024-0145

Arora, N., Dreze, X., Ghose, A., Hess, J., Iyengar, R., Jing, B., Joshi, Y., Kumar, V., Lurie, N., Neslin, S., Sajeesh, S., Su, M., Syam, N., Thomas, J., & Zhang, Z. (2008). Putting one-to-one marketing to work: Personalization, customization, and choice. *Journal of Marketing*, *72*(5), 50–68. DOI: 10.1509/jmkg.72.5.50

Atanasovska, G. (2022). The importance of click rates in your email marketing campaign. Bento. Retrieved from https://bentonow.com/posts/click-rates

Aydin, G., & Silahtaroglu, G. (2021). Insights into mobile health application market via a content analysis of marketplace data with machine learning. PLoS ONE, 16(1 January C7 - e0244302). https://doi.org/DOI: 10.1371/journal.pone.0244302

Baas, J., Schotten, M., Plume, A., Côté, G., & Karimi, R. (2020). Scopus as a curated, high-quality bibliometric data source for academic research in quantitative science studies. *Quantitative Science Studies*, *1*(1), 377–386. DOI: 10.1162/qss_a_00019

Babatunde, S. O., Odejide, O. A., Edunjobi, T. E., & Ogundipe, D. O. (2024). The role of AI in marketing personalization: A theoretical exploration of consumer engagement strategies. *International Journal of Management & Entrepreneurship Research*, *6*(3), 936–949. DOI: 10.51594/ijmer.v6i3.964

Bacilieri, C. (2019). Online insurance and locus of control. *Micro and Macro Marketing*, (3), 591–607. DOI: 10.1431/95044

Bag, S., Srivastava, G., Bashir, M. M. A., Kumari, S., Giannakis, M., & Chowdhury, A. H. (2022). Journey of customers in this digital era: Understanding the role of artificial intelligence technologies in user engagement and conversion. *Benchmarking*, *29*(7), 2074–2098. DOI: 10.1108/BIJ-07-2021-0415

Baldwin, C. (2023).AI email marketing: Transforming engagement, personalization, and ROI for the future. Insider. Retrieved from https://useinsider.com/ai-email-marketing

Banik, B., Banik, S., & Annee, R. R. (2024). AI-driven strategies for enhancing customer loyalty and engagement through personalization and predictive analytics. *International Journal of Machine Learning Research in Cybersecurity and Artificial Intelligence*, *15*(1), 416–447. http://ijmlrcai.com/index.php/Journal/article/view/133/124

Bannister, F., & Connolly, R. (2011). Trust and transformational government: A proposed framework for research. *Government Information Quarterly*, *28*(2), 137–147. DOI: 10.1016/j.giq.2010.06.010

Banytė, J., Lindžiuvienė, J., & Dargytė, G. (2024). *What factors determine the consumer acceptance of AI-based services? the case of Lithuanian consumers*. Smart Innovation, Systems and Technologies.

Becker, J.-M., Cheah, J.-H., Gholamzade, R., Ringle, C. M., & Sarstedt, M. (2023). PLS-SEM's most wanted guidance. *International Journal of Contemporary Hospitality Management*, *35*(1), 321–346. DOI: 10.1108/IJCHM-04-2022-0474

Becker, M., Wiegand, N., & Reinartz, W. J. (2019). Does it pay to be real? Understanding authenticity in TV advertising. *Journal of Marketing*, *83*(1), 24–50. DOI: 10.1177/0022242918815880

Bell, C., Olukemi, A., & Broklyn, P. (2024). AI-driven personalization in digital marketing: Effectiveness and ethical considerations. https://doi.org/DOI: 10.20944/preprints202408.0023.v1

Benitez, J., Henseler, J., Castillo, A., & Schuberth, F. (2019). How to perform and report an impactful analysis using partial least squares: Guidelines for confirmatory and explanatory IS research. *Information & Management*, *103168*. Advance online publication. DOI: 10.1016/j.im.2019.05.003

Benjelloun, A., & Kabak, S. (2024). *Ethical Challenges and Management Implications of Artificial Intelligence in Digital Marketing*. Lecture Notes in Networks and Systems.

Benjelloun, A., & Kabak, S. (2024). *Ethical challenges and managerial implications of artificial intelligence in digital marketing*. Lecture Notes in Networks and Systems.

Benkert, C.-L. (2019). *Ethics & AI: Identifying the ethical issues of AI in marketing and building practical guidelines for marketers*. https://essay.utwente.nl/78303/1/Benkert_BA_BMS.pdf

Bharadwaj, A., Sawy, O. E., Pavlou, P. A., & Venkatraman, N. (2013). Digital Business Strategy: Toward a next generation of insights. *Management Information Systems Quarterly*, *37*(2), 471–482. DOI: 10.25300/misq/2013/37:2.3

Biswas, B., & Sanyal, M. K. (2019). Soft intelligence approaches for selecting products in online market. Proceedings of the 9th International Conference On Cloud Computing, Data Science and Engineering, Confluence 2019 C7 – 8776921.

Blauth, T. F., Gstrein, O. J., & Zwitter, A. (2022). Artificial intelligence crime: An overview of malicious use and abuse of AI. *IEEE Access : Practical Innovations, Open Solutions*, *10*, 77110–77122. DOI: 10.1109/ACCESS.2022.3191790

Blewett, C., & Hugo, W. (2016). Actant affordances: A brief history of affordance theory and a Latourian extension for education technology research. *Critical Studies in Teaching and Learning*, *4*(1), 55–76. DOI: 10.14426/cristal.v4i1.50

Boomy. (2025). Boomy: Create Original Music with AI. https://boomy.com/

Bormane, S., & Blaus, E. (2024). Artificial intelligence in the context of digital marketing communication. *Frontiers in Communication*, *9*, 1411226.

Borsos, Z., Weiss, R. J., Gelly, A., Bailleux, B., Romoff, J., Gutkin, A., & Drossos, L. (2022). AudioLM: A Language Modeling Approach to Audio Generation. arXiv preprint arXiv:2201.12789

Boteva, D. (2023). Advantages and Disadvantages of OTAs in the Distribution System of a Seaside Holiday Hotels. *Izvestia Journal of the Union of Scientists - Varna. Economic Sciences Series*, *12*(1), 239–250. DOI: 10.56065/IJUSV-ESS/2023.12.1.239

Bouchareb, N. (2023). The Role of Artificial Intelligence in Improving Hotels Property Management Systems. *International Journal of Economic Performance*, *06*(02), 554–567.

Breachsense. (n.d.). *5 Data Breach Examples (& Causes to Avoid in 2023)*. Www .breachsense.com. https://www.breachsense.com/blog/data-breach-examples/

Bremner, C. (2023). Revolutionising Travel: ChatGPT and Generative AI Usher in New Era of Automation. *Euromonitor International*. https://www.euromonitor .com/article/revolutionising-travel-chatgpt-and-generative-ai-usher-in-new-era-of-automation?utm_campaign=&utm_content=&utm_medium=Organic&utm_source =linkedin

Brenner, M. (2021). *The Age of Personalization: Digital Marketing Strategies for the Modern Consumer*. Wiley.

Brown, T. B., Mann, B., Ryder, N., Subbiah, M., Kaplan, J., Dhariwal, P., Neelakantan, A., Shyam, P., Sastry, G., Askell, A., Agarwal, S., Herbert-Voss, A., Krueger, G., Henighan, T., Narayan, R., Gao, R., Beck, A., Chen, N., Chen, H., . . . Amodei, D. (2020). Language models are few-shot learners. In Advances in neural information processing systems, 1877–1901.

Bruhn, M., Schoenmüller, V., Schäfer, D., & Heinrich, D. (2012). Brand Authenticity: Towards a Deeper Understanding of Its Conceptualization and Measurement. *Advances in Consumer Research. Association for Consumer Research (U. S.), 40*, 567–576.

Brüns, J. D., & Meißner, M. (2024). Do you create your content yourself? Using generative artificial intelligence for social media content creation diminishes perceived brand authenticity. *Journal of Retailing and Consumer Services, 79*, 103790. DOI: 10.1016/j.jretconser.2024.103790

Buhalis, D. (2003). *eTourism: Information technology for strategic tourism management.* Pearson Education. https://doi.org/DOI: 10.13140/2.1.2274.0804

Buhalis, D. (2020). Technology in tourism-from information communication technologies to eTourism and smart tourism towards ambient intelligence tourism: A perspective article. *Tourism Review, 75*(1), 267–272. DOI: 10.1108/TR-06-2019-0258

Buhas, V., Ponomarenko, I., Buhas, N., & Hulak, H. (2024). Cybersecurity Role in AI-Powered Digital Marketing. *CEUR Workshop Proceedings.*

Buhas, V., Ponomarenko, I., Kazak, O., & Korshun, N. (2024). AI-Driven Sentiment Analysis in Social Media Content. *CEUR Workshop Proceedings.*

Canva. (2025). Canva: Design Anything. Publish Anywhere. https://www.canva.com/

Carloman, A. N., Bermudo, U. V. W., Estilloso, E. M., & Llantos, O. E. (2024). Bundle AI: An Application of Multiple Constraint Knapsack Problem (MCKP) Through Genetic Algorithm (GA). Procedia Computer Science.

Car, T., Šuman, S., & Kliman, A. (2024). Customer Booking Habits and Attitudes Towards AI-Powered Features in Online Travel Agencies. *International Journal of Advances in Computer Science and Technology, 13*(9), 111–117. DOI: 10.30534/ijacst/2024/021392024

Chaffey, D., & Ellis-Chadwick, F. (2019). *Digital Marketing: Strategy, Implementation and Practice*. Pearson Education.

Chamberlain, R., Mullin, C., Scheerlinck, B., & Wagemans, J. (2018). Putting the art in artificial: Aesthetic responses to computer-generated art. *Psychology of Aesthetics, Creativity, and the Arts*, *12*(2), 177. DOI: 10.1037/aca0000136.supp

Charles, V., Rana, N. P., Pappas, I. O., Kamphaug, M., Siau, K., & Engø-Monsen, K. (2024). The Next 'Deep' Thing in X to Z Marketing: An Artificial Intelligence-Driven Approach. *Information Systems Frontiers*, *26*(3), 851–856. DOI: 10.1007/s10796-023-10462-x

Charness, G., & Chen, Y. (2020). Social identity, group behavior, and teams. *Annual Review of Economics*, *12*(1), 691–713. DOI: 10.1146/annurev-economics-091619-032800

Chatterjee, J., Guha Neogi, S., & Saraswat, S. (2024). *Consumer perspectives for purchase intentions of online pharmacy products using generative artificial intelligence*. Lecture Notes in Networks and Systems.

Chatterjee, S., Nguyen, B., Ghosh, S. K., Bhattacharjee, K. K., & Chaudhuri, S. (2020). Adoption of artificial intelligence integrated CRM system: An empirical study of Indian organizations. *The Bottom Line Managing Library Finances*, *33*(4), 359–375. DOI: 10.1108/bl-08-2020-0057

Chatterjee, S., Nguyen, B., Ghosh, S. k., Bhattacharjee, k., & Chaudhuri, S. (2020). Adoption of artificial intelligence integrated CRM system: An empirical study of Indian organizations. *The Bottom Line (New York, N.Y.)*, *33*(4), 359–375. DOI: 10.1108/Bl-08-2020-0057

Chaudhuri, A., & Holbrook, M. B. (2001). The chain of effects from brand trust and brand affect to brand performance: The role of brand loyalty. *Journal of Marketing*, *65*(2), 81–93. DOI: 10.1509/jmkg.65.2.81.18255

Chen, H., Yu, S., Huang, F., Zhu, B., Gao, L., & Qian, C. (2020). Spatio-temporal Analysis of Retail Customer Behavior Based on Clustering and Sequential Pattern Mining. 2020 3rd International Conference on Artificial Intelligence and Big Data, ICAIBD 2020 C7 – 9137465.

Chen, J., Frankwick, G. L., & Zhang, Z. (2022). Adopting Artificial Intelligence to Manage a Turbulent Environment: An Abstract. In Developments in Marketing Science: Proceedings of the Academy of Marketing Science (pp. 223-224). Springer Nature. https://doi.org/DOI: 10.1007/978-3-030-89883-0_61

Chen, J., Zhang, Y., & Wu, Y. (2024). The impact of differential pricing subject on consumer behavior. BMC Psychology, 12(1 C7 - 431). https://doi.org/DOI: 10.1186/s40359-024-01928-x

Cheng, M., Mackenzie, S. H., & Degarege, G. A. (2020). Airbnb impacts on host communities in a tourism destination: An exploratory study of stakeholder perspectives in Queenstown, New Zealand. *Journal of Sustainable Tourism, 30*(5), 1122–1140. DOI: 10.1080/09669582.2020.1802469

Chen, H., Chiang, R. H., & Storey, V. C. (2012). Business intelligence and analytics: From big data to big impact. *Management Information Systems Quarterly*, *36*(4), 1165–1188. DOI: 10.2307/41703503

Chen, N., Li, Z., & Tang, B. (2022). Can digital skills protect against job displacement risk caused by artificial intelligence? Empirical evidence from 701 detailed occupations. *PLoS One*, *17*(11), e0277280. PMID: 36346798

Chen, Y., Prentice, C., Weaven, S., & Hisao, A. (2022). The influence of customer trust and artificial intelligence on customer engagement and loyalty–The case of the home-sharing industry. *Frontiers in Psychology*, *13*, 912339. DOI: 10.3389/fpsyg.2022.912339 PMID: 35992434

Cheredniakova, A., Lobodenko, L., & Lychagina, I. (2021). A Study of advertising content in digital communications: the experience of applying neuromarketing and traditional techniques. Proceedings of the 2021 Communication Strategies in Digital Society Seminar, ComSDS 2021 C7 - 9422887.

Chiarella, S. G., Torromino, G., Gagliardi, D. M., Rossi, D., Babiloni, F., & Cartocci, G. (2022). Investigating the negative bias towards artificial intelligence: Effects of prior assignment of AI-authorship on the aesthetic appreciation of abstract paintings. *Computers in Human Behavior*, *137*, 107406. DOI: 10.1016/j.chb.2022.107406

Chica, M., Cordon, O., Robles, J. F., Garrido, A., Mingot, J., & Damas, S. (2023). Zio: an artificial intelligence digital twin to build virtual markets. *Proceedings of the 2023 IEEE Conference on Artificial Intelligence, CAI 2023*.

Chintalapati, S., & Pandey, S. K. (2022). Artificial intelligence in marketing: A systematic literature review. *International Journal of Market Research*, *64*(1), 38–68. DOI: 10.1177/14707853211018428

Chiu, M. C., Huang, J. H., Gupta, S., & Akman, G. (2021). Developing a personalized recommendation system in a smart product service system based on unsupervised learning model. *Computers in Industry*, *128*, 103421. DOI: 10.1016/j.compind.2021.103421

Choi, Y., & Kim, D. (2024). Artificial Intelligence in The Tourism Industry: Current Trends and Future Outlook. *International Journal on Advanced Science, Engineering and Information Technology*, *14*(6). Advance online publication. DOI: 10.18517/ijaseit.14.6.20452

Cillo, P., & Rubera, G. (2024). Generative AI in innovation and marketing processes: A roadmap of research opportunities. *Journal of the Academy of Marketing Science*. Advance online publication. DOI: 10.1007/s11747-024-01044-7

Cloud, G. (2025). Translation AI. https://cloud.google.com/translate

COCO Consortium. (2025). COCO - Common Objects in Context. https://cocodataset.org/

Coelho, A., Bairrada, C., & Peres, F. (2019). Brand communities' relational outcomes, through brand love. *Journal of Product and Brand Management*, *28*(2), 154–165. DOI: 10.1108/JPBM-09-2017-1593

Cohen, I. G. (2019). Informed consent and medical artificial intelligence: What to tell the patient? Geo. LJ, p. 108, 1425.

Cohen, I. G., & Slottje, A. (2024). Artificial intelligence and the law of informed consent. In Research Handbook On Health, AI, and the Law (pp. 167-182). Edward Elgar Publishing.

Cooter, R. D., & Gilbert, M. (2022). Theory of delegation. In *Public Law and Economics* (pp. 265–304). Academic., DOI: 10.1093/oso/9780197655870.003.0008

Copet, J., Kreuk, F., Gatilov, I., Hsu, W.-N., Polyak, A., Ben-yair, E., Rubenstein, Y., Chou, J.-S., Chen, Y.-A., Polyak, A., Hoffmann, T., Zeghidour, H., & Adi, Y. (2023). AudioCraft: A generative audio library for music and audio compression. arXiv preprint arXiv:2308.10467

Copy.ai. (2025). Copy.ai: AI Writing Tools & Content Generator. https://www.copy.ai/

Crabill, J. (2023, December 6). The Pros And Cons Of AI In Marketing: Focusing On The eLearning Niche. ELearning Industry. https://elearningindustry.com/advertise/elearning-marketing-resources/blog/pros-and-cons-of-ai-in-marketing-tips-for-elearning-marketers

Cui, R. (2024). Optimisation of cross-border e-commerce marketing strategy based on deep learning model. Applied Mathematics and Nonlinear Sciences, 9(1 C7-20230176). https://doi.org/DOI: 10.2478/amns.2023.2.00176

D'Aniello, G., Gaeta, A., Gaeta, M., Lepore, M., Orciuoli, F., & Troisi, O. (2016). A new DSS based on situation awareness for smart commerce environments. Journal of Ambient Intelligence and Humanized Computing, 7(1), 47-61. DOI: 10.1007/s12652-015-0300-0

Daneshjou, R., Smith, M. P., Sun, M. D., Rotemberg, V., & Zou, J. (2021). Lack of transparency and potential bias in artificial intelligence data sets and algorithms: A scoping review. *JAMA Dermatology*, *157*(11), 1362–1369. DOI: 10.1001/jama-dermatol.2021.3129

Davenport, T. H., & Ronanki, R. (2018). Artificial intelligence for the real world. *Harvard Business Review*, *96*(1), 108–116.

Davenport, T., Guha, A., Grewal, D., & Bressgott, T. (2020). How artificial intelligence will change the future of marketing. *Journal of the Academy of Marketing Science*, *48*(1), 24–42. DOI: 10.1007/s11747-019-00696-0

Davis, F., & Davis, F. (1989). Perceived usefulness, perceived ease of use, and user acceptance of information technology. *Management Information Systems Quarterly*, *13*, 319–339. DOI: 10.2307/249008

Davis, J. L., Love, T. P., & Fares, P. (2019). Collective social identity: Synthesizing identity theory and social identity theory using digital data. *Social Psychology Quarterly*, *82*(3), 254–273. DOI: 10.1177/0190272519851025

Davis, N., & Jin, J. (2024). Beyond code: Consumer response to chatbots. *Current Opinion in Psychology*, *58*, C7–C101841. DOI: 10.1016/j.copsyc.2024.101841 PMID: 38981369

De Bruyn, A., Viswanathan, V., Beh, Y. S., Brock, J. K.-U., & Von Wangenheim, F. (2020). Artificial Intelligence and marketing: Pitfalls and opportunities. *Journal of Interactive Marketing*, *51*(1), 91–105. DOI: 10.1016/j.intmar.2020.04.007

De Marcellis-Warin, N., Marty, F., Thelisson, E., & Warin, T. (2022). Artificial intelligence and consumer manipulations: From consumer's counter algorithms to firm's self-regulation tools. *AI and Ethics*, *2*(2), 259–268. DOI: 10.1007/s43681-022-00149-5

Deep, L. (2025). DeepL Translator: World's best AI translator. https://www.deepl.com/translator

Delen, D., & Demirkan, H. (2013). Data, information, and analytics as services. *Decision Support Systems*, *55*(1), 359–363. DOI: 10.1016/j.dss.2012.05.044

Deng, C., & Ravichandran, T. R. (2020). To smile or not? The effect of facial expression on servisse demand in sharing economy platforms. *AMCIS 2020 Proceedings*. 15. https://aisel.aisnet.org/amcis2020/virtual_communities/virtual_communities/15

Devlin, J., Chang, M. W., Lee, K., & Toutanova, K. (2018). BERT: Pre-training of deep bidirectional transformers for language understanding. arXiv preprint arXiv:1810.04805.

Digital, D. (2025). Generative AI in Marketing Content Production. https://www.deloittedigital.com/content/dam/digital/us/documents/insights/insights-20240408-genai-in-marketing-content-production-pov.pdf

Djasurovna, E. S., Obitovich, K. M., & Akramovich, A. I. (2024). Navigating the Digital Landscape: Enhancing Service Discovery and Portability in Digital Marketing Strategies. Lecture Notes in Computer Science (including subseries Lecture Notes in Artificial Intelligence and Lecture Notes in Bioinformatics)

Doanh, D. C., Dufek, Z., Ejdys, J., Ginevičius, R., Korzynski, P., Mazurek, G., & Ziemba, E. (2023). Generative AI in the manufacturing process: Theoretical considerations. *Engineering Management in Production and Services*, *15*(4), 76–89. DOI: 10.2478/emj-2023-0029

Dong, H. (2023). Research Progress and Review on Service Interaction between Intelligent Service Robots and Customers. Proceedings - 2023 International Conference on Service Robotics, ICoSR 2023, Dwivedi, Y. K., Ismagilova, E., Hughes, D. L., Carlson, J., Filieri, R., Jacobson, J.,...Wang, Y. (2021). Setting the future of digital and social media marketing research: Perspectives and research propositions. *International Journal of Information Management*, *59*, C7–C102168. DOI: 10.1016/j.ijinfomgt.2020.102168

Dr, N., & Thilagavathy, E. P. K. (2021). Artificial Intelligence on digital Marketing-An overview. *NVEO - NATURAL VOLATILES & ESSENTIAL OILS Journal | NVEO*, *8*(5), 9895–9908. https://www.nveo.org/index.php/journal/article/view/2772

dtw-python. (2025). dtw-python: Dynamic Time Warping in Python. https://github.com/DynamicTimeWarping/dtw-python

Dubois, D., Jung, S., & Ordabayeva, N. (2021). The psychology of luxury consumption. *Current Opinion in Psychology*, *39*, 82–87. DOI: 10.1016/j.copsyc.2020.07.011

Durmus Senyapar, H. N., Colak, I., & Bayindir, R. (2024). AI-Driven Smart Homes and Smart Grids: Marketing Strategies for Seamless Integration and Consumer Adoption. 12th International Conference on Smart Grid, icSmartGrid 2024.

Easelly. (2025). Easel.ly: Create and Share Visual Ideas Online. https://www.easel.ly/

Egieya, Z. E., Ewuga, S. K., Adegbite, A. O., & Oke, T. T. (2023). The role of virtual and augmented reality in modern marketing: A critical review. *Computer Science & IT Research Journal*, *4*(3), 244–272. DOI: 10.51594/csitrj.v4i3.660

El Koufi, N., & Belangour, A. (2023). Artificial Intelligence Techniques Applied in Precision Marketing: A Survey. *International Conference on Electrical, Computer, Communications and Mechatronics Engineering, ICECCME 2023.*

ElevenLabs. (2025). ElevenLabs: AI Speech Software. https://elevenlabs.io/

Elhajjar, S. (2024). Unveiling the marketer's lens: Exploring experiences and perspectives on AI integration in marketing strategies. *Asia Pacific Journal of Marketing and Logistics*. Advance online publication. DOI: 10.1108/APJML-04-2024-0485

Erevelles, S., Fukawa, N., & Swayne, L. (2016). Big data consumer analytics and the transformation of marketing. *Journal of Business Research*, *69*(2), 897–904. DOI: 10.1016/j.jbusres.2015.07.001

Eriksson, T., Bigi, A., & Bonera, M. (2020). Think with me, or think for me? On the future role of artificial intelligence in marketing strategy formulation. *The TQM Journal*, *32*(4), 795–814. DOI: 10.1108/TQM-12-2019-0303

Exenberger, E., & Bucko, J. (2020). Analysis of Online Consumer Behavior - Design of CRISP-DM Process Model. *AGRIS On-Line Papers in Economics and Informatics*, *12*(3), 13–22. DOI: 10.7160/AOL.2020.120302

Exploring the Ethical Implications of AI-Powered Personalization in Digital Marketing. (2024).. . *Data Intelligence*. Advance online publication. DOI: 10.3724/2096-7004.di.2024.0055

Farid, Y., Chang, C., Marcasciano, M., Di Meglio, F., Rodríguez-Mantilla, I., Nanni, J., & Chen, H. C. (2024). Consent 2.0: Informed choices in the age of artificial intelligence. *Surgery*, *175*(5), 1454–1455.

Felzmann, H., Fosch-Villaronga, E., Lutz, C., & Tamò-Larrieux, A. (2020). Towards transparency by design for artificial intelligence. *Science and Engineering Ethics*, *26*(6), 3333–3361.

Feng, C. M., Park, A., Pitt, L., Kietzmann, J., & Northey, G. (2021). Artificial intelligence in marketing: A bibliographic perspective. *Australasian Marketing Journal*, *29*(3), 252–263. DOI: 10.1016/j.ausmj.2020.07.006

Fernández-Rovira, C., Álvarez Valdés, J., Molleví, G., & Nicolas-Sans, R. (2021). The digital transformation of business. Towards the datafication of the relationship with customers. *Technological Forecasting and Social Change*, *162*, C7–C120339. DOI: 10.1016/j.techfore.2020.120339

Fritz, K., Schoenmueller, V., & Bruhn, M. (2017). Authenticity in branding–exploring antecedents and consequences of brand authenticity. *European Journal of Marketing*, *51*(2), 324–348. DOI: 10.1108/EJM-10-2014-0633

Fu, D., & Fu, K. (2011). Notice of Retraction: Research on European marketing strategies of Huawei and its enlightenment on Chinese enterprise. 2011 2nd International Conference on Artificial Intelligence, Management Science, and Electronic Commerce, AIMSEC 2011—Proceedings C7-6011335, pp. 3254–3258. DOI: 10.1109/AIMSEC.2011.6011335

Fu, M., Wong, C. M., Zhu, H., Huang, Y., Li, Y., Zheng, X., & Vong, C. M. (2018). DAlim: Machine learning-based intelligent lucky money determination for large-scale e-commerce businesses. Lecture Notes in Computer Science (including subseries Lecture Notes in Artificial Intelligence and Lecture Notes in Bioinformatics)

Fukui, Y., & Tabata, T. (2024). Prediction of Consumer Purchases in a Session on an EC Site Considering the Variety of Past Browsing. Lecture Notes in Computer Science (including subseries Lecture Notes in Artificial Intelligence and Lecture Notes in Bioinformatics), Gans, J. S. (2023). Artificial intelligence adoption in a competitive market. *Economica*, *90*(358), 690–705. DOI: 10.1111/ecca.12458

Gabelaia, I. (2023). *The Impact of User-Generated Content on Customer Purchase Intentions of Online Shoppers*. Lecture Notes in Networks and Systems.

Gallego, V., Lingan, J., Freixes, A., Juan, A. A., & Osorio, C. (2024). Applying Machine Learning in Marketing: An Analysis Using the NMF and k-Means Algorithms. Information (Switzerland), 15(7 C7 - 368). DOI: 10.3390/info15070368

Gandomi, A., & Haider, M. (2015). Beyond the hype: Big data concepts, methods, and analytics. *International Journal of Information Management*, *35*(2), 137–144. DOI: 10.1016/j.ijinfomgt.2014.10.007

Gao, X. (2023). KNN-based Precision Marketing Data Mining Algorithm for E-business Platform. Proceedings - 2023 International Conference on Networking, Informatics and Computing, ICNETIC 2023.

Gao, Y., Wang, J., Li, Z., & Peng, Z. (2023). The social media big data analysis for demand forecasting in the context of globalisation: Development and case implementation of innovative frameworks. *Journal of Organizational and End User Computing*, *35*(3). Advance online publication. DOI: 10.4018/JOEUC.325217

Gatys, L. A., Ecker, A. S., & Bethge, M. (2015). A neural algorithm of artistic style. arXiv preprint arXiv:1508.06576

Genadinik, A. (2020). *Digital Marketing: An Essential Guide to Marketing in the Digital World*. Business Expert Press.

Gharib, M., Fakhry, A. E., Ali, A. M., & Abdelhafeez, A., & Hussam Elbehiery. (2024). Single Valued Neutrosophic Sets for Analysis Opinions of Customer in Waste Management. *International Journal of Neutrosophic Science*, *23*(3), 175–185. DOI: 10.54216/ijns.230315

Giannoni, S., Brunstein, D., Guéniot, F., & Jouve, J. (2021). Multichannel distribution strategy of Airbnb hosts. *Annals of Tourism Research Empirical Insights*, *2*(1). Advance online publication. DOI: 10.1016/j.annale.2021.100017

Gilmore, J. H., & Pine, B. J. (2007). *Authenticity: What Consumers Really Want*. Harvard Business Press.

Gkikas, D. C., & Theodoridis, P. K. (2022). AI in Consumer Behavior. In Learning and Analytics in Intelligent Systems (Vol. 22, pp. 147-176). Springer Nature. https://doi.org/DOI: 10.1007/978-3-030-80571-5_10

Glikson, E., & Woolley, A. W. (2020). Human trust in artificial intelligence: Review of empirical research. *The Academy of Management Annals*, *14*(2), 627–660. DOI: 10.5465/annals.2018.0057

Goodfellow, I. J., Pouget-Abadie, J., Mirza, M., Xu, B., Warde-Farley, D., Ozair, S., Courville, A., & Bengio, Y. (2014). Generative adversarial nets. In Advances in neural information processing systems, 2672–2680

Google, A. I. Research. (2025). Conceptual Captions: A Clean Descriptive Captioning Dataset. https://ai.google.com/research/ConceptualCaptions/

Gore, S., & Kumar Mishra, P. (2023). Improvisation of Food Delivery Business by Leveraging Ensemble Learning with Various Algorithms. International Conference on Self-Sustainable Artificial Intelligence Systems, ICSSAS 2023, Proceedings.

Grammarly. (2025). Grammarly: AI-Powered Writing Assistance. https://www.grammarly.com/

Guo, Q, & Mu, L& Lou. (2024). S. Revolutionizing travel experiences: An in-depth analysis of intelligent booking systems and behavioral patterns. *Intelligent Decision Technologies, 18*(2), 1477–1494. DOI: 10.3233/IDT-230625

Gupta, A., & Tomar, K. (2021). Enhancing marketing strategies and analytics through artificial intelligence. Proceedings of 2nd International Conference on Computation, Automation and Knowledge Management, ICCAKM 2021, C7-9357763.

Gupta, R. (2022). Rural marketing transformation through AI-enabled digital platforms. *Indian Journal of Marketing, 52*(4), 34–47.

Gupta, R., Umang, P., & Gupta, S. (2024). *Artificial Intelligence and Its Application in Marketing*. Lecture Notes in Mechanical Engineering.

Gupta, S., & Chokshi, S. (2020). Digital Marketing Effectiveness Using Incrementality. *Communications in Computer and Information Science*.

Gupta, S., Zeballos, J. C., Del Río Castro, G., Tomičić, A., Morales, S. A., Mahfouz, M., Osemwegie, I., Sessi, V. P. C., Schmitz, M., Mahmoud, N., & Inyaregh, M. (2022). Operationalizing Digitainability: Encouraging mindfulness to harness the power of digitalization for sustainable development. In Operationalizing Digitainability: Encouraging mindfulness to harness the power of digitalization for sustainable development. https://doi.org/DOI: 10.20944/preprints202212.0565.v1

Hacker, P. (2023). Manipulation by algorithms. Exploring the triangle of unfair commercial practice, data protection, and privacy law. *European Law Journal, 29*(1-2), 142–175.

Haddaway, N. R., Page, M. J., Pritchard, C. C., & McGuinness, L. A. (2022). PRISMA 2020: An R package and Shiny app for producing PRISMA 2020-compliant flow diagrams, with interactivity for optimised digital transparency and Open Synthesis. *Campbell Systematic Reviews, 18*(2), e1230. DOI: 10.1002/cl2.1230

Hair, J. F., Hult, G. T. M., Ringle, C. M., & Sarstedt, M. (2017). *A Primer on Partial Least Squares Structural Equation Modeling (PLS-SEM)* (2nd ed.). Sage.

Hair, J. F., Ringle, C. M., & Sarstedt, M. (2011). PLS-SEM: Indeed a Silver Bullet. *Journal of Marketing Theory and Practice, 19*(2), 139–152. DOI: 10.2753/MTP1069-6679190202

Hair, J. F., Ringle, C. M., & Sarstedt, M. (2012). Partial Least Squares: The Better Approach to Structural Equation Modeling? *Long Range Planning, 45*(5–6), 312–319. DOI: 10.1016/j.lrp.2012.09.011

Hair, J. F., Ringle, C. M., & Sarstedt, M. (2013). Partial Least Squares Structural Equation Modeling: Rigorous Applications, Better Results and Higher Acceptance. *Long Range Planning*, *46*(1–2), 1–12. DOI: 10.1016/j.lrp.2013.01.001

Hair, J. F., Risher, J. J., Sarstedt, M., & Ringle, C. M. (2019). When to use and how to report the results of PLS-SEM. *European Business Review*, *31*(1), 2–24. DOI: 10.1108/EBR-11-2018-0203

Hair, J. F., Sarstedt, M., Pieper, T. M., & Ringle, C. M. (2012). The Use of Partial Least Squares Structural Equation Modeling in Strategic Management Research: A Review of Past Practices and Recommendations for Future Applications. *Long Range Planning*, *45*(5–6), 320–340. DOI: 10.1016/j.lrp.2012.09.008

Hair, J. F., Sarstedt, M., Ringle, C. M., & Mena, J. A. (2012). An assessment of the use of partial least squares structural equation modeling in marketing research. *Journal of the Academy of Marketing Science*, *40*(3), 414–433. DOI: 10.1007/s11747-011-0261-6

Haleem, A., Javaid, M., Qadri, M. A., Singh, R. P., & Suman, R. (2022). Artificial Intelligence (AI) Applications for marketing: a literature-based Study. *International Journal of Intelligent Networks, 3*(3), 119–132. sciencedirect. https://www.sciencedirect.com/science/article/pii/S2666603022000136

Hartemo, M. (2022). Conversions on the rise - modernizing e-mail marketing practices by utilizing volunteered data. *Journal of Research in Interactive Marketing*, *16*(4), 585–600. DOI: 10.1108/JRIM-03-2021-0090

Hatano, D., Kuroki, Y., Kawase, Y., Sumita, H., Kakimura, N., & Kawarabayashi, K. I. (2019). Non-zero-sum Stackelberg budget allocation game for computational advertising. Lecture Notes in Computer Science (including subseries Lecture Notes in Artificial Intelligence and Lecture Notes in Bioinformatics)

Hawkins, D. I., Mothersbaugh, D. L., & Best, R. J. (2007). *Consumer Behavior: Building Marketing Strategy*. McGraw-Hill/Irwin.

Heath, R. (2009). Emotional engagement: How television builds big brands at low attention. *Journal of Advertising Research*, *49*(1), 62–73. DOI: 10.2501/S0021849909090060

Helgemeir, T., & Cenzano, C. H. (2019). Artificial intelligence in tourism software solutions: Opportunities and challenges until 2024. In K. Jain, S. Sangle, R. Gupta, J. Persis, & M. R. (Eds.), *Managing Technology for Inclusive and Sustainable Growth - 28th International Conference for the International Association of Management of Technology, IAMOT 2019* (pp. 134-142). Excel India Publishers.

Henseler, J., Hubona, G., & Ray, P. A. (2016). Using PLS path modeling in new technology research: Updated guidelines. *Industrial Management & Data Systems, 116*(1), 2–20. DOI: 10.1108/IMDS-09-2015-0382

Henseler, J., Ringle, C. M., & Sarstedt, M. (2015). A new criterion for assessing discriminant validity in variance-based structural equation modeling. *Journal of the Academy of Marketing Science, 43*(1), 115–135. DOI: 10.1007/s11747-014-0403-8

Henseler, J., Ringle, C. M., & Sinkovics, R. R. (2009). The use of partial least squares path modeling in international marketing. In Sinkovics, R. R., & Ghauri, P. N. (Eds.), *Advances in International Marketing* (Vol. 20, pp. 277–319). Emerald Group Publishing Limited., DOI: 10.1108/S1474-7979(2009)0000020014

He, Q. (2022).. . *Design of Marketing Data Mining System Based on AI Lecture Notes on Data Engineering and Communications Technologies, 129*, 133–140. DOI: 10.1007/978-3-030-99616-1_18

Hermann, E. (2022). Leveraging artificial intelligence in marketing for social good—An ethical perspective. *Journal of Business Ethics, 179*, 43–61. DOI: 10.1007/s10551-021-04843-y PMID: 34054170

Hidri, A., Selmi, A., & Hidri, M. S. (2020). Discovery of Frequent Patterns of Episodes within a Time Window for Alarm Management Systems. IEEE Access, 8 C7 - 8955801, 11061-11073. DOI: 10.1109/ACCESS.2020.2965647

hmmlearn. (2025). hmmlearn: Hidden Markov Models in Python. https://hmmlearn.readthedocs.io/en/stable/

Ho, J., Jain, A., & Abbeel, P. (2020). Denoising diffusion probabilistic models. In Advances in neural information processing systems, 6840–6851

Hochreiter, S., & Schmidhuber, J. (1997). Long short-term memory. *Neural Computation, 9*(8), 1735–1780. PMID: 9377276

Hodson, G., & Earle, M. (2017). Social Identity Theory (SIT). In *Encyclopedia of Personality and Individual Differences*. Springer., DOI: 10.1007/978-3-319-28099-8_1185-1

Hoff, K. A., & Bashir, M. (2015). Trust in automation: Integrating empirical evidence on factors that influence trust. *Human Factors, 57*(3), 407–434. DOI: 10.1177/0018720814547570

Holman, L., Head, M., Lanfear, R., & Jennions, M. (2015). Evidence of Experimental Bias in the Life Sciences: Why We Need Blind Data Recording. *PLoS Biology, 13*. Advance online publication. DOI: 10.1371/journal.pbio.1002190

Hsieh, M. Y., Kung, C. Y., Lai, C. S., & Chen, C. T. (2011). Using the QFD to make the most potential marketing strategy by applying innovative wireless technology in a hypercompetitive era. *Key Engineering Materials*.

Hsu, S. F., & Liou, S. (2021). Artificial Intelligence Impact on Digital Content Marketing Research. 2021 9th International Conference on Orange Technology, ICOT 2021

Hu, E. J., Shen, Y., Wallis, P., Allen-Zhu, Z., Li, Y., Wang, S., Wang, L., Chen, M., & Chen, W. (2021). LoRA: Low-Rank Adaptation of Large Language Models. arXiv preprint arXiv:2106.09685

Hu, Y. (2011). Notice of Retraction: Research on the improvement of market competitiveness based on customer value. 2011 2nd International Conference on Artificial Intelligence, Management Science, and Electronic Commerce, AIMSEC 2011—Proceedings C7 - 6010645, 1455–1458. DOI: 10.1109/AIMSEC.2011.6010645

Huang, M. H., & Rust, R. T. (2021). A strategic framework for artificial intelligence in marketing. Journal of the Academy of Marketing Science, pp. 49, 30–50. DOI: 10.1007/s11747-020-00749-9

Huang, S. Y. B., Lee, C. J., & Lee, S. C. (2021). Toward a unified theory of customer continuance model for financial technology chatbots. Sensors, 21(17 C7-5687). DOI: 10.3390/s21175687

Hulland, J. (1999). Use of partial least squares (PLS) in strategic management research: A review of four recent studies. *Strategic Management Journal*, *20*(2), 195–204. DOI: 10.1002/(SICI)1097-0266(199902)20:2<195:AID-SMJ13>3.0.CO;2-7

IBM. (2024, July 25). *AI in Marketing | IBM*. Ibm.com. https://www.ibm.com/think/topics/ai-in-marketing

Ifekanandu, C. C., Anene, J. N., Iloka, C. B., & Ewuzie, C. O. (2023). Influence of artificial intelligence (AI) on customer experience and loyalty: Mediating role of personalization. *Journal of Data Acquisition and Processing*, *38*(3), 1936. DOI: 10.5281/zenodo.98549423

Ilapakurti, A., Vuppalapati, J. S., Kedari, S., Vuppalapati, R., & Vuppalapati, C. (2018a). Adaptive edge analytics for creating memorable customer experience and venue brand engagement, a scented case for Smart Cities. 2017 IEEE SmartWorld Ubiquitous Intelligence and Computing, Advanced and Trusted Computed, Scalable Computing and Communications, Cloud and Big Data Computing, Internet of People and Smart City Innovation SmartWorld/SCALCOM/UIC/ATC/CBDCom/IOP/SCI 2017 - Conference Proceedings.

Ilapakurti, A., Vuppalapati, J. S., Kedari, S., Vuppalapati, R., & Vuppalapati, C. (2018b). *AI infused fragrance systems for creating memorable customer experience and venue brand engagement*. Advances in Intelligent Systems and Computing.

Imanova, G. E., & Imanova, G. (2021). Digital Marketing Technologies Selection Under Z-Environment. Advances in Intelligent Systems and Computing, Jayashree, S., Sidana, N., Pham, L. T., Kunju, L. M., Ratnavalli, B., & Gangodkar, D. (2022). The Progressive Role of Machine learning in Enhancing the Effectiveness of Digital Marketing in Emerging Economies. 2022 2nd International Conference on Advance Computing and Innovative Technologies in Engineering, ICACITE 2022.

Infogram. (2025). Infogram: Create Interactive Charts & Infographics. https://infogram.com/

Irani, H. R., & Nozari, H. (2024). *Smart and sustainable interactive marketing*. IGI Global., DOI: 10.4018/9798369313398

Ivanov, D., Tsipoulanidis, A., & Schönberger, J. (2017). Erratum to: Global supply chain and operations management. In Springer Texts in Business and Economics (pp. E1–E1). Springer International Publishing.

Ivanov, S., & Webster, C. (2019). Conceptual Framework of the Use of Robots, Artificial Intelligence and Service Automation in Travel, Tourism, and Hospitality Companies, Ivanov, S. and Webster, C. (Ed.) *Robots, Artificial Intelligence, and Service Automation in Travel, Tourism and Hospitality* (pp. 7-37). Emerald Publishing Limited. https://doi.org/DOI: 10.1108/978-1-78756-687-320191001

Jagdale, R. S., Shirsat, V. S., & Deshmukh, S. N. (2019). Sentiment analysis on product reviews using machine learning techniques. In Cognitive Informatics and Soft Computing: Proceeding of CISC 2017 (pp. 639-647). Springer Singapore. https://doi.org/DOI: 10.1007/978-981-13-0617-4_61

Jagdale, R., & Deshmukh, M. (2025). Natural Language Processing in Finance: Techniques, Applications, and Future Directions. In Machine Learning and Modeling Techniques in Financial Data Science (pp. 411-434). IGI Global Scientific Publishing. https://doi.org/DOI: 10.4018/979-8-3693-8186-1.ch016

Jain, R., & Singh, P. (2020). AI-powered mobile platforms in rural agriculture: Enhancing productivity and market access. *Agricultural Systems*, •••, 178.

James, C. M., Manoj, D., Pious, G. M., Jose, J. P., & Jeyakrishnan, V. (2021). *Lopels is the AI-based multi-vendor loyalty platform*. Advances in Intelligent Systems and Computing.

Jarek, K., & Mazurek, G. (2019). Marketing and Artificial Intelligence. *Central European Business Review*, *8*(2), 46. DOI: 10.18267/j.cebr.213

Jasper. (2023). *Jasper (formerly jarvis) - #1 AI writing assistant*. Www.jarvis.ai. https://www.jasper.ai/

Jenkins, L. (2018). How to increase email open rates? HubSpot Blog. Retrieved from https://blog.hubspot.com/marketing/increase-email-open-rates

Jha, N., Parekh, D., Mouhoub, M., & Makkar, V. (2020). Customer Segmentation and Churn Prediction in Online Retail. Lecture Notes in Computer Science (including subseries Lecture Notes in Artificial Intelligence and Lecture Notes in Bioinformatics).

Jhaveri, M., Chirputkar, A., & Ashok, P. (2023). The efficacy of artificial intelligence in making the best marketing decisions. International Conference on Innovative Data Communication Technologies and Application, ICIDCA 2023—Proceedings.

Jianjun, M. (2020). Research on collaborative filtering recommendation algorithms based on user behaviour characteristics. Proceedings: 2020 International Conference on Big Data and Artificial Intelligence and Software Engineering, ICBASE 2020 C7-9403763.

Jordan, M. I., & Mitchell, T. M. (2015). Machine learning: Trends, perspectives, and prospects. *Science*, *349*(6245), 255–260. DOI: 10.1126/science.aaa8415 PMID: 26185243

Kachamas, P. (2016). Shaping interactive marketing communication (IMC) through social media analytics and modelling. Lecture Notes in Computer Science (including subseries Lecture Notes in Artificial Intelligence and Lecture Notes in Bioinformatics), Kaponis, A., & Maragoudakis, M. (2022). Data Analysis in Digital Marketing using Machine learning and Artificial Intelligence Techniques, Ethical and Legal Dimensions, State of the Art. ACM International Conference Proceeding Series C7 – 15.

Kadu, S., & Joshi, B. (2022). Text-Based Sentiment Analysis Using Deep Learning Techniques. In Studies in Big Data (Vol. 113, pp. 81-100). Springer Science and Business Media Deutschland GmbH. DOI: 10.1007/978-3-031-10869-3_5

Kar, A. K., & Khatwani, G. (2014). *A group decision support system for selecting a social CRM*. Advances in Intelligent Systems and Computing.

Kasahara, H., Iiyama, M., & Minoh, M. (2017). Transportation mode inference using environmental constraints. Proceedings of the 11th International Conference on Ubiquitous Information Management and Communication, IMCOM 2017 C7 - 83

Kaur, J., Arora, V., & Bali, S. (2020). Influence of technological advances and change in marketing strategies using analytics in the retail industry. *International Journal of System Assurance Engineering and Management, 11*(5), 953–961. DOI: 10.1007/s13198-020-01023-5

Kavitha Devi, M. K., & Venkatesh, P. (2010). Kernel-based collaborative-recommender system for e-purchasing. Sadhana. *Academy Proceedings in Engineering Sciences, 35*(5), 513–524. DOI: 10.1007/s12046-010-0035-8

Keever, S. (2024, August 12). Council Post: AI Is Driving The Future Of SEO: How To Adapt. *Forbes*. https://www.forbes.com/councils/forbesagencycouncil/2024/02/02/ai-is-driving-the-future-of-seo-how-to-adapt/

Keller, R., Stohr, A., Fridgen, G., Lockl, J., & Rieger, A. (2019). Affordance-experimentation-actualisation theory in artificial intelligence research: a predictive maintenance story. In Affordance-Experimentation-Actualization Theory in Artificial Intelligence Research: a Predictive Maintenance Story.

Khanal, K. (2024). Taylor Swift's Branding Strategy: The Economics of Authenticity. In *Compelling Storytelling Narratives for Sustainable Branding* (pp. 230-243). IGI Global. https://doi.org/DOI: 10.4018/979-8-3693-3326-6.ch012

Khatibi, V., Iranmanesh, H., & Keramati, A. (2011). A neuro-IFS intelligent system for marketing strategy selection. *Communications in Computer and Information Science*.

Khondakar, M. F. K., Sarowar, M. H., Chowdhury, M. H., Majumder, S., Hossain, M. A., Dewan, M. A. A., & Hossain, Q. D. (2024). A systematic review on EEG-based neuromarketing: recent trends and analysing techniques. Brain Informatics, 11(1 C7 - 17). DOI: 10.1186/s40708-024-00229-8

Kietzmann, J., Paschen, J., & Treen, E. (2018). Artificial Intelligence in Advertising How Marketers Can Leverage Artificial Intelligence Along the Consumer Journey. *Journal of Advertising Research, 58*(3), 263–267. DOI: 10.2501/JAR-2018-035

Kindermann, R., & Snell, J. L. (1980). *Markov random fields and their applications*. American Mathematical Society.

Kingma, D. P., & Welling, M. (2013). Auto-encoding variational bayes. arXiv preprint arXiv:1312.6114

Kirk, C. P., & Givi, J. (2025). The AI-authorship effect: Understanding authenticity, moral disgust, and consumer responses to AI-generated marketing communications. *Journal of Business Research, 186*, 114984.

Knani, M., Echchakoui, S., & Ladhari, R. (2022). Artificial intelligence in tourism and hospitality: Bibliometric analysis and research agenda. *International Journal of Hospitality Management, 107*, 103317. DOI: 10.1016/j.ijhm.2022.103317

Kock, N. (2016). Hypothesis testing in SEM-based multivariate analyses. *International Journal of e-Collaboration, 12*(3), 1–6.

Kong, H., Wang, K., Qiu, X., Cheung, C., & Bu, N. (2023). 30 years of artificial intelligence (AI) research relating to the hospitality and tourism industry. *International Journal of Contemporary Hospitality Management, 35*(6), 2157–2177. DOI: 10.1108/IJCHM-03-2022-0354

Kordon, A. (2010). Marketing computational intelligence in industry. 2010 IEEE World Congress on Computational Intelligence, WCCI 2010 - 2010 IEEE Congress on Evolutionary Computation, CEC 2010 C7 - 5586356

Kothari, B., & Mani, A. P. (2024). AI-enabled identification of consumer's purchase intention with a practical implementation through analysis of review comments in real time. Multidisciplinary Science Journal, 6(11 C7 - e2024244). https://doi.org/ DOI: 10.31893/multiscience.2024244

Kotler, P., Kartajaya, H., & Setiawan, I. (2024). *Marketing 6.0: O Futuro é Imersivo*. Actual Editora.

Krizhevsky, A., Sutskever, I., & Hinton, G. E. (2012). Imagenet classification with deep convolutional neural networks. In Advances in neural information processing systems, 1097–1105

Kumar, V. V., Devi, G. D., Ajay, U., Sharun, M., & Yukesh, P. (2023). Enhancing smallholder farmer livelihoods through AI-based e-commerce marketing for agricultural products. 2nd International Conference on Sustainable Computing and Data Communication Systems, ICSCDS 2023: Proceedings

Kumar, V., Ashraf, A. R., & Nadeem, W. (2024). AI-powered marketing: What, where, and how? International Journal of Information Management, p. 77 C7-102783. DOI: 10.1016/j.ijinfomgt.2024.102783

Kumar, V., Ramachandran, D., & Kumar, B. (2021). Influence of new-age technologies on marketing: A research agenda. Journal of Business Research, pp. 125, 864–877. DOI: 10.1016/j.jbusres.2020.01.007

Kumar, V., & Reinartz, W. (2016). Creating enduring customer value. *Journal of Marketing, 80*(6), 36–68. DOI: 10.1509/jm.15.0414

Kunekar, P., Usman, M., Veena, C. H., Singla, A., Anute, N., & Polke, N. (2024). Enhancing Advertising Initiatives: Using Machine Learning Algorithms to Engage Targeted Customer. Proceedings of International Conference on Communication, Computer Sciences and Engineering, IC3SE 2024.

Kurolov, M. O. (2022). A systematic mapping study of using digital marketing technologies in health care: The state of the art of digital healthcare marketing. *ACM International Conference Proceeding Series*

Kushnarevych, A., & Kollárová, D. (2023). Development of Artificial Intelligence as a Breakthrough for Personalization in Marketing. *International Conference on Electrical, Computer, Communications and Mechatronics Engineering, ICECCME 2023*. DOI: 10.1109/ICECCME57830.2023.10252550

Kushnarevych, A., & Kollárová, D. (2024, September). The Possibilities of Artificial Intelligence Usage in Loyalty Programs. In *European Conference on Innovation and Entrepreneurship* (Vol. 19, No. 1, pp. 384-390).

Labs, P. (2025). Pika Labs. https://pika.art/

LAION. (2025). LAION Projects. https://laion.ai/projects/

Lakshmipriyanka, A., Harihararao, M., Prasanna, M., & Deepika, Y. (2023). A study on artificial intelligence in marketing. *International Journal for Multidisciplinary Research*, *5*(3), 1–12.

Lamplugh, M. (2024). *The AI marketing playbook: Concepts – Methods – Applications*. Mercury Learning and Information.

LangChain. (2025). LangChain: Building applications with LLMs through composability. https://www.langchain.com/

Laszkiewicz, A., & Kalinska-Kula, M. (2023). Virtual influencers as an emerging marketing theory: A systematic literature review. *International Journal of Consumer Studies*, *47*(6), 2479–2494. DOI: 10.1111/ijcs.12956

Latifi, S. (Ed.). (2024). *ITNG 2024: 21st International Conference on Information Technology–New Generations* (Vol. 1456). Springer. ISBN: 978-3031565991

Laux, J., Wachter, S., & Mittelstadt, B. (2024). Trustworthy artificial intelligence and the European Union AI act: On the conflation of trustworthiness and acceptability of risk. *Regulation & Governance*, *18*(1), 3–32. DOI: 10.1111/rego.12512

Law, R., Lin, K., Ye, H., & Fong, D. (2024). Artificial intelligence research in hospitality: A stateof- the-art review and future directions. *International Journal of Contemporary Hospitality Management*, *36*(6). Advance online publication. DOI: 10.1108/IJCHM-02-2023-0189

Lazaroiu, G., & Rogalska, E. (2023). How generative artificial intelligence technologies shape partial job displacement and labour productivity growth. *Oeconomia Copernicana*, *14*(3), 703–706.

Leavy, S., O'Sullivan, B., & Siapera, E. (2020). Data, power and bias in artificial intelligence. arXiv preprint arXiv:2008.07341.

Lee, J. H. (2021). Changes in marketing brought by AI Proceedings, 2021 21st ACIS International Semi-Virtual Winter Conference on Software Engineering, Artificial Intelligence, Networking, and Parallel/Distributed Computing, SNPD-Winter 2021 C7-9403452.

Lee, V. C. S. (2004). An alternative methodology for mining seasonal patterns using self-organising maps. Lecture Notes in Computer Science (including subseries Lecture Notes in Artificial Intelligence and Lecture Notes in Bioinformatics)

Lee, V. H., Hew, J. J., Leong, L. Y., Tan, G. W. H., & Ooi, K. B. (2020). Wearable payment: A deep learning-based dual-stage SEM-ANN analysis. Expert Systems with Applications, p. 157 C7-113477. DOI: 10.1016/j.eswa.2020.113477

Lee, H., Shin, M., Yang, J., & Chock, T. M. (2024). Virtual Influencers vs. Human Influencers in the Context of Influencer Marketing: The Moderating Role of Machine Heuristic on Perceived Authenticity of Influencers. *International Journal of Human-Computer Interaction*, •••, 1–18. DOI: 10.1080/10447318.2024.2374100

Lee, K., Kim, J., Kim, J., & Kwon, O. (2020). MelGAN: Generative adversarial networks for conditional waveform synthesis. In *Proceedings of the 37th International Conference on Machine Learning*, 4187-4196

Lei, L., Taorong, G., Jindou, Y., Feixiang, G., Tao, X., Tao, C., & Songsong, C. (2021). Research on the strategy of adjustable load resources participating in the distributed trading market. 2021 IEEE 2nd International Conference on Big Data, Artificial Intelligence and Internet of Things Engineering, ICBAIE 2021 C7-9389883

Leigh, T. W., Peters, C., & Shelton, J. (2006). The consumer quest for authenticity: The multiplicity of meanings within the MG subculture of consumption. *Journal of the Academy of Marketing Science*, *34*(4), 481–493. DOI: 10.1177/0092070306288403

Lei, W., Yikai, Y., Jiehui, Z., & Xiaoyi, W. (2020). Predicting consumer behavior in the perspective of consumer neuroscience: Status, challenge, and future. *Guanli Gongcheng Xuebao*, *34*(6), 1–12. DOI: 10.13587/j.cnki.jieem.2020.06.001

Lemon, K. N., & Verhoef, P. C. (2016). Understanding customer experience throughout the customer journey. *Journal of Marketing*, *80*(6), 69–96. DOI: 10.1509/jm.15.0420

Lewis, P., Perez, E., Piktus, A., Petroni, F., Karpukhin, V., Goyal, N., Küttler, H., Lewis, M., Yih, W., & Riedel, S. (2020). Retrieval-augmented generation for knowledge-intensive nlp tasks. In Advances in Neural Information Processing Systems, 9459–9474

Li, M., & Suh, A. (2021, January). Machinelike or humanlike? A literature review of anthropomorphism in AI-enabled technology. In 54th Hawaii international conference on system sciences (HICSS 2021) (pp. 4053-4062).

Li, Y., Murali, P., Shao, N., & Sheopuri, A. (2016). Applying Data Mining Techniques to Direct Marketing: Challenges and Solutions. Proceedings - 15th IEEE International Conference on Data Mining Workshop, ICDMW 2015 C7 – 7395688.

Liang, L. Q., Yu, C. H., & Zhou, X. (2019). The index system of mobile health applications is based on the AHP-Fuzzy comprehensive evaluation method—2019 IEEE Symposium Series on Computational Intelligence, SSCI 2019 C7-9002886.

Liciotti, D., Frontoni, E., Mancini, A., & Zingaretti, P. (2017). Pervasive system for consumer behaviour analysis in retail environments. Lecture Notes in Computer Science (including subseries Lecture Notes in Artificial Intelligence and Lecture Notes in Bioinformatics).

Ling, C. Y., & Che, H. Y. (2021). A study on the establishing data on consumer behavior and lifestyle of singles. *ACM International Conference Proceeding Series*.

LinkedIn. (2025). LinkedIn Marketing Solutions. https://business.linkedin.com/marketing-solutions

Lin, X., Shao, B., & Wang, X. (2022). Employees' perceptions of chatbots in B2B marketing: Affordances vs. disaffordances. *Industrial Marketing Management*, *101*, 45–56.

Liu, Q. (2021). Research on the Intelligent Analysis and Visualization of Webcast Entrepreneurship Data under the E-commerce Mode. Proceedings of the 5th International Conference on I-SMAC (IoT in Social, Mobile, Analytics and Cloud), I-SMAC 2021

Liu, S., Aw, E. C. X., Tan, G. W. H., & Ooi, K. B. (2023). Virtual Influencers as the Next Generation of Influencer Marketing: Identifying Antecedents and Consequences. In Studies in Computational Intelligence (Vol. 1128, pp. 23-39). Springer Science and Business Media Deutschland GmbH. https://doi.org/DOI: 10.1007/978-3-031-48397-4_2

Liu, J. (2024). Marketing strategy matching algorithm under artificial intelligence. *3rd IEEE International Conference on Distributed Computing and Electrical Circuits and Electronics, ICDCECE 2024.*

Liu, L., & Chen, J. (2024). Marketing affordance of social media for product innovation: The role of organisational structures. *Marketing Intelligence & Planning.*

Liu, S., Hu, X., Wang, S. H., Zhang, Y. D., Fang, X., & Jiang, C. (2020). Mixing patterns in social trust networks: A social identity theory perspective. *IEEE Transactions on Computational Social Systems*, *8*(5), 1249–1261. DOI: 10.1109/TCSS.2020.3021179

Liu, Y., & Chen, W. (2021). Optimisation of Brand Marketing Strategy of Intelligent Technology under the Background of Artificial Intelligence. *Mobile Information Systems*, *2021*, C7–C9507917. DOI: 10.1155/2021/9507917

Li, W., & Wang, Y. (2020). Predictive analytics in emerging markets: Applications in Indian agriculture. *Technological Forecasting and Social Change*, •••, 157.

Li, Y. (2024). Optimising the Omni Channel Marketing Strategy of Green Clothing by Integrating Artificial Intelligence and Big Data. *ACM International Conference Proceeding Series*

Li, Y., Chan, J., Peko, G., & Sundaram, D. (2023). Mixed emotion extraction analysis and visualisation of social media text. *Data & Knowledge Engineering*, *148*, C7–C102220. DOI: 10.1016/j.datak.2023.102220

Li, Y., & You, C. (2021). Brand Loyalty Measurement Model Based on Machine Learning Clustering Algorithm. *Journal of Physics: Conference Series.*

Lokalise. (2025). Lokalise: Translation Management System. https://lokalise.com/

Loudly. (2025). Loudly: AI Music Generator. https://loudly.com/

Ltifi, M. (2023). Impact of the E-brand on the Consumer's E-trust, Reliance and Resistance Towards the Chatbot. In Springer Series in Design and Innovation (Vol. 32, pp. 267-292). Springer Nature. https://doi.org/DOI: 10.1007/978-3-031-35385-7_16

Lu, T., & Boutilier, C. (2015). Value-directed compression of large-scale assignment problems. *Proceedings of the National Conference on Artificial Intelligence.*

Lv, H. (2022). Smart Product Marketing Strategy in a Cloud Service Wireless Network Based on SWOT Analysis. *Wireless Communications and Mobile Computing*, *2022*, C7–C7539860. DOI: 10.1155/2022/7539860

Macumber, R., & Durga, V. (2024). Google, SEO and helpful content: How artificial intelligence can be helpful for e-commerce websites. *Journal of Digital & Social Media Marketing.*, *12*(3), 206–206. DOI: 10.69554/rjuw9313

Maharani, W., & Gozali, A. A. (2015). Collaborative Social Network Analysis and Content-Based Approach to Improve the Marketing Strategy of SMEs in Indonesia. *Procedia Computer Science*.

Ma, J., Wang, P., Li, B., Wang, T., Xiang, S. P., & Wang, D. (2024). Exploring User Adoption of ChatGPT: A Technology Acceptance Model Perspective. *International Journal of Human-Computer Interaction*, *41*(2), 1–15. DOI: 10.1080/10447318.2024.2314358

Majeed, S., & Kim, W. G. (2024). Antecedents and consequences of conceptualizing online hyperconnected brand selection. *Journal of Consumer Marketing*, *41*(3), 328–339. DOI: 10.1108/JCM-08-2023-6193

Majumdar, S., & Parida, S. (2021). Bringing AI to the grassroots: Evidence from rural fintech solutions. *The Electronic Journal on Information Systems in Developing Countries*, •••, 87.

Makhlooqa, A., & Mubarakb, M. A. (2024). Artificial intelligence and marketing: Challenges and opportunities. In Technological Innovations for Business, Education and Sustainability (pp. 3-16). Emerald Publishing. DOI: 10.1108/978-1-83753-106-620241001

Malhotra, N. K. (2010). *Marketing Research—An Applied Orientation (6a ed.)* (6.[a]). Prentice Hall.

Malthouse, E., & Copulsky, J. (2023). Artificial intelligence ecosystems for marketing communications. *International Journal of Advertising*, *42*(1), 128–140.

Manca, F., D'Uggento, A. M., & Convertini, N. (2018). Customer segmentation through multiple correspondence analysis. 2018 110th AEIT International Annual Conference, AEIT 2018 C7 - 8577279, Meepung, T., & Kannikar, P. (2022). Artificial Intelligence for Digital Business Performance. 7th International Conference on Digital Arts, Media and Technology, DAMT 2022 and 5th ECTI Northern Section Conference on Electrical, Electronics, Computer and Telecommunications Engineering, NCON 2022, Meftah, M., Ounacer, S., & Azzouazi, M. (2024). Enhancing Customer Engagement in Loyalty Programs Through AI-Powered Market Basket Prediction Using Machine Learning Algorithms. In Engineering Applications of Artificial Intelligence (pp. 319-338). Cham: Springer Nature Switzerland.

Manis, K. T., & Madhavaram, S. (2023). AI-enabled marketing capabilities and the hierarchy of capabilities: Conceptualisation, proposition development, and research avenues. *Journal of Business Research, 157*, C7–C113485. DOI: 10.1016/j.jbusres.2022.113485

Manning, C. D., & Schütze, H. (1999). *Foundations of statistical natural language processing*. MIT Press.

Manyika, J., Silberg, J., & Presten, B. (2019, October 25). *What Do We Do About the Biases in AI?* Harvard Business Review. https://hbr.org/2019/10/what-do-we-do-about-the-biases-in-ai

Maras, M. H., & Alexandrou, A. (2019). Determining authenticity of video evidence in the age of artificial intelligence and in the wake of Deepfake videos. *The International Journal of Evidence & Proof, 23*(3), 255–262. DOI: 10.1177/1365712718807226

Martínez-Rolán, X., & Piñeiro-Otero, T. (2022). Surfing on big data: automation and data mining as a marketing strategy. In *Organisational Innovation in the Digital Age* (pp. 63–85). Springer International Publishing., DOI: 10.1007/978-3-030-98183-9_3

Mayfield, E. (2020). AI-driven email marketing: Boosting open rates and conversions. Navigate the Channel. Retrieved from https://www.navigatethechannel.com/ai-driven-email-marketing

McAuley, J., & Leskovec, J. (2013). Hidden factors and hidden topics: understanding rating dimensions with review text. In *Proceedings of the 7th ACM conference on Recommender systems*, 165–172

McLachlan, G. J., & Peel, D. (2000). *Finite mixture models*. John Wiley & Sons.

Mdoe, A., Mishra, A., & Motahar Hossain, M. (2023). How blockchain and artificial intelligence are changing SME marketing strategies. *Proceedings of the 2023 International Conference on Advanced Computing and Communication Technologies, ICACCTech 2023*.

Meliana, P. (2024, June 4). *The future of marketing: AI transformations by 2025*. ContentGrip; ContentGrip. https://www.contentgrip.com/future-ai-marketing/

Meng, X., & Beninsig, M. A. (2024). Intelligent application utilising facial recognition to determine marketing strategies for shopping mall customers. Proceedings of SPIE, The International Society for Optical Engineering.

Meng, Y. (2025). Attention as Dictionary. https://www.yuan-meng.com/posts/attention_as_dict/

Menidjel, C., Hollebeek, L. D., Leppiman, A., & Riivits-Arkonsuo, I. (2022). Role of AI in enhancing customer engagement, loyalty and loyalty programme performance. In *Handbook of Research on Customer Loyalty* (pp. 316–331). Edward Elgar Publishing.

Meta. (2025). Meta Ads Manager. https://www.facebook.com/business/ads

Microsoft. (2025). Evaluation metrics. https://learn.microsoft.com/en-us/ai/playbook/technology-guidance/generative-ai/working-with-llms/evaluation/list-of-eval-metrics

Mishra, A. (2020). Adoption of cognitive computing solutions in Indian farming communities. *AI & Society*, *35*(4), 983–995.

Mittal, T., Dhiman, A., Singh, V. V., Gupta, A. K., & Kedia, N. (2023). Delving The Role Of Artificial Intelligence-Driven Advertisements On Purchase Intention Of Omnichannel Customers Using SEM. 2023 4th International Conference on Computation, Automation and Knowledge Management, ICCAKM 2023, Moreno-Sandoval, L. G., Sánchez-Barriga, C., Buitrago, K. E., Pomares-Quimbaya, A., & Garcia, J. C. (2018). Spanish Twitter data used as a source of information about consumer food choice. Lecture Notes in Computer Science (including subseries Lecture Notes in Artificial Intelligence and Lecture Notes in Bioinformatics), Motamedi, R. (2024). Integrating Artificial Intelligence and Multichannel Marketing Strategies: Impacts on Consumer Engagement and Brand Loyalty. Business, Marketing, and Finance Open, 1(5), 1-14. https://doi.org/DOI: 10.1111/ijcs.13027

Moffat, D. C. D. C., & Kelly, M. (2006). An investigation into people's bias against computational creativity in music composition. *Assessment*, *13*(11), 1–8.

Morhart, F. M., Malär, L., Guèvremont, A., Girardin, F., & Grohmann, B. (2015). Brand authenticity: An integrative framework and measurement scale. *Journal of Consumer Psychology*, *25*(2), 200–218. DOI: 10.1016/j.jcps.2014.11.006

Moulard, J. G., Garrity, C. P., & Rice, D. H. (2015). What makes a human brand authentic? Identifying the antecedents of celebrity authenticity. *Psychology and Marketing*, *32*(2), 173–186. DOI: 10.1002/mar.20771

Moulard, J. G., Raggio, R. D., & Folse, J. A. G. (2021). Disentangling the meanings of brand authenticity: The entity-referent correspondence framework of authenticity. *Journal of the Academy of Marketing Science*, *49*(1), 96–118. DOI: 10.1007/s11747-020-00735-1

Mueller, S. T. (2020). Cognitive anthropomorphism of AI: How humans and computers classify images. *Ergonomics in Design*, *28*(3), 12–19.

Muminov, H. (2024). Personalization in email marketing: How to increase open rates and engagement. *European Journal of Artificial Intelligence and Digital Economy*, *1*, 36–41. DOI: 10.61796/jaide.v1i8.885

Murphy, J., Gretzel, U., & Pesonen, J. (2019). Marketing Robot Services in Hospitality and Tourism. *Journal of Hospitality and Tourism Technology*, *10*(1), 73–86. DOI: 10.1080/10548408.2019.1571983

Murugesan, S. (2025). Ethical Concerns on AI Content Creation. https://www.computer.org/publications/tech-news/trends/ethical-concerns-on-ai-content-creation

Nam, K., Dutt, C., Chathoth, P., Daghfous, A., & Khan, M. (2021). The adoption of artificial intelligence and robotics in the hotel industry: Prospects and challenges. *Electronic Markets*, *31*(3), 553–574. DOI: 10.1007/s12525-020-00442-3

Napoli, J., Dickinson, S. J., Beverland, M. B., & Farrelly, F. (2014). Measuring consumer-based brand authenticity. *Journal of Business Research*, *67*(6), 1090–1098. DOI: 10.1016/j.jbusres.2013.06.001

Narayanasamy, S. S. A. L., Hajamydeen, A. I., & Ishak, Z. (2019). The theoretical framework of digital marketing and its future availability in Malaysia. 2019 IEEE 9th International Conference on System Engineering and Technology, ICSET 2019—Proceeding C7 – 8906342.

National Qualifications Register. (n.d.). Evidence of need for skilling in the areas of artificial intelligence and machine learning. https://nqr.gov.in/sites/default/files/Annexure%20B_Evidence%20of%20Need.pdf

Naufal, A., Kurniawati, A., & Hasibuan, M. A. (2017). Decision support system of SMB Telkom University roadshow location prioritisation with weighted sum model method. 2016 2nd International Conference of Industrial, Mechanical, Electrical, and Chemical Engineering, ICIMECE 2016 C7 - 7910428

Nazer, L. H., Zatarah, R., Waldrip, S., Ke, J. X. C., Moukheiber, M., Khanna, A. K., & Mathur, P. (2023). Bias in artificial intelligence algorithms and recommendations for mitigation. *PLOS Digital Health*, *2*(6), e0000278.

Ndaguba, E. A., & Van Zyl, C. (2023). Exploring bibliometric evidence of Airbnb's influence on urban destinations: Emotional solidarity, Airbnb supply, moral economy and digital future. *International Journal of Tourism Cities*, *9*(4), 894–922. DOI: 10.1108/IJTC-03-2023-0056

Neal, R. (1990). Connectionist learning of expert systems. *Communications of the ACM*, *33*(3), 42–53.

Neary, B., Horák, J., Kovacova, M., & Valaskova, K. (2018). The future of work: Disruptive business practices, technology-driven economic growth, and computer-induced job displacement. *Journal of Self-Governance and Management Economics*, *6*(4), 19–24.

Nkembuh, N. (2024). Beyond algorithms: A comprehensive analysis of AI-driven personalization in strategic communications. *Journal of Computer and Communications*, *12*, 112–131. DOI: 10.4236/jcc.2024.1210009

Nkomo, N., & Mupa, M. N. (2024). The impact of artificial intelligence on predictive customer behaviour analytics in e-commerce: A comparative study of traditional and AI-driven models. *Iconic Research and Engineering Journals*, *8*(5), 432–439.

Noor, N. (2022). Halal Service Marketing: A Strategic Perspective. In Contributions to Management Science (pp. 11–29). Springer Science and Business Media Deutschland GmbH. DOI: 10.1007/978-3-030-98160-0_3

Norton, D. (2019). *Personalization in Marketing*. Kogan Page Publishers.

Nunes, J. C., Ordanini, A., & Giambastiani, G. (2021). The concept of authenticity: What it means to consumers. *Journal of Marketing*, *85*(4), 1–20. DOI: 10.1177/0022242921997081

Okeleke, P. A., Ajiga, D., Folorunsho, S., & Ezeigweneme, C. (2024). Predictive analytics for market trends using AI: A study in consumer behavior. *International Journal of Engineering Research Updates*, *7*(1), 37–49. DOI: 10.53430/ijeru.2024.7.1.0032

Oke, S. (2008). A literature review on artificial intelligence. *International Journal of Information and Management Sciences*, *19*, 535–570.

Olan, F., Suklan, J., Arakpogun, E. O., & Robson, A. (2024). Advancing Consumer Behavior: The Role of Artificial Intelligence Technologies and Knowledge Sharing. *IEEE Transactions on Engineering Management*, *71*, 13227–13239. DOI: 10.1109/TEM.2021.3083536

Olena, C., Tetiana, T., Violeta, A., Viktoria, K., & Leonid, P. (2024). Use of Artificial Intelligence in the Formation of the Marketing Strategy of the Enterprise—Lecture Notes in Networks and Systems.

Open, A. I. (2025). gpt-2-output-dataset. https://github.com/openai/gpt-2-output-dataset

Open, A. I. (2025a). Sora. https://openai.com/sora

Open, A. I. (2025b). Jukebox. https://openai.com/research/jukebox

Optimizely. (2019). *A/B Testing*. Optimizely.com. https://www.optimizely.com/optimization-glossary/ab-testing/

Osadchaya, E., Marder, B., Yule, J. A., Yau, A., Lavertu, L., Stylos, N., Oliver, S., Angell, R., Regt, A. D., Gao, L., Qi, K., Zhang, W. Z., Zhang, Y., & AlRabiah, S. (2024). To ChatGPT, or not to ChatGPT: Navigating the paradoxes of generative AI in the advertising industry. *Business Horizons*. Advance online publication. DOI: 10.1016/j.bushor.2024.05.002

Otero, E. L., & Gutiérrez, R. C. (2015). *Using social media advertising to increase the awareness, promotion and diffusion of public and private entities*. Advances in Intelligent Systems and Computing.

Özkaynak, Ü., Ercan, Ş., İspir, F. B., Gençoğlu, M. T., & Tanyıldızı, E. (2024). Artificial Intelligence-Based Marble Block Analysis System for Sustainable Green Transformation. 32nd IEEE Conference on Signal Processing and Communications Applications, SIU 2024—Proceedings.

Papavasileiou, V., & Tsadiras, A. (2011). Time variations of association rules in market basket analysis. *IFIP Advances in Information and Communication Technology*.

Parris, D. L., & Guzmán, F. (2023). Evolving brand boundaries and expectations: Looking back on brand equity, brand loyalty, and brand image research to move forward. *Journal of Product and Brand Management*, *32*(2), 191–234. DOI: 10.1108/JPBM-06-2021-3528

Patel, M., & Modi, K. (2020). Exploring Online Ad Images using Deep-Learning Approach. Proceedings of the International Conference on Intelligent Computing and Control Systems, ICICCS 2020 C7-9121175.

Patel, N. (2016). The ultimate guide to conversion rate optimization. Neil Patel Blog. Retrieved from https://neilpatel.com/blog/conversion-rate-optimization/

Patil, B., Ashok, P., & Chirputkar, A. (2024). Artificial Intelligence Powered Paradigm Shift: Revolutionizing Digital Marketing. 4th International Conference on Innovative Practices in Technology and Management 2024, ICIPTM 2024

Patil, D. (2024, November 19). *Artificial intelligence for personalized marketing and consumer behaviour analysis: Enhancing engagement and conversion rates. SSRN*. https://doi.org/DOI: 10.2139/ssrn.5057436

Patil, S. M., Kharat, A. M., Jain, S., Tripathi, V. V. R., Bisen, G. K., & Joshi, A. (2024). Investigating the Influence and Function of Artificial Intelligence in Contemporary Marketing Management: Marketing in the AI Era. *Proceedings of the 3rd International Conference on Advances in Computing, Communication and Applied Informatics, ACCAI 2024*.

Payne, A., & Frow, P. (2005). A strategic framework for customer relationship management. *Journal of Marketing*, *69*, 167–176. DOI: 10.1509/jmkg.2005.69.4.167

Pedersen, C. L., & Ritter, T. (2024). Digital authenticity: Towards a research agenda for the AI-driven fifth phase of digitalization in business-to-business marketing. *Industrial Marketing Management*, *123*, 162–172. DOI: 10.1016/j.indmarman.2024.10.005

Peebles, W., & Xie, S. (2023). Scalable diffusion models with transformers. In *International Conference on Machine Learning*, 28133–28156

Peng, C. C., Wang, Y. Z., & Huang, C. W. (2020). Artificial-Neural-Network-Based Consumer Behavior Prediction: A Survey. 2nd IEEE Eurasia Conference on Biomedical Engineering, Healthcare and Sustainability 2020, ECBIOS 2020 C7 - 9203699

Perez-Vega, R., Kaartemo, V., Lages, C. R., Razavi, N. B., & Männistö, J. (2021). Reshaping the contexts of online customer engagement behavior via artificial intelligence: A conceptual framework. *Journal of Business Research*, *129*, 902–910.

Peruchini, M., da Silva, G. M., & Teixeira, J. M. (2024). Between artificial intelligence and customer experience: a literature review on the intersection. Discover Artificial Intelligence, 4(1 C7 - 4). DOI: 10.1007/s44163-024-00105-8

PeterBrendan. (2025). AdImageNet. https://huggingface.co/datasets/PeterBrendan/AdImageNet

Petty, R., & Cacioppo, J. (1986). The elaboration likelihood model of persuasion. *Advances in Experimental Social Psychology*, *19*, 123–205. DOI: 10.1016/S0065-2601(08)60214-2

Photobucket delivers 24/7 member support with messaging. (2022, March 29). Zendesk. https://www.zendesk.com/customer/photobucket/

Piktochart. (2025). Piktochart: Visual Content Creation Platform. https://piktochart.com/

Pilone, V., Di Pasquale, A., & Stasi, A. (2023). Consumer Preferences for Craft Beer by Means of Artificial Intelligence: Are Italian Producers Doing Well? Beverages, 9(1 C7 - 26). https://doi.org/DOI: 10.3390/beverages9010026

Placani, A. (2024). Anthropomorphism in AI: Hype and fallacy. *AI and Ethics*, •••, 1–8. DOI: 10.1007/s43681-024-00419-4

Ponomarenko, I. V., Pavlenko, V. M., Morhulets, O. B., Ponomarenko, D. V., & Ukhnal, N. M. (2024). Application of artificial intelligence in digital marketing. *CEUR Workshop Proceedings.*

Poornima, N., Sridharan, C., Pavithra, A., Narendiran, R., Vijay, B., & Neelesh, V. S. (2024). Recommender Systems for Personalized Business Marketing: Employing Artificial Intelligence and Business Intelligence in Machine Learning Techniques. Lecture Notes in Electrical Engineering, Qazi, A., Raj, R. G., Tahir, M., Cambria, E., & Syed, K. B. S. (2014). Enhancing business intelligence by means of suggestive reviews. *TheScientificWorldJournal*, *2014*, C7–C879323. DOI: 10.1155/2014/879323

Prada Segura, J. A., & Velandia Daza, J. L. (2021). *Mobile Application to Market Inventories of Small Merchants in the San Victorino Sector in Bogotá: A Strategy Against COVID*. Advances in Intelligent Systems and Computing.

PyMRF. (2025). PyMRF: Python Markov Random Fields Library. https://pymrf.github.io/

Qian, J., & Gao, C. (2011). The application of Data Mining in CRM. 2011 2nd International Conference on Artificial Intelligence, Management Science and Electronic Commerce, AIMSEC 2011—Proceedings C7 – 6010697.

Rabiner, L. R. (1989). A tutorial on hidden Markov models and selected applications in speech recognition. *Proceedings of the IEEE*, *77*(2), 257–286.

Radford, A., Narasimhan, K., Salimans, T., & Sutskever, I. (2018). Improving language understanding by generative pre-training.

Radford, A., Wu, J., Child, R., Luan, D., Amodei, D., & Sutskever, I. (2019). Language models are unsupervised multitask learners. OpenAI blog, 1(8), 9.

Rahaman, S. U. (2024). Real-Time Customer Journey Mapping: Combining AI and Big Data for Precision Marketing. IJLRP-International Journal of Leading Research Publication, 5(7). https://doi.org/g8vkzp

Rai, A. (2020). Explainable AI: From black box to glass box. *Journal of the Academy of Marketing Science*, *48*, 137–141. DOI: 10.1007/s11747-019-00710-5

Rama Krishna, S., Rathor, K., Ranga, J., Soni, A., Srinivas, D., & Anil Kumar, N. (2023). Artificial Intelligence Integrated with Big Data Analytics for Enhanced Marketing. 6th International Conference on Inventive Computation Technologies, ICICT 2023, Proceedings

Ramachandran, K., & Bhattacharya, S. (2020). Rural marketing: Emerging opportunities and challenges in India. *International Journal of Consumer Studies*, *44*(2), 123–134.

Ramirez, M., Khalil, M. A., Can, J., & George, K. (2022). Classification of 'Like' and 'Dislike' Decisions from EEG and fNIRS Signals Using a LSTM Based Deep Learning Network. 2022 IEEE World AI IoT Congress, AIIoT 2022

Rane, N. (2023). Enhancing customer loyalty through Artificial Intelligence (AI), Internet of Things (IoT), and Big Data technologies: improving customer satisfaction, engagement, relationship, and experience. Internet of Things (IoT), and Big Data Technologies: Improving Customer Satisfaction, Engagement, Relationship, and Experience (October 13, 2023). http://dx.doi.org/DOI: 10.2139/ssrn.4616051

Ransbotham, S., Kiron, D., Lafountain, B., & Khodabandeh, S. (2017). Reshaping Business with Artificial Intelligence: Closing the Gap Between Ambition and Action. *MIT Sloan Management Review*.

Rao, H. K., Zeng, Z., & Liu, A. P. (2018). Research on personalised referral service and big data mining for e-commerce with machine learning. 2018 4th International Conference on Computer and Technology Applications, ICCTA 2018

Raskovic, M., & Takacs-Haynes, K. (2021). (Re)discovering social identity theory: An agenda for multinational enterprise internalisation theory. *Multinational Business Review*, *29*(2), 145–165. DOI: 10.1108/MBR-02-2020-0031

Rather, R. A., & Hollebeek, L. D. (2019). Exploring and validating social identification and social exchange-based drivers of hospitality customer loyalty. *International Journal of Contemporary Hospitality Management*, *31*(3), 1432–1451. DOI: 10.1108/IJCHM-10-2017-0627

Ravichandran, M. R., & Kumar, K. (2024). The effectiveness of email marketing for engaging customers. International Journal of Research Publication and Reviews. Retrieved from http://www.ijrpr.com

Rayome, A. (2018). How Sephora is leveraging AR and AI to transform retail and help customers buy cosmetics Beauty retailer Sephora followed customer technology trends to command the cosmetic industry worldwide. Here's an inside look at its successful digital transformation. https://steepnews24.wordpress.com/wp-content/uploads/2018/02/sephora_cover_story_final.pdf

Ricci, F., Shapira, B., & Rokach, L. (2015). *Recommender systems handbook* (2nd ed.). Springer US., DOI: 10.1007/978-1-4899-7637-6

Ringle, C. M., Wende, S., & Becker, J.-M. (2024). SmartPLS 4. Bönningstedt: SmartPLS. Retrieved from https://www.smartpls.com

Rita, S., Kim-Phuc, T., & Sébastien, T. (2021). Long-Term Demand Forecasting System for Demand-Driven Manufacturing. *IFIP Advances in Information and Communication Technology*.

Rodriguez-Sarmiento, L. F., Galpin, I., & Sanchez-Riaño, V. (2024). Mapping Brand Territories Using ChatGPT. *Communications in Computer and Information Science*.

Rohden, S. F., & Espartel, L. B. (2024). Consumer reactions to technology in retail: Choice uncertainty and reduced perceived control in decisions assisted by recommendation agents. *Electronic Commerce Research*, *24*(2), 901–923. DOI: 10.1007/s10660-024-09808-7

Rombach, R., Blattmann, A., Lorenz, D., Esser, P., & Ommer, B. (2022). High-resolution image synthesis with latent diffusion models. In *Proceedings of the IEEE/CVF conference on computer vision and pattern recognition*, 10684–10695

Ronneberger, O., Fischer, P., & Brox, T. (2015). U-net: Convolutional networks for biomedical image segmentation. In *International Conference on Medical image computing and computer-assisted intervention*, 234–241

Rosário, A., Moreira, C., & Macedo, P. (2021). Competitive dynamics of strategic groups in the Portuguese banking Industry, Cuadernos de Gestión, 21(2), 1-15. ISSN: 1131-6837. DOI: <ALIGNMENT.qj></ALIGNMENT>10.5295/cdg.180975ac

Rosário, A., Moreira, C., & Macedo, P. (2021). Competitive dynamics of strategic groups in the Portuguese banking Industry, Cuadernos de Gestión, 21(2), 1-15. ISSN: 1131-6837. DOI: 10.5295/cdg.180975ac

Rosário, A. T., Fernandes, F., Raimundo, R. G., & Cruz, R. N. (2021). Determinants of Nascent Entrepreneurship Development. In Carrizo Moreira, A., & Dantas, J. G. (Eds.), *Handbook of Research on Nascent Entrepreneurship and Creating New Ventures* (pp. 172–193). IGI Global., DOI: 10.4018/978-1-7998-4826-4.ch008

Rosário, A. T., Lopes, P. R., & Rosário, F. S. (2023). Metaverse in Marketing: Challenges and Opportunities. In Khang, A., Shah, V., & Rani, S. (Eds.), *Handbook of Research on AI-Based Technologies and Applications in the Era of the Metaverse* (pp. 204–227). IGI Global., DOI: 10.4018/978-1-6684-8851-5.ch010

Rosário, A., & Casaca, J. (2023). Relationship marketing and customer retention: A systematic literature review. *Studies in Business and Economics*, *18*(3), 44–66. DOI: 10.2478/sbe-2023-0044

Rosário, A., & Dias, J. (2024). Exploring the Landscape of Smart Tourism: A Systematic Bibliometric Review of Internet of Things Literature. *Administrative Sciences*, *14*(22), 22. DOI: 10.3390/admsci14020022

Roy, B., D'Souza, M. S., Bhattacharjee, S., Acharjee, P. B., Thorat, S., & Bhayani, T. (2024). Role of Artificial Intelligence in Influencing Impulsive Buying Behaviour. TQCEBT 2024, 2nd IEEE International Conference on Trends in Quantum Computing and Emerging Business Technologies 2024

Roy, G., & Mandal, S. (2021). Technological disruption in rural India: Role of AI-driven start-ups. *Asia Pacific Journal of Innovation and Entrepreneurship*, *15*(3), 295–311.

Runway, M. L. (2025). RunwayML: Everything you need to make anything you want. https://runwayml.com/

Rustagi, M., & Goel, N. (2022). Predictive analytics: A study of its advantages and applications. IARS'. *International Research Journal*, *12*(1), 60–63.

Rust, R. T., & Huang, M.-H. (2014). The service revolution and the transformation of marketing science. *Marketing Science*, *33*(2), 206–221. DOI: 10.1287/mksc.2013.0836

Saadi, S., & Azdimousa, H. (2024). *Artificial Intelligence and Green Marketing: What Link?* Lecture Notes in Networks and Systems.

Sachar, M., Xiong, M., & Lee, K. C. (2022). Consumer preferences of top-rated over-the-counter acne treatment products: A cohort study. *Archives of Dermatological Research*, *314*(8), 815–821. DOI: 10.1007/s00403-021-02230-1 PMID: 33866436

Sahni, N., Wheeler, S., & Chintagunta, P. (2018). Personalization in email marketing: The role of noninformative advertising content. *Marketing Science*, *37*, 1–23. DOI: 10.1287/mksc.2017.1066

Said, L. B., Bouron, T., & Drogoul, A. (2002). Agent-based interaction analysis of consumer behavior. *Proceedings of the International Conference on Autonomous Agents*.

Sakas, D. P., Giannakopoulos, N. T., Kanellos, N., & Migkos, S. P. (2022). Innovative Cryptocurrency Trade Websites: Marketing Strategy Refinement via Digital Behavior. *IEEE Access : Practical Innovations, Open Solutions*, *10*, 63163–63176. DOI: 10.1109/ACCESS.2022.3182396

Sakoe, H., & Chiba, S. (1978). Dynamic programming algorithm optimization for spoken word recognition. *IEEE Transactions on Acoustics, Speech, and Signal Processing*, *26*(1), 43–49.

Salkovska, J., Batraga, A., Kaibe, L., & Kellerte, K. (2023). Use of Artificial Intelligence in the Digital Marketing Strategy of Latvian Companies—Lecture Notes in Networks and Systems.

Salles, A., Evers, K., & Farisco, M. (2020). Anthropomorphism in AI. *AJOB Neuroscience*, *11*(2), 88–95. DOI: 10.1080/21507740.2020.1740350 PMID: 32228388

Samoili, S., Cobo, M. L., Gómez, E., De Prato, G., Martínez-Plumed, F., & Delipetrev, B. (2020). AI Watch. Defining Artificial Intelligence. Towards an operational definition and taxonomy of artificial intelligence.

Sanchez-Nunez, P., Cobo, M. J., Heras-Pedrosa, C. D. L., Pelaez, J. I., & Herrera-Viedma, E. (2020). Opinion Mining, Sentiment Analysis and Emotion Understanding in Advertising: A Bibliometric Analysis. IEEE Access, 8 C7 - 9141266, 134563-134576. https://doi.org/DOI: 10.1109/ACCESS.2020.3009482

Santos, S., & Gonçalves, H. M. (2021). The consumer decision journey: A literature review of the foundational models and theories and a future perspective. *Technological Forecasting and Social Change*, *173*, C7–C121117. DOI: 10.1016/j.techfore.2021.121117

Saraiva Gonçalves, C., Souza Carneiro, J. D. D., Abadia Reis Rocha, R., & Carvalho de Rezende, D. (2020). The impact of varying educational intervention on consumer understanding and attitude toward reducing sodium in food: Implications for marketing strategies. Journal of Sensory Studies, 35(2 C7 - e12558). https://doi.org/DOI: 10.1111/joss.12558

Sarath Kumar Boddu, R., Santoki, A. A., Khurana, S., Vitthal Koli, P., Rai, R., & Agrawal, A. (2022). An analysis to understand the role of machine learning, robotics and artificial intelligence in digital marketing. Materials Today: Proceedings, pp. 56, 2288–2292. DOI: 10.1016/j.matpr.2021.11.637

Schmidt, P., Biessmann, F., & Teubner, T. (2020). Transparency and trust in artificial intelligence systems. *Journal of Decision Systems*, *29*(4), 260–278.

Schneider, D. M., & Woolley, S. M. (2010). Discrimination of communication vocalizations by single neurons and groups of neurons in the auditory midbrain. *Journal of Neurophysiology*, *103*(6), 3248–3265.

Schwartz, R., Schwartz, R., Vassilev, A., Greene, K., Perine, L., Burt, A., & Hall, P. (2022). Towards a standard for identifying and managing bias in artificial intelligence (Vol. 3, p. 00). US Department of Commerce, National Institute of Standards and Technology.

Selenko, E., Bankins, S., Shoss, M., Warburton, J., & Restubog, S. L. D. (2022). Artificial intelligence and the future of work: A functional-identity perspective. *Current Directions in Psychological Science*, *31*(3), 272–279. DOI: 10.1177/09637214221091823

Senecha, N., & Srivastava, R. (2022). Mentor EduTech: Charting new territories through social media marketing. *Emerald Emerging Markets Case Studies*, *12*(2), 1–32. DOI: 10.1108/EEMCS-09-2021-0310

Septiana Putra, M. F., Aswie, A., Edbert, I. S., & Suhartono, D. (2023). Hybrid Approaches for Customer Segmentation and Product Recommendation. *2023 International Conference on Informatics, Multimedia, Cyber and Information Systems, ICIMCIS 2023*

Setiawan, I., & Purba, H. (2020). A systematic literature review of key performance indicators (KPIs) implementation. *Journal of Industrial Engineering and Management*, *1*, 200–208. DOI: 10.7777/jiemar.v1i3.79

Setor, T. (2021). Information System-Marketing Manager Dyad Presence in Top Management Teams: A Study on Demographic Diversity, Power Disparity and Organizational Performance. *SIGMIS-CPR 2021: Proceedings of the 2021 Computers and People Research Conference*.

Shameem, A., Ramachandran, K. K., Sharma, A., Singh, R., Selvaraj, F. J., & Manoharan, G. (2023). The Rising Importance of AI in Boosting the Efficiency of Online Advertising in Developing Countries. 2023 3rd International Conference on Advance Computing and Innovative Technologies in Engineering, ICACITE 2023.

Sharma, S., Sharma, A., Sharma, Y., & Bhatia, M. (2017). Recommender system using hybrid approach. Proceeding - IEEE International Conference on Computing, Communication and Automation, ICCCA 2016 C7 - 7813722

Sharma, A. (2024). Online Travel Agency (OTA) Platform Usage in the AI Era. *International Journal of Information Management Sciences*, *8*(1), 31–63. https://ijims.org/index.php/home/article/view/86

Sharma, P., & Aggarwal, M. (2019). Analyzing the role of chatbots in customer service: A study of Indian rural consumers. *International Journal of E-Services and Mobile Applications*, *11*(3), 45–63.

Sharma, R., Kumar, A., & Chuah, C. (2021). Turning the blackbox into a glassbox: An explainable machine learning approach for understanding hospitality customer. *International Journal of Information Management Data Insights*, *1*(2), 100050.

Shen, H., Han, Y., Zhang, Z., & Zeng, Z. (2011). Notice of Retraction: Marketing strategies for Chinese public legal services companies. 2011 2nd International Conference on Artificial Intelligence, Management Science and Electronic Commerce, AIMSEC 2011 - Proceedings C7 - 6011125, 3105-3108. DOI: 10.1109/AIMSEC.2011.6011125

Sheth, J. (2021). New areas of research in marketing strategy, consumer behaviour, and marketing analytics: The future is bright. *Journal of Marketing Theory and Practice*, *29*(1), 3–12. DOI: 10.1080/10696679.2020.1860679

Shukla, R. P., Juneja, D., & Monga, S. (2024). *Predictive Analytics in Marketing Using Artificial Intelligence*. Lecture Notes in Networks and Systems.

Siddik, A. Forid, Md. Yong, L. Du, A & Goodell, J. (2025). Artificial intelligence as a catalyst for sustainable tourism growth and economic cycles. *Technological Forecasting and Social Change*, *210*, 123875. DOI: 10.1016/j.techfore.2024.123875

Singhal, K., Singh, J. N., & Sharma, V. (2024). Enabling Autonomous Digital Marketing: A Machine Learning Approach for Consumer Demand Forecasting. Proceedings of the International Conference on Computing, Power, and Communication Technologies, IC2PCT 2024

Singh, K., & Sirdeshmukh, A. (2022). AI-enabled hyperlocal marketing in emerging economies: Opportunities and challenges. *Journal of Retailing and Consumer Services*, •••, 68.

Singh, K., & Tandon, N. (2021). The diffusion of AI-based solutions in India's small-scale industries: A multi-level perspective. *Technology in Society*, •••, 65.

Sinha, M., Fukey, L. N., & Sinha, A. (2021). Artificial Intelligence and Internet of Things readiness: inclination for hotels to support a sustainable environment. In *Cognitive Computing for Human-Robot Interaction* (pp. 327–353). Academic Press.

Siva Balan, R. V., & Kalpana, P. (2023). The role of big data in predicting consumer behavior. In *Big Data: A Road-Map for Successful Digital Marketing* (pp. 111–132). Nova Science Publishers, Inc.

Sivarethinamohan, R. (2023). Exploring the Transformation of digital tourism: trends, impacts, and future prospects. *2023 International Conference on Digital Applications, Transformation and Economy, ICDATE 2023.*

Sleiman, R., Nguyen, Q. T., Lacaze, S., Tran, K. P., & Thomassey, S. (2024). Evaluating the sales potential of new products using machine learning techniques and data collected from mobile applications. *International Journal of Clothing Science and Technology*, *36*(3), 454–473. DOI: 10.1108/IJCST-07-2023-0099

Smith, A. (2018). Cultural influences on consumer behaviour in rural India: Implications for AI-driven marketing strategies. *International Journal of Market Research*, *60*(4), 345–360.

Smith, A., & Jones, B. (2023). Ethical Considerations in AI-Driven Marketing: A Framework for Responsible Personalization. *Journal of Business Ethics*, *174*, 405–421.

Songsangyos, P., Iamamporn, S., & Kongsomlap, T. (2015). A development of decision support system model for sale planning. Proceedings 2015 International Conference on Science and Technology, TICST 2015 C7-7369381.

Soundraw. (2025). Soundraw: AI Music Generator. https://soundraw.io/

Sousa, A., Cardoso, P., & Dias, F. (2024). The Use of Artificial Intelligence Systems in Tourism and Hospitality: The Tourists' Perspective. *Administrative Sciences*, *14*(165), 1–23.

Srivastava, R., Gupta, P., Kumar, H., & Tuli, N. (2023). Digital customer engagement: A systematic literature review and research agenda. *Australian Journal of Management*. Advance online publication. DOI: 10.1177/03128962231177096

Stallone, A., Selva, J., Cordrie, L., Faenza, L., Michelini, A., & Lauciani, V. (2024). ProbShakemap v1. 0: a Python toolbox propagating source uncertainty to ground motion prediction for urgent computing applications. *Authorea Preprints*.

Sterne, J. (2017). *Artificial intelligence for marketing: practical applications*. John Wiley & Sons.

Štilić, A., Nicić, M., & Puška, A. (2023). Check-In to the Future: Exploring the Impact of Contemporary Information Technologies and Artificial Intelligence on the Hotel Industry. *The Business of Tourism, 31*, 5–17. DOI: 10.5937/turpos0-43739

Streamlit. (2025). Streamlit: The fastest way to build and share data apps. https://streamlit.io/

Sung, E. C., Danny Han, D. I., Bae, S., & Kwon, O. (2022). What drives technology-enhanced storytelling immersion? The role of digital humans. *Computers in Human Behavior, 132*, C7–C107246. DOI: 10.1016/j.chb.2022.107246

Sun, L. L. (2023). *Analysis of E-Commerce Live Broadcast Marketing Strategy Based on Big Data Algorithm*. Lecture Notes in Electrical Engineering.

Su, Q. (2018). Research on influencing factors of consumer behavior based on Wechat Stores. *ACM International Conference Proceeding Series*

Su, Q. (2018). Research on influencing factors of consumer behaviour based on Wechat Stores. *ACM International Conference Proceeding Series.*

Surfer, S. E. O. (2025). SurferSEO: AI Content Optimization & SEO Tools. https://surferseo.com/

Su, Y., Wang, E., & Berthon, P. (2023). Ethical Marketing AI? A Structured Literature Review of the Ethical Challenges Posed by Artificial Intelligence in the Domains of Marketing and Consumer Behavior. *Proceedings of the Annual Hawaii International Conference on System Sciences*

Suzuki, R., Ishino, Y., & Takahashi, S. (2018). Characterization of consumers' behavior in medical insurance market with agent parameters' Estimation process using Bayesian network. Lecture Notes in Computer Science (including subseries Lecture Notes in Artificial Intelligence and Lecture Notes in Bioinformatics).

Taqwa, T., Suhendra, A., Hermita, M., & Darmayantie, A. (2016). Implementation of Naïve Bayes method for product purchasing decision using neural impulse actuator in neuromarketing. Proceedings of 2015 International Conference on Information and Communication Technology and Systems, ICTS 2015 C7 – 7379882.

TechTarget. (2023, May). *What is IS (information system or information services)? - Definition from WhatIs.com*. WhatIs.com. https://www.techtarget.com/whatis/definition/IS-information-system-or-information-services

Thamaraiselvi, P., Masih, J., Giri, P., Sridevi, J., Karim Shaikh, I. A., & Prasad, M. V. R. (2024). Analysis of Social Media Marketing Impact on Customer Behaviour Using AI & Machine Learning. *Proceedings of 9th International Conference on Science, Technology, Engineering and Mathematics: The Role of Emerging Technologies in Digital Transformation, ICONSTEM 2024*

The AI Revolution: How Artificial Intelligence is Reshaping Marketing Strategies – IJSREM. (2024). Ijsrem.com. https://ijsrem.com/download/the-ai-revolution-how-artificial-intelligence-is-reshaping-marketing-strategies/

The Role of AI in Marketing and How to Use It. (n.d.). Www.invoca.com. https://www.invoca.com/blog/ai-marketing-how-to-use-it

Thomas, C., & Bhatnagar, P. (2022). Stakeholder collaboration and AI integration in remote rural markets: Evidence from Northern India. *International Journal of Emerging Markets*, *17*(1), 129–147.

Tian, J., Zhang, Y., & Zhang, C. (2018). *Predicting consumer variety-seeking through weather data analytics*. Electronic Commerce Research and Applications., DOI: 10.1016/j.elerap.2018.02.001

Tianyuan, Z., & Moro, S. (2021). *Research Trends in Customer Churn Prediction: A Data Mining Approach*. Advances in Intelligent Systems and Computing.

Tiwari, R. (2023). The impact of AI and machine learning on job displacement and employment opportunities. *International Journal of Engineering Technologies and Management Research*, *7*(1).

Touvron, H., Martin, L., Stone, K., Albert, P., Almahairi, A., Babaei, Y., Bashyal, N., Biswas, S., Lacroix, T., Lavalley, G., & Roux, A. (2024). Llama 3: The Llama 3 Herd of Models. arXiv preprint arXiv:2407.21783

Trandafili, E., Biba, M., & Xhuvani, A. (2013). Profiling social network users with machine learning. *CEUR Workshop Proceedings*.

Tsai, C. Y., Wang, J. C., & Chen, C. J. (2006). A change detection model for credit card usage behaviour. International Conference on Computational Intelligence, Man-Machine Systems and Cybernetics—Proceedings.

Tsai, H. Y. (2024). Bp Neural Network Research on Enterprise Marketing Strategy Combination. *2024 IEEE International Conference on Information Technology, Electronics and Intelligent Communication Systems, ICITEICS 2024* van den Oord, A., Dieleman, S., Zen, H., Simonyan, K., Vinyals, O., Graves, A., Kalchbrenner, N., Senior, A., & Kavukcuoglu, K. (2016). WaveNet: A generative model for raw audio. arXiv preprint arXiv:1609.03499

Van Esch, P., & Stewart Black, J. (2021). Artificial Intelligence (AI): Revolutionizing Digital Marketing. *Australasian Marketing Journal*, *29*(3), 199–203. DOI: 10.1177/18393349211037684

Vaswani, A., Shazeer, N., Parmar, N., Uszkoreit, J., Jones, L., Gomez, A. N., Kaiser, L., & Polosukhin, I. (2017). Attention is all you need. In Advances in neural information processing systems, 5998–6008

Vázquez, S., Muñoz-García, T., Campanella, I., Poch, M., Fisas, B., Bel, N., & Andreu, G. (2014). A classification of user-generated content into consumer decision journey stages. *Neural Networks*, *58*, 68–81. DOI: 10.1016/j.neunet.2014.05.026 PMID: 24996448

Veal, A. J. (2018). *Research Methods for Leisure and Tourism*. Pearson.

Venkatesh, V., & Bala, H. (2012). Adoption and impacts of inter-organizational business process standards: Role of partnering synergy. *Information Systems Research : ISR*, *23*(4), 1131–1157. DOI: 10.1287/isre.1110.0404

Verhoef, P. C., Broekhuizen, T., Bart, Y., Bhattacharya, A., Qi Dong, J., Fabian, N., & Haenlein, M. (2021). Digital transformation: A multidisciplinary reflection and research agenda. *Journal of Business Research*, *122*, 889–901. DOI: 10.1016/j.jbusres.2019.09.022

Verma, K., & Singh, T. P. (2021). AI-based distribution channels in rural supply chains: An empirical analysis. Supply Chain Forum. *International Journal (Toronto, Ont.)*, *22*(4), 381–395.

Verma, S., Sharma, R., Deb, S., & Maitra, D. (2021). Artificial intelligence in marketing: Systematic review and future research direction. *International Journal of Information Management Data Insights*, *1*(1), 100002. DOI: 10.1016/j.jjimei.2020.100002

Vieira, M., Santos, V., & Bacalhau, L. M. (2023). *Systematic Literature Review—Factors of Loyalty and Acceptance in Voice Commerce*. Smart Innovation, Systems and Technologies.

Vij, M., Vij, A., Kumar, P., & Shameem, B. (2024). Impact of AI-Driven Customer Insights on Brand Engagement and Loyalty in Tourism Marketing. *2nd International Conference on Cyber Resilience, ICCR 2024*

Vinaykarthik, B. C. (2022). Design of Artificial Intelligence (AI) based User Experience Websites for E-commerce Application and Future of Digital Marketing. 3rd International Conference on Smart Electronics and Communication, ICOSEC 2022 - Proceedings

Vinnakota, S., Mohan, M. D., Boda, J., Sekuini, J., Mustafa, M., & Madala, H. (2023). Leveraging artificial intelligence in the hospitality industry: Opportunities and challenges. *Asian Journal of Social Science and Management Technology*, *5*(3), 201–210.

Vinod, B. (2016). Big Data in the travel marketplace. *Journal of Revenue and Pricing Management*, *15*(5), 352–359. DOI: 10.1057/rpm.2016.30

Visme. (2025). Visme: Create Visual Content. https://www.visme.co/

Viswanathan, M., & Rosa, J. A. (2019). Understanding subsistence marketplaces: Toward sustainable consumption and entrepreneurship. *Journal of Business Research*, *102*, 607–610.

Vlačić, B., Corbo, L., Silva, S. C., & Dabić, M. (2021). The evolving role of artificial intelligence in marketing: A review and research agenda. *Journal of Business Research*, *128*, 187–203. DOI: 10.1016/j.jbusres.2021.01.055

Volkoff, O., & Strong, D. M. (2017). Affordance theory and how to use it in IS research. In *The Routledge Companion to management information systems* (pp. 232–245). Routledge.

Vyas, A. M. (2024). Exploring the Impact of 'Emotion-Recognition-AI' on Consumer Trust and Satisfaction. 2024 IEEE International Students' *Conference on Electrical, Electronics and Computer Science, SCEECS 2024*.

Wahbeh, S. Y., & Abuelrub, E. E. (2021). Liberty Dental Clinic—the secret behind the most expensive smile creators. In *Corporate Success Stories in the UAE: The Key Drivers behind their Growth* (pp. 93–107). Emerald Group Publishing Ltd., DOI: 10.1108/978-1-80043-578-020211007

Wahid, R., Mero, J., & Ritala, P. (2023). Written by ChatGPT, illustrated by Midjourney: Generative AI for content marketing. *Asia Pacific Journal of Marketing and Logistics*, *35*(8), 1813–1822. DOI: 10.1108/APJML-10-2023-994

Waller, M. A., & Fawcett, S. E. (2013). Data science, predictive analytics, and big data: A revolution transforming supply chain design and management. *Journal of Business Logistics*, *34*(2), 77–84.

Wang, G. A., & Lim, Y. T. (2011). Notice of Retraction: Research on China's Alibaba development. 2011 2nd International Conference on Artificial Intelligence, Management Science and Electronic Commerce, AIMSEC 2011 - Proceedings C7 - 6011136, 2295-2301. DOI: 10.1109/AIMSEC.2011.6011136

Wang, X., & Xu, J. (2011). Notice of Retraction: The study on staff management of service shops. 2011 2nd International Conference on Artificial Intelligence, Management Science and Electronic Commerce, AIMSEC 2011 - Proceedings C7 - 6011303, 3567-3570. DOI: 10.1109/AIMSEC.2011.6011303

Wang, X., & Zhong, W. (2024). Evolution and innovations in animation: A comprehensive review and future directions. Concurrency and Computation: Practice and Experience, 36(2 C7 - e7904). DOI: 10.1002/cpe.7904

Wang, C., Liu, Y., & Zhou, H. (2023). Consumer Consumption Behavioral Model for Business Intelligence Using Artificial Intelligence. *Journal of the Knowledge Economy*. Advance online publication. DOI: 10.1007/s13132-023-01391-w

Wang, H., Kang, B., Peng, L., & Shi, Y. (2022). Analysis and Research on the Marketing Strategy of Agricultural Products Based on Artificial Intelligence. *Mathematical Problems in Engineering*, *2022*, C7–C7798640. DOI: 10.1155/2022/7798640

Wang, H., Wang, J., & Tang, Q. (2018). A review of application of affordance theory in information systems. *Journal of Service Science and Management*, *11*(1), 56–70. DOI: 10.4236/jssm.2018.111006

Wang, W., Li, B., Luo, X., & Wang, X. (2023). Deep Reinforcement Learning for Sequential Targeting. *Management Science*, *69*(9), 5439–5460. DOI: 10.1287/mnsc.2022.4621

Wang, Y., & Wang, H. (2022). *Reinventing the Wheel of Marketing: Assessing the Impact of Artificial Intelligence (AI) on Digital Marketing and Consumer Buying Behavior*. Lecture Notes in Electrical Engineering.

Wedel, M., Bigné, E., & Zhang, J. (2020). Virtual and augmented reality: Advancing research in consumer marketing. *International Journal of Research in Marketing*, *37*(3), 443–465.

Wedel, M., & Kannan, P. K. (2016). Marketing analytics for data-rich environments. *Journal of Marketing*, *80*(6), 97–121. DOI: 10.1509/jm.15.0413

Wei, C. S., Hsu, P. Y., Huang, C. W., Cheng, M. S., & Prassida, G. F. (2020). Devising a Cross-Domain Model to Detect Fake Review Comments. *Communications in Computer and Information Science*.

Wen, Q., Zhou, T., Zhang, C., Chen, W., Ma, Z., Yan, J., & Sun, L. (2022). Transformers in time series: A survey. *arXiv preprint arXiv:2202.07125.*

West, D. M. (2018). *The Future of Work: Robots, AI, and Automation.* Brookings Institution Press.

What are Voice User Interfaces (VUI)? (2017, February 9). The Interaction Design Foundation; Interaction Design Foundation. https://www.interaction-design.org/literature/topics/voice-user-interfaces?srsltid=AfmBOorp7OT2tCl_5LmnxBvcF46rCLw9l33qTL_1K3zfXRG-6arv3j60

Wikipedia. (2025). Recurrent neural network. https://en.wikipedia.org/wiki/Recurrent_neural_network

Wilendra, W., Nadlifatin, R., & Kusumawulan, C. K. (2024). ChatGPT: The AI Game-Changing Revolution in Marketing Strategy for the Indonesian Cosmetic Industry. Procedia Computer Science.

Williams, K. (2023, July 27). *The Pros and Cons of AI in Marketing: An Analysis.* SurveySparrow. https://surveysparrow.com/blog/the-pros-and-cons-of-ai-in-marketing/

Wirtz, J., Tuzovic, S., & Kuppelwieser, V. (2014). The role of artificial intelligence in service innovation. *Journal of Service Management*, *25*(6), 830–848.

Wu, G., Tan, G., Deng, J., & Jiang, D. (2021). Distributed reinforcement learning algorithm of operator service slice competition prediction based on zero-sum Markov game. *Neurocomputing*, *439*, 212–222. DOI: 10.1016/j.neucom.2021.01.061

Wu, W., Wang, X., & Zhang, Y. (2024). Determinants and Effects of Digital Marketing Tools: An Affordance Lens. *SSRN.* https://dx.doi.org/DOI: 10.2139/ssrn.4827567

Xiao, D. (2012). Statistics and analysis of bank customers' financial consumption behaviours. Proceedings: 2012 5th International Symposium on Computational Intelligence and Design, ISCID 2012

Xiao, Z., Qin, Y., Xu, Z., Antucheviciene, J., & Zavadskas, E. K. (2022). The Journal Buildings: A Bibliometric Analysis (2011–2021). [Academic]. *Buildings (Basel, Switzerland)*, *12*(1), 37–52. DOI: 10.3390/ buildings12010037

Xie, D., & He, Y. (2022). Marketing Strategy of Rural Tourism Based on Big Data and Artificial Intelligence. *Mobile Information Systems*, *2022*, C7–C9154351. DOI: 10.1155/2022/9154351

Xu, H. (2022). Intelligent automobile auxiliary propagation system based on speech recognition and AI-driven feature extraction techniques. *International Journal of Speech Technology*, *25*(4), 893–905. DOI: 10.1007/s10772-022-09958-9

Xu, S. (2024). Exploring the impact of personalization in artificial intelligence on digital marketing: Performance evaluation. *Journal of Innovation and Development*, *8*(1), 41–44. DOI: 10.54097/tht8d457

Yadav, B. (2024). Role of Artificial Intelligence in Marketing: A Paradigm Shift. *IJFMR240111924, 6*(1). https://www.ijfmr.com/papers/2024/1/11924.pdf

Yahoo. (2025). Yahoo Webscope Dataset. https://webscope.sandbox.yahoo.com/

Yaiprasert, C., & Hidayanto, A. N. (2023). AI-driven ensemble three machine learning to enhance digital marketing strategies in the food delivery business. *Intelligent Systems with Applications*, *18*, C7–C200235. DOI: 10.1016/j.iswa.2023.200235

Yang, Y., Liu, S., Li, Y., & Jia, J. (2020). Big data marketing: Review and prospect. Xitong Gongcheng Lilun yu Shijian. *Xitong Gongcheng Lilun Yu Shijian*, *40*(8), 2150–2158. DOI: 10.12011/1000-6788-2020-1187-09

Yao, S. (2021). Method and Research of E-commerce Consumers' Purchasing Behavior Forecast and Analysis Based on Machine Learning. *ACM International Conference Proceeding Series*

Youn, S., & Jin, S. V. (2021). "In AI, we trust?" The effects of parasocial interaction and technopian versus luddite ideological views on chatbot-based customer relationship management in the emerging "feeling economy.". Computers in Human Behavior, p. 119 C7-106721. DOI: 10.1016/j.chb.2021.106721

Youssofi, A., Jeannot, F., Jongmans, E., & Dampérat, M. (2024). Designing the digitalized guest experience: A comprehensive framework and research agenda. *Psychology and Marketing*, *41*(3), 512–531. DOI: 10.1002/mar.21929

Yu, X., & Huang, Y. C. (2021). Research on the consumption of different user populations. *ACM International Conference Proceeding Series*

Zaveri, B., & Amin, P. (2019). Augmented and virtual reality: Future of marketing trends. *MANTHAN: Journal of Commerce and Management*, *6*(1), 16–25.

Zeeshan, M., & Saxena, K. (2020). Explorative Study of Artificial Intelligence in Digital Marketing. In Lecture Notes on Data Engineering and Communications Technologies (Vol. 49, pp. 968-978). Springer Science and Business Media Deutschland GmbH. DOI: 10.1007/978-3-030-43192-1_107

Zeghidour, M., Chou, J.-S., Zeiler, N., Zeghidour, H., & Adi, Y. (2021). RAVE: A variational autoencoder for fast and high-quality neural audio synthesis. In ICASSP 2021-2021 IEEE International Conference on Acoustics, Speech and Signal Processing (ICASSP), 316-320

Zehmakan, A. N. (2021). Majority opinion diffusion in social networks: an adversarial approach. *35th AAAI Conference on Artificial Intelligence, AAAI 2021*.

Zhang, J., Wang, Y., Wang, Z., Wang, H., & Lv, X. (2020). Evaluation and classification of travel value of passengers between Wuhan and Yichang based on large samples. Proceedings of 2020 IEEE International Conference on Information Technology, Big Data and Artificial Intelligence, ICIBA 2020 C7-9276961.

Zhang, Y., Pan, K., Huo, Y., Deng, B., & Fu, Y. (2022). Analysis of Power Marketing Strategy Based on Computer Artificial Intelligence Technology. EEI 2022, 4th International Conference on Electronic Engineering and Informatics

Zhang, B. (2024). Innovative exponential TODIM-CoCoSo framework for uncertain multiple-attribute group decision-making in the effectiveness evaluation of short video marketing strategies. *Journal of Intelligent & Fuzzy Systems*, *46*(2), 4029–4042. DOI: 10.3233/JIFS-236767

Zhang, C., & Huang, Z. (2015). Mining tourist motive for marketing development via twice-learning. *Applied Artificial Intelligence*, *29*(2), 119–133. DOI: 10.1080/08839514.2015.993554

Zhang, L., Agrawala, R., & Li, B. (2023). Adding conditional control to text-to-image diffusion models. In *Proceedings of the IEEE/CVF International Conference on Computer Vision*, 3827–3837

Zhuang, Y., Li, X., Sun, Y., & He, X. (2018). A correlation-aware ml-knn algorithm for customer value modeling in online shopping. Lecture Notes in Computer Science (including subseries Lecture Notes in Artificial Intelligence and Lecture Notes in Bioinformatics)

Zhu, J. Y., Park, T., Isola, P., & Efros, A. A. (2017). Unpaired image-to-image translation using cycle-consistent adversarial networks. In *Proceedings of the IEEE international conference on computer vision*, 2223–2232

Ziakis, C., & Vlachopoulou, M. (2023). Artificial Intelligence in Digital Marketing: Insights from a Comprehensive Review. Information (Switzerland), 14(12 C7 - 664). DOI: 10.3390/info14120664

Zuo, Y., Yada, K., & Ali, A. B. M. S. (2017). Prediction of Consumer Purchasing in a Grocery Store Using Machine Learning Techniques. Proceedings - Asia-Pacific World Congress on Computer Science and Engineering 2016 and Asia-Pacific World Congress on Engineering 2016, APWC on CSE/APWCE 2016 C7 – 7941935

About the Contributors

Albérico Travassos Rosário, Ph.D. Marketing and Strategy, Universities of Aveiro (UA), Minho (UM) and Beira Interior (UBI). Post-doctorate - Economics, Management and Industrial Engineering and Tourism, University of Aveiro, with affiliation to the research center GOVCOPP of the University of Aveiro. Master in Marketing and Degree in Marketing, Advertising and Public Relations, degree from ISLA Lisbon Campus. He has the title of Specialist in Marketing and teaches as Assistant Professor with Aggregation at IADE-Faculty of Design, Technology and Communication of the European University and as Guest Assistant Professor with Aggregation at the School of Management and Technology of Santarém (ESGTS) of the Polytechnic Institute of Santarém. He taught at IPAM-Escola de Marketing, ISLA-Instituto Superior de Gestão e Administração de Santarém (ISLA-Santarém), was Director of the Commercial Management Course, Director of the Technical Professional Course (TeSP) of Sales and Commercial Management, Chairman of the Pedagogical Council and Member of the Technical Council and Scientific Researcher of ISLA-Santarém. Consultant on marketing and strategy for SMEs. His main research interests are: Competitive Strategy, Competitive Dynamics, Strategic Groups and Marketing.

Rui Cruz is an Assistant Professor at Universidade Europeia in Lisbon since 2001 and Integrated Researcher at UNIDCOM/IADE, has a PhD in Management and Marketing from the University of Sevilla, Spain. Also has a DEA from the same university and an MBA in Strategic Foresight at IESFF, Lisbon. With over 20 years teaching experience at the service of several higher education institutions in the public and private sector,such as Atlantica University, polytechnic of Setútal and polytechnic of Lisbon, currently accumulates teaching functions at ISECLISBOA. He has held academic management positions in some of the institutions where he has taught, having been the coordinator of the degree and scientific area at the Universidade Europeia and the coordinator of the CTesp of Communication and Marketing at ISECLISBOA. He was also a member of the Pedagogic and Scientific Councils of the European University for several mandates. He is the regent of several disciplines at IADE faculty. Actually teaches academic master's and global undergraduate programs taught in English and Portuguese in the areas of marketing, logistics & supply chain and Business Management. Also teaches subjects related with marketing and digital marketing in Executive Masters and post graduation programs. Advisor and Tutor in master´s dissertations in the areas of marketing, digital marketing and entrepreneurship his research interests are in the areas of business strategy, strategic marketing, industrial and services marketing and relationship marketing and has scientific articles published national and internationally and books published in Portugal and Angola. Professionally, he worked in the field of advertising at the service of large international agencies such as Publicis, ITT marketing services and BBDO in Portugal and abroad, throughout the 80´s. Was also marketing director of one of the largest Portuguese banking groups in the 90´s and business consultant in the areas of strategy and innovation in the first decade of the 21st century

***

Luis José Andrade is a University Professor, Manager, Coacher and Senior Consultant. He is currently Managing Director in the Customer Service area in a leading Business Group in Portugal. His career has been consolidated through the performance of multiple management positions, juxtaposing with the Human Resources and Organizational Consulting, Recruitment and Selection (eg, PGA - Portugália Airlines), specialized training and Coaching in the areas of Customer Care, Organizational Behavior, Marketing Research, Human Resource Management and Management Control. Specialist in the themes of Leadership, Motivation, Quality and processes of continuous improvement. PhD in Labor Sciences, University of Cadiz; Master's and Post-graduate studies in Social and Organizational Psychology (ISCTE) and Psychology Degree in Social Psychology and Organizations (ISPA). He has lectured and coordinated curricular units in the Human Resources, Organizational Behavior, Psychossociology, Marketing field. He has taught and coordinated courses in Human Resources, Organizational Behavior, Psychosociology, Marketing and Market Research and Research Methods. He regularly publishes scientific and opinion articles and is a co-author

Joaquim Casaca is Assistant Professor at IADE, Universidade Europeia, since 2010. He holds a Ph.D. in Management from Universidade Lusíada de Lisboa, a Master's in Management from ISEG - Lisbon School of Economics and Management at the University of Lisbon, a MBA (ISEG), a postgraduate degree in

"Technologies and Information Sciences for Organizations" (ISEG) and a degree in Economics (ISEG). He has developed his teaching activity in the scientific areas of Management, Marketing and Statistics in the Marketing and Advertising degree and several masters in the field of marketing, and in the supervision of master's dissertations. He is an integrated member of UNIDCOM/IADE research center and is a member of the scientific committee of the Observatório do Consumo Consciente – Forúm do Consumo (Conscious Consumption Observatory – Consumer Forum), currently developing research on marketing performance, behavior and development sustainable and conscious consumption. Experienced user in statistical analysis programs such as IBM SPSS Statistics, IBM SPSS AMOS and SmartPLS (structural equation models).

Abdul Hannan Rakib Dalal is an AI researcher, developer, and student, currently pursuing a B.Tech. in Artificial Intelligence & Data Science at Vishwakarma University. He also serves as an NEP SAARTHI for UGC at the Faculty of Science & Technology at Vishwakarma University, Pune His research focuses on AI, ML, IoT, and Predictive Modeling, with a recent publication on optimizing energy efficiency through IoT, IESVE, and machine learning in a Taylor & Francis book. Abdul Hannan is actively working on live projects, including: An examination management system using Excel, streamlining faculty workflows. A dynamic timetable generation software (in progress), optimizing schedules based on faculty and student constraints. He has presented at two conferences and contributed to multiple faculty-led events, continuously striving to bridge AI research with real-world applications.

Gorete Dinis holds a PhD in Tourism, an MSc in Innovation, Planning, and Development Policies, and a BSc in Tourism Management and Planning, all from the University of Aveiro, Portugal. She is the coordinator and a professor for the Master's in Tourism and Digital Communication and the Bachelor's in Tourism at the School of Education and Social Sciences, Polytechnic Institute of Portalegre, Portugal. She is also a member of the Research Center on Health and Social Sciences (CARE), the GOVCOPP research unit, and CITUR Algarve

Maria-Alexandra Foka holds a Bachelor's degree in Marketing and Communication from the Athens University of Economics and Business and a minor in Project Management from DEREE, The American College of Greece, both completed in 2025. She is currently completing a marketing and communication internship, combining academic knowledge with hands-on experience in digital marketing, brand communication, and analytics. Her interests focus on how Artificial

Intelligence can simplify, enhance marketing processes, and make marketing activities more efficient and manageable.

Márcia Grilo has a PhD in Information and Communication Sciences from the University of Nice/Côte d'Azur, France. Adjunct Professor in the Department of Language and Communication Sciences at the Polytechnic Institute of Portalegre and integrated researcher at CARE - Center for Research in Health and Social Sciences (Portalegre) and researcher ICNOVA - Instituto de Comunicação da Nova, Strategic Communication group (Lisbon), Portugal. She is interested in the following areas of research: Organizational Communication and Public Relations; Digital Communication; Communication and Social Change; Internal Communication and Well-being; Political and Religious Communication.

Rajkumar Jagdale is an Assistant Professor and Head of the Department of Computer Science at the Faculty of Science and Technology, Vishwakarma University, Pune. He earned his Ph.D. in Computer Science and IT from Dr. Babasaheb Ambedkar Marathwada University, Chh. Sambhajinagar, Maharashtra, India.With over six years of teaching and research experience, complemented by two years in the industry as Data Scientist, Dr. Jagdale specializes in Sentiment Analysis, Opinion Mining, Text Mining, ML, Big Data Analytics, and RPA. He has made significant academic contributions, with 13 publications in reputable international journals and conferences, and holds one patent related to his research. Dr. Jagdale's work has received notable recognition, including prestigious scholarships such as the JASSO Scholarship to attend a Spring School on "Smart Materials and AI" at Tokushima University, Japan, and the DST Inspire Fellowship from the Department of Science and Technology, Government of India. Additionally, he was awarded a Gold Medal for his exemplary performance in the M.Sc. Computer Science program. He reviewed conference papers and journals and He is member of CSI, ISCA and IAENG.

Luis Miguel holds a PhD in Marketing, from ISCTE-IUL. His main research interest is related to consumer sustainable behaviour and issues such as green marketing recognition of consumer choice. His first degree was in animal production and also holds an MSc in world animal production from the University of Wales. Luis Miguel has taught at ISCTE-IUL since 2014 and at IADE-European University since 2021 in subjects of consumer behaviour, public relations and sustainability.

Ana Margarida Raimundo da Silva is a Master's student in Tourism and Digital Communication at the Polytechnic Institute of Portalegre, in Portugal. At the same time, he is part of the Image and Communication Office of the Municipality of Portalegre, where he develops projects focused on tourism promotion and interaction with the local community. His areas of interest and research include digital marketing strategies, public communication and sustainable tourism development. He graduated in Administrative Consulting from the same Institute in 2004, having completed an internship at the Portalegre City Hall, where he continues to work professionally to this day. In the future, it plans to deepen the relationship between digital communication and tourism promotion, contributing to the appreciation of local resources and heritage.

Ana Vieira holds a degree in Nursing and has over 20 years of experience in healthcare. Driven by her passion for tourism, she decided to venture into a new professional challenge and is currently pursuing a Master's in Tourism and Digital Communication at the Polytechnic Institute of Portalegre. She currently serves as the Operations Director at Portus Alacer – Property Management, an organisation specialising in the management of vacation rentals and the development of authentic tourism experiences in the Alto Alentejo region. Ana is dedicated to providing her clients with exceptional hospitality, crafting experiences that highlight the cultural and natural heritage of the region, with a focus on authenticity and excellence.

Index

E

F

G

I

L

M

O

P

R

S

www.ingramcontent.com/pod-product-compliance
Lightning Source LLC
LaVergne TN
LVHW081532300926
849161LV00006B/1388
* 9 7 9 8 3 6 9 3 9 9 9 4 1 *